Lecture Notes in Computer Science 1895

Edited by G. Goos, J. Hartmanis, and J. van Leeuwen

T0218638

Springer
Berlin
Heidelberg
New York
Barcelona
Hong Kong
London
Milan
Paris
Singapore
Tokyo

Frédéric Cuppens   Yves Deswarte
Dieter Gollmann   Michael Waidner (Eds.)

Computer Security – ESORICS 2000

6th European Symposium
on Research in Computer Security
Toulouse, France, October 4-6, 2000
Proceedings

Springer

Series Editors

Gerhard Goos, Karlsruhe University, Germany
Juris Hartmanis, Cornell University, NY, USA
Jan van Leeuwen, Utrecht University, The Netherlands

Volume Editors

Frédéric Cuppens
ONERA Centre de Toulouse
2 avenue Edouard Belin, 31055 Toulouse Cedex, France
E-mail: cuppens@cert.fr

Yves Deswarte
LAAS-CNRS
7 avenue du Colonel Roche, 31077 Toulouse Cedex 4, France
E-mail: Yves.Deswarte@laas.fr

Dieter Gollmann
Microsoft Research
1 Guildhall Street, Cambridge CB2 3NH, UK
E-mail: diego@microsoft.com

Michael Waidner
IBM Zurich Research Laboratory, Computer Science Department
Manager Network Security and Cryptography
Saeumerstr. 4, 8803 Rueschlikon, Switzerland
E-mail: wmi@zurich.ibm.com

Cataloging-in-Publication Data applied for

Die Deutsche Bibliothek - CIP-Einheitsaufnahme

Computer security : proceedings / ESORICS 2000, 6th European Symposium
on Research in Computer Security, Toulouse, France, October 4 - 6, 2000.
Frédéric Cuppens ... (ed.). - Berlin ; Heidelberg ; New York ; Barcelona ;
Hong Kong ; London ; Milan ; Paris ; Singapore ; Tokyo : Springer, 2000
   (Lecture notes in computer science ; Vol. 1895)
   ISBN 3-540-41031-7

CR Subject Classification (1998): D.4.6, E.3, C.2.0, H.2.0, K.6.5

ISSN 0302-9743
ISBN 3-540-41031-7 Springer-Verlag Berlin Heidelberg New York

Springer-Verlag Berlin Heidelberg New York
a member of BertelsmannSpringer Science+Business Media GmbH
© Springer-Verlag Berlin Heidelberg 2000
Printed in Germany

Typesetting: Camera-ready by author, data conversion by PTP-Berlin, Stefan Sossna
Printed on acid-free paper   SPIN: 10722599   06/3142   5 4 3 2 1 0

Preface

Ten years ago, the first European Symposium on Research in Computer Security was created in Toulouse. It had been initiated by the French AFCET Technical Committee on Information System Security, and mostly by its President, Gilles Martin, who deceased a few months before. Toulouse was a natural choice for its venue, since two of the most important French research teams in security were and still are in Toulouse: ONERA and LAAS-CNRS. At this first symposium, one third of the presented papers were from French authors, while half of the papers came from other European countries.

The second time ESORICS was held, also in Toulouse in November 1992, the number of accepted papers that came from France had decreased by half, equalling the number of US papers, while about two thirds of the papers came from other European countries. It was then recognised that ESORICS was really a European Symposium, and an international steering committee was established to promote the venue of ESORICS in other European countries. This led to the organisation of ESORICS 94 in Brighton, UK; ESORICS 96 in Rome, Italy; and ESORICS 98 in Louvain, Belgium. During these ten years, ESORICS has established its reputation as the main event in research on computer security in Europe.

With this series of biannual events, ESORICS gathers researchers and practitioners of computer security and gives them the opportunity to present the most recent advances in security theory or more practical concerns such as social engineering or the risks related to simplistic implementations of strong security mechanisms.

For its tenth anniversary, ESORICS is coming back to Toulouse, and its success will be reinforced by the conjunction with RAID 2000, the Symposium on Recent Advances in Intrusion Detection. Born as a workshop joined to ESORICS 98, RAID is now an annual event and the most important international symposium in its area. Let us hope that for the next ten years, ESORICS will again visit other European countries and give rise to other successful security spin-offs.

Yves Deswarte

Since the First European Symposium on Research in Computer Security in 1990, ESORICS has become an established international conference on the theory and practice of computer security and the main research-oriented security conference in Europe.

ESORICS 2000 received 75 submissions, all of which were reviewed by at least three programme committee members or other experts. At a two-day meeting of the programme committee all submissions were discussed, and 19 papers were selected for presentation at the conference.

Two trends in computer security became prominent since ESORICS 1998 and thus received special room in the programme: Cybercrime and the lack of dependability of the Internet, and the renaissance of formal methods in security analysis. The former is not reflected by research papers yet, but in order to facilitate discussion we included a panel discussion on "Cybercrime and Cybercops." The latter trend convinced us to allocate two sessions to this topic, namely, on protocol verification and security property analysis.

We gratefully acknowledge all authors who submitted papers for their efforts in maintaining the standards of this conference. It is also our pleasure to thank the members of the programme committee and the additional reviewers for their work and support.

Frédéric Cuppens
Michael Waidner

Killijian (LAAS-CNRS, France), Helger Lipmaa (Nokia Research Center, Finland), Eric Marsden (LAAS-CNRS, France), Fabio Martinelli IAT-CNR, Italy), Renato Menicocci (Fondazione Ugo Bordoni, Italy), Richard Murphy (Mitretek Systems, USA), Valtteri Niemi (Nokia Research Center, Finland), Peng Ning (George Mason University, USA), Kaisa Nyberg (Nokia Research Center, Finland), David Pointcheval (ENS, France), Guillaume Poupard (ENS, France), Roberto Segala (University of Bologna, Italy), Francisco Javier Thayer (MITRE, USA), Andreas Wespi (IBM Research, Switzerland), Ningning Wu (George Mason University, USA), Charles Youman (George Mason University, USA), Lenore Zuck (MITRE, USA).

Organisation Committee

Claire Saurel	ONERA Centre de Toulouse, Co-Chair
Gilles Trouessin	CNAMTS CESSI, Co-Chair
Jérôme Carrère	ONERA Centre de Toulouse
Francine Decavèle	ONERA Centre de Toulouse
Brigitte Giacomi	ONERA Centre de Toulouse
Marie-Thérèse Ippolito	LAAS-CNRS
Rudolphe Ortalo	NEUROCOM
Roger Payrau	ONERA Centre de Toulouse

Table of Contents

Internet Security

Security Property Analysis

Mobile Agents

Checking Secure Interactions of Smart Card Applets[*]

P. Bieber[1], J. Cazin[1], P. Girard[2], J.-L. Lanet[2], V. Wiels[1], and G. Zanon[1]

[1] ONERA-CERT/DTIM
BP 4025, 2 avenue E. Belin,
F-31055 Toulouse Cedex 4, France
{bieber,cazin,wiels,zanon}@cert.fr
[2] GEMPLUS
avenue du pic de Bertagne, 13881 Gémenos cedex, France
{Pierre.GIRARD,Jean-Louis.LANET}@gemplus.com

Abstract. This paper presents an approach enabling a smart card issuer to verify that a new applet securely interacts with already downloaded applets. A security policy has been defined that associates levels to applet attributes and methods and defines authorized flows between levels. We propose a technique based on model checking to verify that actual information flows between applets are authorized. We illustrate our approach on applets involved in an electronic purse running on Java enabled smart cards.

Introduction

A new type of smart cards is getting more and more attractive: multiapplication smart cards. The main characteristics of such cards are that applications can be loaded after the card issuance and that several applications run on the same card. A few operating systems have been proposed to manage multiapplication smart cards, namely Java Card[1], Multos[2] and more recently Windows for Smart Cards[3]. In this paper, we will focus on Java Card. Following this standard, applications for multiapplication smart cards are implemented as interacting Java applets.

Multiapplication smart cards involve several participants: the card provider, the card issuer that proposes the card to the users, application providers and card holders (users). The card issuer is usually considered responsible for the security of the card. The card issuer does not trust application providers: applets could be malicious or simply faulty.

As in a classical mobile code setting, a malicious downloaded applet could try to observe, alter, use information or resources it is not authorized to. Of course,

---

[*] The Pacap project is partially funded by MENRT décision d'aide 98.B.0251
[1] http://java.sun.com/products/javacard
[2] http://www.multos.com
[3] http://www.microsoft.com/smartcard

F. Cuppens et al. (Eds.): ESORICS 2000, LNCS 1895, pp. 1–16, 2000.

a set of JavaCard security functions were defined that severely restrict what an applet can do. But these functions do not cover a class of threats we call illicit applet interactions that cause unauthorized information flows between applets.

Our goal is to provide techniques and tools enabling the card issuer to verify that new applets interact securely with already loaded applets.

The first section introduces security concerns related to multiapplication smart cards. The second section of the paper describes the electronic purse functionalities and defines the threats associated with this application. The third section presents the security policy and information flow property we selected to verify that applets interact securely. The fourth section shows how we verify secure interaction properties on the applets byte-code. The fifth section relates our approach to other existing work.

1   Security Concerns

1.1   Java Card Security Mechanisms

Security is always a big concern for smart cards but it is all the more important with multiapplication smart cards and post issuance code downloading.

Opposed to monoapplicative smart cards where Operating System and application were mixed, multiapplication smart card have drawn a clear border between the operating system, the virtual machine and the applicative code. In this context, it is necessary to distinguish the security of the card (hardware, operating system and virtual machine) from the security of the application. The card issuer is responsible for the security of the card and the application provider is responsible for the applet security, which relies necessarily on the security of the card.

The physical security is obtained by the smart card media and its tamper resistance. The security properties that the OS guarantees are the quality of the cryptographic mechanisms (which should be leakage resistant, i.e. resistant against side channel attacks such Differential Power Analysis [9]), the correctness of memory and I/O management.

A Java Card virtual machine relies on the type safety of the Java language to guarantee the innocuousness of an applet with respect to the OS, the virtual machine [11], and the other applets. However this is guaranteed by a byte-code verifier which is not on board, so extra mechanisms have been added. A secure loader (like OP [18]) checks before loading an applet that it has been signed (and then verified) by an authorized entity (namely the card issuer). Even if an unverified applet is successfully loaded on the card, the card firewall [17], which is part of the virtual machine, will still deny to an aggressive applet the possibility to manipulate data outside its memory space.

To allow the development of multiapplication smart cards, the Java Card has introduced a new way for applets to interact directly. An applet can invoke another applet method through a shared interface. An applet can decide to share or not some data with a requesting applet based on its identifier.

1.2   Applets Providers and End Users Security Needs

Applet providers have numerous security requirements for their applications. Classical one are secret key confidentiality, protection from aggressive applets, integrity of highly sensitive data fields such as electronic purses balances, etc. These requirement are widely covered by the existing security mechanisms at various levels from silicon to secure loaders and are not covered in this paper. However, new security requirements appear with the growing complexity of applets and the ability for applets to interact directly with other applets.

Particularly, application providers do not want information to flow freely inside the card. They want to be sure that the commercial information they provide such as marketing information and other valuable data (especially short term ones such as stock quotes, weather forecast and so on) won't be retransmitted by applets without their consent. For example, marketing information will be collected by a loyalty applet when an end user buys some goods at a retailer. This information will be shared with partner applets but certainly not with competitor applets. However it will certainly be the case that some partners applets will interact with competitor applets. As in the real world trust between providers should not be transitive and so should be the authorized information flows.

So far we have just talked about confidentiality constraints, but integrity should also be considered. For example, corruption of data or of service outputs by an aggressive applet would be an extremely damaging attack for the brand image of an applet provider well-known for its information accuracy and quality of service.

Finally, the end user security requirement will be related mainly with privacy. As soon as medical data or credit card record are handled by the card and transmitted between applets great care should be taken with the information flow ([4] details such a privacy threat).

1.3   Applet Certification

Applet providers and end users cannot control that their information flow requirements are enforced on the card because they do not manage it. Our goal is to provide techniques and tools enabling the card issuer to verify that new applets respect existing security properties defined as authorized information flows.

If the applet provider wants to load a new applet on a card, she provides the bytecode for this applet. The card issuer has a security policy for the card and security properties that must be satisfied. This security policy should take into account the requirements of applet providers and end users. We provide techniques and tools to decide whether the properties are satisfied by the new applet (these techniques are applied on the applet bytecode). If the properties hold, the applet can be loaded on the card; if they do not hold, it is rejected.

2   Electronic Purse

2.1   Electronic Purse Functionalities

A typical example of a multiapplication smart card is an electronic purse with one purse applet and two loyalty applets: a frequent flyer (Air France) application and a car rental (RentaCar) loyalty program. The purse applet manages debit and credit operations and keeps a log of all the transactions. As several currencies can be used (francs and euros for example) this applet also manages a conversion table. When the card owner wants to subscribe to a loyalty program, the corresponding loyalty applet is loaded on the card. This applet must be able to interact with the purse to get to know the transactions made by the purse in order to update loyalty points according to these transactions. For instance, the Air France applet will add miles to the account of the card owner whenever an Air France ticket is bought with the purse. The card owner can use these miles to buy a discounted Air France ticket. Agreements may also exist between loyalty applets to allow exchanges of points. For instance, loyalty points granted by RentaCar could be summed with Air France miles to buy a discounted ticket.

The electronic purse has been chosen as case study for our project. It has been implemented in Java by Gemplus.

2.2   Electronic Purse Threats

We suppose that all the relevant Java and JavaCard security functions are used in the electronic purse. But these functions do not cover all the threats. We are especially interested in threats particular to multiapplication smart cards like illicit applet interactions. An example of illicit interaction in the case of the electronic purse is described on figure 1.

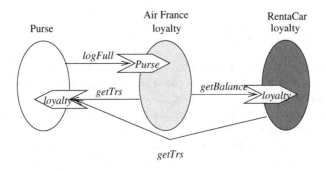

Fig. 1. Applet Interactions

The purse applet has a shared interface for loyalty applets to get their transactions and the loyalty applet has a shared interface for partner loyalty applets to get loyalty points.

A "logfull" service is proposed by the purse to the loyalty applets: when the transaction log is full, the purse calls the *logfull* method of the loyalty applets that subscribed to the service to warn them that the log is full and they should get the transactions before some of them are erased and replaced by new ones. We suppose the Air France applet subscribed to the logfull service, but the RentaCar applet did not. When the log is full, the purse calls the *logfull* method of the Air France applet. In this method, the Air France applet gets transactions from the purse but also wants to update its extended balance that contains its points plus all the points it can get from its loyalty partners. To update this extended balance, it calls the *getbalance* method of the RentaCar loyalty applet. In that case, the car rental applet can guess that the log is full when the Air France applet calls its *getbalance* method and thus get the transactions from the purse. There is a leak of information from the Air France applet to the RentaCar one and we want to be able to detect such illicit information flows. This illicit behaviour would not be countered by the applet firewall as all the invoked methods belong to shared interfaces.

3   Multiapplication Security Policy

3.1   Security Policy

We propose to use a multilevel security policy [4] that was designed for multiapplication smart cards. Each applet provider is assigned a security level and we consider special levels for shared data. On the example of the electronic purse, we have a level for each applet: AF for Air France, P for purse and RC for RentaCar and levels for shared data: $AF + RC$ for data shared by Air France and RentaCar, $AF + P$ for data shared by Air France and purse, etc. The relation between levels $\preceq$ is used to authorize or forbid information flows between applets. In the policy we consider, $AF + P \preceq AF$ and $AF + P \preceq P$, this means that information whose level is $AF+P$ is authorized to flow towards information whose level is P or AF. So shared information from Air France and Purse may be received by Air France and Purse applets. To model that applets may only communicate through shared interfaces, direct flows between levels AF, P and RC are forbidden. So we have: $AF \npreceq P$, $P \npreceq AF$, $AF \npreceq RC$, $RC \npreceq AF$, $P \npreceq RC$ and $RC \npreceq P$.

The levels together with the $\preceq$ relation have a lattice structure, so there are a bottom level *public* and a top level *private*.

3.2   Security Properties

Now we have to define the security properties to be enforced. We have chosen the secure dependency model [1] that applies to systems where malicious applications might communicate confidential information to other applications. Like other information flow models such as non-interference [5], this model ensures that dependencies between system objects cannot be exploited to establish an indirect communication channel. We apply this model to the electronic purse: illicit interactions will be detected by controlling the dependencies between objects of the system.

A program is described by a set of evolutions that associate a value with each object at each date. We note $Ev \subseteq Objects \times Dates \rightarrow Values$ the set of evolutions of a program. The set $Objects \times Dates$ is made of three disjoint subsets: input objects that are not computed by the program, output objects that are computed by the program and are directly observable and internal objects that are not observable. We assume that function lvl associates a security level with input and output objects.

The secure dependency property $SecDep$ requires that the value of output objects with security level l only depends on the value of input objects whose security level is dominated by l:

$$\forall o_t \in Output, \forall e \in Ev, \forall e' \in Ev, e \sim_{aut(o_t)} e' \Rightarrow e(o_t) = e'(o_t)$$

where $aut(o_t) = \{o'_{t'} \in Input \mid t' < t, lvl(o'_{t'}) \preceq lvl(o_t)\}$ and $e \sim_{aut(o_t)} e'$ iff $\forall o'_{t'} \in aut(o_t), e(o'_{t'}) = e'(o'_{t'})$.

This property cannot be directly proved with a model checker such as SMV ([12]) because it is neither a safety or liveness property nor a refinement property. So we look for sufficient conditions of $SecDep$ that are better handled by SMV. By analysing the various instructions in a program, it is easy to compute for each object the set of objects it syntactically depends on. The set $dep(i, o_t)$ contains objects with date $t-1$ used by instruction at program location i to compute the value of o_t. The program counter is an internal object such that pc_{t-1} determines the current instruction used to compute the value of o_t. Whenever an object is modified (i.e. o_{t-1} is different form o_t) then we consider that pc_{t-1} belongs to $dep(i, o_t)$.

Hypothesis 1 *The value of o_t computed by the program is determined by the values of objects in $dep(e(pc_{t-1}), o_t)$:*

$$\forall o_t \in Output, \forall e \in Ev, e' \in Ev, e \sim_{dep(e(pc_{t-1}), o_t)} e' \Rightarrow e(o_t) = e'(o_t)$$

The latter formula looks like $SecDep$ so to prove $SecDep$ it could be sufficient to prove that the security level of any member of $dep(e(pc_{t-1}), o_t)$ is dominated by o_t security level. But $dep(e(pc_{t-1}), o_t)$ may contain internal objects, as lvl is not defined for these objects we might be unable to check this sufficient condition. To overcome this problem we define function $lvldep$ that associates, for each evolution, a computed level with each object. If o_t is an input object then $lvldep(e, o_t) = lvl(o_t)$ otherwise $lvldep(e, o_t) = max\{lvldep(e, o'_{t-1}) \mid o'_{t-1} \in dep(e(pc_{t-1}), o_t)\}$ where max denotes the least upper bound in the lattice of levels.

Theorem 1. *A program satisfies $SecDep$ if the computed level of an output object is always dominated by its security level:*

$$\forall o \in Output, \forall e \in Ev, lvldep(e, o_t) \preceq lvl(o_t)$$

As we want to use model checkers to verify the security properties, it is important to restrict the size of value domains in order to avoid state explosions during verifications. To check security, it is sufficient to prove that the previous property holds in any state of an abstracted program where object values are replaced with object computed levels. If Ev is the set of evolution of the concrete program, then we note Ev^a the set of evolutions of the corresponding abstract program.

Hypothesis 2 *We suppose that the set of abstract evolution Ev^a is such that the image of Ev by abs is included in Ev^a, where $abs(e)(o_t) = lvldep(e, o_t)$ if $o \neq pc$ and $abs(e)(pc_t) = e(pc_t)$.*

Theorem 2. *If $\forall o_t \in Output, \forall e^a \in Ev^a, e^a(o_t) \preceq lvl(o_t)$ then the concrete program guarantees SecDep.*

Proof: Let o_t be an output object and e be a concrete evolution in Ev, by Hypothesis 2 $abs(e)$ is an abstract evolution hence $abs(e)(o_t) \preceq lvl(o_t)$. By definition of abs, $abs(e)(o_t) = lvldep(e, o_t)$ so $lvldep(e, o_t) \preceq lvl(o_t)$ and by applying theorem 1, $SecDep$ is satisfied.

4   Applet Certification

An application is composed of a finite number of interacting applets. Each applet contains several methods. For efficiency reasons, we want to limit the number of applets and methods analysed when a new applet is downloaded or when the security policy is modified.

We first present how we decompose the global analysis of interacting applets on a card into local verifications of a subset of the methods of one applet. Then we explain how the local verifications are implemented.

4.1   Global Analysis Technique

There are two related issues in order to be able to apply the approach in practice: we first have to determine what is the program we want to analyse (one method of one applet, all the methods in one applet, all the methods in all the applets on the card); then we have to identify inputs and outputs and to assign them a level.

We suppose the complete call graph of the application is given. Two kinds of methods will especially interest us because they are the basis of applet interactions: interface methods that can be called from other applets and methods that invoke external methods of other applets. We have decided to analyse subsets of the call graph that include such interaction methods. Furthermore an analysed subset only contains methods that belong to the same applet.

Let us consider for instance the Air France applet. Method *logfull* is an interface method that calls two internal methods: *askfortransactions* and *update*. *askfortransactions* invokes method *gettransaction* of Purse and credit the attribute *balance* with the value of the transactions; *update* invokes method *getbalance* of RentaCar and updates the value of the *extendedbalance* attribute. The program we are going to analyse is the set of 3 methods *logfull*, *askfortransactions* and *update*.

For a given program, we consider as inputs results from external invocations and read attributes. We take as outputs parameters of external invocations and modified attributes. We thus associate security levels with applet attributes and with method invocations between applets. By default, we associate level AF (resp. P and RC) with all the attributes of Air France (resp. Purse and RentaCar) applet. As Air France can invoke the *getbalance* or *debit* methods of RentaCar, we assign the shared security level $RC + AF$ to these interactions. Similarly, as the Purse applet can invoke the *logfull* method of Air France, we associate level $AF + P$ to this interaction. And we associate level $P + AF$ (resp. $P + RC$) to the invocation of *gettransaction* method of the Purse applet by the Air France applet (resp. by RentaCar applet).

We propose an assume-guarantee discipline that allows to verify a set of methods locally on each applet even if the methods call methods in other applets through shared interfaces (see figure 2). For instance, method *update* of applet Air France calls method *getbalance* of RentaCar, we will analyse both methods separately. We check that, in the *update* method of the Air France applet, the level of parameters of the *getbalance* method invocation is dominated by the level of this interaction (i.e. $RC + AF$). And we assume that $RC + AF$ is the level of the result of this method invocation. When we analyse the *getbalance* method in the RentaCar applet, we will check that the level of the result of this method is dominated by the level of the interaction and we will assume that $RC + AF$ is the level of the parameters of the *getbalance* method.

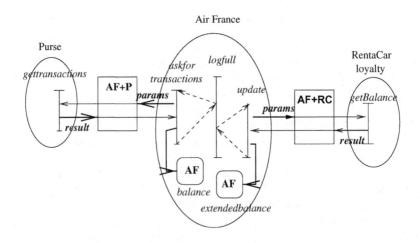

Fig. 2. Assume-Guarantee Verification

We adopt the same discipline for the attributes inside an applet. When an attribute is read, we assume that its level is the security level that was associated with it. When the attribute is modified, we check that the new level is dominated by the security level of this attribute. This assume-guarantee discipline inside an applet allows to verify only a subset of methods of an applet at a time (not the whole set of methods of this applet).

Thanks to this decomposition principle, it is possible to focus the analysis on the new applet that the card issuer wants to download on the cards. If the policy is unchanged there is no need to analyze again the already existing applets because levels associated with input and output objects will not change. If the security policy changes the security level associated with some input or output objects then only methods of already existing applets that use these objects should be checked again.

4.2   Local Analysis Technique

Our method to verify the security property on the application byte code is based on three elements:

- abstraction: we abstract all values of variables by computed levels;
- sufficient condition: we verify an invariant that is a sufficient condition of the security property;
- model checking: we verify this invariant by model checking.

We consider a set of methods at a time. Our approach uses the modularity capabilities of SMV: it first consists in building an SMV module that abstracts a method byte code for each method, then to build a `main` module that contains instances of each of these method abstraction modules and describes the interconnections between these modules. We begin by explaining how we build a module for each method, then we describe the `main` module and finally the properties. We illustrate the approach on the logfull example presented above that involves the analysis of methods *logfull*, *update* and *askfortransactions*.

Method abstraction module.   We illustrate our technique on a simplified version of Air France *update()* method. This method directly invokes method *getbalance* of the RentaCar applet and updates the *extendedbalance* field.

```
Method void update()
    0 aload_0
    1 invokespecial 108 <Method int getbalance()>
    4 istore_1
    5 aload_0
    6 dup
    7 getfield 220 <Field int extendedbalance>
   10 iload_1
   11 iadd
   12 putfield 220 <Field int extendedbalance>
   15 return
```

Abstraction The *update*() byte code abstraction is modelled by an SMV [12] module. This module has got parameters (which are instantiated in the main module):

- *active* is an input of the module, it is a boolean that is true when the method is active (as we consider several methods, we have to say which one is effectively executing);
- *context* is a boolean representing the context level of the caller;
- *param* is an array containing the levels of the parameters of the method;
- *field* is an array containing the levels of the attributes used by the method (only one here *extendedbalance*);
- *method* is an array containing the levels of the results of the external methods invoked by the *update* method (only one here *getbalance*).

The module also involves the following variables:

- *pc*: program counter;
- *lpc*: the level of the program counter, the context level of the method;
- *mem*[*i*]: an array modelling the memory locations;
- *stck*[*i*]: an array modelling the operand stack;
- *sP*: stack pointer;
- *ByteCode*: the name of the current instruction.

The values of the variables are abstracted into levels. Levels are defined in a module called Levels in such a way that a level is represented by a boolean. Hence the types of abstracted variables are boolean or array of boolean. We do not abstract the value of the program counter that gives the sequencing of instructions, we keep unchanged the value of the stack pointer that gives the index of the first empty slot.

```
module update(active, context, param, field, method){
 L: levels;
 pc : -1..9;
 lpc: boolean;
 mem : array 0..1 of boolean;
 stck : array 0..1 of boolean;
 sP : -1..1;
 ByteCode : {invoke_108, load_0, return, nop, store_1, dup,
             load_1, getfield_220,op, putfield_220};
```

The byte code execution starts at program location 0. Initially, the stack is empty, the level of the method parameter is stored in memory location 0. The level *lpc* is initialized to the context level of the caller *context*.

```
init(pc):= 0; init(sP):= 1; init(mem[0]):= param[0];
for (i=0; i< 2; i=i+1) {init(stck[i]) := L.public; }
init(lpc) := context;
```

The control loop defines the value of the program counter and of the current instruction. It is an almost direct translation of the Java byte code. When *pc* is equal to -1 then the execution is finished and the current instruction is nop that does nothing. As in [6], each instruction we consider models various instructions of the Java byte code. For instance, as we do not care about the type of memory and stack locations, instruction *load_0* represents Java instructions (aload_i, iload_i, lload_i,...). Similarly, the *op* instruction models all the binary operations as (iadd, ladd, iand, ior, ...).

```
if (active) {
  (next(pc), ByteCode) :=
    switch(pc) {
      -1: (-1, nop);
      0 : (pc+1, load_0 );
      1 : (pc+1, invoke_108 );
      2 : (pc+1, store_1 );
      3 : (pc+1, load_0 );
      4 : (pc+1, dup );
      5 : (pc+1, getfield_220 );
      6 : (pc+1, load_1 );
      7 : (pc+1, op );
      8 : (pc+1, putfield_220 );
      9 : (-1, return);
  };}
else {next(pc) := pc; next(ByteCode) := nop;}
```

The following section of the SMV model describes the effect of the instructions on the variables. The instructions compute levels for each variable. The *load* instruction pushes the level of a memory location on the stack, the *store* instruction pops the top of the stack and stores the least upper bound of this level and *lpc* in a memory location. The least upper bound of levels $l1$ and $l2$ is modelled by the disjunction of two levels $l1 \vee l2$. The *dup* instruction duplicates on the stack the top of the stack. The *op* instruction computes the least upper bound of the levels of the two first locations of the stack. The *invoke* instruction pops from the stack the parameter and pushes onto the stack the result of this method invocation. Instruction *getfield* pushes on the top of the stack the level of attribute *extendedbalance*. And, finally, instruction *putfield* pops from the stack the level of attribute *extendedbalance*.

```
switch(ByteCode) {
  nop :;
  load_0 : {next(stck[sP]):= mem[0];next(sP):=sP-1;}
  load_1 : {next(stck[sP]):= mem[1];next(sP):=sP-1;}
  store_1 : {next(mem[1]):=(stck[sP+1]|lpc) ;next(sP):=sP+1;}
  dup : {next(stck[sP]):= stck[sP+1]; next(sP):=sP-1;}
  op : {next(stck[sP+2]):=(stck[sP+1]|stck[sP+2]);
```

```
        next(sP):=sP+1};
   invoke_108 : {next(stck[sP]):=method[0];next(sP):= sP+1;}
   getfield_220 : {next(stck[sP+1]):=field[0];}
   putfield_220 : {next(sP):=sP+2;}
   return : ;
   }
```

"Conditional" instructions.   No conditional instruction such as ifne, table switch ... occurs in the example presented above. The behaviour of these instructions is to jump at various locations of the program depending on the value of the top of the stack. As this value is replaced by a level, the abstract program cannot decide precisely which is the new value of the program counter. So an SMV non-deterministic assignment is used to state that there are several possible values for *pc* (generally *pc* + 1 or the target location of the conditional instruction).

It is well known that conditional instructions introduce a dependency on the condition. This dependency is taken into account by means of the *lpc* variable. When a conditional instruction is encountered, *lpc* is modified and takes as new value the least upper bound of its current level and of the condition level. As each modified variable depends on *lpc*, we keep trace of the implicit dependency between variables modified in the scope of a conditional instruction and the condition.

Main module.   We have an SMV module for the *update* method. We can build in a similar way a module for the *gettransactions* method and for the *logfull* method. We also have a module Levels. The SMV main module is composed of two parts: the first part manages the connections between methods (definition of the active method, parameter passing); the second one assigns levels to attributes and interactions.

The main module includes an instance of each of the method abstraction modules and one instance of the level module. To define the active method and describe the activity transfer, we need a global variable *active* from which the activity parameter of the different methods is defined.

```
module main(){
active : {logfull, askfortransactions, update};
L: levels;
m_logfull: logfull((active=logfull));
m_aft: askfortransactions((active=askfortransactions),context_aft,
                        param_aft, field_aft,method_aft);
m_update: update((active=update),context_ud, param_ud,
                field_ud,method_ud);
```

The main module contains a set of equations that define the value of *active* according to the call graph. Initially, the active method is *logfull*. When *askfortransactions* is invoked (m_logfull.ByteCode=invoke_235), method *askfortransactions* becomes active. When it terminates (`m_aft.pc=-1`), logfull becomes active again. When *update* is invoked (`m_logfull.ByteCode=invoke_192`) method *update* becomes active. When this method terminates (`m_update.pc=-1`), *logfull* is active until the end.

When *logfull* invokes *askfortransactions* or *update*, it involves parameter passing between methods. In the example, there is only one parameter in each case, so it is sufficient to copy the top of logfull stack into the parameter array of the invoked method. We also transfer the context level of the caller to the invoked method by copying *lpc* in the *context* parameter.

```
if(m_logfull.ByteCode = invoke_235) {
        next(param_aft[0]) := m_logfull.stck[m_logfull.sP+1];
        next(context_aft) := m_logfull.lpc; }

if(m_logfull.ByteCode = invoke_192) {
        next(param_ud[0]) := m_logfull.stck[m_logfull.sP+1];
        next(context_ud) := m_logfull.lpc; }
```

Remark: the methods in the example do not have result, but in the general case, we would also have to transfer the result (i.e. the top of the stack) from the invoked method to the caller.

It now remains to assign levels to attributes and interactions. In the example, we have two attributes with level *AF*: *balance* (146) which is a parameter of *askfortransactions*, and *extendedbalance* (220) which is a parameter of *update*; and two interactions: *getbalance* (108) between Air France and RentaCar (so its level is $AF + RC$), parameter of *askfortransactions*, and *gettransactions* (179) between Air France and Purse (so its level is $AF + P$), parameter of *update*. Remark: in our boolean encoding of levels, $l1 + l2$ is expressed by $l1\&l2$.

```
field_aft[0] := L.AF;    method_aft[0] := L.AF & L.P;
field_ud[0]  := L.AF;    method_ud[0]  := L.AF & L.RC;
```

Invariant. We explained above how to compute a level for each variable. We also explained what security level we assigned to attributes and interactions. The invariant we verify is the sufficient condition we previously described: the computed level of each output is always dominated by its security level.

For the *update* method we should check two properties : one to verifiy that the interaction between *update* and *getbalance* is correct and the other one to check that *update* correctly uses attribute *extendedbalance*. Property *Smethod_108* means that, whenever the current instruction is the invocation of method *getbalance*, then the level of the transmitted parameters (the least upper bound of *lpc* and the top of the stack) is dominated by the level of the interaction $AF + RC$. In our boolean encoding of levels, $l1$ is dominated by $l2$ if `L.l1` implies `L.l2`. Property *Sfield_220* means that, whenever the current instruction is the modification of field *extendedbalance*, then the level of the new value (the least upper bound of *lpc* and the top of the stack) is dominated by the level of the attribute *AF*.

```
Smethod_108 :
  assert G (m_update.ByteCode=invoke_108 ->
             ((m_update.stck[sP+1]|m_update.lpc) -> L.AF & L.RC));
Sfield_220  :
  assert G (m_aft.ByteCode=putfield_220 ->
             ((m_aft.stck[sP+1]|m_aft.lpc) -> L.AF));
```

For the initial method (here *logfull*), we also have to verify the *Sresult* property which means that whenever the method is finished the level of the return value (the top of the stack) is dominated by the level of the interaction $AF + P$. As *logfull* does not return any value, there is no need to verify this property.

```
Sresult     :
  assert G (m_logfull.ByteCode=return ->
             ((m_logfull.stck[sP+1]|m_logfull.lpc) -> L.AF & L.P));
```

4.3   Analysis

Once we have the abstract model and the invariant, we model check the invariant properties on the model using SMV [12]. If the property does not hold the model checker produces a counter-model that represents an execution of the byte code leading to a state where the property is violated.

A security problem will be detected when checking property *Smethod_108* of method *update*. Indeed, the *logfull* interaction between purse and Air France has $AF + P$ level. The *getbalance* channel has $AF + RC$ level and we detect that the invocation of the *getbalance* method depends on the invocation of the *logfull* method. There is thus an illicit dependency from a variable of level $AF + P$ to an object of level $AF + RC$.

To check all the possible interactions on the example of the electronic purse, we have to do 20 analyses such as the one we presented in this paper. These analyses involve about 100 methods and 60 properties to be verified. The complete (non simplified) version of the logfull interaction contains 5 methods and 8 properties, the verification of each property takes 1s on an Ultra 10 SUN station running Solaris 5.6 with 256 Mbytes of RAM. For the other interactions, 30 properties were checked individually in less than 5s, each of the 20 other properties were verified in less than one minute and the remaining properties are checked individually in less than 3 minutes. We observed that the verification time depends on the number of byte-code lines of methods but SMV was always able to verify the properties in a few minutes. Hence, we think that our technique could be applied to real-world applications because the electronic purse case-study is, by now, a "big" application with respect to smart-card memory size limitations.

5   Related Work

A lot of work has been going on about the analysis of security properties of Java byte code. The major part of this work is concerned with properties verified by

SUN byte code verifier like correct typing, no stack overflow, etc. Among this work, two kinds of approaches can be distinguished depending on the technique used for the verification. Most of the approaches are based on static analysis techniques, particularly type systems [2,16]. One approach has used model checking (with SMV) to specify the correct typing of Java byte code [14]. We also based our approach on model-checking tools because they tend to be more generic and expressive than type-checking algorithms. This allowed us to obtain results faster because we did not have to implement a particular type-checking algorithm. This should also enable us to perform experiments with other security policies and properties.

Recently, several researchers investigated the static analysis of information flow properties quite similar to our secure dependency property but, to our knowledge, none of them applied their work on Java byte-code. Girard et alter [7] defined a type system to check that a programme written in a subset of the C language does not transfer High level information in Low level variables. In [3], the typing relation was related to the secure dependency property. Volpano and Smith [15] proposed a type system with a similar objective for a language that includes threads. They relate their typing relation to the non-interference property. The secure dependency property was compared with non-interference in [1]. Myers and Liskov [13] propose a technique to analyze information flows of imperative programs annotated with labels that aggregate the sensitivity levels associated with various information providers. One of the interesting feature is the declassify operation that allows providers to modify labels. They propose a linear algorithm to verify that labels satisfy all the constraints.

A few pieces of work deal with other kind of security properties. In [8] the authors propose an automatic method for verifying that an implementation using local security checks satisfies a global security property. However, their approach is limited to control flow properties such as Java Virtual Machine stack inspection. The work described in [10] focusses on integrity property by controlling exclusively write operations to locations of references of sensitive objects such as files or network connections.

6   Conclusion and Future Work

In this paper, we have presented an approach for the certification of applets that are to be loaded on a Javacard. The security checks we propose are complementary to the security functions already present on the card. The applet firewall controls the interaction between two applets, while our analysis has a more global view and is able to detect illicit information flow between several applets.

As stated in section 4.3, the complete analysis of the application would concern 20 sets of methods, involving globally about 100 methods. Consequently a lot of SMV models need to be built. Automatization of the production of models is thus mandatory for the approach to be practicable. Such an automatization is relatively straightforward provided that preliminary treatments are made to prepare the model construction, such as construction of the call graph, method name resolution, etc. However, a complete automatization is hardly possible: an interaction with the user will be needed for the definition of security policy and level assignments.

Another interesting issue is the analysis of results. When SMV produces a counter-example for a security property, we have to study how to interpret this counter-example as an execution of the concrete byte code program at the application level.

References

1. P. Bieber and F. Cuppens. A Logical View of Secure Dependencies. *Journal of Computer Security*, 1(1):99–129, 1992.
2. Stephen N. Freund and John C. Mitchell. A type system for object initialization in the java byte code language. In *Proceedings of OOPSLA 98*, 1998.
3. P. Girard. *Formalisation et mise en oeuvre d'une analyse statique de code en vue de la verification d'applications securisees.* PhD thesis, ENSAE, 1996.
4. Pierre Girard. Which security policy for multiapplication smart cards? In *USENIX workshop on smartcard technology*, 1999.
5. J. Goguen and J. Meseguer. Unwinding and Inference Control. In *IEEE Symposium on Security and Privacy*, Oakland, 1984.
6. Pieter H. Hartel, Michael J. Butler, and Moshe Levy. The operational semantics of a java secure processor. Technical Report DSSE-TR-98-1, Declarative systems and Software Engineering group, University of Southampton,Highfield, Southampton SO17 1BJ, UK, 1998.
7. C. O'Halloran J. Cazin, P. Girard and C. T. Sennett. Formal Validation of Software for Secure Systems. In *Anglo-french workshop on formal methods, modelling and simulation for system engineering*, 1995.
8. T. Jensen, D. Le Métayer, and T. Thorn. Verification of control flow based security policies. In *Proceedings of the 20th IEEE Security and Privacy Symposium*, 1999.
9. Paul Kocher, Joshua Jaff, and Benjamin Jun. Differential power analysis: Leaking secrets. In *Advances in Cryptology – CRYPTO'99 Proceedings*. Springer-Verlag, 1999.
10. X. Leroy and F. Rouaix. Security properties of typed applets. In *Proceedings of POPL*, 1998.
11. T. Lindholm and F. Yellin. *The Java Virtual Machine Specification.* Addison Wesley, 1997.
12. K.L. McMillan. *The SMV language.* Cadence Berkeley Labs, 1999.
13. A.C. Myers and B. Liskov. A decentralized model for information flow control. In *Proceedings of the 16th ACM symposium on operating systems principles*, 1997.
14. Joachim Posegga and Harald Vogt. Offline verification for java byte code using a model checker. In *Proceedings of ESORICS*, number 1485 in LNCS. Springer, 1998.
15. G. Smith and D.M. Volpano. Secure information flow in a multi-threaded imperative language. In *Proceedings of POPL*, 1998.
16. Raymie Stata and Martin Abadi. A type system for java bytecode subroutines. In *Proc. 25th Symposium on Principles of Programming Languages*, 1998.
17. Sun Microsystems. *Java Card 2.1 Realtime Environment (JCRE) Specification*, February 1999.
18. Visa. *Open Platform, Card Specification*, April 1999. Version 2.0.

Verification of a Formal Security Model for Multiapplicative Smart Cards[*]

Gerhard Schellhorn[1], Wolfgang Reif[1], Axel Schairer[2],
Paul Karger[3], Vernon Austel[3], and David Toll[3]

[1] Universität Augsburg, Lehrstuhl Softwaretechnik und Programmiersprachen,
D-86135 Augsburg
[2] DFKI GmbH, Stuhlsatzenhausweg 3, D-66123 Saarbrücken
[3] IBM T.J. Watson Research Center, 30 Saw Mill River Rd., Hawthorne, NY 10532

Abstract. We present a generic formal security model for operating systems of multiapplicative smart cards. The model formalizes the main security aspects of secrecy, integrity, secure communication between applications and secure downloading of new applications. The model satisfies a security policy consisting of authentication and intransitive noninterference. The model extends the classical security models of Bell/LaPadula and Biba, but avoids the need for *trusted processes*, which are not subject to the security policy by incorporating such processes directly in the model itself. The correctness of the security policy has been formally proven with the VSE II system.

1 Introduction

Smart cards are becoming more and more popular. Compared to magnetic stripe cards they have considerable advantages. They may not only store data, that can be read and changed from a terminal, but they can also store executable programs. Therefore, anything that can be done with an ordinary computer can be done with a smart card. Their usefulness is limited only by available memory and computational power.

Currently, smart cards used in electronic commerce are single application smart cards: they store applications (usually only one) developed by a *single* provider. The scenario we envision for the future is that of multiapplicative smart cards, where several independent providers, maybe even competitors, have applications (i.e. collections of programs and data files to achieve a certain task) on a single smart card.

As an example, consider three applications: An airline A, which manages electronic flight tickets with the smart card, and two hotel chains H and I which use the smart card as an electronic door opener. A customer would carry the smart card around and show it whenever he visits one of H, I or flies with A. Of course none of the application providers would like to trust the others,

---

[*] Augsburg and DFKI research sponsored by the German Information Security Agency (BSI)

F. Cuppens et al. (Eds.): ESORICS 2000, LNCS 1895, pp. 17–36, 2000.

especially H would not trust his competitor I. Therefore the applications should be completely separate: none of the data H stores for opening doors should be visible or modifiable by I or A.

If two application providers agree, communication should also be possible: Airline A could have a loyalty scheme with H (see Fig. 1), or even with both H and I. Staying in a hotel of H earns a customer loyalty points, which reduces the price to fly with A, but that information must not be available to I. Establishing new communication channels and adding new applications should be possible dynamically: e.g. visiting his bank B, the card holder should be able to add an electronic wallet.

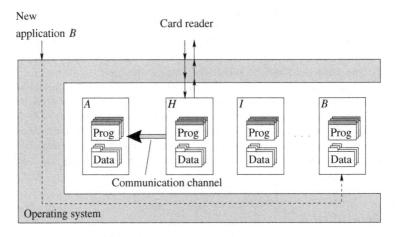

Fig. 1. An example scenario for a multiapplicative smart card

Of course such a scenario raises considerable security issues: How can applications be isolated from each other (e.g. H and its competitor I)? If applications want to communicate, how can communication be allowed without having unwanted information flow (e.g. I should not be able to see loyalty points moving from H to A)? How can it be guaranteed that a dynamically loaded new application does not corrupt existing ones?

In this paper, we present a formal security model that solves these questions for smart cards, as well as cell phones, PDAs, or larger systems. We will model an operating system which executes system calls ("commands"). These system calls are made by applications programs running in user mode on the smart card to an operating system running in supervisor mode on the smart card. They are fundamentally different from the commands defined in ISO/IEC 7816-4 [6] that are commands sent from the outside world to the smart card. The security conditions attached to the commands obey a security policy, which is suitable to solve the problems discussed above. The commands are chosen to be as abstract as possible: There is a command to register authentication information (e.g. a public key) for a new application (one application might have several keys to be able to structure its data into several levels of secrecy and integrity), commands to load and to delete an application program, and file access commands to create, read, write and delete data files. Finally a command to change the secrecy and integrity of a file (according to the security policy) is provided.

The design of the formal security model was influenced by the informal security model [9] developed as part of IBM Research Division's on-going development of a high assurance smart card operating system for the Philips SmartXA chip [15]. The SmartXA is the first smart card chip to have hardware support for supervisor/user modes and a memory management unit. Some more information on potential applications of multiapplicative smart cards with this security model are given in [10]. Our security model was designed to be a generic abstraction from the IBM model that should be useful for other Smart Card providers too. It is compliant with the requirements for an evaluation of operating systems according to the ITSEC evaluation criteria [8] E4 or higher (and comparable Common Criteria [7] EAL5 or higher). The IBM system is designed for even higher assurance levels – ITSEC E5 or E6 or Common Criteria EAL6 or EAL7.

This paper is structured as follows: Sect. 2 describes the security objectives. Sect. 3 introduces the concepts to be implemented on the smart card which are used to achieve the security objectives. We informally define a mandatory security policy based on intransitive noninterference and authentication. Sect. 4 sketches the theory of intransitive noninterference as defined in [16] and explains some extensions. The data structures and commands of the system model are defined in Sect. 5. Sect. 6 discusses how to use the commands of the model for the example above. Sect. 7 discusses the formal verification of the security policy for the model. Sect. 8 compares some of the features of the informal IBM model [9] and the formal model. Finally, Sect. 9 concludes the paper.

2   Security Objectives

The security of a smart card is threatened by a variety of attacks, ranging from physical analysis of the card and manipulated card readers to programs circumventing the OS's security functions, or the OS security functions themselves revealing or changing information that is not intended (covert channels). In the model described in this paper we will be concerned with the question whether the operating system's functionality on the level of (abstract) system calls can guarantee the security requirements. We will therefore assume that operating system calls are atomic actions (this should be supported by hardware, e.g. a supervisor mode of the processor). We will not address physical threats to the card itself or to the card readers. Also, threats on the level of, e.g. memory reuse or register usage in the machine code will not be considered.

Our model addresses the following security objectives.

O1: Secrecy/integrity between programs of the same or different applications.
O2: Secure communication between applications.
O3: Secure downloading of code.

Application providers need to have guarantees that the data and programs they store on the card and pass to and receive from card readers are handled such that their secrecy and integrity is guaranteed: their code and data neither be observable nor alterable by other programs. This guarantees that secret data produced by one application's program cannot be leaked to another application, and that programs of one application can not be crashed by other application's corrupt data. Some application providers will additionally want to classify their programs and data into different levels of security and integrity. The OS should also guarantee that data are handled in a way that respects these different security and integrity levels. This is useful, e.g., in case a small number of programs operate on highly sensitive data and the rest only operate on insensitive data. In this case only a small fraction of the code has to be checked to handle the sensitive data correctly, because the bulk of the programs are guaranteed by the OS not to be able to access the sensitive data at all.

Some application providers will want their programs to exchange data with other applications in a controlled way, i.e. only in a way that has been mutually agreed on by the providers. The objective of secure communication asserts that data can only be communicated between applications if both application providers agree with the communication and with the form in which the data is communicated. It also implies that the communication cannot be observed or manipulated by other programs. We only consider communication through storage channels, timing channels are not in the scope of the model.

Our model does not impose restrictions on transitive communications: if application A sends some information to B (which assumes that they both have agreed), it no longer has any influence on what B does with the information. B could send it to any application C, even one hostile to A, if it has agreed with C to do so. Since it is not clear that this problem can be addressed technically we assume that providers who have explicitly agreed to exchange data have set up contracts to prevent such potential fraud by non-technical means.

Secure communication of application programs with card readers should be supported by the OS. However, this involves security considerations for devices outside the card and is not in the scope of the model described in this paper: we assume that a reliable communication between programs and card readers is implemented by the programs but will not consider the OS services needed to achieve this. Using the terminology of [19] we define all applications on the card to be within the security perimeter (to be in the "controlled application set"), while all devices outside the card are untrusted subjects.

All the objectives described above should not be threatened by programs that are dynamically loaded onto the card.

3   Security Concepts

In this section we define the concepts for security, which should be implemented on the smart card as an infrastructure. We define security claims over these concepts, which ensure that the 3 security objectives given in the previous section are met. The security claims will be proven formally for our model.

Secrecy and integrity (objective O1) are common objectives of security models. Usually variants of the well-known mandatory security models of Bell/LaPadula [2] and Biba [3] are used for this purpose. We assume the reader is familiar with them and their use of access classes (consisting of an access level and a set of access categories) to define the secrecy and integrity classification of files (objects) as well as the clearance of subjects. In our case applications will act as subjects. They will get disjoint sets of access categories (in the simplest case, application names and access categories coincide). This results in separated applications, where communication is completely prohibited.

One problem with this classical approach is that adding communication channels (objective O2) in such a Bell/LaPadula model will violate the security policy (simple security and *-property). Of course it is possible to add "trusted processes" (like it was done in the Multics-instance of the Bell/LaPadula [2] or in [12]), which are considered to be outside the model (i.e. properties of the security policy are proved ignoring them). But one of our main security objectives is to include such secure communication in the verified model.

Our solution to this problem consists of two steps. The first part is to use the following idea from the IBM operating system [9] (similar ideas are also given in [17] and [12]): Instead of giving a subject two access classes (icl, scl) as clearance (one for integrity and one for secrecy), we define the clearance of a subject to be four access classes $(ircl, srcl, iwcl, swcl)$: The first two are used in reading operations, the other two in writing operations.

Usual application programs will have the same access classes for reading and writing ($ircl = iwcl$ and $srcl = swcl$). A communication channel from application A to application B is realized by a special program, called a *channel program* with two different pairs of access classes: the pair used for reading will have the clearance of A, while the one used for writing will have the clearance of B. This will allow the channel to read the content of a file from A and to write it into a file, which can then be read by B.

The second part consists in defining a new security policy, which generalizes the one of the Bell/LaPadula and Biba model. We will show, that the model satisfies the following security policy:

A subject A with clearance (ircl$_A$,iwcl$_A$,srcl$_A$,swcl$_A$) can transfer information to a subject B with clearance (ircl$_B$,iwcl$_B$,srcl$_B$,swcl$_B$) if and only if iwcl$_A \geq$ ircl$_B$ and swcl$_A \leq$ srcl$_B$

Formally, we will prove that our security model is an instance of an intransitive noninterference model. Corollaries from this fact are that without communication channels, the model is an instance of the Bell/LaPadula as well as of the Biba model (objective O1) and that if a channel is set up as described above, it exactly allows communication from A to B (objective O2). The proof also implies that our model is free of covert storage channels. This is in contrast to pure Bell/LaPadula-like models, which require an extra analysis for covert storage channels (see [13]).

To accommodate secure downloading of applications (and of channel programs; objective O3), we have to add a second concept to our model: authentication. We will base authentication on a predefined function *check* for digital signatures. Loaded data d will have to be signed with a signature s, such that calling $check(k,s,d)$ with a key k stored on the card yields true. Since issues of cryptography are outside the scope of a formal model, we do not specify the types of s and k (one possible interpretation of k is a public key of RSA cryptography, and that s is a signature for d which can only be given using the corresponding private key). Instead we only make the following basic assumption: From a successful check it can be deduced that the person who stored k previously on the card has signed d, and therefore agreed to loading d.

Under the basic assumption, our authentication scheme will guarantee the following two properties for downloading applications:

– The card issuer can control which applications are loaded onto the card.
– The owner of an application has agreed to loading each of his programs. All other programs, which he has not agreed to being loaded, can not interfere with the application.

In particular, it is guaranteed that if the application owner does not want any communication with other applications, the application will be completely isolated. Also, the second property implies that any channel program between two applications A and B must have been authenticated by both A and B.

4   Noninterference

This section first repeats the main definitions of the generic noninterference model as defined by Rushby [16]. Following Rushby, we will sketch that a simple Bell/LaPadula model, where the system state consists of a set of subjects with an access class as clearance and a set of objects with an access class as classification, is an instance of the model. To define our smart card security model as an instance of noninterference, we had to make small modifications to the generic model. They resulted in a generalization of Rushby's main theorem, which is given at the end of the section.

The system model of noninterference is based on the concept of a state machine, which starts in a fixed initial state *init* and sequentially executes commands (here: OS commands, i.e. system calls). Execution of a command may alter the system state and produces some output. The model does not make any assumptions on the structure of the system or on the set of available commands. The model is specified algebraically using functions *exec*, *out* and *execl*; for a system state *sys* and a command *co*, $exec(sys, co)$ is the new system state and $out(sys, co)$ is the generated output. $execl(sys, cl)$ (recursively defined using *exec*) returns the final state of executing a list *cl* of commands.

To define security it is assumed that each command co is executed by a subject with a certain *clearance*[1] D which is computable as $D = dom(co)$. The general model of noninterference makes no assumptions about the structure of clearances. They are just an abstract notion for the rights of a subject executing a command. Also note, that subjects are not defined explicitly in the generic model, since only their clearance matters for security.

A security policy is defined to be an arbitrary relation $\rightsquigarrow$ on clearances. $A \rightsquigarrow B$ intuitively means that a subject with clearance A is allowed to pass information to a subject with clearance B ("A interferes with B"), whereas $A \not\rightsquigarrow B$ means that commands executed by A will have no effect on B.

For the Bell/LaPadula instance of the model, the clearance of a subject is defined as usual as an access class, and the $\rightsquigarrow$-relation coincides with the less-or-equal relation on access classes (a subject with lower clearance can pass information to one with higher clearance, but not vice versa). The $\rightsquigarrow$-relation is therefore *transitive* in this case. The big advantage of a noninterference model over a Bell/LaPadula model is that it is possible to define interference relations, which are *not* transitive[2]. This is what we need for the smart card security model, to model communication: we want an application A to be able to pass information to another application B via a channel program C, i.e. we want $A \rightsquigarrow C$ and $C \rightsquigarrow B$. But we do not want information to be passed from A directly to B, i.e. we want $A \not\rightsquigarrow B$.

Informally, security of a noninterference model is defined as the requirement that the outcome of executing a command co does not depend on commands that were previously executed by subjects which may not interfere with the subject of co, i.e. $dom(co)$.

To formalize this, a function *purge* is defined. $purge(cl,B)$ removes all commands "irrelevant for B" from the commandlist cl. The output to a command co then must be the same, whether cl or $purge(cl,dom(co))$ are executed before it. Formally, a system is defined to be secure, if and only if for all commandlists cl and all commands co

$$out(execl(init,cl),co) = out(execl(init,purge(cl,dom(co))),co) \qquad (1)$$

holds. For a transitive interference relation the definition of *purge* is simple: a command co can be purged if and only if $dom(co) \not\rightsquigarrow B$. For the simple Bell/LaPadula instance, Rushby[16] shows that this definition of security is equivalent to simple security and the $\star$-property. Therefore the simple Bell/LaPadula model is an instance of transitive noninterference.

The definition of security for an intransitive noninterference model (i.e. a noninterference model with an intransitive interference relation) also requires to prove property (1), but the definition of commands, which must be purged

---

[1] The clearance of a subject is called *security domain* in [16]. We avoid this term since it is also used with a different meaning in the context of Java security.

[2] an intransitive interference relation is also possible in domain and type enforcement models [4], [1], but these models do not have a uniform, provable definition of security, which rules out covert channels.

is more complicated: Consider the case mentioned above, where we have two applications A, B and a channel program C with $A \rightsquigarrow C$ and $C \rightsquigarrow B$, but $A \not\rightsquigarrow B$. Now according to the original definition of *purge*, first executing three commands $[co_1, co_2, co_3]$ with $dom(co_1) = A$, $dom(co_2) = C$ and $dom(co_3) = A$, and then looking at the output for a fourth command co executed by B should give the same result as looking at the output to co after only executing co_2: *purge* will remove both co_1 and co_3 since their clearance (in both cases A) does not interfere with B. But removing co_1 is wrong, since command co_1 could make some information of A available for C (since $A \rightsquigarrow C$), and the subsequent command co_2 could pass just this information to B (since $C \rightsquigarrow B$). Finally co could just read this information and present it as output.

Therefore co_1 may affect the output of co and should not be purged. In contrast, co_3 should be purged, since no subsequent commands can pass information to B (the domain of co). The definition of *purge* must be modified, such that its result is $[co_1, co_2]$. The question whether a command is allowed to have a visible effect on some subject after some more commands have been executed now becomes dependent on these subsequently executed commands. Therefore a set of clearances *sources(cl,B)*, which may pass information to B during the execution of a list of commands cl is defined. The first command, co, of a commandlist $[co|cl]$ then does not interfere with clearance B directly or indirectly (and may therefore be purged) if and only if it is not in *sources*(cl, B).

We will give extended versions of *sources* and *purge* for our variant of the model below, which has Rushby's definitions as special cases. Defining a variant of the noninterference model was necessary to make our smart card security model an instance. Two modifications were necessary.

The first is a technical one: the system states we will consider in the smart card security model will have invariant properties, that will hold for all system states reachable from the initial state. Therefore, instead of showing proof obligations for *all* system states, it is sufficient to show them for system states with the invariant property only.

The second modification is more substantial: We do not assume that the clearance of a subject executing a command can be computed from the command alone, since usually the clearance of a subject is stored in the system state. Therefore we must assume that function $dom(sys,co)$ may also depend on the system state. Making the *dom*-function dependent on the system state requires that *sources* and *purge* must also depend on the system state. Our definitions are:

$$sources(sys, [\,], B) = \{B\}$$

$$sources(sys, [co|cl], B) = \begin{cases} \{dom(sys, co)\} \cup sources(exec(sys, co), cl, B) \\ \quad \text{if } dom(sys, co) \rightsquigarrow A \\ \quad \text{for any } A \in sources(exec(sys, co), cl, B) \\ sources(exec(sys, co), cl, B) \quad \text{otherwise} \end{cases}$$

and

$$purge(sys, [\,], B) = [\,]$$

$$purge(sys, [co|cl], B) = \begin{cases} purge(sys, cl, B) \\ \quad \text{if } dom(sys, co) \notin sources(sys, [co|cl], B) \\ [co|purge(exec(sys, co), cl, B)] \quad \text{otherwise} \end{cases}$$

Security is now defined as:

$$out(execl(init, cl), co) = \\ out(execl(init, purge(cl, dom(execl(init, cl), co))), co) \tag{2}$$

Rushby's definitions are the special case, where none of the functions *dom*, *sources* and *purge* depends on the system state. It is easy to see that for transitive interference relations the simple definition of *purge* coincides with the definition given above.

For our definition, we proved the following generalization of Rushby's "Unwinding theorem" (Theorem 7 on p. 28 in [16]).

Theorem 1. If a relation $\overset{A}{\sim}$ and a predicate *inv* can be defined, such that the conditions

1. $\overset{A}{\sim}$ is an equivalence relation
2. $inv(sys) \wedge inv(sys') \wedge sys \overset{dom(sys,co)}{\sim} sys' \rightarrow out(sys, co) = out(sys', co)$
   (system is output consistent)
3. $inv(sys) \wedge dom(sys, co) \not\rightsquigarrow A \rightarrow sys \overset{A}{\sim} exec(sys, co)$
   (system locally respects $\rightsquigarrow$)
4. $inv(sys) \wedge inv(sys') \wedge sys \overset{A}{\sim} sys' \wedge sys \overset{dom(sys,co)}{\sim} sys'$
   $\rightarrow exec(sys, co) \overset{A}{\sim} exec(sys', co)$
   (system is weakly step consistent)
5. $sys \overset{A}{\sim} sys' \rightarrow (dom(sys, co) \rightsquigarrow A \leftrightarrow dom(sys, co) \rightsquigarrow A)$
   (commands respect $\rightsquigarrow$)
6. $sys \overset{dom(sys,co)}{\sim} sys' \rightarrow dom(sys, co) = dom(sys', co)$
   (commands respect equivalence $\sim$)
7. $inv(init)$ (initially invariant)
8. $inv(sys) \rightarrow inv(exec(sys, co))$ (invariance step)

are all provable, then the system is secure, i.e. property (2) holds.

The theorem allows to reduce the proof of property (2), which talks globally about all possible commandlists, to eight local properties for every command. It uses an equivalence relation $sys \overset{A}{\sim} sys'$ on system states, which intuitively says, that two system states *sys* and *sys'* "look the same" for a subject with clearance *A*. In the simple Bell/LaPadula instance of the model this is true if the files readable by *A* are identical.

5 The Formal Model

This section describes the formal security model in detail. First, we informally describe the data structures that form the system model. Then, we will describe the set of commands (OS calls) and their security conditions. Finally, we will give the formal properties we proved for the system model.

The main data structure used in the model is the system state. It consists of three components: a *card key*, the *authentication store* and the *file system*.

The card key is not modifiable. It represents authentication information that is necessary for any application to be downloaded onto the card. The card key could be the public key of the card issuer, but it could also contain additional information, e.g. the public keys of some certifying bodies, that are allowed to certify the integrity level of subjects (this is another idea used in the IBM system [9]), or it could contain the key of the card user. We assume that the card key is fixed, before the operation system is started (either already when the card is manufactured, or when the card is personalized).

The second component is the authentication store. It stores authentication information for every access category, for which there are files on the card. Usually we will have one authentication information per application, but it is also possible to allocate several access categories for one application (presumed the card issuer agrees).

The third, main component is the file system. An important decision we have taken in modeling the file system is to abstract from the structure of directories. Instead we have modeled only the classification of directories. This has the disadvantage that we must assume directories to exist when needed. On the other hand this makes the model more generic, since we do not need to fix a concrete directory structure like a tree or an (acyclic) graph. Note that adding a directory structure would only require to verify that creating and removing directories does not cause covert channels. All other commands and their security conditions (e.g. the compatibility property, see the next section) would remain unchanged.

The file system uniquely addresses files with file identifiers (which could be either file names together with an access path, or physical addresses in memory). Files contain the following five parts of information:

- The classification (secrecy and integrity access class) of the directory, where the file is located.
- The classification (secrecy and integrity access class) of the file itself.
- The file content, which is not specified in detail (usually a sequence of bytes or words).
- An optional security marking (i.e. a classification, consisting of four access classes). Files with a security marking act as subjects and objects (in the sense of Bell/LaPadula). Data files do not carry a security marking. They only have the role of objects.

Access classes consist of an access level (a natural number) and a set of access categories (i.e. unique application names), as usual in Bell/LaPadula-like models.

Access classes are partially ordered, using the conjunction of the less-or-equal ordering on levels, and the subset-ordering on sets of categories. The lowest access class *system-low* consists of level 0 and an empty category set. To have a lattice of access classes we add a special access class *system-high*, which is only used as the integrity level of the top-level directory.

The system starts in an initial state with an empty authentication store and an empty file system. Note that there is no "security officer" (or a "root" using UNIX terminology) who sets up the initial state or maintains the security policy. Such a supervisor is assumed in many security models, but in contrast to a stationary computer there is no one who could fill this role after the smart card has been given to a user.

The system now executes OS commands. The commands are grouped in two classes: *createappl*, *loadappl* and *delappl* are invoked by the OS itself as an answer to external requests, while *read*, *write*, *create*, *remove* and *setintsec* are called by a currently running (application or channel) program.

Our model can be viewed as a simple instance of a domain and type enforcement (DTE) model (see [4], [1]) with two domains "OS" and "application", where the domain interaction table (DIT) is set such that only the OS domain may create or delete subjects and the domain definition table (DDT) for the domain "application" is set according to the interference relation (the domain "OS" can not access files).

The command *createappl* creates a new access category, which acts as the name of a new application. *loadappl* loads the main file of an application (or a channel). The file gets a classification as security marking, and therefore can act as a subject in the model. *delappl* removes such a file. To access files, we use the commands *create* to create a new one, *read* to read its content, *write* to overwrite it, and *remove* to delete the file. Usual operating systems will have more low-level commands (like opening and closing files, or commands to read only the next byte of a file) to support an efficient memory management, but since the security conditions for opening a file would be exactly the same as for our *read* command, we have chosen the more abstract version. Finally, the command *setintsec* modifies the integrity and secrecy classification of a file.

The commands *read*, *write*, *create*, *remove* and *setintsec* are called by a currently running application or channel program (the current subject). To model this current subject, their first argument is a file identifier which points to the currently running program (a file with a security marking). We call a file identifier, which points to a program, a *program identifier*, and denote it as *pid*. The security marking of the file determines the clearance of the current subject.

It is not necessary to model the currently running program as an extra component of the system state, since files with a security marking are stored in directories with secrecy *system-low* and integrity *system-high* (we do not consider "secret subjects"). Therefore, switching between applications has no security conditions, and the additional argument *pid* which is given to each command can be freely chosen.

We will now give a detailed listing of the operating system commands available. For each command we first define its functionality (new system state and output), if all security conditions are fulfilled. Otherwise, all commands return *no* as output and leave the system state unchanged. Second, for each command a precise definition of the security conditions is given. To make the security conditions easily readable, we will use predicates *read-access(pid, fid, sys)*, *write-access(pid, fid, sys)*, *dir-read-access(pid, fid, sys)* and *dir-write-access(pid, fid, sys)*. These describe in which circumstances a subject *pid* is allowed to see, read or write a file *fid* given a system state *sys*. For the predicates to hold, it is required that

- *pid* points to a file in the file system of *sys*, which has a security marking consisting of the four access classes (*ircl,iwcl,srcl,swcl*) for integrity/secrecy read/write. Remember that these markings characterize the clearance of the subject executing the command.
- *fid* points to a file in the file system of *sys* which has access classes *icl* and *scl* for integrity/secrecy, and whose directory has classification *idcl* and *sdcl*.
- For *read-access fid* must be readable by *pid*, i.e. $ircl \leq icl$ and $scl \leq srcl$.
- For *write-access fid* must be writable by *pid*, i.e. $icl \leq iwcl$ and $swcl \leq scl$.
- For *dir-read-access* the directory of *fid* must be readable by *pid*, i.e. $ircl \leq idcl$ and $sdcl \leq srcl$.
- For *dir-write-access* the directory of *fid* must be writable by *pid*, i.e. $idcl \leq iwcl$ and $swcl \leq sdcl$.

Note that *dir-read-access* determines whether a file *fid* is visible to the currently running application *pid* (i.e. whether its existence is known), while *read-access* gives access to the contents of a file.

create(pid,iac,sac). Subject *pid* creates a new file with empty content and no security marking in a directory with classification *iac* and *sac* for integrity and secrecy. The classifications of the new file are set to the read classifications of *pid*. The new file name is returned as output.

Security conditions: pid must point to a file with marking (*ircl, iwcl, srcl, swcl*) and a directory that has classification (*iac,sac*) must be readable and writable by *pid*, i.e. $ircl \leq iac$, $sac \leq srcl$, $iac \leq iwcl$ and $swcl \leq sac$ must hold.

remove(pid,fid). Program *pid* deletes the file named by *fid* from the file system. The resulting output is *yes* on success, *no* on failure.

Security conditions: dir-read-access(pid, fid, sys) and *dir-write-access(pid, fid, sys)* must hold. Note that *dir-write-access* implies, that *fid* has no secrecy marking, since such files are stored in a directory with integrity = *system-high*.

setintsec(pid,fid,iac,sac). Program *pid* sets the classification of file *fid* to be *iac* for integrity and *sac* for secrecy. The command returns *yes* as output.

Security conditions:

1. *dir-read-access(pid, fid, sys)*.

2. *dir-write-access*(*pid*, *fid*, *sys*).
3. *write-access*(*pid*, *fid*, *sys*).
4. Either one of the following two conditions holds:
   - The new integrity access class *iac* is not higher than the old integrity access class of the file, and the new secrecy class *sac* is not lower than the old secrecy class of *fid* (downgrading integrity and upgrading secrecy is allowed).
   - *fid* is readable by *pid*, i.e. *read-access*(*pid*, *fid*, *sys*) holds, the new integrity class is not higher than the integrity class of its directory and the new secrecy class is not lower than the secrecy class of its directory (upgrading integrity and downgrading secrecy is allowed for for *readable* files, as long as compatibility is not violated. Note that *dir-write-access* together with compatibility assures, that *pid*'s new integrity/secrecy will not be higher/lower than the write integrity/secrecy).

write(pid,fid,c). Program *pid* overwrites the file content of file *fid* to be *c*. The command returns *yes* as output.

Security conditions: fid must point to a file with no security marking. The conditions *dir-read-access*(*pid*, *fid*, *sys*) and *write-access*(*pid*, *fid*, *sys*) must hold.

read(pid,fid). Program *pid* reads the contents of file *fid*, which are returned as output. The system state is unchanged.

Security conditions: dir-read-access(*pid*, *fid*, *sys*) and *read-access*(*pid*, *fid*, *sys*) is required.

createappl(au, au'). A new application name (an access category) *ap* (relative to the ones that exist in the authentication store) with associated authentication information *au* is created, stored in the authentication store. *ap* is returned as output.

Security conditions: It is checked, whether the card issuer allows a new application with authentication information *au*. This is done with *check(ck,au',au)* using the additionally given key *au'* (a digital signature for *au* given by the card issuer) and the key *ck* of the card issuer that is stored on the card.

loadappl(au,st,d,c,iac,sac). A new program with clearance *d* and content *c* is loaded (added to the file system). Its security classes become *iac* and *sac*. The integrity/secrecy classification of the files directory is set to *system-high* and *system-low*. The new file identifier is returned.

Security conditions:
First the authorization of the card issuer for downloading the application is checked using the digital signature *au* by calling *check(ck, au, (d, c, iac, sac))* (note that the full information (*d,c,iac,sac*) to be stored on the card must be signed). Then a check is done for every access category *an* (= application name) that is contained in any of the four access classes of the clearance *d*. For each such name *st* must contain an appropriate digital signature *au'* and calling *check(au", au', (d, c, iac, sac))* must yield true, where *au"* is the key for *an* stored in the authentication store of the card. These checks make sure that any application which may be interfered, agrees to the downloading of the application.

delappl(au,st,fid). The file, to which *fid* points, is deleted. The command returns *yes* as output.

Security conditions: fid must have a security marking *d*. Otherwise, the security conditions are the same as for the loadappl command, except that the argument (*d,c,iac,sac*) for the *check* function is computed from the file *fid*.

6   How to Use the Model

In this section, we revisit the example from the introduction. We discuss how the commands of the previous section are used to establish the scenario of an airline A, which exchanges loyalty points with hotel chains H and I, and how the security policy is used.

We start with an empty smart card, that only stores a card key, which we assume to encode authentication information for the card issuer and the card holder. As a first action, we use *createappl* to store authentication information (a public key) for each of the three applications. Since we do not want the application to be structured internally, one call to *createappl* for each application is sufficient. Each returns one (new) access class for the application. The call to *createappl* is checked against the card key, so it is made sure that card issuer and card holder agree to creating the access classes, which we call A, H and I in the following.

To load an application program for each application, *loadappl* is called (there may be several programs for each application). The loaded application programs are checked to be signed by A, H and I respectively. Loading a new version of an application program can be done by calling *delappl* and then *loadappl* at any time.

After the application programs have been loaded, they can now be called freely (calling an application program is not security relevant, so the security model does not contain a special command). Each can freely create and modify files, using the *create, read, write* and *delete* commands.

The security policy ensures that the three applications will be completely separate, i.e. reading or writing files of another application, even by accident, is impossible.[3] No communication between the applications is possible, even if new applications are loaded, since we assume that no one else can guess the signature of A, H and I.

If H wants to transfer loyalty points to A, both A and H have to agree to load a channel program[4]. The channel program will have a read access class (both for integrity and secrecy) of H, and a write access class of A. Therefore to load it, both A and H must sign it. Of course this channel program should be checked carefully by both parties to do the following: When called, it should

---

[3] It is impossible, because the three secrecy access classes for A, H, and I are all disjoint. Bell/LaPadula also permits an access class to dominate another. For example, if access class X > Y, then information could flow from Y to X.

[4] Channel programs are called guard programs in [9]. They have also be called downgrading programs or sanitizers in various military applications.

read a file given by H to ensure that it has a suitable format, containing only information about loyalty points. This is possible, since the channel program has read access. Then it should call *setintsec* to change both the integrity and the secrecy access class of the file from H to A. Thereby the file is moved from the set of files accessible for H to those accessible by A, and application A can subsequently read the loyalty points.

The security policy ensures that the channel program can only transfer information from H to A. No other communication will be possible as long as no other pair of applications agrees to loading another channel program. The actions of the channel program will be completely invisible to the other hotel I.

Finally, to establish the scenario of the introduction, I and A will load another channel program, and bank B will create another application with *createappl* and *loadappl*. Maybe the bank as application provider will need two access classes, to run two applications (maybe one for the electronic wallet and one for online banking). Then it will call *createappl* twice. The bank might also use various secrecy and integrity levels for its files. Then the security policy will guarantee that the applications of the bank will respect Bell/LaPadula secrecy and Biba integrity internally.

Additional examples of using the model can be found in [10], where the model is shown in an electronic purse example and in several possible messaging scenarios.

7   Verification

The smart card security model described in Sect. 5 and the modified generic model of noninterference were formally specified using the VSE II system [5].

The noninterference model as described in Sect. 4 consists of about 200 lines of algebraic specification, and Theorem 1 was proved similarly to [16].

The smart card security model of Sect. 5 was also specified algebraically with 800 lines. A full specification of both models can be found in [11]. The following three main security claims were verified:

- The card issuer controls which applications are loaded onto the card, i.e. any application loaded on the card was signed by the card issuer.
- The owner of each application has signed each of his programs, when it was loaded. No program, which he has not agreed to loading, can interfere with the application.
- The smart card model is an instance of the noninterference model.

For the first proof we basically have to show, that each authentication information stored in the authentication store has been checked for agreement of the card issuer. This is done by induction on the number of executed commands, since the authentication store is modified only by adding new entries in *createappl*.

For the proof of the second property, note that an application, which first allocates an access category A as its application name with *createappl*, and then loads an application file with the set of access categories in all four access classes set to {A} can be interfered only by other applications, which have A in their category set of integrity write clearance (provided the third property holds!). Therefore it is sufficient to check, that any file with a security marking that contains an access category A, has been checked to be signed by A when it was loaded. This can again be proved by induction on the number of executed commands, similar to the first property.

The proof that shows that the smart card model is an instance of noninterference is much more complicated. The main problem here is to find definitions of the noninterference relation $\rightsquigarrow$, the equivalence relation $\overset{A}{\sim}$ and the system invariant inv such that Theorem 1 holds. Sect. 3 requires that we define $A \rightsquigarrow B$ as $iwcl_A \geq ircl_B$ and $swcl_A \leq srcl_B$, but the other two definitions have to be found incrementally by proof attempts. We tried several versions, which lead to unprovable goals. Analyzing such an unprovable goal always resulted in a concrete system state, which our definitions classified as secure and a sequence of commands that lead to an insecure state. We then had to decide, whether the security conditions of one of the involved commands was wrong, or whether our definitions of $\overset{A}{\sim}$ and inv were still insufficient.

For the final system invariant we use the conjunction of the two properties:

1. Compatibility property: Each file has an integrity (secrecy) classification that is at most (at least) the integrity (secrecy) classification of its directory
2. Visibility property: All files with a security marking are stored in a directory with integrity/secrecy classification system-high/system-low

The first property is common in mandatory security models (e.g. the Multics instance of Bell/LaPadula uses it too). The second property is necessary since we want to be able to switch freely between applications (see previous section).

The final definition of the equivalence relation $sys \overset{A}{\sim} sys'$, which says, which system states "look the same for a subject with clearance A" consists of the following four properties:

1. The authentication store and the card key must be the same in both system states.
2. The loaded files, which have a security marking, must be the same.
3. The set of files visible for A must be the same, i.e. the set of filenames for which a file exists in a directory which A can read, must be the same. Their classifications and directory classifications must be the same.
4. The files which A can read in both system states must be identical. Not only must they have the same security marking (this follows already from the second property), the same classification and the same directory classification (because of compatibility this is implied by the third property), but also their content must be identical.

With these three definitions of $\rightsquigarrow$, inv and $\overset{A}{\sim}$ we were able to verify the eight preconditions of Theorem 1. Each of the proofs split into subproofs for each of the eight commands.

About a month of work was needed to reach a fully verified security policy, most of the time was spent to verify that the model is an instance of noninterference. During this time several specification errors were found. Many of them were typing errors, but a few of them were errors in the security conditions, which had not shown up during a careful informal analysis by several people. There were some minor errors, that were easy to correct, e.g. that the integrity classification of a newly created file has to be set to the read integrity of the caller, not its write integrity.

The most problematic security conditions we found are those of the *setintsec* command, which modifies the classification of a file. Originally there were separate commands to set integrity and secrecy, but this results in the following problem: If we want both to upgrade secrecy and to downgrade integrity, after executing the first command the files' secrecy will be too high to downgrade integrity. Weakening the conditions of *setintegrity* to allow integrity downgrading for files, whose secrecy has been upgraded resulted in covert channels. It was interesting to see, that these covert channels are not possible in a pure Bell/LaPadula and Biba setting, but that they are specific to using subjects (channels), which have different access classes for reading and writing.

8   The IBM Model

The IBM model [9] addresses two issues that are not in the current version of the formal model. The first on assignment of integrity levels is a purely practical issue that cannot really be formalized. The second on execution control is simply not formalized at this time.

The first issue is that the Biba integrity model does not model any real practical system. Unlike the Bell/LaPadula model that developed from existing military security systems, the Biba integrity model developed purely from a mathematical analysis of the security models. However, Biba did not suggest how to actually decide which programs were deserving of a high integrity access class and which were not. This has made practical application of the Biba model very difficult.

In section 3, we required that developers and card issuers digitally sign the applications, using the function *check*. This is much as is done in Java and ActiveX security approaches. However, the IBM informal model goes beyond this. If an application has been independently evaluated and digitally signed by a certifying body, then we can grant it a higher level of integrity, without having to depend on the reputation of the developer or the skills of the card issuer. For example, we could define integrity levels for ITSEC-evaluated [8] applications. The Commercially Licensed Evaluation Facility (CLEF) would evaluate the application and the certifying body would digitally sign the application and its ITSEC E-level. A card issuer (such as a bank) might lay a requirement on vendors who want to download applications onto their cards. The application must have received an ITSEC evaluation at a policy-determined level to be acceptable. Common criteria evaluations [7] would be equally acceptable.

There could be provisions for less formal evaluations than full ITSEC. For example, a commercial security laboratory could check an application for obvious security holes (buffer overflows and the like) and for Trojan horses or trapdoors. While not as formal as an ITSEC evaluation, it might be sufficient for loyalty applications.

There is one problem with using more than one kind of evaluation criteria. If an application has been evaluated under one criteria, and another application has been evaluated under a very different criteria, then if a user wishes to download both of those application onto the same card, it is not clear how to compare the integrity classes. If the two criteria have defined mappings (such as the E levels of the ITSEC and the EAL levels of the Common Criteria), then there is not a problem. However, if the card issuer chose to use some very different and incompatible criteria, then downloading of other applications that were ITSEC evaluated might be difficult.

The second issue is control of execution permissions. The original Biba model prevents high integrity applications from reading low-integrity data, in fear that the application might be compromised in some form. This makes it difficult to describe applications that have been designed with high integrity to specifically process low integrity data input and to rule on its appropriateness. This processing of low integrity data is called sanitization. However, in the process of allowing a high integrity application to sanitize low integrity data, we do NOT want to allow a high integrity application to execute low integrity code, either deliberately or accidentally[5].

As discussed in section 3, we support sanitization for both secrecy and integrity by assigning four access classes to each subject ($ircl,srcl,iwcl,swcl$), the first two for reading and the last two for writing. In the traditional Bell/LaPadula and Biba models, execution is always associated with reading, but that association would allow a high integrity subject that was sanitizing low integrity data to also execute low integrity program code. Therefore, for integrity only, the IBM model associates execute permission with write permission, rather than read permission. Separating the execute permission from the read permission originated in the program integrity model of Shirley and Schell [18] which was in turn based on the protection ring mechanism of Multics [14]. The policy was further developed in the GEMSOS security model [17] that specified a range of levels within which integrity downgrading could occur.

The combined access rules are shown in Fig. 2. Recall that subjects have four access classes, while objects have only two[6]. The execute permission rule specified in the figure is for a normal program to program transfer[7].

---

[5] Most buffer overflow attacks come from violating this rule.

[6] Subjects can sometimes be treated as objects. Details on this can be found in [9].

[7] The IBM operating system also supports another operation, called CHAIN, which is a way to start a separate process executing at some other integrity and secrecy access class. The intended use of CHAIN is to start a guard or sanitization process or for a guard process to start a recipient of sanitized information. Details of CHAIN are omitted here, for reasons of space, but can be found in [9].

Read permission
  $srcl$ (subject) $\geq scl$ (object) and $ircl$ (subject) $\leq icl$ (object)

Write permission
  $swcl$ (subject) $\leq scl$ (object) and $iwcl$ (subject) $\geq icl$ (object)

Execute permission
  $srcl$ (subject) $\geq scl$ (object) and $iwcl$ (subject) $\leq icl$ (object)

The target program of a transfer runs at the integrity level of the caller. A high integrity program cannot call or transfer to lower integrity code.

Fig. 2. Access Control Rules

9   Conclusion

We have defined a generic security model for the operating system of a multiapplicative smart card. The model formalizes the main security aspects of secrecy, integrity, secure communication between applications and secure downloading of new applications. The two main theoretical results are that intransitive noninterference is a suitable framework for such models and that authentication can be integrated in the model.

We found that formal verification was extremely helpful in analyzing the security model. We were able to remove all covert channels from the model, even ones that we had not found during a thorough informal analysis. The six weeks required for formal specification and verification of the model are a reasonable effort to achieve this result.

There is still work to do. One important question we have left open is to formalize the communication of applications on the card with the outside world. This issue would require to extend the security model to include security aspects of the outside world, e.g. the authentication of card readers. We also would have liked to compare our security policy for downloading with the upcoming VISA standards (which were not available to us yet). Finally, extending the model to be applicable to Java Cards will also require further research.

References

1. L. Badger, D. F. Sterne, D. L. Sherman, K. M. Walker, and S. A. Haghighat. Practical domain and type enforcement for UNIX. In *1995 IEEE Symposium on Security and Privacy*, pages 66–77, Oakland, CA, May 1995. URL: http://www.tis.com/docs/research/secure/secure_dte_proj2.html.
2. D. E. Bell and L. J. LaPadula. Secure Computer Sytems: Unified Exposition and Multics Interpretation. Technical Report ESD–TR–75–306, The MITRE Corporation, HQ Electronic Systems Division, Hanscom AFB, MA, March 1976. URL: http://csrc.nist.gov/publications/history/bell76.pdf.
3. K. J. Biba. Integrity Considerations for Secure Computer Sytems. Technical Report ESD–TR–76–372, The MITRE Corporation, HQ Electronic Systems Division, Hanscom AFB, MA, April 1977.
4. W. E. Boebert and R. Y. Kain. A practical alternative to hierarchical integrity policies. In *8th National Computer Security Conf.*, pages 18–27, Gaithersburg, MD, 1985. National Computer Security Center and National Bureau of Standards.

5. D. Hutter, H. Mantel, G. Rock, W. Stephan, A. Wolpers, M. Balser, W. Reif, G. Schellhorn, and K. Stenzel. Vse : Controlling the complexity in formal software developments. In *Applied Formal Methods — FM-Trends 98*. LNCS 1641, 1998.

6. Identification cards - identification cards - interrelated circuit(s) cards with contacts - part 4: Inter-industry commands for interchange. ISO/IEC 7816-4, International Standards Organization, 1995.

7. Information technology - security techniques – evaluation criteria for IT security. ISO/IEC 15408, International Standards Organization, 1999. URL: http://csrc.nist.gov/cc.

8. ITSEC. *Information Technology Security Evaluation Criteria, Version 1.2*. Office for Official Publications of the European Communities, Brussels, Belgium, 1991.

9. P. A. Karger, V. Austel, and D. Toll. A new mandatory security policy combining secrecy and integrity. RC 21717, IBM Research Division, T. J. Watson Research Center, Yorktown Heights, NY, 15 March 2000. URL: http://domino.watson.ibm.com/library/CyberDig.nsf/home.

10. P. A. Karger, V. Austel, and D. Toll. Using a mandatory secrecy and integrity policy on smart cards and mobile devices. In *(EUROSMART) Security Conference*, pages 134–148, Marseille, France, 13-15 June 2000. RC 21736 available at http://domino.watson.ibm.com/library/CyberDig.nsf/home.

11. F. Koob, M. Ullmann, S. Wittmann, G. Schellhorn, W. Reif, A. Schairer, and W. Stephan. A generic security model for multiapplicative smart cards — final report of the SMaCOS project. to appear as BSI report.

12. T. F. Lunt, P. G. Neumann, D. Denning, R. R. Schell, M. Heckman, and W. R. Shockley. Secure distributed data views – vol.1: Security policy and policy interpretation for a class A1 multilevel secure. Technical Report SRI-CSL-88-8, SRI International, Menlo Park, CA, August 1988.

13. J. McLean. Security models. In J. Marciniak, editor, *Encyclopedia of Software Engineering*. Wiley & Sons, 1994. URL: http://chacs.nrl.navy.mil/publications/CHACS.

14. Elliott I. Organick. *The Multics System: An Examination of Its Structure*. The MIT Press, Cambridge, MA, 1972.

15. Philips semiconductors and IBM research to co-develop secure smart cards: Highly secure operating system and processor, suitable for multiple applications. URL: http://www.semiconductors.philips.com/news/content/file_384.html, Feb. 1999.

16. J. Rushby. Noninterference, Transitivity, and Channel-Control Security Policies. Technical Report CSL-92-02, SRI International, Menlo Park, CA, 1992. URL: http://www.csl.sri.com/~rushby/reports/csl-92-2.dvi.Z.

17. R. Schell, T. F. Tao, and M. Heckman. Desingning the GEMSOS security kernel for security and performance. In *8th National Computer Security Conference*, pages 108–119, Gaithersburg, MD, 30 September - 3 October 1985. DoD Computer Security Center and National Bureau of Standards.

18. L. J. Shirley and R. R. Schell. Mechanism sufficiency validation by assignment. In *1981 Symposium on Security and Privacy*, pages 26–32, Oakland, CA, 27–29 April 1981. IEEE Computer Society.

19. D. F. Sterne and G. S. Benson. The controlled application set paradigm for trusted systems. In *1995 National Information Systems Security Conference*, Baltimore, Maryland, 1995. National Computer Security Center and National Institute of Standards and Technology. URL: http://www.tis.com/docs/research/secure/secure_dte_proj2.html.

How Much Negotiation and Detail Can Users Handle?
Experiences with Security Negotiation and the Granularity of Access Control in Communications

Kai Rannenberg

Microsoft Research Cambridge, UK
`kair@microsoft.com`

Abstract. Tailor made security is being enabled by more options for specifying security policies and enhanced possibilities for negotiating security. On the other side these new options raise the complexity of transactions and systems: Users can be overwhelmed, which can lead to less security than before. This paper describes conclusions from a case study and trial of a personal reachability and security manager for telephone based communication. The device helped to negotiate and balance security requirements. The study analysed how much negotiation and detail users could handle during their day-to-day transactions and how they could be supported. Some results are strongly related to more 'classic' security techniques like access control that are becoming more and more interactive: When users learn to understand the consequences of their access control decisions and can tune their policies these mature to a satisfying level. When users see advantages for their daily activities they are willing to invest more time into understanding additional complexity.

1 Introduction: Non-expert Users and Security Technology

Security technology tends to become more powerful and to open more options for specifying individual and fine-grained security policies. Moreover enhanced communication facilities allow negotiating the security properties of transactions. As participants often have different and conflicting interests, these negotiations are important. But more options also raise the complexity of transactions and systems, users can be overwhelmed [Gong99, p. 150], which can lead to less security then before [WhiTyg99]. Therefore it is important to see how much negotiation and detail users can handle during day-to-day transactions and how to support them in this. Usability for non-expert users can even be an important factor in the decision whether or not to implement a security mechanism.

This paper describes conclusions from a case study on the negotiation of reachability and relates them to more 'classic' security techniques, especially access control. The study was part of a larger project on multilateral security (see

F. Cuppens et al. (Eds.): ESORICS 2000, LNCS 1895, pp. 37–54, 2000.

Section 2). It focussed on personal telephone reachability and security management, an approach that aims at avoiding annoying calls and securing telephone
communication (Section 3 and 4): Callees (receivers of a call) can formulate
general and security requirements for accepting calls. Callers can use several options to demonstrate the importance or urgency of their call. The reachability
and security manager was used in a trial by more than 30 users in public healthcare (doctors, nurses etc.), most of them neither computer nor security literate
(Section 5).

While the main security goals of the reachability manager (avoid annoying
calls but don't force the callers to deliver all information all the time) do not
exactly match 'classic' security requirements, the configuration of one's own
reachability and security requirements has some striking similarities to computer
and data access control. So some of the experiences of how users reacted to the
complexity introduced into their 'telephone life' seem to be useful in a broader
sense. Therefore Section 6 discusses some of the results from the study and puts
them into relation to fundamental issues of access control, negotiation in general,
and issues of security perception.

2   Multilateral Security and Negotiation

The 'Kolleg Security in Communications' [MülRan99] aimed at 'Multilateral Security' for communications: All parties in a transaction, e.g. a telephone call,
should be able to formulate and enforce their security interests [RaPfMü99].
This was considered to be especially important for open communication systems, where different parties, e.g. subscribers, providers, or network operators,
have different and maybe even conflicting interests. One approach was to make
technology offer options and facilitate negotiations to balance one's own security
requirements against those from others.

2.1   The Example: Annoying Calls and the Caller ID Conflict

One example that had strongly influenced the work was the conflict regarding
Caller ID displays in telephone communication. Caller ID displays had in the
early 90's led to an extensive public discussion[1].

One side argued that the security and privacy interests of callers were violated if their telephone numbers were displayed at the called persons' (callees')
side. For example, other people on the callee side could get knowledge of the
caller calling. Also the callees themselves could misuse the collected numbers for
advertisement calls, or an unlisted telephone number could become public.

---

[1] Caller ID displays are connected to a telephone line, e.g. integrated into the telephone
itself, and show the number of the calling telephone line when a call comes in. Modern
telephones also easily allow storage and further processing of incoming Caller IDs. A
more precise term would be 'Calling Line Number', but Caller ID is generally used
[Caller ID].

The other side argued that Caller ID would just balance the power between caller and callee properly. It would especially protect callees from annoying and harassing calls, as at least some information would now be given to them. Otherwise the callees would have almost no protection[2] against being woken up in the middle of the night by some malevolent or nosy caller[3].

The introduction of options for the callers to switch off Caller ID (either per call or per default) did not solve the problem: Callees would tend to generally reject calls without Caller IDs, as they had no other selection criteria and this then was the simplest solution. So the callers would be forced to display the Caller ID anyway.

This situation gave rise to the idea of 'Reachability Management' (Section 3): Computer and communication technology should be able to give callees more options to decide whether a call was welcome, and to protect themselves from unwelcome calls. It should also give callers more options to show the importance and urgency of their calls. Additional features allowed users to specify security features for their calls (see Section 4 on Security Management)

3 Reachability Management

Reachability management offers callees the possibility to specify the circumstances, under which they are willing to receive a call. This specification, together with the information callers provide during the call request, is the basis for the decision whether the callee is immediately notified of the call, e.g. whether the telephone bell rings (cf. Figure 1). Reachability management was sometimes being described as a "Secretary for those who cannot afford a real one". Most versions of the reachability management were implemented on Newton PDAs connected to GSM telephones. This allows for reachability management even in situations when no secretary could be around. Additionally some stationary reachability managers were connected to ISDN lines.

This section describes the selection and negotiation of the data being transmitted during the signalling phase of a communication request (see Section 3.1). It also shows how callers can describe their communication request adapted to their situation (3.2), and how callees are able to configure their reachability needs in various ways (3.3). More information can be found in e.g. [ReDaFR97].

3.1 Options for the Negotiation of Reachability

The prototype that was implemented facilitates negotiation of the following attributes:

---

[2] Except unplugging or switching off the phone.

[3] There is also quite some marketing interest behind the introduction of caller ID, but this issue is left out here for the moment.

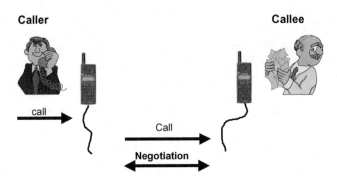

Fig. 1. Communication supported by a Reachability Management System

- How the communication partners are known to each other (anonymously, through a pseudonym, by their real identity)[4].
- The urgency or purpose of the communication request seen from each of the communication partners' point of view.
- The existing security requirements and the mechanisms used to secure the current communication (see Section 4).

Several options allowed specifying the urgency and importance of a communication request:

- *Statement of urgency based on self-assessment:* The caller indicates a certain degree of urgency. This assessment may be very subjective and only relevant with regard to the current situation of the callee. Therefore, this option was implemented as a further inquiry (cf. 3.2).
- *Specification of a subject or topic:* The topic of a desired communication can give the callee an indication of how important the communication is. The callee's reachability manager can only evaluate this specification automatically if the caller and callee have previously negotiated a list of subjects and situations.
- *Specification of a role:* The caller can indicate that he is calling in a certain role (or with a specific qualification), for example in fulfilling a certain task. This role is contained in the 'identity cards' of the identity management subsystem. When a particular identity card is selected for personal identification the role in which one is communicating is also selected. The callee may also be addressed in one of several different roles: these are essentially divided into private (private network subscriber, club member) and professional (physician in the hospital, hospital nurse) roles.

---

4   An integrated 'Identity Management' allowed to administer real names, pseudonyms, and roles (e.g. 'Member of hospital administration' or 'Manager of a sports club') as well as certificates for these.

- *Presentation of a voucher:* In certain situations one may want calls of particular persons to be given priority, e.g. when waiting for a call to be returned. A caller can issue a call voucher for this purpose. Subsequently, the callee can use this voucher in order to receive preference for his return call.
- *Offering a surety:* In order to emphasize the seriousness of his communication request and his statement regarding the urgency, the caller may offer a (possibly negotiated) amount of money as a surety. "Satisfaction guaranteed or this money is yours!" is the philosophy of this feature. If the callee does not agree with the caller's evaluation of the urgency, he can keep the money or, e.g. donate it to a charity. The callee may use this option, for example, if the caller did not want to disclose his identity. This option is implemented as a further inquiry (cf. Section 3.2).

A call only gets through if the caller's offer matches the requirements of the callee. Otherwise the callee's reachability manager can offer other options, for example to leave a message or a return call request (optionally together with a voucher).

3.2   Performing a Call – Caller's View of Reachability Management

To set up a call, the caller first has to choose his communication partner. The reachability manager supports the caller with a personal subscriber directory (phone book) or an integrated 'public' directory. Persons contacted frequently may be assigned a short code. Then the call set-up dialogue (cf. Figure 2) appears. This enables the caller to specify his identity, the reason for the call and its urgency, as well as to submit a voucher for a callback (if one is available).

Before the callee is personally involved, the communication request is evaluated and negotiated by his reachability manager. Depending on the rules established in the configuration of the callee's reachability (cf. 3.3) the caller's reachability manager will continue by displaying (cf. Figure 3):

- A connection set-up dialogue telling that the callee is notified;
- A message saying that the call was denied; or
- An additional inquiry.

The inquiry dialogues used when establishing a connection include:

- Inquiry regarding identity: if the callee wants to be informed of the identity, a selection of the caller's own certificates appears (cf. Figure 3 top left). The caller may choose not to supply identity information. In this case the callee gets the message that the caller explicitly wants to remain anonymous.
- Inquiry regarding urgency (cf. Figure 3 top right): the callee leaves the decision of whether or not to put through the call up to the caller. The caller receives a short text message and the choice of either cancelling the call (in order to avoid any disturbance in the situation described) or to insist on performing the call (because, in his opinion, it is urgent enough).

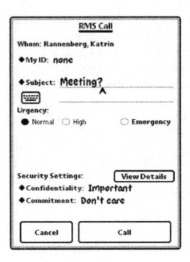

Fig. 2. Call set-up dialogue

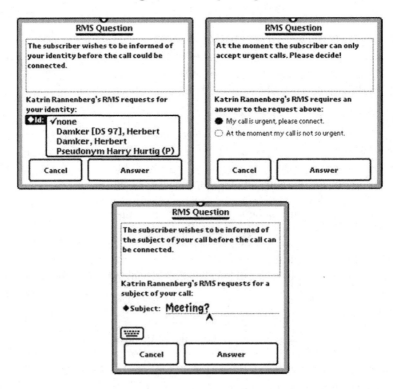

Fig. 3. Inquiry dialogues on caller's reachability manager – initiated by callee's reachability manager

- Inquiry regarding the subject (cf. Figure 3 bottom): if the callee wants to be informed of the subject and the caller didn't previously give any details, a text-input field appears.
- Inquiry regarding a surety: in order to emphasize the seriousness of a communication request, the callee may ask the caller to remit an amount of money as a surety. The caller may comply (and remit the amount requested), or reject the request.

If the call is rejected, the caller sees a call rejection dialogue. This informs him about the reason for the rejection and offers him various opportunities to continue, e.g. the prototype offers an opportunity to leave a message or a callback request (in form of a text message with a return call voucher attached). A message editor and a simple folder system were implemented in the prototype.

3.3 Configuring Reachability – Callee's View of Reachability Management

In the personal configuration of his reachability manager the user determines the various reactions to incoming calls (communication requests). He defines, which information the reachability manager will request from a caller, in order to evaluate the communication request. A likely example would be that the callee's reachability manager requests the identification of the caller, or a surety from an unidentified caller. Subscribers configure their reachability for different situations of daily life or the working environment by defining a set of rules for each situation. When using the reachability manager they then switch between these predefined situations.

The left side of Figure 4 shows the set of rules applying to the sample situation 'Meeting'; the right side shows the dialogue for defining rules. Each individual rule establishes the subscriber's role (business or private) and the conditions that have to be fulfilled (e.g. call from a particular subscriber). The reaction to incoming calls (e.g. connect, deny, divert or make further inquiry) is also defined for each case. Because the rules are evaluated top down, their order within a particular situation is important and, therefore, may be changed as required. The last rule of each situation becomes the default rule for the situation. It describes the reaction to be taken when no other rule applies. The prototype also contained other concepts, such as 'situation independent rules' being evaluated with top priority in any situation, but these proved to be too complex in the simulation study (cf. Section 5 and Section 6).

4 Security Management

Which security measures are to be used in a communication is situation-dependent and the partners may view this controversially. This issue was addressed by the negotiation concept of *security management* [GaGrPS97,Pordes98]. Users can independently decide whether to use security measures or not and negotiate this

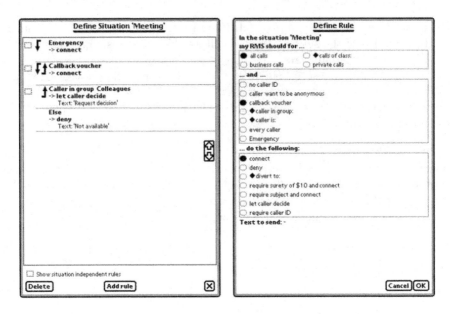

Fig. 4. Configuration of a situation and definition of a rule

with their partners. The security management is embedded in the reachability management system and aims at being easy-to-handle, even though the technical security mechanisms are fairly complex.

4.1 Security Characteristics, Requirements, and Offers

The prototype used in the simulation study did not provide all possible security measures for telephone communication, but offered examples of some particularly important measures[5]. *Encryption* and *Unobservability* provide protection of the communication connection and, therefore, affect both communication partners equally. On the other hand, a user can provide *Authentication* and *Acknowledgement* of a call without the partner doing the same.

Although only a few security measures were offered, they yield numerous possible combinations for each call. For reasons of usability the security measures were grouped into the dimensions *Confidentiality* and *Commitment*. Confidentiality contains the measures encryption and unobservability. Commitment contains

---

[5] It should be noted that some of the security functions offered were not actually implemented, as the focus of the project was on experiences on negotiation. End-to-end voice call encryption would have required special telephone hardware instead of 'off-the-shelf' GSM mobile phones. Measures for unobservability would have required too substantial changes in the GSM communication infrastructure. However the prototype contained a crypto facility for signing and verifying text messages and certificates.

the measures authentication and acknowledgement. Users are then able to select the requested levels of confidentiality and commitment, which the system maps to the various security measures (cf. Figure 2). However, it was also possible to set the various measures directly ('self-defined').

4.2 Three Step Coordination

In principle, the negotiation of security requirements can be carried out in any number of steps, including further inquiries from the caller or the callee. For ease of handling a simple model was implemented:

1. The caller makes a security proposal in the call template. This proposal contains the security measures he requests and those he is prepared to take. This is transmitted to the callee's reachability management system.
2. The callee's security manager compares the proposal with his security requirements and preferences. He then produces a coordinated and modified counterproposal.
3. The caller's security manager compares the proposal and counterproposal and puts the call through if both match. Otherwise the caller is asked whether he accepts the callee's proposal.

4.3 Security Scope

To avoid repeated inquiries or frequent failures of negotiation, both parties specify additional conditions, e.g. whether to take specific security measures if requested, or if a personal security requirement can be ignored, if necessary. This is done by means of a three-level schema of attributes associated locally with security requirements and security offers. Security requirements can be assigned the attributes 'mandatory', 'if possible', 'don't care' and security offers the attributes 'don't care', 'if necessary', 'never'.

To avoid the caller having to disclose requirements and offers immediately, the scope of the security is not communicated directly. Instead, the caller (or his/her security manager) overplays the requirements and underplays the offers in the first negotiation step. Only two levels of the local three-level setting are transmitted. The attribute 'if possible' is transmitted as 'mandatory', i.e. the requirement is described as non-negotiable. The attribute 'if necessary' is transmitted as 'never', making the offer non-negotiable. If the callee's counterproposal does not match the caller's proposal, the security manager can lower the original security requirements (without having to re-consult the caller) and put the call through. Only if this fails the caller is asked regarding the counterproposal.

5 Testing and Trialling

The reachability and security manger was tested and trialled in several ways:

1. A one-day 'tele-roleplay' (Teleplanspiel) took place before the first implementations started: Kolleg participants all over Germany had to solve telecommunicative tasks. They had reachability managers available, which were played by colleagues, but to simulate a machine-like interface they could interact with them only via paper based forms that they had to complete according to certain rules. The aim of the tele-roleplay was to test features and the concept of stepwise negotiation.
2. Several versions of the reachability manager underwent professional usability tests by psychologists to ease their handling [DuENRS99].
3. The largest test was the simulation study 'Reachability and Security Management in Health Care' in which more than 30 real test persons used the technology under realistic conditions.

This paper concentrates on the simulation study, as this was the largest trial and brought the most advanced results. It shortly describes the concept of simulation studies (Section 5.1) and gives an overview of the environment (5.2), the participants (5.3), the cases and set-up (5.4), and the course of the study and the methods of observation and analysis (5.5). A more detailed description of the simulation study can be found in [AmBlBR99,PoRoSc99,RoHaHe99].

5.1   Simulations Studies

Simulation studies follow the principle 'Highest proximity to reality without damage': Qualified persons from the field under investigation act as 'expert test persons'. They are observed over a set period of time working independently with prototype technical devices in an environment, which closely resembles reality. This means

- Real tasks, which have been devised on the basis of real problems;
- Really affected persons and cooperation partners, which are, however, played by test persons;
- Real attacks and breakdowns, the damage of which, however, is restricted to the context of the simulation;
- Real test cases, which likewise only produce, simulated consequences.

5.2   The Simulation Environment

For several reasons the simulation took place in the Heidelberg (Germany) health care system:

- The healthcare informatics had some sense for security issues considering the sensitive data they were handling in their patient records;
- Reachability management was an issue in the hospital: Doctors usually carried pagers to be available when being away from their office. These pagers were seen as a constant nuisance as they only transmitted very limited information: a telephone number to be called and the signal whether the request

was 'urgent' or 'very urgent'. So very often doctors were forced to 'jump to a not so near telephone' only to find out that the call was not even half as urgent as the caller perceived. Reachability management was also an issue with general practitioners who were in the process of deploying mobile phones to use when they were visiting patients at home.

– The hospital already experimented with PDAs. They were used to ease mobile access to electronic patient records and other information as well as to enhance the communication, e.g. to send requests for drugs or special examinations to the hospital pharmacy or the radiology department. Testing of this software was part of the study.

5.3   The Participants and the Set-Up

31 'expert test persons' from different healthcare organizations participated. A large group was physicians from eight different medical departments of Heidelberg University Hospital. Nurses from two wards, one head nurse and one administrative officer joined them. Two general practitioners, together with their assistants, also took part. Their participation was important in order to observe the use of mobile technology in outpatient care and to investigate the co-operation beyond organizational borders, e.g. between the general practitioners and the hospital physicians, when a patient was referred to the hospital or sent home again. It was also possible to investigate the co-operation between hospital staff and outpatient care at the patients' homes as two nurses engaged in aftercare participated.

All 'expert test persons' participated from their usual places of work and also during other activities including meetings, conferences, transporting of patients, and shopping. The devices were used in cafes, in corridors, in elevators, on bicycles, in cars and in trains.

Due to the fact that neither real patients, nor real patient data should be used during the evaluation of technology it was necessary to create simulation tasks for the 'expert test persons' based on real tasks. These simulated tasks were prepared in advance and presented to the test users during the simulation week, together with a number of special communication tasks.

In order to offer the expert test persons a close-to-reality communication environment, 10 scientists from the research projects acted as their counter-parts. They also used the prototype technology and played the roles of friends, patients, relatives, administrative persons, and staff from the professional doctor's association and health insurance institutions (altogether 75 virtual users). Another 25 persons took part by working in the user and technical support, observing the distributed 'expert test persons' and playing the patient roles. Altogether, 76 people were involved in the simulation study.

5.4   The Cases

The 'expert test persons' processed 21 medical cases during the simulation week. They were asked to add to the information available for a simulation patient by ordering specific examinations or consultation. The simulated cases were initiated by a simulation patient who appeared at the doctor's office or by an electronic referral together with a letter of admission. When examinations or consultation were ordered, the requested information (laboratory results, radiology results) was transferred to the central patient database. The physician treating the patient could access this information. For some patients additional information regarding previous stays in hospital was available. The 'expert test persons' were entirely free in respect of actions or decisions. The only control the 'simulation directors' exercised over the course of the simulation was that of assuming some roles (for example patient, relative, senior physicians or administrative person), or by providing specific information.

Apart from these extensive medical cases (70 examination requests, 42 examination reports), about 60 smaller communication tasks were carried out – each of them with three to ten communication contacts. These tasks were, for instance, information requests from the hospital management, requests of a health insurance company, questions from relatives, invitations from club members, or unsolicited offers from an insurance agent or an investment broker.

5.5   Course of the Study, Observation, and Analysis

Altogether, roughly 2000 telephone contacts took place during the simulation week and around 1000 test messages were exchanged. Numerous changes in the configurations of the reachability and the security management system were made[6]. About 50% of the messages were encrypted and nearly 50% were digitally signed. One example, a faked warning with a faked signature certificate from a non-existing pharmacy reporting problems with a certain drug, shows how near to reality the cases were: The message created so much discussion and involvement among the participants that some administrative officers considered to ask for stopping the study.

In order to obtain the individual experiences of the different test users and to analyse them for future use of the technology, the following instruments were used (among others and only with agreement of the users):

- Observation of the behaviour of the test persons during processing of the simulation cases;
- Daily group discussions about experiences and specific design aspects;
- Analysis of the logged communication data;
- A questionnaire administered after the simulation week (over 80% return);
- A post-survey in the form of two-hour intensive interviews.

---

[6] This includes only the documented transactions, probably more actions took place that were neither documented nor reported.

6   Reachability as an Example for Controlled Complexity and Advanced Access Control

The general positive outcome was that users accepted the extra complexity, as they saw a high personal benefit for their daily communication tasks (6.1). This could prove useful for other forms of access control (6.2). An increasing awareness of security issues could be noted (6.4), but also some limits of the concept of negotiation showed up clearly (6.3).

6.1   Making Users Migrate into Managing More Complex Controls

Reachability as well as security management introduces additional complexity into what used to be 'a simple phone call'. In general users accepted the extra complexity, as they saw a high personal benefit for their daily communication tasks. However different users used rather different ways to cope with the complexity and to find the configurations they liked best:

- Some users never changed the pre-configured situation rule sets ('connect every call', 'no calls', and 'meeting').
- Many participants created some new situations or changed rules in existing situations.
- Some users created a large number of situations in advance trying to match the real-life situations they could envisage (e.g. 'visiting a patient', 'office work', or 'stand-by') but reduced this number later after having gained more experience.

In the end most users regarded three to five different situations as a useful number, e.g. three levels of reachability similar to the phases of a traffic light (green, yellow, red) and some personal extras.

There seems to be the important lesson that the general positive reaction to the challenge of configuring one's own reachability was based on the fact that users were offered some variety: They could upgrade from simple settings but also use the full power of the tool to find out about requirements they might have[7]. So interesting compromises between earlier extremes turned out:

- Original 'normal' telephones that did not offer any options at all had been considered as too primitive. The same had been true for the pagers used in the hospital, which had too limited facilities (cf. 5.2).
- Early versions of the reachability manager included all options the developing computer scientists could think of. They failed already in the usability tests for being much too complex.
- So the version used in the simulation study aimed at a mixture of expressive power and entry-level ease to encourage as many users as possible to use as many features as they could.

---

[7] Users could theoretically also downgrade to the 'normal' situation without reachability manager, but this wasn't observed.

Switching between telephone and email communication, e.g. for leaving a message when callees were not available, did not cause any confusion among the users. On the contrary, this feature was very popular. Callers could write and correct their messages more easily than with a normal voice mail system. Callees could more easily overview and digest incoming messages and also take advantage of the callback vouchers.

Two other aspects also encouraged users to experiment with the more sophisticated functionality:

- A lot of the functions could easily be tested without producing any harm to the equipment or any data.
- Manual filtering was still possible and allowed users to deny a call, even when the rules would have let it through.

There was some demand for an assistance function warning users when they had specified 'suspicious' combinations, e.g. illogical rule sets or more than one situation in which all calls were blocked.

However there was much more demand for improving the switching of the activated reachability situation or level. In order to avoid complicated actions, hardware buttons can be designated for quick and easy switching between reachability levels. Mobile phones now move into this direction when offering buttons for switching the ringer to 'silent'.

There could also be a reminder function to be activated when the user switches to a reachability level with strong filtering. This reminder function could prevent the user from forgetting to switch back to a more communicative reachability level. A more powerful step could be to let the mobile device analyse body movement patterns or other biometric data of its wearer. For example movement patterns like driving a car or riding a bicycle could restrict the reachability, while movement patterns like working at a desk could ease reachability.

6.2   Reachability Management as a Form of Access Control

Reachability management can be seen as a special form of access control, defining the rules for external access to internal resources, especially to the telephone bell, whose ringing usually has a strong influence on the next-minute activities of the people around and can be rather disruptive.

Therefore it is useful to look into the developments in other areas of access control. This holds especially for areas, where mandatory access control policies are not very feasible, e.g. as private or small office users don't have a security administrator at hand and also might not wish to be restricted on their own computer. They then act as their own security administrators and often have to learn by trial and error. This was already shown in the area of encryption software, even for programs that aim at easy usability like PGP 5.0. In [WhiTyg99] several cases are described where users did not understand the concepts of the software they used. Consequently they made crucial mistakes that could have caused exactly the risk the software should have protected against[8].

An example directly from the area of access control is controlling executable web content, which aims at protecting local systems and data against possible malicious behaviour of web content from insecure areas, e.g. from the Internet. Early Java sandbox approaches were very restricted, but easy to use and configure. Recent technology, e.g. the JDK 1.2 security architecture, is much more powerful and allows a much finer granularity of access control, but its "overall complexity might appear overwhelming to the non-expert computer user" [Gong99, p. 150].

The next useful step might be an interface delivering useful standard and start-up settings but also some freedom to explore the full functionality. This especially holds as more and more access control policies are not only a question of 'granted' or 'not granted' but

- Include some negotiation with the claimer and other parties, e.g. when authorisation or payment information has to be checked before access is granted;
- Embrace accompanying measures such as extended audit in cases when access is granted[9].

Also including the dimension of time that has been tested extensively in reachability management becomes more important: e.g. accesses can be more easily allowed during office hours (as support is easier at hand) or after office hours (as the potential damage on business processes is lower).

Controlling executable web content has another set of similarities with reachability management, resulting from a certain fuzziness of the problem, at least in practice:

- In many cases it is not decidable, what would be the 'right' decision: Granting access to an applet, whose security properties are unclear, might cause damage or not; denying access can be the only way to be safe, but can also reduce the productivity of the workflow. Many users don't understand the security options of applet access control anyway, but have to allow some things to get their work done. So they are always risking that something goes wrong. Granting or denying access to caller can always be the wrong decision, as one never knows what the person on the other side is up to.
- In many cases the damage is limited: Having to reboot the computer or to reinstall some software after an aggressive applet caused problems is a

---

[8] For example PGP users did not understand the concept of public key infrastructures and the fact, that confidential messages had to be encrypted with the public key of the communication partner, so they failed to use this key thus sending the message unprotected.

[9] One example is the 'grey list' of identifiers of 'dubious' mobile terminals as specified in the GSM standards: subscribers registering with a terminal that is found in the grey list usually get access, but are tracked intensively, as terminals registered in the grey list are usually stolen mobile phones.

nuisance, but not catastrophic, and one can very often recover. Getting an unwanted call because the reachability management did not work as intended, can happen, but there is almost always 'a new game' to start over with.

There are also properties of reachability management that make it different from 'classical' access control:

- A 'one time wrong' might not be tolerable due to the consequences, e.g. for highly confidential data.
- Allowing users to control every successful access (i.e. the option to manually deny calls) was very popular with callees. It is probably not so popular with many administrators of large databases who have other things to do than to confirm every access. However users browsing around the WWW are quite accustomed now to windows that pop up rather unexpectedly and ask for details or extra authorisation.

Altogether the degree of the differences depends largely on the application environment, and so it can be useful in access control areas to look for a migration path along the experiences made with reachability management.

6.3   The Limits of Negotiation

Negotiation about options was generally welcomed. However there are limits to it, especially when a feature becomes very popular. The option to receive a receipt for the fact that one was calling but not being let through, was particular popular with users who had a lot of outgoing communication. They saw these receipts as useful defence in case callees would complain why a time-critical decision had been taken without checking back with them. However callees tended to be less willing to hand over 'non-reachability receipts' to avoid what they considered misuse.

An illustrative example was the following: Doctors, who had taken in a new patient at the reception, had to reach somebody at a ward to ask for a free bed before they could transfer the patient there. Busy wards usually did not put too much priority on answering the phone. So with reachability management the doctors tended to send a message that they required a bed and had not got through. Wards claimed that this was simply shifting problems over to them and not a cooperative way to do business and use the information they gave out. Subsequently it became harder to get 'non-reachability receipts' from them.

When callees had configured their reachability managers to not issue 'non-reachability receipts' callers asked for third parties to document their call attempts. While this can be solved easily (some users simply took bystanders as witnesses for not getting through) it also shows a limit of negotiation. One cannot really negotiate about proofs for being ignored. On the other side one can negotiate a lot of information out of the other party when one is in high demand.

The project group had envisaged this problem beforehand, but no general solution was seen[10]. Therefore the group was rather interested how things would turn out in 'real life' and how important the 'principal problem' would be in practice. It turned out that callees were most keen on the 'subject' information accompanying a call, and that callers had other things to do than to investigate the reachability settings of their counterparts.

There is also another non-negotiable issue: Negotiating about the unobservability of a single transaction does not make sense, when the negotiation contains the character of the transaction.

6.4   Security Perception Issues

It showed that the awareness of security issues increased over time, partially because of incidents, partially because users got a deeper understanding of the technology. However users understood 'confidentiality' of a call in a far broader sense than the developers had intended it. They had thought in 'classic' telephone communication protection terms, meaning that 'confidentiality' would apply protection against eavesdropping. Users expected that 'confidentiality' would also mean that the other side had been properly authenticated and had agreed to not publish the content of the call later.

Another observation was that many users intuitively coupled authorisation and identification issues: The concept that authorisation can make sense even without identification, e.g. when a compensation for eventual damage is prepaid, was perceived only by a few, who thought about situations where it was advisable not to come up with one's own identity.

Misunderstandings like these correspond with reports in [WhiTyg99] on users misunderstanding terms and concepts of encryption and public key infrastructures (cf. 6.2) and seem to be a rather common problem. One might like to ask for more security education, but this is only one side of the problem. There is at least one lesson for developers: To avoid confusion one should check whether technical terms like 'confidential' are already reserved in the application environment. If so, it is useful to either look for other terms or to make very clear which level (e.g. technical communication or application area customs and ethics) is meant when a certain term is used.

7   Conclusions

Usability of security mechanisms showed to be not an issue of offering *the* right solution to users, as *the* users don't exist, but to offer something for different users in different stage of interest, understanding, and competence. The simulation study gave good evidence that the features and implementation of reachability management complied with users' requirements. Users learned to understand the consequences of their access control decisions and tuned their policies so these matured to a satisfying level. Therefore the experiences should be useful in other access control areas, especially when circumstances require that more complex

---

[10]   Except turning back to the 'old' telephone system with no context information being transmitted

mechanisms are introduced. Negotiation showed to be a helpful feature, though one should not think that offering parties the flexibility to negotiate the issues could solve every problem.

Acknowledgments. Thanks go to my colleagues in the Kolleg 'Sicherheit in der Kommunikationstechnik' for their work there. I would also like to thank Dieter Gollmann for e.g. broadening my horizon regarding access control and Michael Roe, Fabien Petitcolas, and Roger Needham for helping to re-reflect and advance the Kolleg's ideas.

References

[AmBlBR99]   Elske Ammenwerth, Hans-Bernd Bludau, Anke Buchauer, Alexander Roßnagel: Simulation Studies for the Evaluation of Security Technology; pp. 547 - 560 in [MülRan99]

[Caller ID]   http://www.markwelch.com/callerid.htm

[DuENRS99]   Cornelius Dufft, Jürgen Espey, Hartmut Neuf, Georg Rudinger, Kurt Stapf: Usability and Security; pp. 531 - 545 in [MülRan99]

[GaGrPS97]   Gunther Gattung, Rüdiger Grimm, Ulrich Pordesch, Michael J. Schneider: Persönliche Sicherheitsmanager in der virtuellen Welt. S. 181-205 in Mehrseitige Sicherheit in der Kommunikationstechnik. Günter Müller, Andreas Pfitzmann (eds), Vol. I, Bonn et al. 1997

[Gong99]   Li Gong: Inside Java 2 Platform Security: Architecture, API Design and Implementation; Addison-Wesley; Reading et al 1999

[MülRan99]   Günter Müller, Kai Rannenberg: Multilateral Security in Communications; Addison-Wesley-Longman; München et al. 1999; ISBN-3-8273-1360-0

[Pordes98]   Ulrich Pordesch: Negotiating security among end users: concept and test in a simulation study, Computer Networks and ISDN-Systems 30/1998, 1597 - 1605.

[PoRoSc99]   Ulrich Pordesch, Alexander Roßnagel, Michael J. Schneider: Simulationsstudie "Mobile und sichere Kommunikation im Gesundheitswesen", DuD 1999, p. 76

[RaPfMü99]   Kai Rannenberg, Andreas Pfitzmann, Günter Müller: IT Security and Multilateral Security; pp. 21-29 in [MülRan99]

[ReDaFR97]   Martin Reichenbach, Herbert Damker, Hannes Federrath, Kai Rannenberg: Individual Management of Personal Reachability in Mobile Communication; pp. 163-174 in Louise Yngström, Jan Carlsen: Information Security in Research and Business; Proceedings of the IFIP TC11 13th International Information Security Conference (SEC'97): 14-16 May 1997, Copenhagen, Denmark; Chapman & Hall, London; ISBN 0-412-8178-02

[RoHaHe99]   Alexander Roßnagel, Reinhold Haux, Wolfgang Herzog (eds), Mobile und sichere Kommunikation im Gesundheitswesen, Braunschweig, Vieweg, 1999

[WhiTyg99]   Alma Whitten, Doug Tygar: Why Johnny Can't Encrypt: A Usability Evaluation of PGP5.0; Proceedings of the 8th USENIX Security Symposium, August 1999

Secure Anonymous Signature-Based Transactions

Els Van Herreweghen

IBM Research, Zurich Research Laboratory, 8803 Rüschlikon, Switzerland
evh@zurich.ibm.com

Abstract. Electronic commerce protocols often require users to reveal their identities and other information not necessary for reasons of security. Some applications such as contract signing are often argued to require a signer's authenticated identity; but this authentication may give the recipient a false feeling of security if certificate registration procedures do not guarantee a mapping to a liable person, or correctness of certificate data. In this paper, we propose a separation of identity from liability. Liability-aware certificates allow certificate issuers to make explicit which liabilities it takes with respect to the transaction, the certificate data or the signer's identity. We illustrate their use in the design of a pseudonym service providing pseudonym certificates for secure anonymous transactions.

1 Introduction

Many electronic commerce services and protocols are not designed with the goal of protecting the privacy or anonymity of end users. In fact, they often require the user to give a lot of information not strictly necessary for reasons of security. Such information can be present in the certificates certifying the user's public key.

As the collection and exploitation of information becomes more of a concern, users are less willing to give out information. It is therefore desirable to re-examine the need for giving out certain information items as part of business processes. Necessary is only the information from which the recipient of a digital signature (representing a payment, an auction bid, a contract) derives trust that the payment is valid, that the bidder will pay upon winning the bid, that the signer is liable to execute the contract. Most often, this trust is not based on the signer's identity. Rather, it is based on the identity and trustworthiness of the authority certifying the signer's key, thereby implicitly or explicitly 'vouching' for transactions made with that key.

Also, the liability of certification authorities with respect to certificate registration procedures is often unclear. When a party relying on a signature requires that it be made by a certified 'real' identity, there may be an assumption but no guarantee that a legal person can be held liable for this signature. Rather than receiving a signature by an authenticated 'real' identity certified under uncertain

F. Cuppens et al. (Eds.): ESORICS 2000, LNCS 1895, pp. 55–71, 2000.

liability rules, it would be more useful for the relying party to have the certifier's guarantee that a legal person can be held liable for the signature.

In this paper, we demonstrate a separation of identity from liability and certification. We transform a number of signature-based protocols into pseudonymized versions. We show how to provide maximal security for the relying party by including issuers' liabilities into signers' certificates. We distinguish between liability for data in the certificate, liability for transactions made with the certificate, and liability to reveal a signer's real identity under specified conditions.

The outline of the paper is as follows. In Section 2, we introduce the concept by describing a pseudonym server transforming certificates in a generic account-based payment system into single-use pseudonym certificates. We show that it is possible for the payment recipient to have a guarantee of payment, without affecting the protocol, and without introducing any liability for the pseudonym server. In Section 3, we discuss the value of certificates and signatures for more general applications, and introduce a liability-aware certificate format. In Section 4, this certificate format is used in the design of a generic pseudonym server, issuing pseudonym certificates for a potentially large set of applications. Section 5 discusses related work and suggestions for future research; Section 6 concludes the paper.

2   Pseudonymizing a Generic Payment System

The generic payment protocol in Figure 1 follows the model of the iKP [1,2] and SET [3] protocols. Its exact format, however, is derived from the requirements for disputable payment protocols in [4]. After presenting the protocol, we analyze its implicit guarantees and liabilities. We then introduce a pseudonym server (PS) into this system and design a pseudonymized version of the payment protocol. The goal is to preserve existing payment guarantees for the relying party while minimizing the pseudonym server's liability.

2.1   The Generic Payment Protocol

The participants in the protocol are C (Customer), M (Merchant) and A (Acquirer). C's certificate $CERT_C$ is issued by I (Issuer) and specifies I's liability for payments made using $CERT_C$; I's certificate $CERT_I$ is assumed to be issued by a root certification authority.

We use the following notation:

SK_X, PK_X: X's secret signature key and public key in a digital signature scheme.
$S_X(M)$: Signature with SK_X over message M – does not include M.
$E_Y(M)$: Encryption of M under Y's public encryption key.
$CERT_X$: X's public-key certificate (certifying PK_X).
role: Role in the payment system ('customer', 'merchant', 'issuer', 'acquirer').

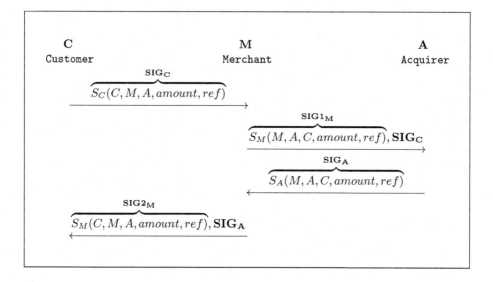

Fig. 1. Generic payment protocol

With SIG_C, C authorizes a payment to M, who then adds its own signature $SIG1_M$ to form an authorization request. SIG_A constitutes A's authorization response. M creates a payment receipt $SIG2_M$ and sends this together with SIG_A to C.

The parameter ref contains at least a transaction identifier trx_id and a transaction time, possibly also a goods description or a hash thereof. We only represent the actual signatures; which of the components of a signature are actually sent as part of the protocol messages, or as part of a previous negotiation protocol, is not relevant to this discussion: it is assumed that the verifier of a signature possesses the data constituting the signed message (including the necessary certificates to verify them).

M may verify SIG_C to validate the correctness of transaction data. M's payment guarantee, however, is derived from A's authorization SIG_A. A's authorization, in turn, is based on the validity of SIG_C, the contents of $CERT_C$ and $CERT_I$, and the terms of the contract between A and I. The combination of $CERT_C$, $CERT_I$ and this contract provide A with a guarantee such as "I will honor validly constructed payments with PK_C up to an amount of \$1000 subject to the condition that $CERT_C$ nor $CERT_I$ were on a revocation list accessible by A at the time A authorized the transaction". As I may not be able to verify exactly when A authorized the payment, I may allow a maximum processing delay : "...were on a revocation list 12 hours before A presents the transaction to I for clearance".

Liabilities or revocation conditions may not actually be part of existing certificates; rather, they are part of contracts, implicit agreements or implicit procedures and are thus implicitly present in a certificate. We can then represent a certificate $CERT_X$, issued by Y [1]:

$$CERT_X = S_Y(role, X, PK_X, Y, L = \{amount, condition\})$$

where L stands for Y's liability for transactions made with PK_X. L consists of an amount and possibly the conditions related to revocation.

In the example above, assuming that I is directly certified by a root authority:

$$CERT_C = S_I(customer, C, PK_C, I, L = \{amount=\$1000, maxdelay = 12 \text{ hrs}\})$$
$$CERT_I = S_{root}(issuer, I, PK_I, root, L = \{amount=\$10,000, maxdelay = 12 \text{ hrs}\})$$

2.2   Requirements for a Secure Pseudonymized Version

We now develop a pseudonymized version of the above generic payment protocol. C, possessing a long-term payment certificate $CERT_C$, can obtain one-time pseudonym certificates $CERT_P$ from a pseudonym server PS, allowing C to make payments under the pseudonym P and remain anonymous towards M and A. (We assume that we cannot change the existing payment infrastructure and thus that the interface between C and I, such as registration, account definition and payment processing, is fixed. In this infrastructure, C has a non-anonymous account with I, and I expects a valid payment order to be linked to that account. Therefore, we do not consider anonymity of C towards I. However, the constructions introduced to anonymize C towards M and A can also be applied to anonymize C towards I if we relax the previous assumption and allow a change to the interface between C and I.) PS, of course, needs to be a recognized issuer in the specific payment system in order for $CERT_P$ to be considered a valid certificate by the relying party.

We first list the different criteria against which we will measure the pseudonymized version.

Guarantees towards relying party (A). A valid signature SIG_P over a transaction has the same guarantee of payment as a valid signature SIG_C over the same transaction.

For general signature-based protocols (as discussed in Sections 3 and 4), a relying party may want the pseudonym certificate to express the conditions (e.g., fraudulent behavior) under which it can obtain a real identity of the signer. In the specific case of a payment protocol, however, we assume that only the guarantee of payment is relevant to the relying party. It should therefore be unnecessary to ever reveal the real identity of even a dishonest or fraudulent C to A (or M).

---

[1] The notation for liability is intuitive and does not define a specific format or language. The certificate format is merely a symbolic representation; additional information such as expiration time, attributes etc. are represented only when relevant to the discussion.

No extra risk for I. I wants proof of C's payment authorization even if the payment is made under pseudonym P: if I does not trust PS, I has no reason to debit C's account for pseudonymous payments under a pseudonym P which allegedly represents C. Even if I trusts PS (e.g., I operates PS as a service), I may need to prove C's authorization to a third party, e.g. in order to protect itself against repudiation by C.

Minimal trust by C in PS. PS should protect C's privacy and not give away information about C, or reveal the linking between C and the pseudonyms it uses. PS may publish privacy policies stating to which end, under which conditions and to whom PS may reveal which information about C. As mentioned in the first requirement, PS should never have to reveal any information about C to M or A. (Of course, if PS ever has a dispute with C, PS may need to reveal C's identity to a third party.) It is difficult to enforce and verify the PS's compliance with its privacy policies; C has to trust PS to adhere to them. This requirement holds for the various pseudonym server scenarios in this paper, and we will not repeat it when discussing their security.

Another of C's requirements is for PS not to be able to frame C. This requirement seems easy to fulfill if C is allowed to issue its own pseudonym private keys. We will see, however, that PS may have an interest in issuing the pseudonym private keys if it wants to limit its own risk.

Minimal risk for PS. PS is liable for transactions made with certificates it issued. PS can rigorously limit that liability, e.g., by issuing single-use $CERT_P$ only after receiving a valid SIG_C from C. Then, when PS is held liable for a payment $(CERT_P, SIG_P)$, it can show (to I or a to a third party) a payment $(CERT_C, SIG_C)$ for which I is liable. Still, revocation issues need to be taken into account: for PS to assume no liability at all, the possibility should be excluded that $CERT_P$ can be valid after $CERT_C$ has been revoked.

In the following sections, we investigate different possibilities for pseudonymizing the previous protocol, with different impact on liability of PS, on efficiency, and on PS's infrastructure requirements for revocation.

2.3 Design for Maximum Security: PS Online, $CERT_P$ Linked to Transaction

In this first design, PS issues a different pseudonym key pair (PK_P, SK_P), pseudonym certificate $(CERT_P)$ and signature SIG_P for C for each transaction. PS is thus always on-line and participates in the transaction. The pseudonym certificate is linked to the specific transaction; this guarantees that it can be used only once.

Description of the protocol. The P-M-A transaction in the pseudonymized protocol is the same as the C-M-A transaction in the original protocol, with

C's identity, signature and certificate replaced by P's identity, signature and certificate. M and A see P as customer; and PS as the issuer of P's certificate:

$SIG_P = S_P(P,M,A,time,amount,ref)$
$SIG1_M = S_M(M,A,P,time,amount,ref)$
$SIG_A = S_A(M,A,P,time,amount,ref)$
$SIG2_M = S_M(P,M,A, time,amount,ref)$

PS issues SIG_P only after having received and validated a transaction signature SIG_C from C. SIG_C is PS' proof of C's commitment to the transaction. PS includes SIG_C in $CERT_P$, allowing I to check SIG_C: this protects PS against repudiation by C and protects C against framing by PS.

New certificates introduced in the system are then:

$CERT_{PS}$ is a root-issued issuer certificate:
$$CERT_{PS} = S_{root}(issuer, PS, PK_{PS}, root, L_{root}).$$
$CERT_P = S_{PS}(customer, P, PK_P, PS, L_{PS}, issuer\_data)$

with issuer_data $= E_I(SIG_C, C)$, the encryption of C's identity and transaction signature. It can only be decrypted by I and provides I with proof of C's authorization.

The resulting protocol is depicted in Figure 2. To highlight the difference with the original version, we also show the transport of certificates belonging to C (and I) and P (and PS).

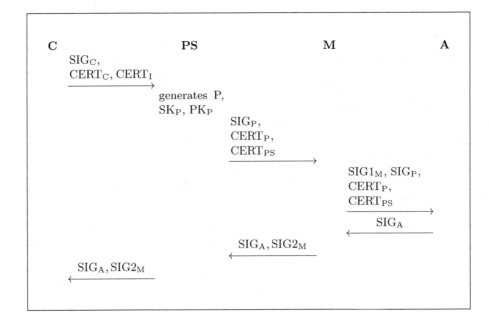

Fig. 2. Pseudonymized payment protocol: on-line PS, one-time pseudonym certificate

The settlement between A and I (not shown in the figure) may be done at a later point in time. Depending on A's 'awareness' of pseudoymized certificates, A may initiate a settlement with PS by sending {SIG_P, $CERT_P$} to PS and PS sending issuer_data to I. Alternatively, A directly sends issuer_data to I.

To hide the linking between C and P also towards outsiders, the channel between C and PS additionally needs to be encrypted. Also, traffic anonymizers or MIXes [5,6,7] used on the C-PS and C-M channels can help to unlink the pseudonym request from the pseudonym use, and to hide the linking of C or P to a network address. These extensions apply to the different pseudonym server designs in this paper but are not discussed here.

The 'receipts' $SIG2_M$ and SIG_A don't include C's identity; C may thus not be able to use them as transaction receipts. One could allow C to prove the linking between C and P by including such a proof (e.g., a hash H(C,P,ref)) in $CERT_P$ and by PS returning $CERT_P$ to C together with SIG_A and $SIG2_M$. Still, this solution requires C to reveal its real identity when proving its participation in the transaction. This can only be avoided by changing the way receipts are used. E.g., C could prove ownership of a receipt $SIG2_M$ or SIG_A, not by proving a linking between C and P but by dynamically proving knowledge of a secret associated with P while showing the receipt. Such a secret could be SK_P or another secret key associated with P, and would be securely communicated by PS to P. This alternative is a topic for future research.

Security analysis. We now analyze the above protocol in terms of the requirements in Section 2.2.

Guarantees towards relying party (A). We define a valid (SIG_P, $CERT_P$, $CERT_{PS}$) to constitute the same payment guarantee as in the original system, i.e., PS is liable to honor a valid SIG_P under the condition of $CERT_P$ and $CERT_{PS}$ not being revoked.

No extra risk for I. I only clears payments based on a valid SIG_C, proof of C's transaction commitment.

Minimal trust by C in PS. PS cannot frame C, as I only accepts payments containing a valid SIG_C.

Minimal risk for PS. PS does not take any risk at all as long as it only issues $CERT_P$ for a valid SIG_C and checks that $CERT_C$ is not on any revocation list. This ensures that any valid SIG_P is based on a valid SIG_C, i.e., any payment which is acceptable to A will be honored by I, and thus PS can transfer any liability to I. PS only increases its risk (up to the amount in $CERT_P$) by not acting honestly or correctly.

The absence of risk for PS strongly depends on PS issuing the pseudonym key pair. If C were allowed to issue his own (SK_P, PK_P), it would be possible for C to generate a SIG_P inconsistent with SIG_C, causing liabilities for PS not covered by I.

Discussion. The model of PS issuing pseudonym keys and certificates for every new transaction provides maximum security to all the parties, and a total absence of risk for the PS. For reasons of efficiency, however, it may be desirable for C to obtain pseudonym certificates ahead of time, such as to avoid contacting PS for every transaction. The next section describes such an alternative solution and its security features.

2.4   Alternative Design: Offline PS

Allowing C to obtain certificates ahead of time has two direct consequences. First, the pseudonym certificate can no longer be linked to a specific transaction, and thus has to be valid for a certain amount of time. Second, as C makes the actual pseudonym payment without PS's involvement, C has to issue the pseudonym key pair. This introduces major risks:

1. PS cannot enforce a linking between SIG_C and SIG_P. Or, PS cannot enforce that P's payment valid for A contains C's payment acceptable to I.
2. After issuing $CERT_P$, $CERT_C$ can be revoked, which leaves PS with the liability for payments with $CERT_P$ until $CERT_P$ is revoked or no longer valid.

The second problem can be addressed in either of the following ways:

- PS issues very short-lived pseudonym certificates (e.g., $CERT_P$ lifetime is smaller than the revocation delay of $CERT_C$). Then, even if $CERT_C$ is revoked, any outstanding $CERT_P$ will be invalid by the time I refuses payments with $CERT_C$. This solution, however, defeats the purpose of C obtaining certificates some time before the actual transaction.
- PS revokes pseudonym certificates by posting Certificate Revocation Lists (CRLs) to the appropriate CRL directories. It should then frequently verify revocation status of parent certificates $CERT_C$ of outstanding pseudonym certificates $CERT_P$, and revoke pseudonym certificates as needed.

In order to address the first problem, PS has to take the role of an insurer, resort to risk management strategies, and charge for the service accordingly. Alternatively, PS may require a deposit or guarantee from C equal to PS's liability for the pseudonym certificate. Neither solution, however, gives I or a third party a proof of transaction by C. The protocol in Figure 3 constructs such a proof by C committing to the pseudonym (keys) as part of the pseudonym retrieval procedure; this commitment $S_C(CERT_C, PK_P,...)$ may be encrypted for I and included in $CERT_P$, in a way similar to SIG_C in the protocol in Figure 2. Such a scenario changes the dispute handling rules of the protocol: with the combination of SIG_P and the commitment, I as well as an external verifier should conclude that C authorized the payment. It may also solve the first problem: if PS includes the same liability in $CERT_P$ as in $CERT_{PS}$, PS again can transfer liability to I for every payment valid to A.

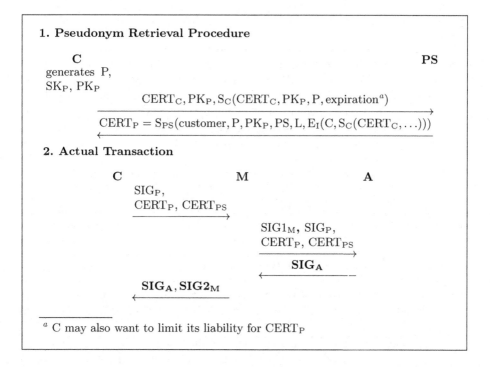

1. Pseudonym Retrieval Procedure

C   PS

generates P,
SK_P, PK_P

$$CERT_C, PK_P, S_C(CERT_C, PK_P, P, expiration^a)$$
⟶

$$CERT_P = S_{PS}(customer, P, PK_P, PS, L, E_I(C, S_C(CERT_C, \ldots)))$$
⟵

2. Actual Transaction

C   M   A

SIG_P,
$CERT_P$, $CERT_{PS}$
⟶

$SIG1_M$, SIG_P,
$CERT_P$, $CERT_{PS}$
⟶

SIG_A
⟵

SIG_A, $SIG2_M$
⟵

---

[a] C may also want to limit its liability for $CERT_P$

Fig. 3. Pseudonymized payment protocol: off-line PS

Security Features

Guarantees towards relying party (A). We define, as in the previous solution, a valid (SIG_P, $CERT_P$, $CERT_{PS}$) to represent a payment guarantee for A, on condition that $CERT_P$ or $CERT_{PS}$ are not revoked.

No extra risk for I. From $CERT_P$ and the encrypted commitment, I can derive C's identity and commitment to P and PKp; from SIG_P, P's authorization of the transaction. Thus I takes no extra risk on condition that a potential external verifier applies the same verification rules.

Minimal trust by C in PS. PS cannot frame C, as C generates the pseudonym keys.

Minimal risk for PS. If PS takes care of the revocation problem (immediately revoking $CERT_P$ in case of a revoked $CERT_C$) and makes sure not to take more liability in $CERT_P$ than I takes in $CERT_C$, PS again limits its liability.

2.5 Discussion

The designs in Sections 2.3 and 2.4 both provide equal guarantees towards the relying party but show some tradeoffs between PS's liability, and changes of infrastructure and efficiency. An off-line PS serving pseudonym certificates ahead of time may be a more efficient solution. In this case, PS has to limit its liability by taking care of timely revocation of pseudonym certificates, and by requiring that the user commit to the pseudonym key. This commitment has to be recognized by an external verifier in order for I to prove the user's authorization through P.

An on-line PS issuing transaction-linked certificates is a less efficient solution but allows PS to rigorously minimize its liability without requiring any changes in verification and dispute handling infrastructure, and without requiring PS to handle revocation issues.

3 Generalized Signatures and Liabilities

The pseudonym server designs in the previous section are specific for the payment protocol and assume that the user already has a long-term certificate for use in this protocol.

When dealing with more general signatures, such as digitally signed contracts, it may no longer be possible to attach a fixed value to the transaction, as we did in the case of payments. The party relying on a signed contract may also attach a value to the guarantee that the signer is a liable person whose identity will be revealed under certain conditions, or to the correctness of certain attributes in the signer's certificate.

A generic digital signature (with corresponding certificate) can be represented as:

$$\mathbf{CERT_S} = S_I(\text{Pid, role, S, } PK_S, \text{ I, attrs}), \quad \mathbf{SIG_S} = S_S(\text{trx\_data, trx\_id})$$

with

Pid, role: the protocol identifier and S's role;
S: the signer (of the contract, auction bid, payment, ...);
I: the certificate issuer certifying PK_S;
trx_data: describing the type and contents of the transaction;
trx_id: a unique transaction identifier (similar to the ref parameter).

SIG_S expresses S's commitment either to the correctness of trx_data, or to the execution of some action described in trx_data, such as payment or contractual obligation. A verifier V can hold S (or, I through $CERT_S$) liable for this commitment. In order to determine the potential value of such a liability, we describe the different damages to V that can be incurred:

– V may suffer loss if attrs in $CERT_S$ are not correct; e.g., attrs specify a quality label of S as a registered construction company and SIGs represents a bid for constructing a building.

- V may suffer loss if data in trx_data is incorrect; this may be relevant if S's commitment is a commitment to data rather than to an action or contract.
- If trx_data represents an action or contractual obligation, V suffers loss if the promise (contract) expressed in trx_data is not kept (executed). In the special case of the contract being a payment, it can be the value of the payment.

In order to express I's or S's liability for data (attrs or trx_data), it should be possible to attach a value to their correctness. Also, their correctness should be publicly verifiable, or, it should be specified which third party or arbiter can judge this.

3.1   Liability-Aware Certificates

The possible losses described above can be covered by liabilities included into certificates:

$$\text{CERT}_S = S_I(\text{Pid, role, S, PK}_S, \text{I, attrs, L})$$

L, the issuer's liability, consists of a set (0 or more) of individual components, each of which have one of the following types: Ld (related to data liability), Lt (related to transaction liability) and Li (related to identity liability). Other than a type, each component has an amount, a condition for liability, and an indication of which party can evaluate the condition.

Some examples of individual liability components are:

- a liability {type = Ld, amount = \$1000, condition = attrs, verifier = Arbiter} indicates that the certificate issuer takes a liability of \$1000 for any certificate attributes which are found to be incorrect by Arbiter.
- a liability {type = Ld, amount = \$1000, condition = trx_data, verifier = Arbiter} indicates that the certificate issuer takes a liability of \$1000 for any trx_data signed by the certificate holder which are found to be incorrect by Arbiter.
- a liability {type = Lt, amount = \$1000, condition = any, verifier = Arbiter} indicates that the certificate issuer takes a liability of \$1000 if Arbiter evaluates the transaction (e.g., the contract execution) as failed.
- a liability {type = Li, amount = \$10000, condition = trx_data, verifier = Arbiter} indicates that the certificate issuer is liable for revealing the real identity of a signer (who is a liable person) if Arbiter evaluates trx_data to be false or not executed. Failure to reliably reveal a real identity makes the issuer liable to compensate \$10000.

Following are some additional examples of the use of liabilities in specific applications:

- A liability in a user certificate for a SET-like payment system could look as follows:

L = {{type=Lt, amount=\$1000, condition=(revocation_delay=12hrs), verifier=Arbiter}}.
Here, the only liability taken by the issuer is to honor payments up to \$1000 as long as the revocation condition is fulfilled. The issuer does not take any liability for attributes or for revealing a signer's identity.

– A liability in a certificate of a construction company used for contract signing could be:
L = {{type=Ld, amount=\$1000, condition=attrs, verifier=Arbiter},
{type=Li, amount=\$10000, condition=trx_data, verifier=Arbiter}}.
The issuer takes no liability for the transaction (or its execution); it takes a liability of \$1000 for any false attributes, and guarantees, with a penalty of \$10000, to reveal the real name of a signer if the contract is not executed as asserted by the verifier.

The above examples are meant to demonstrate the concept; in a detailed design, the expression of individual liabilities and conditions may require more complex statements.

In the following section, we now describe the design of the pseudonym server. We use the liability-aware notation for long-term and pseudonym certificates.

4   A Generic Pseudonym Server

We would like a generic pseudonym server to fulfill following requirements:

1. The pseudonym server issues certificates that can be used in a set of different protocols, such as contract signing, auction, payment.
2. The pseudonym server can serve certificates in a protocol-independent manner, i.e., does not play an active role in composing protocol-specific signatures.
3. The pseudonym certificates are not necessarily linked to a specific transaction, allowing for pseudonym certificates to be acquired ahead of time.
4. The one-time user of a pseudonymous service or protocol need not have a long-term certificate for that protocol, i.e., a user registered with the pseudonym server may request one-time pseudonym certificates for a number of protocols. E.g., the PS could be a service provided by a user's Internet Service Provider (ISP) and the user can obtain a one-time SET certificate for a specific payment.

A user S of such a pseudonym service has a long-term certificate $CERT_S$ recognized by or issued by PS, and can obtain pseudonym certificates from PS for different protocols and transactions. Figure 4 shows such a pseudonymized transaction. The CERT_REQ - CERT_RES exchange constitutes the core PS functionality. The other flows illustrate the possible use of pseudonymized certificates within a specific transaction: in an optional CERT_PROP flow, the verifier V sends to S the proposed certificate format; the last flow containing SIG_P is S's actual transaction commitment using pseudonym P.

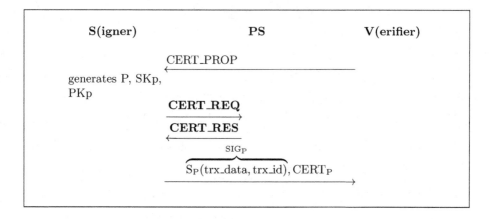

Fig. 4. Generic pseudonym server

4.1   CERT_REQ, CERT_RES

We now describe the message and certificate formats in more detail; the design choices are then clarified when analyzing the security of the pseudonymous transaction.

$CERT_S = S_I(pid_S, role_S, S, PK_S, I, attrs_S, L_{I-S})$

with L_{I-S} the set of liabilities I takes for data in $CERT_S$ and transactions with $CERT_S$.

$CERT_P = S_{PS}(pid_P, role_P, P, PK_P, PS, attrs_P, L_{PS-P})$

with L_{PS-P} the set of liabilities PS takes for data and transactions with $CERT_P$.

$CERT_P$ may be linked to a specific transaction by specifying a transaction identifier as part of the various liability conditions. This limits the risk taken by PS, and may make it unnecessary for PS to have to deal with revoking $CERT_P$. Note that PS can be the same entity as I, in which case S simply has a long-term account with PS. This can be the case if the PS service is offered by a ISP.

$CERT\_REQ = S_C(CERT\_REQ, pid_P, role_P, P, PK_P, PS, attrs_P, L_{PS-P})$, $CERT_S$
$CERT\_RES = CERT_P$

With CERT_REQ, S communicates the desired certificate contents to PS, and at the same time commits to signatures made with SKp in the context of the requested $CERT_P$. It can thus be seen as a secure registration procedure where S takes liability for PK_P and the $CERT_P$ not yet received, in a way provable by PS.

PS's decision to issue $CERT_P$ depends on its evaluation of risk. This depends on the liabilities in the requested $CERT_P$, whether it is valid for only one or more transactions, the contract terms between S and PS, whether or not S has an account with PS, etc. The processing of CERT_REQ, therefore, may involve additional communication between S and PS, such as PS asking for some guarantee or deposit.

4.2   The Liabilities in CERT$_P$

In some cases, the expected liabilities in CERT$_P$ can be derived by V and/or S from transaction features, such as the amount of a payment or auction bid. More complex liabilities may be determined by V on a per-transaction basis. V may have to explicitly communicate expected liabilities to S, as shown with the CERT_PROP flow in Figure 4.

Such a message could have a similar format as a CERT_REQ and can be signed by V:

$$S_V(CERT\_PROP,\ldots,L)$$

in which case it may a binding commitment, part of the contract between S (P) and V.

Security Features. We now analyze the CERT_REQ - CERT_RES flows with respect to the security features listed in Section 2.2, omitting the issuer-specific requirement which was specific for the payment system.

Guarantees towards relying party V. The relying party V receiving a signature SIG$_S$ in a transaction has a guarantee of I's liabilities in CERT$_P$, thus of receiving liability amounts or the real identity of the signer.

Minimal trust of C in PS. As S generates pseudonym keys and commits to them using its private signature key SK$_S$, PS is not able to frame S.

PS absorbs minimal risk. In case of a dispute, PS can prove S's commitment to a pseudonym key, and thus S's involvement in a transaction with that key. The remaining risk depends on the possibilities for PS to 'recover' liabilities from I or S. This depends on contracts between S and PS (or between S and I).

4.3   Example: Auction

We illustrate the above principles with one more example. In this example, an ISP plays the role of PS for its registered users, billing them for this service through the existing billing relationship. Registered users have a limited liability credit with the PS. A user S, registered with the ISP, wants a pseudonym certificate to bid on a last minute vacation offer with an auction service. The auction service accepts anonymous or pseudonymous bids under the condition that payment is guaranteed, the bidder's age is above 18, and the winning bidder's identity will be revealed to the auction service.

S has a long-term certificate CERT$_S$ and private key SK$_S$ with which to authenticate to the ISP/PS. This long-term certificate may contain values of (or references to) maximum liabilities PS is willing to take for this user, attributes of the user (such as age) which PS has verified upon registration and is willing to vouch in a pseudonym certificate.

The pseudonym certificate (and, similarly, CERT_REQ) could look as follows:

CERT$_P$ = S$_{PS}$(CERT_REQ, e-auction, bidder, P, PK$_P$, PS, attrs={{age>18}}, L={{Ld, \$100, none, Arbiter},{Lt, \$300, none, Arbiter}, {Li, \$300, condition(auction_id), Arbiter}}).

This expresses that PS takes a liability of \$100 for the correctness of age, gives a payment guarantee of \$300 for the transaction, and guarantees to reveal S's identity on condition of winning the auction with identifier auction_id. Assuming that PS can prove S's age to be over 18 to Arbiter, and PS has proof of S's real identity, the risk taken by PS is limited to the transaction amount (\$100), which may be below S's credit limit, in which case PS doesn't need additional deposits or guarantees from S.

5   Related and Future Work

In this paper, we focused on existing systems based on X.509 [8] or similar certificates, on introducing explicit liability statements into these certificates, and on optimal control of the pseudonym server over its liabilities. Though the pseudonym server cannot frame users, it still has to be trusted with a large amount of information about users, their transactions, and the linking of their pseudonyms. Pseudonym systems based on blind signatures [9,10]) can provide stronger anonymity guarantees and require less trust in the pseudonym server than the designs presented in this paper. They can provide protection against specific forms of user misbehavior (such as double-spending a coin [11]) through cryptographic constructs that cause the identity of a misbehaving user to be revealed. It is interesting to investigate to which extent such pseudonym systems can support the functionality we provided in this paper. The potential complexity of liability conditions (such as the ones for revealing identities), however, seems to suggest the existence of a trusted party evaluating them, which does not fit with blind signature schemes. Also, blind signatures may make it much harder for an issuer or pseudonym server to control the usage of a pseudonym certificate and thus its liability.

This paper has introduced a concept rather than a full design, and leaves several topics open for investigation. The liability types may need to be refined as more complex electronic negotiations and transactions are defined. Expressing liability contents, such as conditions and verifiers, was done using an intuitive notation; a language and notation need to be developed.

The choice to use pseudonyms as identifiers in certificates was made for reasons of compatibility with the existing certificate formats. It would be possible to remove also those pseudonyms from certificates and use strictly anonymous certificates.

It should also further be investigated how to use traffic anonymizers (such as [5]) or MIXes [6,7] to provide unlinkability between the request for and the actual use of a pseudonym.

6 Conclusion

In this paper, we have separated the notion of identity from liability, by suggesting that certificates explicitly specify liabilities needed by the party relying on a digital signature. We have illustrated this principle by introducing a pseudonym server that acts as an intermediate certificate issuer in existing certificate-based systems. The pseudonym certificates provide a relying party with clear guarantees, while the pseudonym server itself can calculate its own risk and minimize it through appropriate contracts with or deposits from requesting users.

We demonstrated the separation of identity from liability by applying it to the anonymization of existing transactions. It is, however, equally applicable in non-anonymous systems, where the presence of a certified identity may cause relying parties to make incorrect assumptions about liability guarantees. Also in these cases, making certifiers' liabilities explicit may help clarify objective guarantees, avoid unexpected liability gaps, and enhance trust.

References

1. Bellare, M., Garay, J.A., Hauser, R., Herzberg, A., Krawczyk, H., Steiner, M., Tsudik, G., Waidner, M. iKP – A Family of Secure Electronic Payment Protocols. In: Proc. First USENIX Workshop on Electronic Commerce. USENIX Assoc., Berkeley (1995) 89-106.
2. Bellare, M., Garay, J., Hauser, R., Herzberg, A., Krawczyk, H., Steiner, M., Tsudik, G.,Van Herreweghen, E., Waidner, M. Design, Implementation and Deployment of the iKP Secure Electronic Payment System. IEEE J. Sel. Areas in Commun. **18**, April 2000 issue, in press.
3. Mastercard and Visa. SET Secure Electronic Transactions Protocol, Version 1.0. Book One: Business Specifications; Book Two: Technical Specification; Book Three: Formal Protocol Definition. May 1997. Available from http://www.setco.org/download.html.
4. Asokan, N., Van Herreweghen, E., Steiner, M. Towards a Framework for Handling Disputes in Payment Systems. In: Proc. 3rd USENIX Workshop on Electronic Commerce, Boston, MA. USENIX Assoc., Berkeley (1998) 187-202.
5. The Anonymizer. http://www.anonymizer.com.
6. Gülçü, C., Tsudik, G. Mixing e-mail With Babel. In: Proc. 1996 Symposium on Network and Distributed System Security. IEEE Society Press, Los Alamitos (1996) 2-16.
7. Pfitzmann, A., Pfitzmann, B., Waidner, M. ISDN-Mixes: Untraceable Communication with Very Small Bandwidth Overhead. In: CI/ITC Conf.: Communication in Distributed Systems, Mannheim, Germany, February 1991. Informatik-Fachberichte 267. Springer-Verlag, Heidelberg (1991) 451-463.
8. ISO/IEC 9594-8 (X.509): OSI - The Directory - Authentication Framework.

9. Chaum, D. Security Without Identification: Transaction Systems to Make Big Brother Obsolete. Commun. ACM **28** (1985), No. 10.
10. Lysyanskaya, A., Rivest, R., Sahai, A. Pseudonym Systems. Master's Thesis, MIT Laboratory for Computer Science (1999).
11. Chaum, D., Fiat, A., Naor, M. Untraceable Electronic Cash. In: Advances in Cryptology – Eurocrypt'89. Springer-Verlag, Berlin (1989) 319-327

Metering Schemes for General Access Structures

Barbara Masucci[1] and Douglas R. Stinson[2]

[1] Dipartimento di Informatica ed Applicazioni, Università di Salerno,
84081 Baronissi (SA), Italy, masucci@dia.unisa.it
http://www.dia.unisa.it/~masucci
[2] Department of Combinatorics and Optimization, University of Waterloo,
Waterloo, Ontario, N2L 3G1, Canada, dstinson@cacr.math.uwaterloo.ca
http://www.cacr.math.uwaterloo.ca/~dstinson

Abstract. A *metering scheme* is a method by which an audit agency is able to measure the interaction between servers and clients during a certain number of time frames. Naor and Pinkas [9] considered schemes in which any server is able to construct a *proof* if and only if it has been visited by at least a number, say h, of clients in a given time frame. In this paper we construct metering schemes for more general access structures, which include *multilevel* and *compartmented* access structures. Metering schemes realizing these access structures have useful practical applications: for example, they can be used to measure the interaction of a web site with a specific audience which is of special interest. We also prove lower bounds on the communication complexity of metering schemes realizing general access structures.

Keywords: Distributed Audit, Metering, Security, Cryptography, Entropy.

1 Introduction

The growing popularity of the Internet is driving various applications, several of which are commercially oriented. One such commercial application is advertising. Most of the revenues of web sites come from advertisement payments. Access data are usually collected at web sites, which have control over the collecting process and stored data. Since the owners of the web sites can charge higher rates for advertisements by showing a higher number of visits, they have a strong economic incentive to inflate the number of visits. Consequently, web advertisers should prevent web sites displaying their ads from inflating the count of their visits. In a typical scenario there are many servers and clients, and an audit agency whose task is to measure the interaction between the servers and the clients.

Franklin and Malkhi [6] were the first to consider the metering problem in a rigourous theoretical approach. Their solutions offer only a "lightweight security" and cannot be applied if servers and clients have a strong commercial interest to falsify the metering results. Subsequently, Naor and Pinkas [9] proposed *metering schemes* in which a server is able to compute a proof for a certain time frame if and only if it has been visited by a number of clients larger than or equal

F. Cuppens et al. (Eds.): ESORICS 2000, LNCS 1895, pp. 72–87, 2000.

to some threshold h in that time frame. Recently, different kinds of metering schemes have been proposed. Metering schemes for ramp structures [1,5] have been introduced in order to reduce the overhead to the overall communication due to the metering process. Metering schemes with pricing [1,8], which allow to count the exact number of visits received by each server, and dynamic multi–threshold metering schemes [2], which are metering schemes in which there is a different threshold for any server and any time frame, have been introduced in order to have a more flexible payment system.

The measures considered in previous metering schemes are simple thresholds. In other words, these measures can distinguish between two cases: either the server has received at least a required number of visits or it has not. A more general situation is when we have a set Γ of subsets of clients, called an *access structure*, and the audit agency wants to verify if a server has received visits by at least a subset in Γ (the subsets in Γ are called *qualified subsets*).

In this paper we prove that it is possible to construct a metering scheme realizing any monotone access structure. Moreover, we provide lower bounds on the communication complexity of any metering scheme realizing a monotone access structure. Afterwards, we concentrate our attention on two particular kinds of access structures, *multilevel* and *compartmented* access structures. These access structures have useful practical applications. For example, metering schemes realizing these access structures can be used to measure the interaction of a web site with a specific audience which is of special interest. These schemes can be used, for example, by an editor of text books who pays a web site to host her advertisements and is interested in knowing how many professors visited the site.

2   Metering Schemes for General Access Structures

A *metering scheme* consists of n clients, say $C_1, \ldots, C_n$, m servers, say $S_1, \ldots, S_m$, and an audit agency A whose task is to measure the interaction between the clients and the servers in order to count the number of client visits that any server has received. Metering schemes considered by Naor and Pinkas [9] are specified by a threshold h: the audit agency wants to count if in any time frame the number of visits received by servers is greater than or equal to h. A more general situation is when we have a set Γ of subsets of clients and the audit agency wants to verify if a server has received visits by at least a subset in Γ.

Let $\{C_1, \ldots, C_n\}$ be the set of clients. An *access structure* on $\{C_1, \ldots, C_n\}$ is a set $\Gamma = \{A_1, \ldots, A_\ell\}$ of subsets of clients, i.e., $A_r \subseteq \{C_1, \ldots, C_n\}$ for $r = 1, \ldots, \ell$. The subsets in Γ are called *qualified subsets*. In a metering scheme realizing the access structure Γ any server which has been visited by at least a qualified subset of clients in Γ in a time frame is able to provide the audit agency with a proof for the visits it has received. The access structure that we consider in this paper are *monotone*, i.e., they satisfy the following property: if $A_r \in \Gamma$ and $A_r \subseteq A_z \subseteq \{C_1, \ldots, C_n\}$, then $A_z \in \Gamma$. Indeed, if a server receives visits by a subset A_z of clients which contains a qualified subset A_r, then it can reconstruct its proof by ignoring the information provided by clients in $A_z \setminus A_r$.

The general form of a metering scheme is the following: There is an *initialization phase* in which the audit agency provides each client with some piece of information. For any $i = 1, \ldots, n$, we denote by c_i the information that the audit agency A gives to the client $\mathcal{C}_i$. Moreover, we denote by C_i the set of all possible values of c_i. Given a set of clients $\mathcal{A}_r = \{\mathcal{C}_{i_1}, \ldots, \mathcal{C}_{i_k}\} \subseteq \{\mathcal{C}_1, \ldots, \mathcal{C}_n\}$, where $i_1 < i_2 < \ldots < i_k$, we denote by A_r the cartesian product $C_{i_1} \times \cdots \times C_{i_k}$. A *regular operation* consists in a client visit to a server during a time frame. During such a visit the client gives to the visited server a piece of information which depends on its private information, on the identity of the server, and on the time frame. For any $i = 1, \ldots, n$, $j = 1, \ldots, m$, and $t = 1, \ldots, \tau$, we denote by $c_{i,j}^t$ the information that the client $\mathcal{C}_i$ sends to the server $\mathcal{S}_j$ when visiting it in time frame t. Moreover, we denote by $C_{i,j}^t$ the set of all possible values of $c_{i,j}^t$. Let $B = \{1, \ldots, \beta\} \subseteq \{1, \ldots, s\}$ be a set of server indices. Given a set of clients $\mathcal{A}_r = \{\mathcal{C}_{i_1}, \ldots, \mathcal{C}_{i_k}\} \subseteq \{\mathcal{C}_1, \ldots, \mathcal{C}_n\}$, where $i_1 < i_2 < \ldots < i_k$, we denote by $A_{r,B}^t$ the cartesian product $C_{i_1,1}^t \times \cdots \times C_{i_k,1}^t \times \cdots \times C_{i_1,\beta}^t \times \cdots \times C_{i_k,\beta}^t$. At the end of any time frame t there is a *proof computation stage*. For any $j = 1, \ldots, m$ and $t = 1, \ldots, \tau$, we denote by p_j^t the proof computed by the server $\mathcal{S}_j$ when it has been visited by at least a qualified set of clients in time frame t. Moreover, we denote by P_j^t the sets of all values that p_j^t can assume. Given a set of server indices $B = \{1, \ldots, \beta\} \subseteq \{1, \ldots, s\}$, we denote by P_B^t the cartesian product $P_1^t \times \cdots \times P_\beta^t$. Finally, there is a *proof verification stage* in which the audit agency A verifies the proofs received by servers. If the proof received from a server at the end of a time frame is correct, then A pays the server for its services.

We consider a scenario in which a certain number $c \leq n$ of clients and $s \leq m$ of servers can be *corrupt*. A corrupt server can be assisted by corrupt clients and other corrupt servers in computing its proof. Let $\mathcal{C}_{i_1}, \ldots, \mathcal{C}_{i_c}$ be the corrupt clients. We assume that any qualified subset of clients $\mathcal{A}_r \in \Gamma$ contains $c_r \leq c$ corrupt clients, that is, $|\mathcal{A}_r \cap \{\mathcal{C}_{i_1}, \ldots, \mathcal{C}_{i_c}\}| = c_r < |\mathcal{A}_r|$, for any $r = 1, \ldots, \ell$. A corrupt client $\mathcal{C}_i$ can donate to a corrupt server the whole information received from the audit agency during the initialization phase. At time frame t, a corrupt server can donate to another corrupt server the information that it has received during time frames $1, \ldots, t$. For any $j = 1, \ldots, m$ and $t = 1, \ldots, \tau$, we denote by $V_j^{[t]}$ all the information known by a corrupt server $\mathcal{S}_j$ in time frames $1, \ldots, t$. We also define $V_j^{[0]} = \emptyset$.

In this paper with a boldface capital letter, say $\mathbf{X}$, we denote a random variable taking value on a set denoted by the corresponding capital letter X according to some probability distribution $\{Pr_{\mathbf{X}}(x)\}_{x \in X}$. The values such a random variable can take are denoted by the corresponding lower letter. Given a random variable $\mathbf{X}$ we denote with $H(\mathbf{X})$ the Shannon entropy of $\{Pr_{\mathbf{X}}(x)\}_{x \in X}$ (for some basic properties of entropy, consult the Appendix).

We formally define metering schemes for general access structures by using the entropy approach, as done in [1,5,8,2].

Definition 1. *A metering scheme realizing the access structure $\Gamma = \{\mathcal{A}_1, \ldots, \mathcal{A}_\ell\}$ is a method to measure the interaction between n clients $\mathcal{C}_1, \ldots, \mathcal{C}_n$ and m server*

$\mathcal{S}_1, \ldots, \mathcal{S}_m$ *during τ time frames in such a way that the following properties are satisfied:*

1. *For any time frame t, any client is able to compute the information needed to visit any server in time frame t:*
   Formally, it holds that $H(\mathbf{C}_{i,j}^t | \mathbf{C}_i) = 0$ for $i = 1, \ldots, n$, $j = 1, \ldots, m$, and $t = 1, \ldots, \tau$.
2. *For any time frame t, any server $\mathcal{S}_j$ which has been visited by a qualified subset of clients $\mathcal{A}_r \in \Gamma$ in time frame t can compute its proof for time frame t:*
   Formally, it holds that $H(\mathbf{P}_j^t | \mathbf{A}_{r,j}^t) = 0$, for $j = 1, \ldots, m$, $r = 1, \ldots, \ell$, and $t = 1, \ldots, \tau$.
3. *Let $\mathcal{S}_1, \ldots, \mathcal{S}_\beta$ be a coalition of $1 \le \beta \le s$ corrupt servers and let $B = \{1, \ldots, \beta\}$. Let $\mathcal{C}_1, \ldots, \mathcal{C}_\alpha$ be a coalition of $\alpha \le c$ corrupt clients, where $|\{\mathcal{C}_1, \ldots, \mathcal{C}_\alpha\} \cap \mathcal{A}_r| = \alpha_r \le c_r$, for any $r = 1, \ldots, \ell$. Assume that in some time frame t each server in the coalition has been visited by a set of clients $\mathcal{D} \subset \mathcal{A}_r$, where $|\mathcal{D}| < |\mathcal{A}_r| - \alpha_r$ for any $r = 1, \ldots, \ell$. Then, the servers in the coalition have no information on their proofs for time frame t:*
   Formally, it holds that $H(\mathbf{P}_B^t | \mathbf{C}_1 \ldots \mathbf{C}_\alpha \mathbf{D}_B^t \mathbf{V}_B^{[t-1]}) = H(\mathbf{P}_B^t)$.

Notice that Naor and Pinkas [9] considered metering schemes realizing the access structure $\Gamma = \{\mathcal{A} \subseteq \{\mathcal{C}_1, \ldots, \mathcal{C}_n\} : |\mathcal{A}| \ge h\}$. Such an access structure is called a *threshold access structure*.

2.1 Lower Bounds on the Communication Complexity

In this subsection we provide lower bounds on the communication complexity of metering schemes. In order to prove our results we will resort to the two following technical lemmas.

Lemma 2. *Let $\mathbf{X}$ and $\mathbf{Y}$ be two random variables such that $H(\mathbf{X}|\mathbf{Y}) = 0$. Then, for any two random variables $\mathbf{Z}$ and $\mathbf{W}$, it holds that $H(\mathbf{W}|\mathbf{XYZ}) = H(\mathbf{W}|\mathbf{YZ})$.*

Lemma 3. *Let $\mathbf{Y}$, $\mathbf{Z}$, and $\mathbf{W}$ be three random variables such that $H(\mathbf{W}|\mathbf{YZ}) = 0$ and $H(\mathbf{W}|\mathbf{Y}) = H(\mathbf{W})$. Then, it holds that $H(\mathbf{Z}|\mathbf{Y}) = H(\mathbf{W}) + H(\mathbf{Z}|\mathbf{YW})$.*

The next lemma immediately follows from Definition 1.

Lemma 4. *Let Γ be an access structure on $\{\mathcal{C}_1, \ldots, \mathcal{C}_n\}$, let $\mathcal{X} = \{\mathcal{C}_{i_1}, \ldots, \mathcal{C}_{i_k}\}$ be a set of $k \le n$ clients, let $\mathcal{S}_1, \ldots \mathcal{S}_\beta$ be $\beta \le m$ servers and let $B = \{1, \ldots, \beta\}$. Then, in any metering scheme realizing Γ it holds that*

$$H(\mathbf{X}_B^t | \mathbf{X}) = 0,$$

for any $t = 1, \ldots, \tau$.

Proof. We have that

$$H(\mathbf{X}_B^t|\mathbf{X}) = H(\mathbf{C}_{i_1,B}^t \cdots \mathbf{C}_{i_k,B}^t|\mathbf{C}_{i_1} \cdots \mathbf{C}_{i_k})$$

$$\leq \sum_{r=1}^{k} \sum_{j=1}^{\beta} H(\mathbf{C}_{i_r,j}^t|\mathbf{C}_{i_r}) \text{ (from (7) and (8) of Appendix)}$$

$$= 0 \text{ (from Property 1 of Definition 1).}$$

□

The next lemma will be a useful tool to prove a lower bound on the size of the information distributed to servers from clients during a visit.

Lemma 5. *Let Γ be an access structure on $\{\mathcal{C}_1,\ldots,\mathcal{C}_n\}$, let $\mathcal{A}_r \in \Gamma$ be a qualified set, let $\mathcal{C}_i \in \mathcal{A}_r$, and let $\mathcal{E}_r = \mathcal{A}_r \setminus \{\mathcal{C}_i\}$. Let $\mathcal{S}_1,\ldots\mathcal{S}_\beta$ be $\beta \leq m$ servers and let $B = \{1,\ldots,\beta\}$. Then, in any metering scheme realizing Γ it holds that*

$$H(\mathbf{C}_{i,B}^t|\mathbf{E}_{r,B}^t \mathbf{V}_B^{[t-1]}) \geq H(\mathbf{P}_B^t),$$

for any $t = 1,\ldots,\tau$.

Proof. Let $\mathcal{C}_1,\ldots,\mathcal{C}_\alpha$ be a coalition of $\alpha \leq c$ corrupt clients other than $\mathcal{C}_i$, and let $\mathcal{D}_r \subset \mathcal{E}_r$ be a set of $|\mathcal{A}_r| - \alpha_r - 1$ clients such that $\mathcal{D}_r \cap \{\mathcal{C}_1,\ldots,\mathcal{C}_\alpha\} = \emptyset$. Assume that $\{\mathcal{C}_1,\ldots,\mathcal{C}_\alpha\} \cap \mathcal{A}_r = \{\mathcal{C}_1,\ldots,\mathcal{C}_{\alpha_r}\}$. We have that

$$H(\mathbf{C}_{1,B}^t \cdots \mathbf{C}_{\alpha,B}^t|\mathbf{C}_1 \ldots \mathbf{C}_\alpha \mathbf{C}_{i,B}^t \mathbf{D}_{r,B}^t \mathbf{V}_B^{[t-1]}) \leq H(\mathbf{C}_{1,B}^t \cdots \mathbf{C}_{\alpha,B}^t|\mathbf{C}_1 \ldots \mathbf{C}_\alpha)$$

$$\text{(from (8) of Appendix)}$$

$$= 0 \text{ (from Lemma 4).}$$

Applying Lemma 2 with $\mathbf{X} = \mathbf{C}_{1,B}^t \cdots \mathbf{C}_{\alpha,B}^t$, $\mathbf{Y} = \mathbf{C}_1 \ldots \mathbf{C}_\alpha \mathbf{C}_{i,B}^t \mathbf{D}_{r,B}^t \mathbf{V}_B^{[t-1]}$, and $\mathbf{W} = \mathbf{P}_B^t$ we get

$$H(\mathbf{P}_B^t|\mathbf{C}_1 \ldots \mathbf{C}_\alpha \mathbf{C}_{i,B}^t \mathbf{D}_{r,B}^t \mathbf{V}_B^{[t-1]}) = H(\mathbf{P}_B^t|\mathbf{C}_{1,B}^t \cdots \mathbf{C}_{\alpha,B}^t \mathbf{C}_1 \ldots \mathbf{C}_\alpha \mathbf{C}_{i,B}^t \mathbf{D}_{r,B}^t \mathbf{V}_B^{[t-1]})$$

$$\leq H(\mathbf{P}_B^t|\mathbf{C}_{1,B}^t \cdots \mathbf{C}_{\alpha_r,B}^t \mathbf{C}_{i,B}^t \mathbf{D}_{r,B}^t)$$

$$\text{(from (8) of Appendix, since } \alpha_r \leq \alpha)$$

$$= 0.$$

The last equality follows from Property 2 of Definition 1, since $\{\mathcal{C}_1,\ldots,\mathcal{C}_{\alpha_r}\} \cup \{\mathcal{C}_i\} \cup \mathcal{D}_r = \mathcal{A}_r$. From Property 3 of Definition 1 we have that

$$H(\mathbf{P}_B^t|\mathbf{C}_1 \ldots \mathbf{C}_\alpha \mathbf{D}_{r,B}^t \mathbf{V}_B^{[t-1]}) = H(\mathbf{P}_B^t).$$

Therefore, applying Lemma 3 with $\mathbf{Y} = \mathbf{C}_1 \ldots \mathbf{C}_\alpha \mathbf{D}_{r,B}^t \mathbf{V}_B^{[t-1]}$, $\mathbf{Z} = \mathbf{C}_{i,B}^t$, and $\mathbf{W} = \mathbf{P}_B^t$, we get

$$H(\mathbf{C}_{i,B}^t|\mathbf{C}_1 \ldots \mathbf{C}_\alpha \mathbf{D}_{r,B}^t \mathbf{V}_B^{[t-1]}) = H(\mathbf{P}_B^t) + H(\mathbf{C}_{i,B}^t|\mathbf{C}_1 \ldots \mathbf{C}_\alpha \mathbf{D}_{r,B}^t \mathbf{V}_B^{[t-1]} \mathbf{P}_B^t)$$

$$\geq H(\mathbf{P}_B^t) \text{ (from (5) of Appendix).} \tag{1}$$

We have that

$$H(\mathbf{C}^t_{1,B} \cdots \mathbf{C}^t_{\alpha,B} | \mathbf{C}_1 \ldots \mathbf{C}_\alpha \mathbf{D}^t_{r,B} \mathbf{V}^{[t-1]}_B) \leq H(\mathbf{C}^t_{1,B} \cdots \mathbf{C}^t_{\alpha,B} | \mathbf{C}_1 \ldots \mathbf{C}_\alpha)$$
$$\text{(from (8) of Appendix)}$$
$$= 0 \text{ (from Lemma 4).}$$

Therefore, applying Lemma 2 with $\mathbf{X} = \mathbf{C}^t_{1,B} \cdots \mathbf{C}^t_{\alpha,B}$, $\mathbf{Y} = \mathbf{C}_1 \ldots \mathbf{C}_\alpha \mathbf{D}^t_{r,B} \mathbf{V}^{[t-1]}_B$ and $\mathbf{W} = \mathbf{C}^t_{i,B}$, we get

$$H(\mathbf{C}^t_{i,B} | \mathbf{C}_1 \ldots \mathbf{C}_\alpha \mathbf{D}^t_{r,B} \mathbf{V}^{[t-1]}_B) = H(\mathbf{C}^t_{i,B} | \mathbf{C}^t_{1,B} \cdots \mathbf{C}^t_{\alpha,B} \mathbf{C}_1 \ldots \mathbf{C}_\alpha \mathbf{D}^t_{r,B} \mathbf{V}^{[t-1]}_B)$$
$$\leq H(\mathbf{C}^t_{i,B} | \mathbf{C}^t_{1,B} \cdots \mathbf{C}^t_{\alpha_r,B} \mathbf{D}^t_{r,B} \mathbf{V}^{[t-1]}_B)$$
$$\text{(from (8) of Appendix, since } \alpha_r \leq \alpha)$$
$$= H(\mathbf{C}^t_{i,B} | \mathbf{E}^t_{r,B} \mathbf{V}^{[t-1]}_B). \tag{2}$$

The last equality holds since $\mathcal{E}_r = \mathcal{D}_r \cup \{\mathcal{C}_1, \ldots, \mathcal{C}_{\alpha_r}\}$. Therefore, the lemma follows from inequalities (2) and (1). □

The next corollary provides a lower bound on the size of the information distributed to servers from clients during a visit.

Corollary 6. *Let Γ be an access structure on $\{\mathcal{C}_1, \ldots, \mathcal{C}_n\}$. Then, in any metering scheme realizing Γ it holds that*

$$H(\mathbf{C}^t_{i,j}) \geq H(\mathbf{P}^t_j)$$

for any $i = 1, \ldots, n$, $j = 1, \ldots, m$, and $t = 1, \ldots, \tau$.

If the proofs for the servers are uniformly chosen in a finite field F, i.e., $H(\mathbf{P}^t_j) = \log |F|$ for any $j = 1, \ldots, m$ and $t = 1, \ldots, \tau$, then from Corollary 6 and from (4) of Appendix it holds that $\log |C^t_{i,j}| \geq \log |F|$ for any $i = 1, \ldots, n$, $j = 1, \ldots, m$, and $t = 1, \ldots, \tau$. In order to prove a lower bound on the size of the information distributed to clients we need the next lemma.

Lemma 7. *Let Γ be an access structure on $\{\mathcal{C}_1, \ldots, \mathcal{C}_n\}$, let $\mathcal{X} \subseteq \{\mathcal{C}_1, \ldots, \mathcal{C}_n\}$, let $\mathcal{S}_1 \ldots, \mathcal{S}_\beta$ be a coalition of $\beta \leq s$ corrupt servers and let $B = \{1, \ldots, \beta\}$. Then, in any metering scheme realizing Γ it holds that*

$$H(\mathbf{X}) \geq \sum_{t=1}^{\tau} H(\mathbf{X}^t_B | \mathbf{V}^{[t-1]}_B).$$

Proof. We have that

$$H(\mathbf{X}^1_B \cdots \mathbf{X}^\tau_B | \mathbf{X}) \leq \sum_{t=1}^{\tau} H(\mathbf{X}^t_B | \mathbf{X}) \text{ (from (7) of Appendix)}$$
$$= 0 \text{ (from Lemma 4).}$$

Therefore, applying Lemma 3 with $\mathbf{Z} = \mathbf{X}$ and $\mathbf{W} = \mathbf{X}_B^1 \ldots \mathbf{X}_B^\tau$ we get

$$
\begin{aligned}
H(\mathbf{X}) &= H(\mathbf{X}_B^1 \ldots \mathbf{X}_B^\tau) + H(\mathbf{X}|\mathbf{X}_B^1 \ldots \mathbf{X}_B^\tau) \\
&\geq H(\mathbf{X}_B^1 \ldots \mathbf{X}_B^\tau) \text{ (from (5) of Appendix)} \\
&= H(\mathbf{X}_B^1) + \sum_{t=2}^\tau H(\mathbf{X}_B^t|\mathbf{X}_B^1 \ldots \mathbf{X}_B^{t-1}) \text{ (from (6) of Appendix)} \\
&\geq \sum_{t=1}^\tau H(\mathbf{X}_B^t|\mathbf{V}_B^{[t-1]}).
\end{aligned}
$$

$\square$

The next lemma provides a lower bound on the size of the information distributed to clients during the initialization phase in metering schemes.

Lemma 8. *Let Γ be an access structure on $\{\mathcal{C}_1, \ldots, \mathcal{C}_n\}$. Let $\mathcal{S}_1 \ldots, \mathcal{S}_\beta$ be a coalition of $\beta \leq s$ corrupt servers and let $B = \{1, \ldots, \beta\}$. Then, in any metering scheme realizing Γ it holds that*

$$
H(\mathbf{C}_i) \geq \sum_{t=1}^\tau H(\mathbf{P}_B^t)
$$

for any $i = 1, \ldots, n$

Proof. Let $\mathcal{A}_r \in \Gamma$, let $\mathcal{C}_i \in \mathcal{A}_r$ and let $\mathcal{E}_r = \mathcal{A}_r \setminus \{\mathcal{C}_i\}$. We have that

$$
\begin{aligned}
H(\mathbf{C}_i) &\geq \sum_{t=1}^\tau H(\mathbf{C}_{i,B}^t|\mathbf{V}_B^{[t-1]}) \text{ (from Lemma 7)} \\
&\geq \sum_{t=1}^\tau H(\mathbf{C}_{i,B}^t|\mathbf{E}_{r,B}^t\mathbf{V}_B^{[t-1]}) \text{ (from (8) of Appendix)} \\
&\geq \sum_{t=1}^\tau H(\mathbf{P}_B^t) \text{ (from Lemma 5).}
\end{aligned}
$$

$\square$

If the proof sequences of the corrupt servers are statistically independent, then the next corollary holds. For the sake of simplicity we state this result for the simple case where $H(\mathbf{P}_{j_1}^{t_1}) = H(\mathbf{P}_{j_2}^{t_2})$ for all $j_1, j_2 \in \{1, \ldots, m\}$ and $t_1, t_2 \in \{1, \ldots, \tau\}$. We denote this common entropies by $H(\mathbf{P})$. However, our result apply to the general case of arbitrary entropies on the proofs.

Corollary 9. *Let Γ be an access structure on $\{\mathcal{C}_1, \ldots, \mathcal{C}_n\}$. Let $\mathcal{S}_1 \ldots, \mathcal{S}_s$ be a coalition of s corrupt servers. Then, in any metering scheme realizing Γ in which the sequences of the proofs of the servers $\mathcal{S}_1, \ldots, \mathcal{S}_s$ are statistically independent, it holds that*

$$
H(\mathbf{C}_i) \geq s\tau H(\mathbf{P})
$$

for any $i = 1, \ldots, n$.

If the random variable $\mathbf{P}$ is uniformly distributed in a finite field F, i.e., $H(\mathbf{P}) = \log |F|$, then from Corollary 9 and from (4) of Appendix it holds that $\log |C_i| \geq s\tau \log |F|$ for any $i = 1, \ldots, n$.

2.2 A Protocol for Metering Schemes Realizing General Access Structures

In this subsection we will show that for any monotone access structure it is possible to construct a metering scheme realizing it. The construction uses as building blocks threshold metering schemes proposed by Naor and Pinkas [9]. The proofs are points of a finite field $GF(q)$ where q is a sufficiently large prime number. Let $\Gamma = \{\mathcal{A}_1, \ldots, \mathcal{A}_\ell\}$ be a monotone access structure on $\{\mathcal{C}_1, \ldots, \mathcal{C}_n\}$. We denote with "$\circ$" an operator mapping each pair (j, t), with $j = 1, \ldots, m$ and $t = 1, \ldots, \tau$, to an element of $GF(q)$ and having the property that no distinct two pairs (j, t) and (j', t') are mapped to the same element. The protocol is the following:

- **Initialization:**
  The audit agency A chooses a polynomial $P_1(x, y)$ over $GF(q)$, which is of degree $h_1 - 1$ in x and $s\tau - 1$ in y. For $r = 2, \ldots, \ell$, A chooses a polynomial $P_r(x, y)$ over $GF(q)$, which is of degree $h_r - 1$ in x and $s\tau - 1$ in y and such that $P_r(0, y) = P_1(0, y)$. Afterwards, for any $r = 1, \ldots, \ell$, A gives the polynomial $P_r(i, y)$ to each client $\mathcal{C}_i \in \mathcal{A}_r$.

- **Regular Operation for Time Frame t:**
  When a client $\mathcal{C}_i$ visits a server $\mathcal{S}_j$ during a time frame t it gives the values $P_r(i, j \circ t)$, for any $r \in \{1, \ldots, \ell\}$ such that $\mathcal{C}_i \in \mathcal{A}_r$, to $\mathcal{S}_j$.

- **Proof Generation and Verification:**
  If during a time frame t a server $\mathcal{S}_j$ has received visits from a qualified set $\mathcal{A}_r$, for some $r \in \{1, \ldots, \ell\}$, then it can interpolate the polynomial $P_r(x, j \circ t)$ and compute the proof $P_r(0, j \circ t)$. When the audit agency receives the value $P_r(0, j \circ t)$ it can easily verify if this is the correct proof for server $\mathcal{S}_j$.

Analysis of the Scheme. Now we prove that the proposed scheme is a metering scheme realizing the access structure Γ.

First, we prove that Property 1 of Definition 1 is satisfied. For any $i = 1, \ldots, n$, the information given by the audit agency to the client $\mathcal{C}_i$ consists of the univariate polynomials $P_r(i, y)$, for any $r \in \{1, \ldots, \ell\}$ such that $\mathcal{C}_i \in \mathcal{A}_r$. For any $j = 1, \ldots, m$ and $t = 1, \ldots, \tau$, the information given to the server $\mathcal{S}_j$ by client $\mathcal{C}_i$ during a visit in time frame t is obtained by evaluating the univariate polynomials $P_r(i, y)$ at $j \circ t$, for any $r \in \{1, \ldots, \ell\}$ such that $\mathcal{C}_i \in \mathcal{A}_r$. Hence, for any time frame t, each client can compute the piece to be given to any visited server.

Now, we prove that Property 2 of Definition 1 is satisfied. Let $\mathcal{A}_r \in \Gamma$ be a qualified subset of clients. Assume that during a time frame t a server $\mathcal{S}_j$ receives visits from all clients in $\mathcal{A}_r$. Since $|\mathcal{A}_r| = h_r$, then the server can interpolate the polynomial $P_r(x, j \circ t)$. Afterwards, the server can compute its proof $P_r(0, j \circ t)$ for time frame t.

Finally, we prove that Property 3 of Definition 1 is satisfied. We consider the worst possible case, in which s corrupt servers and c corrupt clients decide to cooperate at time frame τ. Let $\mathcal{A}_r \in \Gamma$ be a qualified subset of clients and let c_r be the number of corrupt clients in $\mathcal{A}_r$. Assume that during time frame τ each corrupt server $\mathcal{S}_j$ in the coalition has received $g_{j,r} \leq h_r - c_r - 1$ regular visits from clients in the subset $\mathcal{A}_r \in \Gamma$. In order to compute its proof for time frame τ any server $\mathcal{S}_j$ should be able to interpolate either the univariate polynomial $P_r(x, j \circ \tau)$ or the bivariate polynomial $P_r(x, y)$ for some $r \in \{1, \ldots, \ell\}$. Therefore, we consider the two following cases:

Case 1. The server $\mathcal{S}_j$ tries to interpolate a polynomial $P_r(x, j \circ \tau)$, for some $r \in \{1, \ldots, \ell\}$.
Let $r \in \{1, \ldots, \ell\}$. Each corrupt client $\mathcal{C}_i$ in $\mathcal{A}_r$ donates the polynomial $P_r(i, y)$ to $\mathcal{S}_j$ from which $\mathcal{S}_j$ can compute the value $P_r(i, j \circ \tau)$. Since there are c_r corrupt clients in $\mathcal{A}_r$, $\mathcal{S}_j$ can compute c_r values of $P_r(x, j \circ \tau)$ in addition to those provided by the $g_{j,r}$ visits performed by non corrupt clients in $\mathcal{A}_r$. Consequently, the overall number of points of $P_r(x, j \circ \tau)$ known to $\mathcal{S}_j$ is less than or equal to $h_r - 1$. Therefore, $\mathcal{S}_j$ obtains a linear system of $h_r - 1$ equations in h_r unknowns. For any choice of a value in $GF(q)$, there is a univariate polynomial $Q_r(x, j \circ \tau)$ of degree $h_r - 1$, which is consistent with this value and with the information held by $\mathcal{S}_j$. Since there are q such polynomials, the probability of $\mathcal{S}_j$ in guessing its proof for time frame τ is at most $1/q$.

Case 2. The coalition of servers try to interpolate a polynomial $P_r(x, y)$ for some $r \in \{1, \ldots, \ell\}$.
We consider the worst possible case in which any corrupt server $\mathcal{S}_j$ in the coalition has collected the maximum possible information during the previous time frames $1, \ldots, \tau - 1$. In other words, for any time frame $t = 1, \ldots, \tau - 1$, the server $\mathcal{S}_j$ has been visited by at least a qualified set of clients, that is, there exists some index r, such that $\mathcal{S}_j$ has interpolated the polynomial $P_r(x, j \circ t)$. We consider the worst possible case in which the index r is the same for any time frame $t = 1, \ldots, \tau - 1$. This means that the information collected by each corrupt server $\mathcal{S}_j$ during the previous time frames is equivalent to the h_r coefficients of each polynomial $P_r(x, j \circ t)$, for any $t = 1, \ldots, \tau - 1$. The information that a corrupt client $\mathcal{C}_i$ donates to a corrupt server is equivalent to the $s\tau$ coefficients of the polynomial $P_r(i, y)$, for any $r \in \{1, \ldots, \ell\}$ such that $\mathcal{C}_i \in \mathcal{A}_r$. Then, the overall information on $P_r(x, y)$ held by the servers $\mathcal{S}_1, \ldots, \mathcal{S}_s$ consists of

$$c_r s\tau + s(\tau - 1)h_r + \sum_{j=1}^{s} g_{j,r} - c_r s(\tau - 1) \tag{3}$$

points. The first term of (3) is the information donated by the c_r corrupt clients in $\mathcal{A}_r$, the second term is the information collected by the

s corrupt servers during time frames $1, \ldots, \tau - 1$, the third term is the information provided by client visits at time frame τ, and the last term is the information which has been counted twice. Since $g_{j,r} \leq h_r - c_r - 1$ for $j = 1, \ldots, s$, then expression (3) is less than or equal to $h_r s \tau - s$. Therefore, the servers obtain a system of $h_r s \tau - s$ equations in $h_r s \tau$ unknowns. For any choice of s values in $GF(q)$, there is a bivariate polynomial $Q_r(x, y)$ of degree $h_r - 1$ in x and $s\tau - 1$ in y, which is consistent with these values and with the information held by the servers. Since there are q^s such polynomials, then the corrupt servers $\mathcal{S}_1, \ldots, \mathcal{S}_s$ have probability at most $1/q^s$ of guessing their proofs for time frame τ.

Efficiency of the Scheme. We now want to consider the efficiency of the scheme constructed in Subsection 2.2. For any client $\mathcal{C}_i$, let d_i be the number of sets $\mathcal{A} \in \Gamma$ such that $\mathcal{C}_i \in \mathcal{A}$. In the proposed scheme the information distributed to client $\mathcal{C}_i$ by the audit agency consists of $d_i s \tau$ points of $GF(q)$. The information given from client $\mathcal{C}_i$ to a server $\mathcal{S}_j$ during a visit in a time frame consists of d_i points of $GF(q)$.

If we construct a metering scheme realizing a threshold access structure Γ with threshold h by using the previous scheme, then the information distributed to each client by the audit agency consists in $\binom{n-1}{h-1} s \tau$ points of $GF(q)$, while the information distributed by any client to any server during a visit consists in $\binom{n-1}{h-1}$ points of $GF(q)$. This construction is very inefficient, compared to the construction proposed by Naor and Pinkas [9]. Indeed, in Naor and Pinkas' scheme the information distributed to each client by the audit agency consists only in $s\tau$ points of $GF(q)$, while the information distributed by any client to any server during a visit consists in a single point of $GF(q)$. Therefore, in general, the construction of Subsection 2.2 gives schemes which are not optimal with respect to the communication complexity.

3   Metering Schemes for Targeted Audience

In this section we concentrate our attention on two particular kinds of access structures, *multilevel access structures* and *compartmented access structures*. These access structures, introduced by Simmons in [11] and further investigated in [3] and [7], have useful practical applications. Metering schemes realizing these access structures can be used to measure the interaction of a web site with a specific audience which is of special interest. These schemes can be used, for example, by an editor of text books who pays a web site to host her advertisements and is interested in knowing how many professors visited the site.

3.1   Multilevel Access Structures

Consider the following situation: there are two disjoint classes, L_1 and L_2, where the clients in L_1 are professors and the ones in L_2 are PhD students. We require that a server containing information related to a research topic can reconstruct its proof for a time frame t if it receives at least two visits from professors or three visits from PhD students in that time frame. Now, assume that the server is visited by one professor and two PhD students during a time frame t: then, it would be probably unacceptable that the server would be not able to reconstruct its proof for time frame t. In this situation what is needed is a metering scheme in which the information provided by clients in different classes is related. This means that the information provided by clients in a certain class should be useful not only when combined with information provided by clients in the same class, but also when combined with information provided by clients in all lower level classes.

In a *multilevel access structure* there are u disjoint classes of clients (also called *levels*), $L_1, \ldots, L_u$, where each class $L_r \subseteq \{C_1, \ldots, C_n\}$ is associated to a positive integer $h_r \leq n_r = |L_r|$, for $r = 1, \ldots, u$, and such that $h_1 < h_2 < \cdots < h_u$. A multilevel access structure consists of those subsets which contain at least h_r clients all of level *at most* L_r for some $r \in \{1, \ldots, u\}$. Therefore, in any metering scheme realizing a multilevel access structure, any server is able to compute its proof for a given time frame if and only if it has received at least h_r visits from clients of level *at most* L_r for some $r \in \{1, \ldots, u\}$ during that time frame. Of course, the audit agency must know the identities of all participants in order to set up a metering scheme for a multilevel access structure.

In a multilevel access structure the information provided by clients in a level L_z to servers during their visits should be more valuable than the information provided by clients in levels L_r, with $r > z$, in order to compute a proof. A trivial way to realize schemes with this property could be the following: the audit agency distributes more information to clients in high level classes. In this case the pieces distributed to clients in high level classes are more valuable because they contain more information about the servers' proofs. The disadvantage of this solution is that it penalizes clients in high level classes by requiring them to handle more information than clients in low level classes. Since we are interested in the efficiency of metering schemes, we would like to have schemes in which the size of the information distributed to clients is the same, even though the pieces provided to servers by some clients may be more effective in computing a proof than others.

A Protocol for Metering Schemes Realizing Multilevel Access Structures.

In this subsection we will prove that for any multilevel access structure it is possible to construct a metering scheme realizing it. Let Γ be a multilevel access structure with u levels $L_1, \ldots, L_u$ and let $h_r \leq n_r = |L_r|$ be the threshold associated to level L_r, for any $r = 1, \ldots, u$. Let $h_1 < h_2 < \cdots < h_u$. The protocol is the following:

- **Initialization:** The audit agency A chooses a polynomial $P_u(x, y)$ over $GF(q)$, which has degree $h_u - 1$ in x and $s\tau - 1$ in y. Afterwards, for any $r = 1, \ldots, u - 1$, A constructs the polynomial $P_r(x, y)$ of degree $h_r - 1$ in x and $s\tau - 1$ in y, by truncating the polynomial $P_u(x, y)$ at degree $h_r - 1$. For any $r = 1, \ldots, u$ and for any client $C_i \in L_r$, A picks a value $x_i \in GF(q)$

and constructs the h_u-dimensional vector $v_i = (1, x_i, x_i^2, \ldots, x_i^{h_r-1}, 0, \ldots, 0)$, which is made public (we will explain later how A chooses the value x_i for any client C_i). Afterwards, A gives the polynomial $P_r(x_i, y)$ to any client $C_i \in L_r$.

- **Regular Operation for Time Frame** t:
  When a client $C_i \in L_r$ visits a server S_j during a time frame t, it gives the value $P_r(x_i, j \circ t)$ to S_j.

- **Proof Generation and Verification:**
  Let $r \in \{1, \ldots, u\}$ and let $C_{i_1}, \ldots, C_{i_{h_r}}$ be h_r clients of level *at most* L_r visiting a server S_j in time frame t. Suppose that there is no subset of this set of clients which contains h_z clients of level *at most* L_z, for any $1 \leq z < r$. Let M be the $h_r \times h_u$ matrix with rows $v_{i_1}, \ldots v_{i_{h_r}}$, where v_{i_k} is the h_u-dimensional vector corresponding to client C_{i_k}, for $k = 1, \ldots, h_r$; let $b = (b_0, \ldots, b_{h_r-1})$ be the h_r-dimensional vector whose elements are the coefficients of the polynomial $P_r(x, j \circ t)$, and let d be the h_r-dimensional vector containing the visits from clients $C_{i_1}, \ldots, C_{i_{h_r}}$ to server S_j in time frame t. The server S_j obtains a system of h_r equations in h_r unknowns, whose matrix form is $Mb = d$. This system has a unique solution over $GF(q)$, constituted by the h_r coefficients $b_0, \ldots, b_{h_r-1}$ of the polynomial $P_r(x, j \circ t)$, if and only if the matrix M is nonsingular, i.e., if and only if the vectors $v_{i_1}, \ldots v_{i_{h_r}}$ are independent. In this case the server can compute all the coefficients $b_0, \ldots, b_{h_r-1}$ of the polynomial $P_r(x, j \circ t)$, and reconstruct its proof $P_r(0, j \circ t) = b_0$. When the audit agency receives the value $P_r(0, j \circ t)$, for some $r \in \{1, \ldots, u\}$, from server S_j then it can easily verify if this is the correct proof for server S_j in time frame t.

In the next lemma, following the line of Theorem 1 in [3], we prove that for any multilevel access structure there is a method for the audit agency to choose the x_i's in such a way that, for any $r \in \{1, \ldots, u\}$, any h_r vectors corresponding to clients of level *at most* L_r are independent.

Lemma 10. *Let Γ be a multilevel access structure with u levels $L_1, \ldots, L_u$ and let $h_r \leq n_r = |L_r|$ be the threshold associated to level L_r, for any $r = 1, \ldots, u$. Let $h_1 < h_2 < \cdots < h_u$. Let $n = \sum_{r=1}^{u} n_r$ be the total number of clients. If $q > (h_u - 1)\binom{n}{h_u-1}$ then it is possible to choose the values $x_1, \ldots, x_n$ associated to the clients $C_1, \ldots, C_n$ in such a way that for any $r \in \{1, \ldots, u\}$, any h_r vectors corresponding to clients of level at most L_r are independent.*

Proof. Let v_0 be the h_u dimensional vector $(1, 0, \ldots, 0)$. Let $C_1 \in L_z$, for some $z \in \{1, \ldots, u\}$. The audit agency chooses the value $x_1 \in GF(q)$ in such a way that the h_u dimensional vectors $v_1 = (1, x_1, x_1^2, \ldots, x_1^{h_z-1}, 0, \ldots, 0)$ and v_0 are independent.

Suppose the audit agency has chosen the value x_i for any client C_i with $1 \leq i < k \leq n$, and let $C_k \in L_r$ for some $r \in \{1, \ldots, u\}$. Let Ω_k be the set of subspaces spanned by some subset of size $h_r - 1$ of the k vectors $v_0, \ldots, v_{k-1}$. It is easy to see that $|\Omega| < \binom{k}{h_r-1}$. Then, the audit agency A picks the value x_k in $GF(q)$ in such a way that the h_u dimensional vector $v_k = (1, x_k, x_k^2, \ldots, x_k^{h_r-1}, 0, \ldots, 0)$ is not in any of the subspaces in Ω_k. To see that this is possible, let $R \in \Omega_k$, and let $w = (w_0, w_1, \ldots, w_{h_r-1}, 0 \ldots, 0)$ be a normal vector to R. Then the equation $\sum_{i=0}^{h_r-1} w_i x^i = 0$ has at most $h_r - 1$ solutions over $GF(q)$.

Since there exist at least h_r clients of level L_r, for any $r = 1, \ldots, u$, it follows that we need $q > (h_u - 1)\binom{n}{h_u-1}$ in order to be able to choose the x_i's as explained above. Now, consider a set of h_r vectors corresponding to h_r clients of level *at most* L_r and suppose that there is no subset of this set which contains z participants of level *at most* L_z, for any $z < r$. Then, by construction, the h_r vectors are independent.   □

It is easy to see that the proposed scheme is a metering scheme realizing the multilevel access structure Γ. Indeed, following the line of Subsection 2.2 we can prove that Properties 1, 2, and 3 of Definition 1 are satisfied.

Efficiency of the Scheme. In the proposed scheme the information distributed to any client C_i by the audit agency consists of $s\tau$ points of $GF(q)$. The information given from client C_i to any server S_j during a visit consists of a single point of $GF(q)$. It is easy to see that the scheme of Subsection 3.1 meets the bounds of Corollary 6 and Lemma 8, and hence it is optimal with respect to the communication complexity.

One other issue to consider is the amount of computation needed for the audit agency to set up a metering scheme realizing a multilevel access structure. The problem of the scheme we have presented is that it requires the audit agency to do many checks to be sure that the points x_i's are in the right positions (i.e., that the vectors associated to any set of h_r clients all of level *at most* L_r are independent). Brickell [3] has proposed different ways to choose the x_i's which do not require such checking. It is easy to modify our metering scheme, since we only need to modify the initialization phase according to the constructions proposed by Brickell [3]. These constructions involve irreducible polynomials over $GF(q^\gamma)$, where $\gamma = uh_u^2$ and q is a prime such that $q > |L_r| + 1$ for any $r = 1, \ldots, u$. In particular, Brickell proved that the x_i's can be constructed in time polynomial in $(|L_1|, \ldots, |L_u|, q)$.

3.2 Compartmented Access Structures

Consider the following situation: there are two disjoint compartments, L_1 and L_2, where the clients in L_1 are professors and the ones in L_2 are PhD students. We require that a server containing information related to a research topic can reconstruct its proof for a time frame t if it receives at least two visits from professors *and* three visits from PhD students in that time frame. Now, assume that the server is visited by one professor during a time frame t. Then, no matter how many PhD students concur, the reconstruction of the proof for a server should be inhibited unless it receives at least a visit from another professor.

In a *compartmented access structure* there are u disjoint classes of clients (also called *compartments*), $G_1, \ldots, G_u$, where each class $G_r \subseteq \{C_1, \ldots, C_n\}$ is associated to a positive integer $h_r \leq n_r = |G_r|$, for $r = 1, \ldots, u$. The compartmented access structure consists of those subsets which contain at least h_r clients from compartment G_r, *for any* $1 \leq r \leq u$. Therefore, in any metering scheme realizing a compartmented access structure, any server $\mathcal{S}_j$ is able to compute its proof for a given time frame if and only if it has received at least h_r visits from clients in compartment G_r, *for any* $1 \leq r \leq u$, during that time frame.

A Protocol for Compartmented Access Structures. In this subsection we will prove that for any compartmented access structure it is possible to construct a metering scheme realizing it. Let Γ be a compartmented access structure with u compartments $G_1, \ldots, G_u$ and let $h_r \leq n_r = |G_r|$ be the threshold associated to compartment G_r, for any $r = 1, \ldots, u$. The protocol is the following:

- **Initialization**:
  The audit agency A chooses u independent polynomials $P_1(x, y), \ldots, P_u(x, y)$ over $GF(q)$, where for any $r = 1, \ldots, u$, the polynomial $P_r(x, y)$ has degree $h_r - 1$ in x and $s\tau - 1$ in y. For any $r = 1, \ldots, u$, A gives the polynomial $P_r(i, y)$ to each client $\mathcal{C}_i \in G_r$.

- **Regular Operation for Time Frame** t:
  When a client $\mathcal{C}_i \in G_r$ visits a server $\mathcal{S}_j$ during a time frame t, it gives the value $P_r(i, j \circ t)$ to $\mathcal{S}_j$.

- **Proof Generation and Verification**:
  Assume that in time frame t a server $\mathcal{S}_j$ has received visits from at least h_r clients in the compartment G_r, for any $r = 1, \ldots, u$. Then, the server $\mathcal{S}_j$ can interpolate the polynomial $P_r(x, j \circ t)$ and compute the value $P_r(0, j \circ t)$ for any $r = 1, \ldots, u$. Finally, $\mathcal{S}_j$ can compute the value $\sum_{r=1}^{u} P_r(0, j \circ t)$, which is its proof for time frame t. When the audit agency receives the value $\sum_{r=1}^{u} P_r(0, j \circ t)$ from server $\mathcal{S}_j$ then it can easily verify if this is the correct proof for server $\mathcal{S}_j$ in time frame t.

It is easy to see that the proposed scheme is a metering scheme realizing the compartmented access structure Γ. Indeed, following the line of Subsection 2.2 we can prove that Properties 1, 2, and 3 of Definition 1 are satisfied.

Efficiency of the Scheme. In the proposed scheme the information distributed to client $\mathcal{C}_i$ by the audit agency consists of $s\tau$ points of $GF(q)$. The information given from client $\mathcal{C}_i$ to any server $\mathcal{S}_j$ during a visit consists of a single point of $GF(q)$. It is easy to see that the scheme of Subsection 3.2 meets the bounds of Corollary 6 and Lemma 8, and hence it is optimal with respect to the communication complexity.

4   Conclusions

In this paper we have considered metering schemes in which it is necessary for the servers to know the identities of visiting clients in order to reconstruct their proofs. A nice property for a metering scheme would be to enable *client and server anonymity*. Client anonymity is possible in some particular situations: in a threshold access structure, visits can be anonymous, provided that the servers do not know the correspondence between the values i and the client C_i. In multilevel and compartmented access structures, anonymity can be preserved "within levels" and "within compartments", respectively.

Moreover, in this paper we have assumed that clients provide correct shares when they visit servers. In a practical implementation of a metering scheme, some method of authentication should be used. However, the method of authentication used would be, in general, independent of the specific metering scheme and it could be incorporated as an additional feature in any metering scheme, if desired.

Acknowledgements. We would like to thank the anonymous referees for their useful comments. This work was done while the first author was visiting the Department of Combinatorics and Optimization at the University of Waterloo. She wants to thank the Department for its hospitality. The research of the second author is supported by the Natural Sciences and Research Council of Canada under grants NSERC-IRC 216431-96 and NSERC-RGPIN 203114-98.

References

1. C. Blundo, A. De Bonis, and B. Masucci, *Bounds and Constructions for Metering Schemes*, Technical Report, Università di Salerno, October 1999.
2. C. Blundo, A. De Bonis, B. Masucci, and D. R. Stinson, *Dynamic Multi-Threshold Metering Schemes*, Technical Report CORR **2000-18**, Centre for Applied Cryptographic Research, University of Waterloo, 2000.
3. E. F. Brickell, *Some Ideal Secret Sharing Schemes*, The Journal of Combinatorial Mathematics and Combinatorial Computing, Vol. **6**, pp. 105–113, 1989.
4. T. M. Cover and J. A. Thomas, Elements of Information Theory. John Wiley & Sons, 1991.
5. A. De Bonis and B. Masucci, *An Information Theoretic Approach to Metering Schemes*, to appear in "IEEE International Symposium on Information Theory (ISIT 2000)".
6. M. Franklin and D. Malkhi, *Auditable Metering with Lightweight Security*, Journal of Computer Security, Vol. **6**, No. 4, pp. 237–225, 1998.
7. H. Ghodosi, J. Pieprzyk, and R. Safavi-Naini, *Secret Sharing in Multilevel and Compartmented Groups*, in "Australasian Conference on Information Security and Privacy - ACISP '98", LNCS, Vol. **1438**, pp. 367–378, 1998.
8. B. Masucci and D. R. Stinson, *Efficient Metering Schemes with Pricing*, Technical Report CORR **2000-06**, Centre for Applied Cryptographic Research, University of Waterloo, 2000.
9. M. Naor and B. Pinkas, *Secure and Efficient Metering*, in "Advances in Cryptology - EUROCRYPT '98", LNCS, Vol. **1403**, pp. 576–590, 1998.
10. A. Shamir, *How to Share a Secret*, Communications of the ACM, Vol. **22**, pp. 612–613, 1979.
11. G. J. Simmons, *How to (Really) Share a Secret*, in "Advances in Cryptology - CRYPTO '88", LNCS, Vol. **403**, pp. 390–448, 1988.

Appendix - Information Theory Background

In this section we review the basic concepts of Information Theory used in our definitions and proofs. For a complete treatment of the subject the reader is advised to consult [4].

Given a probability distribution $\{Pr_{\mathbf{X}}(x)\}_{x \in X}$ on a set X, we define the *entropy* [1] of $\mathbf{X}$, as $H(\mathbf{X}) = -\sum_{x \in X} Pr_{\mathbf{X}}(x) \log Pr_{\mathbf{X}}(x)$. The entropy satisfies the following property:

$$0 \leq H(\mathbf{X}) \leq \log |X|, \tag{4}$$

where $H(\mathbf{X}) = 0$ if and only if there exists $x_0 \in X$ such that $Pr_{\mathbf{X}}(x_0) = 1$; whereas $H(\mathbf{X}) = \log |X|$ if and only if $Pr_{\mathbf{X}}(x) = 1/|X|$, for all $x \in X$.

Given two sets X and Y and a joint probability distribution on their cartesian product, the *conditional entropy* $H(\mathbf{X}|\mathbf{Y})$, is defined as

$$H(\mathbf{X}|\mathbf{Y}) = -\sum_{y \in Y} \sum_{x \in X} Pr_{\mathbf{Y}}(y) Pr(x|y) \log Pr(x|y).$$

From the definition of conditional entropy it is easy to see that

$$H(\mathbf{X}|\mathbf{Y}) \geq 0. \tag{5}$$

Given n sets $X_1, \ldots, X_n$ and a joint probability distribution on their cartesian product, the entropy of $\mathbf{X}_1 \ldots \mathbf{X}_n$ satisfies

$$H(\mathbf{X}_1 \ldots \mathbf{X}_n) = H(\mathbf{X}_1) + \sum_{i=2}^{n} H(\mathbf{X}_i|\mathbf{X}_1 \ldots \mathbf{X}_{i-1}). \tag{6}$$

Given $n+1$ sets $X_1, \ldots, X_n, Y$ and a joint probability distribution on their cartesian product, the entropy of $\mathbf{X}_1 \ldots \mathbf{X}_n$ given $\mathbf{Y}$ satisfies

$$H(\mathbf{X}_1 \ldots \mathbf{X}_n|\mathbf{Y}) \leq \sum_{i=1}^{n} H(\mathbf{X}_i|\mathbf{Y}). \tag{7}$$

Given $n+2$ sets $X_1, \ldots, X_n, Y, Z$ and a joint probability distribution on their cartesian product, the *conditional mutual information* $I(\mathbf{Y}; \mathbf{Z}|\mathbf{X}_1 \ldots \mathbf{X}_n)$ between $\mathbf{Y}$ and $\mathbf{Z}$ given $\mathbf{X}_1, \ldots, \mathbf{X}_n$ is defined as

$$I(\mathbf{Y}; \mathbf{Z}|\mathbf{X}_1 \ldots \mathbf{X}_n) = H(\mathbf{Y}|\mathbf{X}_1 \ldots \mathbf{X}_n) - H(\mathbf{Y}|\mathbf{X}_1 \ldots \mathbf{X}_n \mathbf{Z})$$

and enjoys the following property: $I(\mathbf{Y}; \mathbf{Z}|\mathbf{X}_1 \ldots \mathbf{X}_n) \geq 0$, from which one gets

$$H(\mathbf{Y}|\mathbf{X}_1 \ldots \mathbf{X}_n) \geq H(\mathbf{Y}|\mathbf{X}_1 \ldots \mathbf{X}_n \mathbf{Z}). \tag{8}$$

---

[1] All logarithms in this paper are to the base 2.

A Typed Access Control Model for CORBA

Gerald Brose[*]

Institut für Informatik
Freie Universität Berlin, D–14195 Berlin, Germany
brose@inf.fu-berlin.de

Abstract. Specifying and managing access rights in large distributed systems is a non–trivial task. This paper presents a language–based approach to supporting policy–based management of access rights. We develop an object–oriented access model and a concrete syntax that is designed to allow both flexible and manageable access control policies for CORBA objects. We introduce a typed construct for access rights called *view* that allows static type checking of specifications and show how a realistic example policy is expressed using our notation.
Keywords: Access control, roles, types, CORBA.

1 Introduction

Due to the heterogeneity inherent in open distributed systems such as CORBA [OMG99], security requirements cannot be enforced by operating systems with their established set of mechanisms alone. Rather, it is the middleware that has to provide platform–independent security services. The correct design and implementation of security mechanisms according to the Object Management Group's (OMG) *Security Service Specification* [OMG98] are not, however, the only technical challenges in ensuring proper overall protection in a distributed object system.

The design, specification, and implementation of security policies and the management of the corresponding access rights at runtime are both error–prone and security–critical. There are few methods or tools that provide adequate support for application designers and security administrators in distributed object systems. The main problems are ensuring scalability while at the same time allowing the description of fine–grained accesses, which requires appropriate grouping constructs. A related problem is manageability. To make large numbers of fine–grained access rights manageable, it is necessary not just to group these rights but also to provide abstractions that represent the underlying policies. Otherwise, the inherent logic is lost and administrators are left with just "raw data". Unfortunately, the existing access control model for CORBA as specified in [OMG98] is inadequate in all these respects [Kar98,Bro99].

In this paper, we are concerned with support for specifying access control policies. In general terms, an access control policy is a description of which

---

[*] This work is funded by the German Research Council (DFG), grant No. LO 447/5–1.

F. Cuppens et al. (Eds.): ESORICS 2000, LNCS 1895, pp. 88–105, 2000.

accesses are allowed and which are denied. In a more technical, but still abstract sense, an access control policy is a set of rules that, when parameterized with access control information, is evaluated by an access decision function to yield a boolean result, i.e. an access is either allowed or denied. We take a language–based approach to the problem of specifying and managing access control policies and devise a formal notation that allows designers and administrators to deal with abstractions that are adequate for their tasks. Our aim is to reap all the benefits of language support like documentation, structuring, type–safety, reuse, and enhanced communication between developers and administrators.

An interesting aspect of this work is that providing a usable and manageable environment has implications for the underlying access model. Existing access control models [HRU76,San92,BN89], which have been designed to make certain safety properties tractable or to allow certain classes of security policies that were not expressible in other models, either do not apply well to CORBA or do not support high–level language constructs that help writing specifications. The contributions of this paper are the introduction of a typed grouping concept for access rights called *view* and the definition of a view–based access control language for CORBA that allows static type–checking to ensure the consistency of specifications. The resulting model is intended to serve as a basis for the development of a comprehensive set of tools.

The rest of this paper is structured as follows. Our access model is presented and discussed in section 2. Section 3 contains a realistic example for a policy with dynamic rights changes. Related work is discussed in section 4. The paper concludes with a brief summary and an outlook on future work.

2   A View–Based Access Control Model

To address the scalability and manageability problems outlined in section 1 we need to define the appropriate grouping concepts and abstractions. While the main contribution of this paper is a typed grouping construct for access rights, our policy language also relies on roles as a concept for grouping users. Rather than introducing a new role model, we describe a few basic assumptions for suitable role–based authentication systems in the context of our model. The remainder of this section then introduces our access control model both formally and in a concrete syntax, the *view policy language* VPL [Bro99].

2.1   Roles

To support flexible development, deployment, and management of policies in potentially diverse environments, we cannot rely on the actual identity of users because they are not known in advance. With regard to object invocations, the most suitable abstraction for users is that of a *role* as it allows us to concentrate on the specific, logical function in which a principal is operating on application or system objects. Our notion of role is different from the widely–used role concept in role–based access control (RBAC) [SCFY96] where roles represent a combination of user groups with sets of authorizations, or just a set of authorizations [FK92].

We use the term role as a synonym for actors as in use case diagrams. In other words, roles are sets of users and group principals based on their common aspects in different interaction contexts. We assume a public–key based service that issues privilege attribute certificates that represent role membership [HBM98] to principals upon request and whose signature is trusted by the access decision function. A security service like [OMG98] can then manage access sessions between callers and objects so that objects always see "users in roles" rather than individual users.

Role names for sets of users are declared in `roles` clauses as in Fig. 1. If we wanted to write a policy that describes accesses to objects representing resources in a university setting, we might want to refer to principals in roles such as lecturer, student, or examiner.

```
roles
     head, lecturer, student, examiner
role assertion
     card( examiner and student) == 0;
     card( head ) == 1
```

Fig. 1: Roles and role assertions

In addition to referring to logical actors, some policies may make assumptions on the way roles are structured, and on the way membership is granted. Role assertions express requirements on the authentication service used to authenticate users in roles and can be written as in Fig. 1. Here, we require that the intersection of `examiner` and `student` is empty, i.e. the authentication service must ensure that no principal who is a member of role `student` is ever granted membership in role `examiner`. Another possible assertion is that membership in certain roles, e.g. the role `head` in the example, is only ever granted to a single principal.

A deployer of a policy must check that role membership is certified in accordance with the assertions expressed in the policy. The assignment of individual users or whole user groups to roles is not expressed in a static policy description but is performed at deployment time. In case the authentication service does not already offer certificates for the roles listed in a policy specification, the deployer can perform a simple renaming operation for role identifiers to map them onto existing roles, e.g., to map an existing role `professor` onto role `lecturer`. If existing roles do not map well, new roles need to be set up in the authentication service.

2.2   Views

To address the requirements outlined in section 1 we propose an object–oriented access model based on *views*. A view is a named set of access rights. These access rights are both permissions or denials for operations on objects. While access decisions are made based on individual rights, views are the units of description and of granting or revoking.

The need for such a concept is motivated by the observation that it is not adequate to describe object systems using a limited set of generic rights such as "read", "write", and "execute". Thus, unlike the classical access matrix model [Lam74] or the standard CORBA access model [OMG99], individual rights in our model directly correspond to operations in the target object's interface. While this allows access policies that are more expressive and suitable for object–oriented systems, it also introduces additional complexity because the set of access rights is open and potentially very large. To make these access rights manageable, we need to exploit their inherent structure.

An important property of views is that they are typed by the object interface they control. Views are defined as part of the policy specification. Figure 2 shows an example of a view definition in VPL. Views are defined as access controls for a particular IDL interface, which is referenced in the controls–clause of the view definition.

```
view NameResolver controls CosNaming::NamingContext {
    allow
        resolve;
        list;
};
```

Fig. 2: A view definition

In the example, the view `NameResolver` controls the IDL type `CosNaming::NamingContext`, which is the IDL interface for the CORBA name service [OMG97]. Permissions are listed after the keyword `allow`, denials would be introduced by `deny`. In the example, only operations to list the name bindings in the context and to resolve a name are allowed.

More formally, let U be the set of user identifiers (i.e., public keys) and $ROLE$ the set of roles. At any one time, a user interacts with an object in a single role, so we define the set of subjects $S : U \times ROLE$ as users in roles. Let O be the set of objects and V the set of views. We model a system's protection state as a tuple (S, O, M), where $S \subseteq S$, $O \subseteq O$ and $M : S \times O \to \mathbb{P}(V)$ is an access matrix, $\mathbb{P}$ denoting the power set. The matrix entry $M_{(s,o)}$ contains subject s's views on object o.

Let $Mode = \{allow, deny\}$ be the set of rights modes, $Prio = \{strong, weak\}$ the set of priorities and Op the set of operation names. Priorities are used for conflict resolution as described below. We define the set of rights as $R = Op \times Mode \times Prio$. A right $r \in R$ is thus a tuple (op, m, p), so any right has a corresponding operation, a priority and is either a permission or a denial.

The set of views V is defined as $\mathbb{P}(R) \times T$, where T denotes the set of object types. A view $V \in V$ is thus a tuple (R, T), i.e. a set of rights and a controlled object type. We define a number of restrictions for views that ensure their well–

formedness. We demand that the operations for all rights in a view are operations of the object type controlled by the view (1). Also, views may only contain one right definition for any given operation, so a view has no conflicting rights (2).

Let the function $rights : \mathcal{V} \to \mathbb{P}(\mathcal{R})$ associate a view with its rights. The function $controlled : \mathcal{V} \to \mathcal{T}$ maps a view to its controlled object type, and function $ops : \mathcal{T} \to \mathbb{P}(Op)$ maps an object type to the set of its operation names. Note that in CORBA IDL, $ops(t)$ is indeed a set, i.e. all operation names in a type must be unique, so overloading of operation names is not possible.

$$\forall\, v \in \mathcal{V} \; : \forall\, (op, m, p) \in rights(v) : op \in ops(controlled(v)) \tag{1}$$

$$\forall\, v \in \mathcal{V} \; : \forall\, (op_i, m_i, p_i), (op_j, m_j, p_j) \in rights(v) :$$
$$op_i = op_j \Rightarrow m_i = m_j \wedge p_i = p_j \tag{2}$$

Matrix entries must be well–typed, i.e. they must satisfy condition (3), which ensures that views entered into the access matrix are always applicable to the object in the matrix's column. i.e. that the object has the same type or a subtype of the view's controlled type. Subtyping of object types is denoted by $\sqsubseteq$ and has the usual substitution semantics.

$$\forall v \in \mathcal{V}, o \in \mathcal{O}, s \in \mathcal{S} : v \in M_{(s,o)} \Rightarrow type(o) \sqsubseteq controlled(v) \tag{3}$$

For each object access the views held by the calling subject are checked to determine whether they contain a permission for the requested operation. If they do and, as explained in 2.3, no denials override this permission, the access is granted.

View extension. Like object types, views may be directly or indirectly related through extension so that definitions can be reused. A derived view inherits all its base view's rights — both permissions and denials — and may also add new rights. These added rights may only increase the permissions in the view, however. It is not possible to declare any denials in a derived view.

The semantics of view extension is thus one of monotonically adding permissions, just like interface inheritance adds operations to interfaces and never removes them. As a result, a derived view is substitutable for any of its base views. For the access decision function, this means that if a subject holds multiple views, only the most derived views need to be checked for permissions.

In VPL, extension is expressed by listing base view names after a colon. In the example in Fig. 3, all view definitions directly or indirectly extend `NameResolver`, so they inherit the permission for the operation `resolve` and additionally permit the operations listed in their own definitions.

In the example, the view `NameBinder` extends `NameResolver` by additionally allowing the `bind` operation. The view `NamingContextManager` allows two more operations: new contexts can be created with `new_context` or created and at the same time bound to a given name with `bind_new_context`. Note that

```
view NameBinder: NameResolver {
    allow
        bind;
};

view NamingContextManager: NameBinder {
    allow
        new_context;
        bind_new_context;
};
```

Fig. 3: View extension

`NamingContextManager` does not have an explicit `controls` clause, the control-led type is inherited from its base view. In the case of multiple base views, the controlled object type must be listed explicitly.

Formally, extension on views is denoted by $\leqslant$ ("extends") and has the following properties:

$$\forall \, v, w \in \mathcal{V} : v \leqslant w \Rightarrow$$

$$controlled(v) \sqsubseteq controlled(w) \land rights(w) \subseteq rights(v) \land \tag{4}$$

$$\forall (op, m, p) \in rights(v) \setminus rights(w) : m = allow \tag{5}$$

Property (4) requires a derived view to control the same or a more derived object type than its base views and that it has at least as many rights. Property (5) requires all rights introduced in the derived view to be permissions. Note that we do not exclude extension of multiple base views here. View hierarchies can thus be designed along object type inheritance hierarchies.

2.3   Implicit Authorizations, Denials, and Conflict Resolution

An implicit authorization [RBKW91] is one that is implied by other authorizations whenever a grouping construct is used for granting. If, e.g., a view v on an object is granted to a role, this implies granting v to every individual user who may take on this role.

While it is more convenient to specify general access rules this way than to grant each of the implied authorizations individually, it must also be possible to express exceptions to rules, e.g., that users in one particular role are denied one particular operation on an object. Because the absence of a permission cannot be used to override an existing permission, it is necessary to define a means by which negative authorizations [Sti79] or denials can be explicitly specified, as shown in Fig. 4.

If it is possible to define both permissions and denials, conflicts can arise, some of which may represent exceptions. We now describe a strategy that determines whether, in a given conflict situation, the denial or the permission takes precedence. Our conflict resolution strategy relies on the extension relation between views and on explicit priorities in view definitions.

```
view BaseView controls T {          view DerivedView : BaseView {
    allow                               allow
        op_1;                               op_4;
        op_2;                               strong op_3; // incorrect
    deny                                };
        strong op_3;
        op_4;
};
```

Fig. 4: Denials and explicit priorities

Priorities in our model can only take one of two values: strong or weak. As in [RBKW91], the intention of marking a right as "strong" is that it should not be possible for another right to override the strong right in case of conflicts. As an example for explicit priorities, consider again Fig. 4. In the definition of the view BaseView, the keyword strong marks the denial for operation op_3 and the permission for the same operation in DerivedView as "strong"; all remaining rights in both views are weak.

To control how derived views may redefine inherited rights, we add a restriction to the definition of derived views: A derived view may only redefine weak rights. Strong rights may not be redefined:

$$\forall\, v, w \in \mathcal{V}:\ v \leqslant w \Rightarrow \forall\, (op, m', p') \in rights(v), (op, m, p) \in rights(w):$$
$$m' \neq m \Rightarrow p = weak \tag{6}$$

Property (6) allows redefinitions that change an inherited right's mode, but because of property (5) only denials can be redefined as permissions and not vice versa. A redefinition may also be used to make a right strong without changing the right mode, so that it cannot be further redefined in derived views. When we check the definitions in Fig. 4 using (6), DerivedView is found to be incorrect because the strong denial of op_3 in BaseView cannot be redefined.

Conflict resolution. Basically, conflicts between a permission p and a denial d can only arise in two cases. The first case is that the views that contain the definition of p and d are related by extension. In this case, the more derived view takes precedence.

Two views are only related by extension if one view is directly on the path along the extension hierarchy from a view to the root of hierarchy. Otherwise, two views are unrelated even if they have a common ancestor. In the case that conflicting views are not related, the stronger right takes precedence. If the two conflicting rights' priorities are both weak, the denial takes precedence. To guarantee that a strong permission cannot be overridden in a conflict, however, requires static analysis of view definitions to detect potential conflicts. In case such a potential conflict is discovered, those view definitions that could potentially violate the semantics of "strong" must be rejected.

For the data model defined by OMG IDL, we can statically detect view definitions with potentially inconsistent rights definitions. A type checker can reject specifications or at least print warnings if potentially conflicting definitions are both strong. For two unrelated views, conflicts between rights definitions are only possible if their controlled object types are either equal or related by inheritance. This is the only way that two identical operation names can refer to the same operation in an IDL interface. Note that this restriction on the data model, which prevents interfaces inheriting operations with the same name from different supertypes, is not present in other languages, e.g., in Java. If we were to use Java as the distributed object model, a type checker would not be able to guarantee that a strong right cannot be overridden.

If the following condition holds, we must reject the specification:

$$\exists\, v, w \in \mathcal{V} : v \not< w \land v \not> w \land\ T_v = controlled(v) \land T_w = controlled(w)\ \land$$
$$(T_v \sqsubseteq T_w \lor T_v \sqsupseteq T_w)\ \land \exists\, (op1, m1, p1) \in rights(v), (op2, m2, p2) \in rights(w) :$$
$$op1 = op2 \land m1 \neq m2 \land p1 = strong \land p2 = strong \tag{7}$$

Note that checking this condition requires system–level analysis, i.e., all existing views must be checked. To make this analysis and the administration of views in general practical, we assume that the scope of object type extensions and the visibility of view definitions is restricted by the boundaries of policy management domains [Slo94]. We do not further address domains as a grouping concept for objects in this paper, but it is obvious that manageability of large–scale systems depends on appropriate domain management concepts.

The resolution strategy presented above is simple, flexible and sound. It is possible to express both denials and permissions as the exceptional case, and the use of explicit priorities is straightforward. The downside of this approach is that some view definitions must be rejected simply because of their potential for conflict, even if the conflicts might never actually arise.

2.4   Dynamic Rights Changes

A system's protection state is usually not constant. Objects and subjects are added to or deleted from a system, and rights may be granted and revoked for the purposes of delegation of responsibility or as part of an application–specific security policy. We distinguish the following three cases:

1. *Discretionary granting* or revocation occurs when a grantor explicitly calls a grant operation provided by the security service, thereby inserting views into or removing views from access matrix entries.
2. *Automatic granting* or revocation is performed implicitly by the security service. This occurs when operations are invoked that were defined as triggers in an application–specific policy such as *Chinese Wall* [BN89].
3. *Delegation* occurs implicitly during the course of an operation invocation when the target object delegates the call to another object. This might

require to pass on security attributes of the caller, such as role membership certificates. A number of different delegation policies are possible here
[OMG98], which also depend on whether the target object has security attributes of its own. We do not describe delegation in more detail here. Suffice
it to say that, in general, these attributes do not correspond to rights, so
no new rights are added to the system. Rather, receiving subjects may now
qualify for membership in additional roles and thus gain additional access
rights.

Discretionary Granting. A granting subject can pass on only views that it
possesses and that are also marked as grantable. Rights granted in this way are
restricted to permissions, so a subject cannot restrict another subject's allowed
operations by granting its own denials. With this restriction, there is no need for
recipients to explicitly accept granted views. A simple example is given in Fig.
5.

```
view GrantableView controls T {
    allow
        grant {tech_staff, janitor};
        enter;
};
```

Fig. 5: A grantable view

To allow for explicit, discretionary granting the view `GrantableView` is marked grantable by allowing the operation `grant`. While grant is in fact a meta–
right that corresponds to the `enter` command in matrix models such as [HRU76,
San92], it is modeled just as any other right and may be both a permission or a
denial. It can also be marked as strong.

Additionally, we assume a relation $grantable\_to: \mathcal{V} \times ROLE$ which lists legal
recipient roles for a view. In VPL, this relation is expressed by parameterizing
`grant` with a set of roles that may receive this view. If no recipient roles are
given, a view can be granted without restrictions, otherwise the view may only
be entered into $M_{(s,o)}$ if $s = (u, r)$ and r is one of the target roles.

As mentioned above, an additional restriction for well–formed views is that
a grantable view must not contain denials:

$$\forall\, v \in \mathcal{V}: \; \exists\, (grant, allow, p) \in rights(V) \Rightarrow \; \neg\, \exists\, (op, deny, q) \in rights(V)\,(8)$$

By inserting a view v into $M_{(s,o)}$, a grantor effectively acquires a right on the
matrix entry $M_{(s,o)}$ that allows him to again remove that view at his discretion,
which potentially leads to further revocations if the grantee has passed on the
view after receiving it.

One potential problem with our approach is that a matrix entry is a *set* of
views, so if a grantor passes on a view that the grantee already possesses, the
grantor would acquire the right to delete that right at any time — such as in the

very instance the view was granted. In effect, it would be possible for a grantor to revoke all those views from another subject that both the grantee and the grantor possess. This can be avoided if we change the model so that either matrix entries are multisets, or if a grantor only acquires revoke rights on views that the grantee does not already possess. For practical reasons, we chose the latter solution because it requires no additional bookkeeping.

Automatic granting. It is appropriate to describe discretionary granting in a view definition because the ability to grant a view depends only on the possession and grantability of a view. This is not so for automatic granting or delegation, however. Both delegation and automatic granting depend only on the invocation of a particular operation and could thus be described in an extended interface notation or as IDL annotations. For better integration with other parts of the policy specification we introduce a new language construct schema.

As an example, we describe how an owner status is assigned to the subject calling a factory object's create operation. For this example, we rely on the two IDL interfaces Document and DocumentFactory in Fig. 6.

```
interface Document {                    interface DocumentFactory {
   void read(out string text);             Document create();
   void write(in string text);          };
};
```

Fig. 6: Interfaces Document and DocumentFactory

Figure 7 lists the view and schema definitions. To give owner status for a newly created object to the caller of the create operation on a DocumentFactory object, the schema for DocumentFactory has a grants clause for the create operation. This clause specifies that a view Owner on the result object is to be granted to caller. result and caller are reserved identifiers with the obvious meanings. Schema rules must also be able to refer to out parameters of the operation in case it is necessary to modify views on objects passed to the caller this way. In these cases, the schema can use the name of the formal parameter, which is unique in the operation context. This is not shown in the figure.

An Owner view, which gives access to all operations in the interface, allows the unrestricted granting of this view to other subjects. To also illustrate automatic revocation the schema also contains a revokes clause which specifies that a User view is to be revoked from the caller, thereby removing his right to call the create operation again.

A number of points are worth noting about schemas. First, while schemas do introduce dynamic state changes whose consequences for a particular policy might be hard to predict, they do not introduce new conflicts. This is only possible through the definition of new views. Thus, resolvability of all potential conflicts between rights is still preserved. Second, the grants and revokes clauses can be regarded as operation postconditions with respect to the protection state of the policy domain as they describe an operation's effect on this protec-

```
view Reader controls Document {
   allow
      read;
}
view Owner: Reader {
   allow
      grant;
      write;
}
view User controls DocumentFactory {
   allow
      create;
}

schema DocumentFactory {
   create
      grants
         Owner on result to caller;
      revokes
         User on this from caller;
};
```

Fig. 7: Views and schema for document creation

tion state. Third, an implementation of this concept must be able to undo the effects of these clauses if they occur in an invocation context that is later aborted, e.g., because of lack of permissions for a subsequent operation invocation or because of an exception.

3 An Example Policy

As a case study in VPL we present an application–specific policy for a system that supports programme committees in reviewing papers for a conference.[1] This system is a simple workflow application and supports the following procedure:

1. Authors may submit papers until the deadline is reached. The programme committee (PC) chair assigns a number of reviewers to each paper. This assignment process is not explicitly supported.
2. Reviewers write and submit reviews. After a reviewer has submitted a review for a paper, he may read other reviews for the same paper — but not before he submits. He may now also modify his own review, but not others. (The idea is to shield each reviewer from other reviewers' influence until he commits, but to allow the resolution of conflicts between reviews before the final PC meeting.)

---

[1] This example is designed after a similar system called CyberChair which is being used by the ECOOP conferences. For details see http://wwwtrese.cs.utwente.nk/CyberChair/

3. The final decision for each paper — approval or rejection — must be unanimous. (The resolution of all remaining conflicts is left to the involved reviewers and is not explicitly supported.)

3.1   Application Design

We can derive use cases or scenarios directly from the above description. Even if, in simple cases like this one, a use case–model is not strictly necessary, it is useful for the design of the application's security policy. In this example, the following scenarios occur (the respective actors and interfaces are listed in brackets):

1. Change of processing phases (PC chair, Conference)
2. Submission of papers (authors, Conference)
3. Reviewing (Reviewers, Conference, Paper, Review)

```
interface Conference {
    void callForPapers();
    void deadlineReached();
    void makeDecision();
    void submitPaper(in string paper);
    void listPapers(out string list);
    Paper getPaper(in long paper);
};
```

Fig. 8: Interface Conference

The identified actors are not represented in the system. Notification of authors is via e–mail and not through remote invocation. Figures 8 and 9 list the necessary object interfaces in CORBA IDL.

The main process starts when the PC chair issues a call for papers by invoking callForPapers(). Papers are submitted as arguments of the operation submitPaper() and represented as strings. The conference object creates objects of type Paper from these strings. When the chair has called deadlineReached() to finish the submission phase, reviewers can retrieve submissions by calling getPaper() and giving a reference number as an argument. The operation listPapers() is called to list available papers with their reference numbers.

```
interface Paper {                          interface Review {
    void read (out string text);               void read(out string text);
    Review submitReview(                       void update(in string text);
        in string review,                  };
        in long reviewer);
    void listReviews(out string list);
    Review getReview(in long reviewer);
};
```

Fig. 9: Interfaces Paper and Review

The interface `Paper` allows reading and listing reviews that have already been submitted for this paper. Reviewers who submit by calling `submitReview()` get a `Review` object in return which they can then modify if necessary. After calling `submitReview()` they may also retrieve the reviews of other reviewers using `getReview()`.

3.2   Policy Design

Using the actors identified above we can directly derive the role declarations in Fig. 10. The role `author` is meant to be available to all users excluding those that have been assigned membership in role `chair` — which may only be done for a single principal. Membership in role `chair` implies membership in role `reviewer`.

```
roles
    chair, author, reviewer
role assertion
    author implies not chair;
    chair implies reviewer;
    card( chair ) == 1
```

Fig. 10: Roles and assertions

Static policy aspects. Designing views for the scenarios sketched above is straightforward. We define the views in Fig. 11 to capture the static aspects of this policy.

```
view Member controls Conference {          view ReviewPaper controls Paper {
    allow                                      allow
        listPapers;                                read;
        getPaper;                                  listReviews;
}                                          }
view Chair: Member {
    allow
        callForPapers;
        deadlineReached;
        makeDecision;
}
```

Fig. 11: Views

There are two views for reviewers: `Member` controls objects of type `Conference`, and the view `ReviewPaper` controls `Paper` objects. A `Member` view on conference objects allows listing as well as retrieving papers, a `ReviewPaper` view on paper objects allows reading and listing information about reviews that have been submitted so far. Another view `Chair`, that extends the member view that controls `Conference`, defines the rights to switch between the processing stages.

To assign initial views on all objects of a type to roles, VPL has a keyword `holds` as shown in Fig. 12. If an object's type can be inferred from the view, it need not be listed explicitly. It is possible, however, to assign a view on subtypes of the view's controlled object type. The scope of an object type extension is assumed to be restricted by the boundaries of the management domain.

```
chair holds Chair;
reviewer, chair holds ReviewPaper on Paper, read on Review;
```

Fig. 12: Initial views

Here, the chair holds an initial `Chair` view for all `Conference` objects in the domain, but the extension of `Conference` is supposed to contain just a singleton. At the same time, reviewers and the chair hold two more views, viz. `ReviewPaper` on all `Paper` objects and another, anonymous view that allows reading all reviews: `read` is simply a shorthand notation for:

`view _ controls Review { allow read; }`

Since, at this stage, reviewers have no views that would allow to retrieve papers using `getPaper` or to retrieve reviews using `getReview`, these operations will in effect only be usable after a `Member` view has been granted.

Dynamic aspects. The most interesting feature of this policy are the changes in the protection state when reviews are submitted: before this point, reviewers may not read other reviews; from then on, they may. Which accesses are permitted thus depends on earlier accesses, similar to the *Chinese Wall* policy [BN89]. To describe transitions like these that are directly connected to changes in the application state, we use schemas. In this example there are two schemas, one for the conference interface and one for submissions.

The `Conference` schema describes how the protection state changes in reaction to operations on the conference object. If `callForPapers` is called, views are assigned to authors that allow to submit papers. These views are again anonymous and only contain the permission for the operation `submitPaper`. In addition, the `Member` view on the conference object is assigned to reviewers. After the deadline for submissions is reached, the permission to submit papers is revoked. At the same time, reviewers receive views that allow them to submit reviews. Finally, when the reviewing process is ended by the chair calling `makeDecision`, reviewers may no longer submit reviews.

The `Paper` schema defines that the right to submit a review for this `Paper` object is revoked for the caller so that only one review may be submitted per reviewer. When submitting, reviewers receive new views that allow to retrieve other reviews for this paper.

```
schema Conference {
   callForPapers
      grants
         submitPaper on this to author;
         Member on this to reviewer;
   deadlineReached
      grants
         submitReview on Paper to reviewer;
      revokes
         submitPaper on this from author;
   makeDecision
      revokes
         submitReview on Paper from reviewer;
}
schema Paper {
   submitReview
      grants
         update on result to caller;
         getReview on this to caller;
      revokes
         submitReview on this from caller;
}
```

Fig. 13: Schemas

4   Related Work

Language approaches to protection have been know since the 1970s. An early approach is [JL78] which uses ADTs for enforcing protection. Here, however, protection is part of an implementation and not described separately. Another language–based and also object–oriented model for non–distributed environments is [RSC92]. This model does distinguish between different classes of principals but again does not separate policy specifications from application implementation.

The concept of *views* as an access control concept was first used for a distributed object system in [Hag94]. Views are also used for protection in relational and object–oriented databases[SLT91]. Their use for access control purposes resembles the use of type abstraction as a protection concept. Unlike database views that can span multiple types, a view in our model is restricted to objects of a single IDL type. Joining views on different IDL types $T_1, ..., T_n$ can, however, be modeled by specifying an additional IDL interface T that extends $T_1, ..., T_n$ and defining a view on T. Another difference is that database views may define content–specific access controls, e.g., by stating that an attribute may only be read if its value is above a certain threshold. While this is a possible extension to our model, it is not possible in its current form.

PolicyMaker [BFL96] is a generic skeleton language for policy statements in which filter programs can be embedded. Applications perform access checks themselves by querying a policy database that evaluates unstructured request strings according to the filters. While this approach addresses distributed systems and can model complex trust relations between keys, it does not impose structure on policy specifications nor offer any kind of type checking for policy statements.

Grouping privileges into named protection domains to enhance support for the security management of relational databases has been proposed in [Bal90]. Our approach is similar, but more fine–grained and more modular: named protection domains inherently group not only privileges but also objects, and may even group users. Views describe authorizations on individual objects and combine with more appropriate management concepts for users and objects, viz. roles and domains. We believe that protection domains are not applicable to the richer data models of distributed object systems.

A general framework for defining arbitrary access control policies is proposed in [JSSB97] where policies are formulated as a set of rules in a logic–based language. This model leaves open all design decisions about how implicit authorizations are derived, how rights propagate in groups, which conflict resolution strategies are used and how priorities are employed. Rules for these questions have to be defined first as part of a policy library. The data model for protected objects is also left open and has to be described separately. The protection state is extended with a history component that logs all accesses as facts in a database in order to enable state–based policies like *Chinese Wall*. This model exhibits a more complex concrete syntax than ours, policy specifications are less structured.

Adiron [Adi], a vendor of CORBA Security products, provides an access control language with their product, but this language is not object–oriented and also limited to the restricted standard model of access control in CORBA.

5 Summary and Future Work

In this paper we presented a new access control model based on a typed grouping construct for rights called *view*. We introduced a concrete syntax, VPL, that allows application developers and security administrators to specify access control policies for CORBA domains at an abstract language level and gave an example of how a specific access policy can be expressed using our notation. The model might be extended with a more general priority system in the future.

We are currently working on a partial implementation of the CORBA Security Service for our own CORBA implementation JacORB [Bro97] and on integrating our model with this implementation to prove its feasibility and practical value. Other current and future work includes refining our notion of domains and defining language constructs that allow the composition of domains and their policies, e.g., into domain hierarchies. Building on these concepts, we intend to develop management tools for policy domains.

Acknowledgments. I would like to thank Peter Löhr for many valuable discussions. I would also like to thank the anonymous referees for helpful suggestions.

References

[Adi]   Adiron. http://www.adiron.com/.

[Bal90]   Robert W. Baldwin. Naming and grouping privileges to simplify security management in large databases. In *Proc. IEEE Symposium on Research in Security and Privacy*, pages 116–132, 1990.

[BFL96]   Matt Blaze, Joan Feigenbaum, and Jack Lacy. Distributed trust management. In *Proc. IEEE Symposium on Security and Privacy*, pages 164–173, 1996.

[BN89]   David Brewer and Michael Nash. The chinese wall security policy. In *IEEE Symposium on Security and Privacy*, pages 206–214, 1989.

[Bro97]   Gerald Brose. JacORB — design and implementation of a Java ORB. In *Proc. International Conference on Distributed Applications and Interoperable Systems (DAIS'97)*, pages 143–154, Cottbus, Germany, September 1997. Chapman & Hall.

[Bro99]   Gerald Brose. A view–based access model for CORBA. In Jan Vitek and Christian Jensen, editors, *Secure Internet Programming: Security Issues for Mobile and Distributed Objects*, LNCS 1603, pages 237–252. Springer, 1999.

[FK92]   David Ferraiolo and Richard Kuhn. Role–based access control. In *Proc. 15th National Computer Security Conference*, 1992.

[Hag94]   Daniel Hagimont. Protection in the Guide object–oriented distributed system. In *Proc. ECOOP 1994*, LNCS, pages 280–298. Springer, 1994.

[HBM98]   R. J. Hayton, J. M. Bacon, and K. Moody. Access control in an open distributed environment. In *Proc. IEEE Symposium on Security and Privacy*, pages 3–14, 1998.

[HRU76]   M.H. Harrison, W.L. Ruzzo, and J.D. Ullman. Protection in Operating Systems. *Communications of the ACM*, 19(8):461–471, 1976.

[JL78]   Anita Jones and Barbara Liskov. A language extension for expressing constraints on data access. *Communications of the ACM*, 21(5):358–367, May 1978.

[JSSB97]   Sushil Jajodia, Pierangela Samarati, V. S. Subrahmanian, and Elisa Bertino. A unified framework for enforcing multiple access control policies. In *Proc. International Conference on Management of Data*, pages 474–485, 1997.

[Kar98]   Günter Karjoth. Authorization in CORBA security. In *Proc. ESORICS'98*, pages 143–158, 1998.

[Lam74]   Butler W. Lampson. Protection. *ACM Operating Systems Rev.*, 8(1):18–24, January 1974.

[OMG97]   OMG. *CORBAservices: Common Object Services Specification*, November 1997.

[OMG98]   OMG. *Security Service Revision 1.5*, November 1998.

[OMG99]   OMG. *The Common Object Request Broker: Architecture and Specification, Revision 2.3*, June 1999.

[RBKW91]   Fausto Rabitti, Elisa Bertino, Won Kim, and Darrel Woelk. A model of authorization for next–generation database systems. *ACM Transactions on Database Systems*, 16(1):88–131, March 1991.

[RSC92]   Joel Richardson, Peter Schwarz, and Luis-Filipe Cabrera. CACL: Efficient fine–grained protection for objects. In *Proc. OOPSLA 1992*, pages 263–275, 1992.

[San92]   Ravi S. Sandhu. The typed access matrix model. In *Proc. IEEE Symposium on Security and Privacy*, pages 122–136, 1992.

[SCFY96]   Ravi S. Sandhu, Edward J. Coyne, Hal L. Feinstein, and Charles E. Youman. Role–based access control models. *IEEE Computer*, 29(2):38–47, 1996.

[Slo94]   Morris Sloman. Policy driven management for distributed systems. *Journal of Network and Systems Management*, 2(4), 1994.

[SLT91]   Marc H. Scholl, Christian Laasch, and Markus Tresch. Updatable views in object–oriented databases. In *Proc. 2. Int. Conf. on Deductive and Object–Oriented Databases*, number 566 in LNCS, pages 189–207, Berlin, Germany, 1991. Springer.

[Sti79]   Helmut G. Stiegler. A structure for access control lists. *Software — Practice and Experience*, 9:813–819, 1979.

Safety Analysis of the Dynamic-Typed Access Matrix Model

Masakazu Soshi

School of Information Science, Japan Advanced Institute of Science and Technology
1-1 Asahidai, Tatsunokuchi-machi, Nomi-gun, Ishikawa 923-1292, JAPAN
soshi@jaist.ac.jp

Abstract. The safety problem in access matrix models is the one to determine whether or not a given subject can eventually obtain an access privilege to a given object. Unfortunately, little is known about protection systems for which the safety problem is decidable, except for strongly constrained systems (e.g., monotonic systems). Therefore, we propose the Dynamic-Typed Access Matrix Model, which extends Typed Access Matrix model by allowing the type of an object to change dynamically. DTAM model has an advantage that it can describe non-monotonic protection systems for which the safety problem is decidable. In this paper, we formally define DTAM model and then discuss various aspects of it.

Keywords: access control, access matrix model, safety problem, computational complexity, decidability

1   Introduction

Today a huge amount of valuable information is being processed and stored by computers and it is of great importance to establish security in such environments. A security model gives us a framework that specifies computer systems (or protection systems) precisely from a security point of view.

One of the most widely-accepted security models is an *access matrix model*. In an access matrix model, a protection system is characterized by a collection of *subjects* (e.g., users or processes) and *objects* (e.g., files or I/O devices). Access control is enforced according to an *access matrix* A, which has a row for each subject and a column for each object, and $A[s, o]$ maintains the set of access modes that subject s is authorized to perform on object o.

Harrison et al. first formalized security property of protection systems in the access matrix model (HRU model) as the *safety problem* [4].[1] The safety problem is the one to determine whether or not a given subject can eventually obtain an access privilege to a given object. Generally speaking, unfortunately, the safety problem is undecidable [4,7]. This is primarily due to the fact that the

---

[1] For lack of space, here we present some relevant work only briefly. See the excellent historical review in [6] for further details.

F. Cuppens et al. (Eds.): ESORICS 2000, LNCS 1895, pp. 106–121, 2000.

access matrix model has broad expressive power and that the number of newly created objects can be infinite. Little is known about protection systems for which the safety problem is decidable, except for strongly constrained systems (e.g., monotonic systems, where no new entities can be created and no revocation of privileges are allowed). For example, Sandhu developed the Typed Access Matrix (TAM) Model [6], which has a wide variety of decidable safety cases, but most of which are limited to monotonic systems. However, since security policies in existent computer systems are not monotonic, it would be difficult to apply the safety analysis of monotonic systems to real systems.

Therefore, we propose the Dynamic-Typed Access Matrix (DTAM) Model, which extends TAM model by allowing the type of an object to change dynamically. DTAM model has an advantage that it can describe non-monotonic protection systems for which the safety problem is decidable. In order to show this, first we introduce a *type relationship (TR) graph*. Then we show that the safety problem for non-monotonic systems becomes decidable if, roughly speaking, the TR graphs of the systems have no cycle with respect to parent-child relationship between objects.[2] Moreover, if we impose on this situation additional restrictions that no new objects are permitted to be created, the safety problem becomes NP-hard. The decidable safety cases discussed in this paper fall outside the known decidable ones in previous work.

The remainder of the paper is structured as follows. We formalize DTAM model in Section 2 and make a thorough investigation of the safety property of DTAM model in Section 3. Section 4 discusses various topics on DTAM model and then finally we conclude this paper in Section 5.

2   Dynamic-Typed Access Matrix Model

In this section we give a formal description of the Dynamic-Typed Access Matrix (DTAM) model.

2.1   Basic Concepts

Definition 1. *Objects are defined as passive entities, e.g., files or I/O devices, which are protected by the security control mechanism of a computer system, and* subjects *as active entities, e.g., users or processes, which access objects. The current set of subjects and objects are denoted by S and O, respectively. We assume $S \subseteq O$. Each member of the set $O - S$ is called a* pure object *[6].*

Every object has its own *identity* inherently. Hence, for instance, no object can be created repeatedly as the identical one. In this paper, the identities of a subject and an object are represented by s and o, respectively ($s \in S$, $o \in O$).

Definition 2. *Every object has a type, which can be changed dynamically. L is a finite set of all types. In particular, we denote a set of types of subjects by L_S ($L_S \subseteq L$). We assume $1 \leq |L_S| \leq |L|$.*

---

[2] The precise condition for this case will be given in Section 3.

For example, L_S may consist of three user types, *programmer*, *system-engineer*, and *project-manager*. In addition, we can take $file_{trade-secrets}$ and $file_{public}$ for examples of types of pure objects.

Next we define the type function as follows:

Definition 3. *First we define the function which returns the type of a subject as* $f_S : S \to L_S$. *Next we define the function which returns the type of a pure object as* $f_O : (O - S) \to (L - L_S)$. *Now we can define the* type function $f_L : O \to L$, *which associates a type with every object, as follows:*

$$f_L(o) = \begin{cases} f_S(o) & \text{if } o \in S, \\ f_O(o) & \text{otherwise.} \end{cases}$$

Note that mapping from objects to their types expressed by f_L may vary as time elapses because object types can be dynamically changed.

Definition 4. Access modes *are kinds of access that subjects can execute on objects (e.g., read, write, own, and execute) and a finite set of access modes are denoted by R.*

Using Definition 4, an access matrix can be defined as follows:

Definition 5. *An* access matrix A *is a matrix which has a row for each subject and a column for each object. An element $A[s, o]$ of A stores the set of access modes ($A[s, o] \subseteq R$) that subject s is authorized to exercise on object o.*

Now we can define a protection state (or state for short) of a system as follows:

Definition 6. *A* protection state *is defined by (S, O, A, f_L) and denoted by Q.*

2.2   Primitive Operations and Commands

The way in which a protection system evolves by activities of subjects is modeled by incremental changes of the protection state, which are made by executing a sequence of commands. In this section, we first define primitive operations in order to give the definition of commands.

Definition 7. *The definition of* primitive operations *is given in Table 1, where the states just before and after a primitive operation executes are indicated by (S, O, A, f_L) and (S', O', A', f_L'), respectively.*

Most notable primitive operations in DTAM model are **change type of subject** s **to** l_s' and **change type of object** o **to** l_o'. It is often desirable to change the type of an object dynamically to specify security policies in real computer systems [2,5]. For the example in Section 2.1, if a user who is a programmer is promoted, first to the position of a system engineer, and next to a project manager, then such a situation is easily expressed by dynamically changing the user type accordingly. Dynamically changeable types are also advantageous in safety analysis (Section 3).

We shall define commands based on Definition 7.

Table 1. DTAM primitive operations

Primitive Operations	Conditions	New States
enter r **into** $A[s,o]$	$s \in S$ $o \in O$ $r \in R$	$S' = S,\ O' = O$ $A'[s,o] = A[s,o] \cup \{r\}$ $A'[s',o'] = A[s',o']$ if $(s',o') \neq (s,o)$, for all $s' \in S,\ o' \in O$ $f_L'(o') = f_L(o')$ for all $o' \in O$
delete r **from** $A[s,o]$	$s \in S$ $o \in O$ $r \in R$	$S' = S,\ O' = O$ $A'[s,o] = A[s,o] - \{r\}$ $A'[s',o'] = A[s',o']$ if $(s',o') \neq (s,o)$, for all $s' \in S,\ o' \in O$ $f_L'(o') = f_L(o')$ for all $o' \in O$
change type of subject s **to** l_s'	$s \in S$ $l_s' \in L_S$	$S' = S,\ O' = O$ $A'[s',o] = A[s',o]$ for all $s' \in S,\ o \in O$ $f_L'(s) = l_s'$ $f_L'(o) = f_L(o)$ if $o \neq s$, for all $o \in O$
change type of object o **to** l_o'	$o \in O - S$ $l_o' \in L - L_S$	$S' = S,\ O' = O$ $A'[s,o'] = A[s,o']$ for all $s \in S,\ o' \in O$ $f_L'(o) = l_o'$ $f_L'(o') = f_L(o')$ if $o' \neq o$, for all $o' \in O$
create subject s' **of type** l_s	$s' \notin O$ $l_s \in L_S$	$S' = S \cup \{s'\},\ O' = O \cup \{s'\}$ $A'[s,o] = A[s,o]$ for all $s \in S,\ o \in O$ $A'[s',o] = \phi$ for all $o \in O$ $A'[s,s'] = \phi$ for all $s \in S'$ $f_L'(s') = l_s$ $f_L'(o) = f_L(o)$ for all $o \in O$
create object o' **of type** l_o	$o' \notin O$ $l_o \in L - L_S$	$S' = S,\ O' = O \cup \{o'\}$ $A'[s,o] = A[s,o]$ for all $s \in S,\ o \in O$ $A'[s,o'] = \phi$ for all $s \in S$ $f_L'(o') = l_o$ $f_L'(o) = f_L(o)$ for all $o \in O$
destroy subject s	$s \in S$	$S' = S - \{s\},\ O' = O - \{s\}$ $A'[s',o] = A[s',o]$ for all $s' \in S',\ o \in O'$ $f_L'(o) = f_L(o)$ for all $o \in O'$
destroy object o	$o \in O - S$	$S' = S,\ O' = O - \{o\}$ $A'[s,o'] = A[s,o']$ for all $s \in S',\ o' \in O'$ $f_L'(o') = f_L(o')$ for all $o' \in O'$

Definition 8. *A* command *is a computational unit which has the form:*

command $\alpha(x_1 : l_1, x_2 : l_2, \ldots, x_k : l_k)$
   if $r_1 \in A[x_{k_{s1}}, x_{k_{o1}}] \wedge r_2 \in A[x_{k_{s2}}, x_{k_{o2}}] \wedge \ldots \wedge r_m \in A[x_{k_{sm}}, x_{k_{om}}]$
   then $op_1;\ op_2;\ \ldots;\ op_n$
end

Here α *is the name of the command, and* x_1, x_2, $\ldots$, x_k *are formal parameters of* α *whose types are given by* l_1, l_2, $\ldots$, l_k, *respectively. Furthermore,* k_{s1}, k_{s2}, $\ldots$, k_{sm}, k_{o1}, k_{o2}, $\ldots$, k_{om} *are integers between 1 and* k. r_1, r_2, $\ldots$, r_m *are* *access modes and op_1, op_2, ..., op_n are primitive operations. We assume that k, m, and n are finite. CM denotes a finite set of commands.*

*As defined above, a command consists of the condition and the body. Condition of a command is the predicate placed between **if** and **then** in the command, where we can specify the conjunction of multiple condition expressions. However, a command does not necessarily have the condition. A command with no condition is said to be an* unconditional command. *A condition expression in the condition of a command tests for the presence of an access mode in a cell of A. Finally, the* body *of a command is the sequence of the primitive operations contained in the command.*

A command is invoked by replacing all formal parameters of the command with actual parameters (i.e., objects) of the appropriate types. After that, if the condition of the command and all of the conditions of the primitive operations in the body are evaluated to true in terms of the actual parameters, then the command (more precisely, the primitive operations in the body with actual parameters) can be executed. Otherwise, the command cannot be executed. Furthermore, we assume that every execution of commands is serial and atomic.

2.3   Authorization Schemes and Protection Systems

In this section we define an authorization scheme and a protection system, which are abstractions of security policies and computer systems, respectively [6]:

Definition 9. *An* authorization scheme *is defined by (L_S, L, R, CM). Furthermore, A* protection system *(or simply* system*) consists of an authorization scheme and an initial state (S_0, O_0, A_0, f_{L_0}).*

Next we consider monotonicity and non-monotonicity of authorization schemes and protection systems.

Definition 10. *An authorization scheme whose commands do not contain primitive operations **destroy**, **delete**, and **change type** is said to be* monotonic. *An authorization scheme which is not monotonic is said to be* non-monotonic. *Furthermore, if the authorization scheme of a system is monotonic, the system is said to be* monotonic, *otherwise* non-monotonic.

This completes the formalization of DTAM model.

3   Safety Analysis

In this section we shall study the safety problem in DTAM model thoroughly.

3.1   Preliminaries

First in this section we present some preliminaries that make the analysis easier.

Definition 11. Normalization of command $\alpha(x_1 : l_1, x_2 : l_2, \ldots, x_k : l_k)$ is to perform the following two transformations on α for every formal parameter x_i $(1 \leq i \leq k)$. However, if α has no **change type of subject** (or **object**) x_i in its body, then the two transformations have no effect on it with respect to x_i. In the description below, we assume for simplicity that x_i is a subject. If x_i is a pure object, we transform α in the similar manner.

[**Transformation 1**] If α has only one **change type of subject** x_i, then the transformation 1 has no effect on it with respect to x_i. Otherwise, α includes in the body more than one **change type of subject** x_i. Now we extract from the body of α every **change type of subject** x_i but the last one.

[**Transformation 2**] In this stage we assume that the transformation 1 has already been applied to α. Let us assume that with respect to x_i, the body of α now contains **create subject** x_i of type l_i and **change type of subject** x_i to l_i' (if it is not the case, Transformation 2 has no effect with respect to x_i). Now we extract **change type of subject** x_i to l_i' from the body and transform **create subject** x_i of type l_i into **create subject** x_i of type l_i'. Furthermore, we replace the type of formal parameter x_i of α with l_i'. As a result, we have $\alpha(x_1 : l_1, x_2 : l_2, \ldots, x_i : l_i', \ldots, x_k : l_k)$ instead of the original α.

Transformation 1 and 2 *optimize* commands with respect to **change type**, i.e., take the net effects of the sequences of the primitive operations. So the following theorem is rather obvious:

Theorem 1. *Given any command $\alpha(x_1 : l_1, x_2 : l_2, \ldots, x_k : l_k)$ and protection state Q, if α can be run on Q and Q changes into a state Q' by executing α, then command $\alpha'(x_1 : l_1', x_2 : l_2', \ldots, x_k : l_k')$, which is the normalization of α, can also be run on Q and Q changes into Q' by executing α'.*

Proof. For the sake of brevity, we assume that every formal parameter x_i of α is a subject. If it is a pure object, we can prove the theorem in the same way.

Concerning Transformation 1, for each x_i, every **change type of subject** x_i in the body of α has no effect on the execution of other primitive operations in the body. Thus, only the last **change type of subject** x_i is significant and the results of execution of α and that of α' on Q are the same.

Now notice that for each x_i, there is at most one **create subject** x_i in the body of α because no subject can be created repeatedly as the identical one (see also Section 2.1). Furthermore, before **create subject** x_i, there must exist no primitive operation which accesses x_i, i.e., **enter/delete** for an element of A corresponding to x_i, **change type of subject** x_i, and **create/destroy subject** x_i. Therefore, Transformation 2 does not cause any difference between the results of execution of α and that of α', but possibly does between the formal parameters of x_i in α and in α'. However, the latter difference is not significant in type checking of formal and actual parameters in α and α' since the actual parameter subject corresponding to x_i does not exist until α (or α') is executed on Q.

Finally, recall that Transformation 1 and 2 does not make any change in the condition part of α. As a result if the condition of α holds true on Q, then so does the condition of α'. This completes the proof.   □

By Theorem 1, we can easily show the next corollary:

Corollary 1. *Set of reachable states from the initial state of a protection system do not change even if all commands in the command set of the system are normalized.*

The most important result of Theorem 1 (or Corollary 1) is that we have only to consider commands each of which contains at most one **change type** operation with respect to each formal parameter. This makes the following safety analysis easier. Hence hereafter we assume that all commands are normalized unless otherwise explicitly stated.

Now we introduce a type relationship (TR) graph for safety analysis of DTAM model. For that purpose, first we define parent-type relationships between types.

Definition 12. *If the body of $\alpha(x_1 : l_1, x_2 : l_2, \ldots, x_k : l_k)$ has* **create subject** x_i *of type* l_i *or* **create object** x_i *of type* l_i *$(1 \le i \le k)$, then we define l_i as a* child type *with respect to* **create** *in α. If l_i is not a child type with respect to* **create** *in α, then l_i is said to be a* parent type *with respect to* **create** *in α. In particular, if every l_i $(1 \le i \le k)$ is a child type with respect to* **create***, all l_i are said to be* orphan types.

Definition 13.   – *If the body of $\alpha(x_1 : l_1, x_2 : l_2, \ldots, x_k : l_k)$ has* **change type of subject** x_i *to l_i' or* **change type of object** x_i *to l_i' $(1 \le i \le k)$, then l_i' is said to be a* child type *with respect to* **change type** *in α and l_i is said to be a* parent type *with respect to* **change type** *in α.*
    – *If the body of $\alpha(x_1 : l_1, x_2 : l_2, \ldots, x_k : l_k)$ has neither* **change type of subject** x_i *nor* **change type of object** x_i *and l_i is a parent type with respect to* **create** *in α $(1 \le i \le k)$, then l_i is said to be a* parent type *with respect to* **change type** *in α as well as a* child type *with respect to* **change type** *in α. In this case the types of the parent and the child are the same.*

In order to demonstrate what parent-child relationships between types are like, let us consider the following three commands α_1, α_2, and α_3:

command $\alpha_1(x_1 : l_1^s, x_2 : l^o)$
    create object x_2 **of type** l^o
    change type of subject x_1 **to** l_2^s
end

command $\alpha_2(x : l_2^s)$
    change type of subject x **to** l_1^s
end

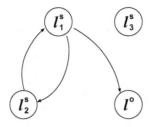

Fig. 1. Example of TR graph

command $\alpha_3(x : l_3^s)$
   create subject x **of type** l_3^s
end

First let us consider α_1. l_1^s is a parent type with respect to **create** in α_1 and a parent type with respect to **change type** in α_1. Also l_2^s is a child type with respect to **change type** in α_1. l^o is a child type with respect to **create** in α_1. In α_2, l_2^s is a parent type with respect to **create** in α_2 and a parent type with respect to **change type** in α_2. Furthermore, l_1^s is a child type with respect to **change type** in α_2. Concerning α_3, we see that l_3^s is an orphan type. It is evident from α_3 that any command that has an orphan type must be unconditional and we can execute the command on any protection state. In consequence, we can create objects of an orphan type infinitely.

Now we are ready to define a type relationship (TR).

Definition. 14. *A type relationship (TR) graph $RG = (V_R, E_R)$ is a directed graph defined as follows:*

- *V_R is a set of vertices and $V_R = L$.*
- *E_R ($\subseteq V_R \times V_R$) is a set of edges and for each pair of v_1, $v_2 \in V_R$, a edge from v_1 to v_2 exists in E_R if and only if either of the following two conditions holds:*
  - *for some command α, v_1 is a parent type with respect to **create** in α and v_2 is a child type with respect to **create** in α, or*
  - *for some command α, v_1 is a parent type with respect to **change type** in α and v_2 is a child type with respect to **change type** in α.*

For example, we show in Figure 1 TR graph for the three commands α_1, α_2, α_3 in this section .

3.2   Safety Analysis of Non-monotonic Protection Systems (I)

Let us again consider TR graph depicted in Figure 1. Furthermore we assume that a subject s of type l_1^s exists in a state. Now we can create from the state an infinite number of pure objects o_1, o_2, ..., by executing $\alpha_1(s, o_1)$, $\alpha_2(s)$,

$\alpha_1(s, o_2)$, $\alpha_2(s)$, ... In addition, as stated in Section 3.1, we can create objects of an orphan type infinitely. In summary, the existence of cycles[3] and orphan types in a TR graph is closely related to whether or not the number of objects in a protection system is finite, which in turn heavily influences the decidability of the safety problem as mentioned in Section 1.

In this section we shall show that DTAM model can describe non-monotonic systems for which the safety problem is decidable.

First of all we define creating commands [6] and parent-child relationships between objects.

Definition 15. *If command* α *contains* **create subject** *or* **create object** *operations in its body, we say that* α *is a* creating command, *otherwise a* noncreating command.

Definition 16. *If command* $\alpha(x_1 : l_1, x_2 : l_2, ..., x_k : l_k)$ *can be executed by substituting* o_1, o_2, ..., o_k *for* x_1, x_2, ..., x_k *and the execution creates some new objects, then we say that* o_i *(1 $\leq$ i $\leq$ k) is a* parent *if* l_i *is a parent type with respect to* **create** *in* α, *otherwise that* o_i *is a* child. *A* descendant *of object* o *is recursively defined as* o *itself or a child of a descendant of* o. *If object* o_1 *is a descendant of object* o_2, o_2 *is said to be an* ancestor *of* o_1.

Note that even a pure object can be a parent of other objects by definition.

Now we can prove the following lemma:

Lemma 1. *Suppose a TR graph has no cycle that contains parent types with respect to* **create** *in creating commands. In such a case, given any creating command* $\alpha(x_1 : l_1, x_2 : l_2, ..., x_k : l_k)$, *if* l_i *(1 $\leq$ i $\leq$ k) is a parent type with respect to* **create** *in* α, *then* α *must have* **change type of subject** x_i *to* l_i' *or* **change type of object** x_i *to* l_i' *in its body such that* $l_i \neq l_i'$.

Proof. Suppose that for some creating command $\alpha(x_1 : l_1, x_2 : l_2, ..., x_k : l_k)$ and some i (1 $\leq$ i $\leq$ k), l_i is a parent type with respect to **create** in α and α does not have **change type of subject** x_i **to** l_i' or **change type of object** x_i **to** l_i' in its body such that $l_i \neq l_i'$. In that case, l_i is a parent type as well as a child type with respect to **change type** by Definition 13. Consequently the TR graph must contain at least one self-loop with vertex l_i by Definition 14. This is a contradiction.   □

Lemma 1 means that the execution of a creating command α must change the type of every actual parameter (object) into another type if the type of the corresponding formal parameter is a parent type with respect to **create** in α. However, the converse of Lemma 1 is not true.

Using Lemma 1, we can prove Lemma 2:

Lemma 2. *The number of objects in arbitrary protection state of a protection system has an upper bound, provided that:*

---

[3] Throughout this paper, we regard a (self-)loop as a special case of cycles, i.e., a cycle of length one.

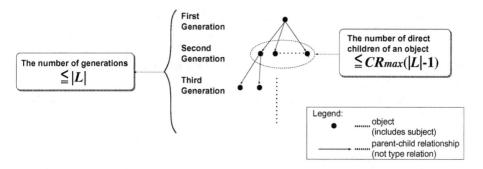

Fig. 2. Descendants of an object

1. *the authorization scheme of the system has no orphan type, and*
2. *the TR graph of the system has no cycle that contains parent types with respect to* **create** *in creating commands.*

Proof. Since there are no orphan types, every child type with respect to **create** has the corresponding parent type with respect to **create**. Therefore, every object in the system is a descendant of an object in the initial state $Q_0 = (S_0, O_0, A_0, f_{L0})$.

For command α, let $CR(\alpha)$ be the total number of **create subject** and **create object** operations in the body of α. Furthermore, let CR_{max} be the maximum value of $CR(\alpha)$ ($\alpha \in CM$). By Definition 8, CR_{max} is finite.

Now, with respect to some object o in a protection state, let us consider the number of descendants of o (see Figure 2).[4]

First we consider the maximum number of direct children of o. We see that only at most $|L| - 1$ times we can execute creating commands with o as input. The reason for this is as follows. If we can execute some creating command α with o as its actual parameter, then the type of the corresponding formal parameter must be always a parent type with respect to **create** in α since o is already existent. Therefore, by Lemma 1, a type of o must be changed to another type after α with o is executed. So if we can execute such creating commands more than $|L| - 1$ times, then in the execution sequence of the commands, at least two types assigned to o must be the same. However, this implies that in the TR graph there exists a cycle that contains several types assigned to o, all of which are parent types with respect to **create** in creating commands. This contradicts the assumption 2 of Lemma 2. Therefore, the number that creating commands with o as input can be executed is at most $|L| - 1$ and as a consequence the number of direct children of o during the lifetime of the system is given by at most $CR_{max} \times (|L| - 1)$.

---

[4] Note that Figure 2 is *not* a TR graph. Please do not be confused in the following discussion.

Next we discuss the maximum number of generations of descendants of o. The number of the generations is less than or equal to $|L|$. The reason is that if it is greater than $|L|$, in descendants of o there exist two objects that are of the same type. This also implies that the TR graph has a cycle with parent types with respect to **create** and causes a contradiction.

From the discussions above, an upper bound of the number of descendants of an object is given by:

$$1 + (CR_{max}(|L| - 1)) + (CR_{max}(|L| - 1))^2 + \ldots + (CR_{max}(|L| - 1))^{|L|-1}$$

$$= \begin{cases} \dfrac{(CR_{max}(|L| - 1))^{|L|} - 1}{CR_{max}(|L| - 1) - 1} & \cdots \text{ where } CR_{max}(|L| - 1) > 1 \\ |L| & \cdots \text{ where } CR_{max}(|L| - 1) = 1 \\ 1 & \cdots \text{ where } CR_{max}(|L| - 1) = 0. \end{cases}$$

Consequently, the number of objects in arbitrary protection state of the protection system has an upper bound O_{max}, which is given by:

$$O_{max} = \begin{cases} |O_0| \dfrac{(CR_{max}(|L| - 1))^{|L|} - 1}{CR_{max}(|L| - 1) - 1} & \cdots \text{ where } CR_{max}(|L| - 1) > 1 \\ |O_0||L| & \cdots \text{ where } CR_{max}(|L| - 1) = 1 \\ |O_0| & \cdots \text{ where } CR_{max}(|L| - 1) = 0. \end{cases}$$

$\square$

From Lemma 2, we can derive Theorem 2:

Theorem 2. *The safety problem for protection systems is decidable, provided that:*

1. *the authorization schemes of the systems have no orphan type, and*
2. *the TR graphs of the systems have no cycle that contains parent types with respect to* **create** *in creating commands.*

Proof. By Lemma 2, the number of objects in arbitrary protection states of the systems in Theorem 2 is finite. This implies that the number of distinct protection states of such a system is also finite, which is proved as follows.

Let n_s and n_o denote the numbers of subjects and objects, respectively. Then the access matrix A has n_s rows and n_o columns and can express at most $(2^{|R|})^{n_s n_o}$ distinct states of authorization since each element of A can have at most $2^{|R|}$ distinct states. In regard to f_L, the maximum number of ways in which f_L maps objects to object types is given by:

$$\begin{cases} |L_S|^{n_s} (|L| - |L_S|)^{n_o - n_s} & \text{if } |L_S| < |L| \\ |L_S|^{n_s} & \text{otherwise. (i.e., } |L| = |L_S|) \end{cases}$$

From the discussions above, an upper bound of the number of distinct protection states of the system is given by (recall that a protection state is defined by a four-tuple (S, O, A, f_L)):

$$
\begin{cases}
\sum_{n_o=0}^{O_{max}} \sum_{n_s=0}^{n_o} \left\{ \binom{O_{max}}{n_s} \binom{O_{max} - n_s}{n_o - n_s} 2^{|R|n_s n_o} |L_S|^{n_s} (|L| - |L_S|)^{n_o - n_s} \right\} \\
\qquad \cdots \text{if } |L_S| < |L| \\
\sum_{n_s=0}^{O_{max}} \left\{ \binom{O_{max}}{n_s} 2^{|R|n_s{}^2} |L_S|^{n_s} \right\} \qquad \cdots \text{otherwise. (i.e., } |L| = |L_S|)
\end{cases}
$$

In other words, the number of different states is finite. Therefore, we can check whether or not a particular subject has a particular right for a particular object in every reachable state from the initial state by using, say, depth-first search. □

By the proof above, we see that whenever the conditions given in Theorem 2 are satisfied, the safety problem is decidable regardless of the kinds of primitive operations in command bodies. Namely, Theorem 2 shows the existence of new non-monotonic systems where the safety problem is decidable.

3.3   Safety Analysis of Non-monotonic Protection Systems (II)

In this section, we again discuss the safety problem for non-monotonic systems in Theorem 2, but with further restriction that they have no creating commands.

Theorem 3. *The safety problem is NP-hard for protection systems, provided that:*

1. *the authorization schemes of the systems have no creating command,[5] and*
2. *the TR graphs of the systems have no cycle.*

Proof. First we present the subset sum problem [3]:

> Given a finite set M, a size function $w(m) \in Z^+$ for each $m \in M$, positive integer N. Is there a subset $M' \subseteq M$ such that the sum of the sizes of the elements in M' is exactly N?

The subset sum problem is known to be NP-complete. Hereafter we assume that $M = \{m_1, m_2, \ldots, m_n\}$ and $\sum_{i=1}^{n} w(m_i) = I$. Furthermore, let $w_1, w_2, \ldots, w_k$ be the set of distinct values of $w(m_1), w(m_2), \ldots, w(m_n)$. Without loss of generality, we assume that $w(m_1) \leq w(m_2) \leq \ldots \leq w(m_n)$ and $w_1 < w_2 < \ldots < w_k$. This implies that $1 \leq w(m_1) = w_1$.

Given this subset sum problem and a protection system that satisfies the conditions in Theorem 3, we run the *authorization scheme construction algorithm* (AC algorithm for short), which is given in Figure 3. Two **while** statements in the figure ((1) and (6)) compute L_S and CM, respectively, and the commands $\alpha_{N,end}$ and $\alpha_{i,j}$ (i and j are variables) are defined as follows:

command $\alpha_{N,end}(x : l_N^s)$
　　enter r **into** $A[x, x]$
　　　change type of subject x **to** l_{end}^s
end

---

[5] Such protection systems do not have orphan types.

$L_S \leftarrow \{l_0^s\}; C \leftarrow \{l_0^s\};$

while $C \neq \phi$ **do begin**   /* (1) */

    From $C = \{l_{i_1}^s, l_{i_2}^s, \ldots, l_{i_l}^s\}$, choose $l_{i_a}^s$ whose subscript i_a is

        the smallest of $\{i_1, i_2, \ldots, i_l\}$ and set $i \leftarrow i_a$.

    $C \leftarrow C - \{l_i^s\};$ /* (2) */

    for $j \leftarrow 1$ **to** k **do begin**   /* (3) */

        if $i + w_j \leq I$ **then begin**   /* (4) */

            $L_S \leftarrow L_S \cup \{l_{i+w_j}^s\}; C \leftarrow C \cup \{l_{i+w_j}^s\};$ /* (5) */

        end

        else goto END1

    end;

END1:

  end;

$CM \leftarrow \{\alpha_{N,end}\}; C \leftarrow L_S;$

while $C \neq \phi$ **do begin**   /* (6) */

    From $C = \{l_{i_1}^s, l_{i_2}^s, \ldots, l_{i_l}^s\}$, choose $l_{i_a}^s$ whose subscript i_a is

        the smallest of $\{i_1, i_2, \ldots, i_l\}$ and set $i \leftarrow i_a$.

    $C \leftarrow C - \{l_i^s\};$

    for $j \leftarrow 1$ **to** n **do begin**

        if $i + w(m_j) \leq I$ **then** $CM \leftarrow CM \cup \{\alpha_{i,j}\}$ **else goto** END2

    end;

END2:

  end;

$R \leftarrow \{r\}; L_S \leftarrow L_S \cup \{l_N^s, l_{end}^s\}; L \leftarrow L_S \cup \{l_1^o, l_2^o, \ldots, l_n^o, l_{end}^o\};$

Fig. 3. Algorithm for authorization scheme construction

command $\alpha_{i,j}(x_1 : l_i^s, x_2 : l_j^o)$

    change type of subject x_1 **to** $l_{i+w(m_j)}^s$

    change type of object x_2 **to** l_{end}^o

end

For example, let us consider the case that $M = \{m_1, m_2, m_3\}$, $w(m_1) = 2$, $w(m_2) = 3$, $w(m_3) = 3$. Shown in Figure 4 is the TR graph of the authorization scheme generated by AC algorithm. For the sake of simplicity, the parts of the graph for types of pure objects and parent-child relationships in command $\alpha_{N,end}$ are not drawn in Figure 4.

Now we consider whether AC algorithm eventually stops or not. Regarding **while** statement (1) of AC algorithm, l_i^s whose subscript i is the smallest is removed from C in step (2) and $l_{i+w_j}^s$ is added to C in step (5). However, since the condition in step (4) ensures that a subscript of each element of C is not greater than I, C becomes empty eventually and **while** statement (1) surely terminates. With respect to **while** statement (6), it also stops in the end. The computational complexity of AC algorithm is $O(In)$.

We are now in a position to consider the polynomial-time reducibility from the subset sum problem to the safety problem in Theorem 3. For that purpose, we

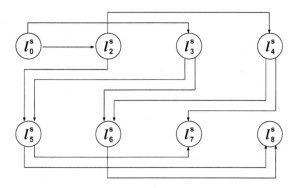

Fig. 4. TR graph generated by AC algorithm

- $S_0 = \{s\}$
- $O_0 = S_0 \cup \{o_1, o_2, \ldots, o_n\}$
- For every pair of $s \in S_0$ and $o \in O_0$, $A_0[s, o] = \phi$
- $f_{L0}(s) = l_0^s$, $f_{L0}(o_i) = l_i^o$ $(1 \leq i \leq n)$

Fig. 5. Initial state of $\mathcal{P}$

consider the protection system $\mathcal{P}$, which has the authorization scheme generated by AC algorithm. The initial state of $\mathcal{P}$, (S_0, O_0, A_0, f_{L0}), is given in Figure 5. In the rest of this section we reduce the subset sum problem to the safety problem for $\mathcal{P}$, which is a restricted case of the safety problem in Theorem 3.

Let us assume the subset sum problem has a solution $M' = \{m_{j_1}, m_{j_2}, \ldots, m_{j_l}\}$. That is, $M' \subseteq M$ and $w(m_{j_1}) + w(m_{j_2}) + \ldots + w(m_{j_l}) = N$. In such a case, for subject s and pure objects $o_{j_1}, o_{j_1}, \ldots, o_{j_l}$, we can execute commands $\alpha_{0,j_1}(s, o_{j_1})$, $\alpha_{w(m_{j_1}),j_2}(s, o_{j_2})$, $\alpha_{w(m_{j_1})+w(m_{j_2}),j_3}(s, o_{j_3})$, $\ldots$, and finally $\alpha_{w(m_{j_1})+w(m_{j_2})+\ldots+w(m_{j_{l-1}}),j_l}(s, o_{j_l})$ one by one. According to the execution, the type of s changes from l_0^s to $l_{w(m_{j_1})}^s$, $l_{w(m_{j_1})+w(m_{j_2})}^s$, $\ldots$, $l_{w(m_{j_1})+w(m_{j_2})+\ldots+w(m_{j_l})}^s = l_N^s$ in turn. Finally, for subject s, we can invoke command $\alpha_{N,end}(s)$, and s acquires the privilege r. If the subset sum problem has no solution, the type of s can never be l_N^s and r is not granted to s.

On the other hand, suppose that s can possess the privilege r in $\mathcal{P}$. Namely, for s, $o_{j_1}, o_{j_2}, \ldots, o_{j_l}$, we can run commands $\alpha_{a_0,j_1}(s, o_{j_1})$, $\alpha_{a_1,j_2}(s, o_{j_2})$, $\ldots$, $\alpha_{a_{l-1},j_l}(s, o_{j_l})$ in this order and the type of s is changed into $l_{a_l}^s = l_N^s$. Finally we can execute $\alpha_{N,end}(s)$ and s gets r. Note that $0 = a_0 < a_1 < \ldots < a_l = N$ holds.

At this time, let us assume that $\alpha_{0,i}$ $(1 \leq i \leq n)$ takes the following form:

command $\alpha_{0,i}(x_1 : l_0^s, x_2 : l_i^o)$
    change type of subject x_1 **to** $l_{z_i}^s$
    change type of object x_2 **to** l_{end}^o
end.

Thus we have z_1, z_2, ..., z_n and for every i ($1 \le i \le n$), we set $w(m_i)$ to z_i. Consequently, we have $M = \{m_1, m_2, ..., m_n\}$, $w(m_1)$, $w(m_2)$, ..., $w(m_n)$.

Now, by the authorization scheme of $\mathcal{P}$, we see that for every b ($1 \le b \le l$), $a_b - a_{b-1} = w(m_{j_b})$ holds and by adding each side of these equations we obtain:

$$N = w(m_{j_1}) + w(m_{j_2}) + \ldots + w(m_{j_l}).$$

Then $M' = \{m_{j_1}, m_{j_2}, \ldots, m_{j_l}\}$ is exactly a solution of the subset sum problem. $\square$

4   Discussion

The reason for the decidability of Theorem 2 can be informally summarized as follows: recall that the TR graphs have no cycle that contains parent types with respect to **create** in creating commands in the theorem. So if the current type of o is a parent type with respect to **create** in α, the execution of creating command α must change the type of every actual parameter object o of α into a type that o has never experienced. To put it in another way, creating commands make 'irreversible' changes on types of parent objects. It is this irreversibility in creating objects that makes the safety analysis decidable; The type change in creating objects is irreversible, so that the number of times such type changes occur is finite since the total number of types is finite by assumption. In consequence, the number of objects is finite (Lemma 2) and the safety problem becomes decidable.

In non-monotonic systems in Theorem 2, it is possible that the systems reach a state where we can no longer create new objects. However, generally speaking, it is a good practice to reevaluate security policies continuously [1], so the state could be a possible candidate point of time for such reevaluation.

Although the number of objects in the systems of Theorem 2 is finite, because the TR graphs can have cycles as long as the cycles do not contain parent types with respect to **create** in creating commands, it is possible to execute commands infinite times in such systems. In that case, the lifetimes of the systems are infinite.

Finally, it should be noted again that the safety problem is generally undecidable and most of decidable safety cases in previous work are for monotonic systems. On the other hand, the decidable cases in Theorem 2 and in Theorem 3 are for non-monotonic systems and fall outside the known decidable ones. Especially, we have shown that the safety problem in Theorem 3 belongs to a well-known complexity class, namely, NP-hard. However, in practice safety analysis is intractable unless it has polynomial time complexity. So further research is needed for non-monotonic systems where the safety analysis is decidable in polynomial time.

5   Conclusion

In this paper, we have proposed the Dynamic-Typed Access Matrix (DTAM) Model, which extends TAM model by allowing the type of an object to change dynamically. DTAM model has an advantage that it can describe non-monotonic protection systems where the safety problem is decidable. In order to show this, first we have introduced a type relationship (TR) graph, with which we express both parent-child and transition relationships among types. Next we have shown that the safety problem becomes decidable in a non-monotonic system, provided that some restrictions are imposed on it. Moreover, we have shown that the safety problem becomes NP-hard when no new entities are permitted to be created. The decidable safety cases discussed in this paper fall outside the known decidable ones in previous work.

In subsequent research, we will go on investigating other non-monotonic systems where the safety analysis is decidable, especially, in polynomial time.

Acknowledgments. The author would like to thank the anonymous referees for valuable and helpful comments on this paper.

References

1. D. Bailey. A philosophy of security management. In M. D. Abrams, S. Jajodia, and H. J. Podell, editors, *Information Security: An Integrated Collection of Essays*, pages 98–110. IEEE Computer Society Press, 1995.
2. S. N. Foley, L. Gong, and X. Qian. A security model of dynamic labeling providing a tiered approach to verification. In *Proceedings of the IEEE Symposium on Security and Privacy*, pages 142–153, 1996.
3. M. R. Garey and D. S. Johnson. *Computers and Intractability – A Guide to the Theory of NP-completeness.* W. H. Freeman and Co., 1979.
4. M. A. Harrison, W. L. Ruzzo, and J. D. Ullman. Protection in operating systems. *Commun. ACM*, 19(8):461–471, Aug. 1976.
5. C. Meadows. Policies for dynamic upgrading. In S. Jajodia and C. E. Landwehr, editors, *Database Security, IV: Status and Prospects*, pages 241–250. Elsevier Science Publishers B. V (North-Holland), 1991.
6. R. S. Sandhu. The typed access matrix model. In *Proceedings of the IEEE Symposium on Security and Privacy*, pages 122–136, May 1992.
7. R. S. Sandhu. Undecidability of the safety problem for the schematic protection model with cyclic creates. *J. Comput. Syst. Sci.*, 44(1):141–159, Feb. 1992.

A Formal Model for Role-Based Access Control Using Graph Transformation *

Manuel Koch, Luigi V. Mancini, and Francesco Parisi-Presicce

Dip. Scienze dell'Informazione, Universitá degli Studi di Roma *La Sapienza*
Via Salaria 113, 00198 Roma, Italy, {carr,lv.mancini,parisi}@dsi.uniroma1.it

Abstract. Role-Based Access Control (RBAC) is supported directly or in a closely related form, by a number of products. This paper presents a formalization of RBAC using graph transformations which is a graphical specification technique based on a generalization to nonlinear structures of classical string grammars. The proposed formalization provides an intuitive description for the manipulation of graph structures as they occur in information systems access control, a specification of static and dynamic consistency conditions on graphs and graph trasformations, a uniform treatment of user roles and administrative roles, and a detailed analysis of the decentralization of administrative roles. Moreover, the properties of a given RBAC specification can be verified by employing one of the graph transformation tools available.

1 Introduction

The activities within a computer system can be viewed as a sequence of operations on objects. One of the primary purposes of security mechanisms is *access control* (AC) which consists of determining and enforcing which active entities, e.g processes, can have access to which objects and in which access mode.

This paper focuses on Role-Based Access Control (RBAC), an AC mechanism described in [SBM99]. It appears that RBAC tries to match the need of many organizations to base AC decisions on the roles assigned to users as part of the organization. In this context RBAC facilitates the administration of AC decisions while making the process less error-prone. A formal analysis of RBAC would be useful for the following reasons:

1. prove the properties of a given RBAC specification: RBAC consists of a family of conceptual models and the most advanced ones include role hierarchies, constraints, and decentralized administration of roles; this complexity requires a formal setting to ensure that a RBAC specification meets basic correctness properties of the system.

2. compare different AC models: for example, to better meet the needs of a specific application one could compare the pros and cons of discretionary AC, mandatory AC and RBAC;

---

* partially supported by the EC under TMR Network GETGRATS,Esprit WG APP-LIGRAPH, and by the Italian MURST.

F. Cuppens et al. (Eds.): ESORICS 2000, LNCS 1895, pp. 122–139, 2000.
© Springer-Verlag Berlin Heidelberg 2000

3. predict the system behavior in combining different AC policies: for example, to support *role transition*, that is the means for moving towards RBAC in coexistence with previous models of AC.

This paper presents a formalization of RBAC using graph transformations which is a graphical specification technique based on a generalization of classical string grammars [Roz97] to nonlinear structures. The advantages of using the graph transformation formalism are: an intuitive visual description of the manipulation of graph structures as they occur in the AC; an expressive specification language, which allows, for example, the detailed specification of various schema for decentralizing administrative roles; a specification of static and dynamic consistency conditions on graphs and graph transformations; a uniform treatment of user roles and administrative roles; an executable specification that exploits existing tools [EEKR99] to verify the properties of a given graph-based RBAC description.

The issues addressed in this paper include: the presentation of a formal framework for RBAC which allows the specification and verification of consistency requirements; the discussion of some open problems, such as the revocation cascade of users membership when administrative roles are decentralized, and a comparison of several possible solutions. In particular, this paper focuses on the issue of (decentralized) administration of user/role assignment and revocation in the RBAC model; the administration of permission/role assignment and revocation, discussed in [NO99] for the case of one administrator, is not explicitly treated here, but can be described in a similar way. The comparison of different AC policies within the graph grammar formalism and the analysis of the system behavior in combining different AC policies are the subject of another paper [KMPP00].

The rest of this paper is organized as follows. Section 2 overviews the basic notions of graph transformations. Section 3 describes the graph based modeling of RBAC. Section 4 shows how to prove the graph based correctness of a RBAC specification and briefly discusses the use of constraints. In section 5, we show that the formalism is sufficiently expressive to describe possible solutions to some nontrivial open problems mentioned in [San98], such as the decentralized administration of roles. To our knowledge, this was an open issue, now solved here at the specification level with a proposal of different solutions, compared in section 6. Section 7 contains some concluding remarks and additional comparison with existing work.

2   Graph Transformation

A graph consists of a set of nodes and a set of edges. Edges are directed, i.e. they run from a node (the *source* of the edge) to a node (the *target* of the edge). Each node and each edge has a *type*. Several nodes and edges of the same type may occur in one graph. Figure 1 depicts a graph with four node types and only one edge type. The node types are u, s, r and ar and will be used to describe the role-based access control model introduced later on. Nodes of type

u represent users, nodes of type r are roles, nodes of type ar are administrative roles and nodes of type s model sessions. A detailed explanation of the graph model follows in Sec. 3. This section focuses on the main components of graph transformation, which are a *transformation rule* and a *transformation step*. We introduce the concepts in this section only informally. A detailed (also formal) introduction can be found in the handbook to graph transformation [Roz97]. A

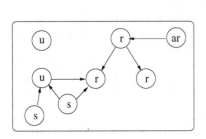

Fig. 1. *A RBAC state graph.*

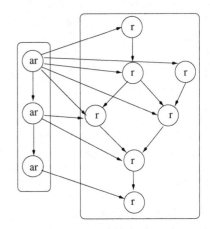

Fig. 2. *Administrative role hierarchy graph (left) and role hierarchy graph (right).*

graph represents a state of a system, for example a security system based on roles as shown in Fig. 1. State changes are specified by graph transformation rules, called just *rules* in the following. A rule is formally given by a *graph morphism* $r : L \to R$, where both L and R are graphs, called *left-hand side* and *right-hand side*, respectively. A graph morphism consists of an injective partial mapping r_n between the sets of nodes and an injective partial mapping r_e between the sets of edges of L and R. The mappings must be compatible with the graph structure and the types. Compatible with the graph structure means that whenever the mapping for edges is defined for an edge e, the mapping for nodes is defined for the source s and the target t node of the edge e and $r_n(s)$ and $r_n(t)$ are the source and target nodes of the edge $r_e(e)$ in the right-hand side. Compatible with the type means that nodes and edges are mapped only to nodes and edges of the same type. If the mappings are total, we call the graph morphism *total*. The graph L describes which objects a graph G must contain for the rule $r : L \to R$ to be applicable to G. Nodes and edges of L for which the partial mappings are undefined are deleted by the rule. Nodes and edges of L for which the partial mappings are defined are preserved and have an image in R. Nodes and edges of R without a preimage in L are newly created.

The complete set of rules for the RBAC model is given in Section 3 and 5. We choose now two of them to explain the application of rules. The first rule is given by **add to role** in Fig. 4. The intended meaning of this rule is to make a user a member of a role. The membership of a user to a role is modeled by an edge, from the u to the r node, that this rule must create. The assignment of a user to a role takes place by an administrative role that is responsible for the role. In our graph model, responsibility is indicated by an edge from the ar to the r node. So, the left-hand side L consists of one node of type ar, one of type r and one of type u, and an edge between the ar node and the r node to show the responsibility. The dashed edge between the u and the r node represents a *negative application condition*. A negative application condition represents a structure that, as a whole, must not occur in G for the application of the rule. For the rule **add to role**, a membership edge between the u and r nodes must not exist in G before the rule application. If the unwanted structure occurs, then the negative application condition is not satisfied. Note that the presence of a part only of the unwanted structure is acceptable: for example in the rule **veto deletion** in Fig. 9, there could be a senior role, provided that it is not assigned to the user.

Whereas **add to role** is a preserving rule (the graph morphism for the rule is total, so that the rule does not delete anything), the rule **remove user** (see Fig. 4) removes a user from the system. Since we do not want to have active sessions that do not belong to any user, also all the sessions of the deleted user must be closed. Therefore, the left-hand side of **remove user** consists of a user node u connected to a session node s. The double circle around the s node (these nodes are called *set nodes*) specifies that the rule has to be applied to *all* session nodes s connected to the user; this means, in particular, that the rule can be applied also to users without active sessions. The right-hand side of the rule is empty to specify the deletion of the user with all her/his sessions.

The application of a rule $r : L \to R$ to a graph G takes place in four steps:
1. Find the left-hand side L as a subgraph in G. The subgraph is denoted by $L(G)$.
2. If there is a negative application condition that is not satisfied (that is, L(G) can be extended in G to an unwanted structure) then stop.
3. Remove all nodes and edges from $L(G)$ that are not present in R.
4. Add all nodes and edges in R that are not present in L. The nodes occuring both in L and in R are used to connect the new parts to the old ones.

The left-hand side L of the rule **add to role** occurs several times in the graph of Fig. 1. One possible matching is shown in Fig. 3 by the gray node pattern. For simplicity, labels on nodes have been omitted from graph and rules in the example and only their types are shown. In concrete graphs (like the one in Fig. 6), nodes have unique labels (e.g., specific names for users and roles) and there is no ambiguity on the application of a rule to a graph, since matching nodes have the same labels. Next, we have to check the negative application condition of the rule that requires that there is no edge between the u and the r node. Since the edge does not exist for the given matching, the rule is applied. It deletes nothing and inserts the edge between the nodes determined by the match of L. The transformed graph contains a new edge indicating that the gray user is a member of the gray role.

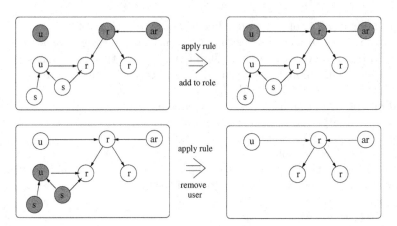

Fig. 3. *Application of rule* `add to role` *(top) and rule* `remove user` *(bottom).*

We now apply the rule `remove user` to this new graph. We can apply it to the upper or to the lower user node, and in Fig. 3 the lower node is chosen (again node labels can be used to avoid ambiguity). Since this user has two active sessions, they also have to be removed. The double circle in the rule *remove user* requires that we match all the sessions of the user, and it is not enough to match only one session or none at all. Note that set nodes can be given a variable label that can match any label in a concrete graph [PEM87]. There is no negative application condition to check. We delete the whole gray part, since a node or an edge does not exist in the right-hand side of `remove user`. Notice that the deletion of the right session node leaves a dangling edge, i.e., an edge without a source node. The same is true for the edge between the gray user and the connected role node. Since dangling edges are not allowed by the definition of graphs, dangling edges are automatically deleted in the graph transformation semantics as well.

In Section 3 the concept of a *path* is used. A path in a graph is a sequence of edges, where the target node of each edge in the sequence coincides with the source node of its successor edge in the sequence. We denote paths between two nodes by an edge equipped by ∗ for paths of arbitrary length including length 0 or a + for paths that have at least length 1 (see for example the rules in Fig. 4).

Graph transformations are supported by several tools described in [EEKR99]. They provide mainly graphical editors to insert/draw the graphs, to specify rules with negative application conditions and a graph transformation machine to apply rules.

3   Role-Based Access Control

This section concerns with the specification of the **ARBAC97** model introduced by Sandhu et al in [SBM99] using graph transformations. The graph model includes administrative roles as well as inheritance of roles. In the **ARBAC97** model, the (administrative) role hierarchy is given by a partial order over (administrative) roles. In Figure 2 an example of an administrative role hierarchy (on the left-hand side) and a role hierarchy (on the right-hand side) is shown, where the hierarchies are given by graphs. Roles as well as administrative roles are given by nodes of type r and ar, respectively, and edges between roles show the inheritance relation. Graphs generalize the notion of a partial order, and by defining specific rules one could restrict the graph structure to any role hierarchy. Additionally, Figure 2 shows edges between administrative roles and user roles, representing the authorization to modify the user role by the administrative role. The set of roles reachable by such edges from an administrative role is the *range* of the administrative role. For instance, the range of the upper administrative role is given by the upper five roles, whereas the lower administrator has the authorization only for the lowest role. The use of a set of roles to represent a range differs from the approach of [SBM99], where the range is represented by an interval over the partial order, and ranges of junior administrators are required to be subranges of the senior administrator. The approach proposed there is not particularly suited to manage dynamic changes in administrator's ranges. We discuss these problems and others in a later section in more detail. Our approach is more general since the concept of an interval can be seen as a particular assignment of administrative roles to user roles. Moreover, our approach allows the modelling of administrators with disjoint role responsibility.

A user can be a member of a role and authorized for a role: a user is authorized for a role, if the role is inherited from a role to which the user is assigned. A user can establish a session during which the user activates a subset of roles of which she/he is a member. Note that the concept of sessions corresponds to the notion of *subjects* in the classical AC terminology. Role management, that is the creation and deletion of roles as well as assignment and revocation of users and permissions to roles, is the responsibility of *administrative roles*. The basic operations of the RBAC model are *add user, remove user, add assignment, remove assignment, add inheritance, remove inheritance, add role, remove role, add session, remove session, activate role* and *deactivate role*. All these operations are now modeled by graph transformation rules (see Fig. 4). The resulting graph specification uses a weak revocation, meaning that the deletion of a user from a role is not propagated to roles higher in the hierarchy; this corresponds to the URA97 model in [San98].

add user and **remove user**: The rule **add user** has an empty left-hand side, since users can be created at any time. The result of the rule is a new user represented by a node of type u. The rule **remove user** removes a user by deleting the corresponding user node u. To ensure that there are no active sessions of this user after the deletion of the user, all his/her sessions are deleted as well. This is indicated by the double circled session node in the left-hand side of rule **remove user**. The interpretation is that *all* sessions connected to the user are deleted. The deletion of the session implies the deletion of all the connections to roles that the session has, this is guaranteed by the graph trasformation approach chosen. The roles themselves remain.

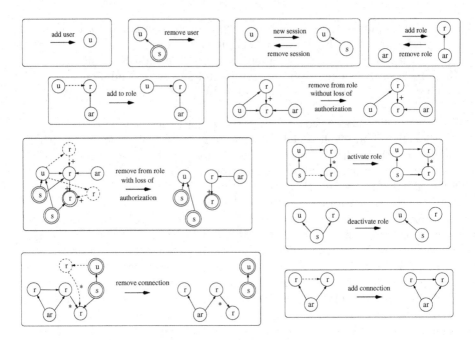

Fig. 4. *Graph rules for the RBAC Model.*

add session and **remove session**: A session is graphically presented by a node of type s. It has always a connection to one user. The rules for the creation and deletion of sessions are **new session** and **remove session**. A session node s is immediately connected by an edge to the user who is using s. A session can be deleted at any time regardless of the presence of active roles of the session. The session is deleted by removing the session node. This implies that all session-to-role edges are deleted as well, automatically.

add role and **remove role**: The creation of roles is modeled by the rule **add role**. Roles are added and removed by administrative roles. The new role becomes an element of the administrator's range indicated by the edge shown in the rule. The deletion of a role is only possible by an administrative role responsible for that role. Then, the r node and the connecting edge are removed.

add assignment and **remove assignment**: The assignment of users to roles is modeled by the rule **add to role**. To ensure that only an administrator responsible for the role assigns the user, an ar node connected to the r node is required. An administrator assigns a user to a role by connecting the user node and the role node by an edge, called *assignment edge*. Then, the user becomes a member of this role. This is allowed if and only if the user is not already a member of role r, specified by the negative application condition indicated by the dashed assignment edge. The deletion of the assignment edge does not necessarily remove the authorization of the user u for the role r. In particular, if there is an assignment edge to a higher role which is inherited by r, then u remains authorized for r. This case is modeled by the graph rule **remove from**

`role without loss of authorization`. The rule requires that u is assigned to a role higher in the hierarchy. The $+$ at the edge between the two roles indicates a non empty path in the role hierarchy. It ensures that the two role nodes are different. In this case, the assignment edge can be simply deleted from the lower role. No other actions are necessary since the user is still authorized for it. On the contrary, if the higher role does not exist, the user looses the authorization for the role r. This implies that r must leave all sessions of the user. Moreover, all roles that are transitively authorized by the deleted assignment have to be deactivated from all the user sessions unless user u gets the authorization from another role of which u is a member. The left-hand side of the rule `remove from role with loss of authorization` requires that the user not be a member of a higher role in the hierarchy, as specified by the negative application condition indicated by the dashed upper role. In addition, all roles that inherit the role where the assignment edge is removed (indicated by the roles reachable by a $+$ path) and that are not authorized by other roles (indicated by the dashed lower role) have to be removed from the sessions of the user as well.

activate role and **deactivate role**: A user can activate any role r for which she/he is authorized. A user is authorized for r, if there is a path starting with an assignment edge and ending in r. The corresponding graph rule is `activate role`. An edge between the session node and the role node shows that the role is active in the session. This edge is created by the user of the session. The star $*$ at the edge between the roles indicate a (possibly empty) path through the role hierarchy. An empty path indicates that a user can also activate a role to which she/he is directly assigned. Role r can only join a session if r is not already a member of that session, as indicated by the dashed edge between the session node and the role node. The deactivation of a role from a session is specified by deleting the edge between the session and the role node.

add inheritance and **remove inheritance**: if the administrative role is authorized for two roles r and r', then an administrative role can establish a new inheritance relation between them. The inheritance relation is indicated by an edge between the two roles. The rule `add connection` adds this edge if it does not exist already. The deletion of an inheritance relation may cause a user to loose the authorization for some of his inheriting roles. In particular, a user looses these autorizations if and only if there are no other paths from that user to the role r'. In this case, the roles have to be deactivated from the sessions. The corresponding rule `remove connection` removes edge (r,r') and deactivates the roles of all sessions of all users that do not have the authorization for this role through another path of the role hierarchy (a negative application condition indicated by the dashed objects). Note that an administrator can only add roles within her/his range because a newly created role must be connected to roles for which the administrator is already responsible (see the rule `add connection`).

4   Graph-Based Correctness of RBAC

We now show how the graphical formalism can be used to prove the correctness of a RBAC specification. We clarify the graphical concepts with a running example taken from [GB98]. There, a set of properties is given that defines the consistency requirement for a RBAC database. A state of the RBAC database having these properties is consistent. One property out of this set is

(1) $\forall u \in USERS, \forall r_1, r_2 \in ROLES, r_1, r_2 \in active\_roles(u) \Rightarrow (r_1, r_2) \notin dsd.$

The *dynamic separation of duties* (*dsd*) is a relation on roles. Roles related by a *dsd* relation must not be active in the same session of a user at the same time.

In [GB98], the semantics of the basic operations of the RBAC model is specified using both set theory and additional logical conditions. It is also shown that a given RBAC specification is correct in the following sense: if the RBAC database is in a consistent state, then the database remains in a consistent state after the operation is performed. The specification of the *activate roles* operation in [GB98] (where it is called *addActiveRoles*) is reported below. Note that to prevent the operation *activate roles* from violating the property (1) an additional logical condition must be used.

addActiveRoles
Arguments:
   user, roleset
Semantics:
   $active\_roles' = (active\_roles \backslash$
   $\{user \mapsto active\_roles(user)\}) \cup$
   $\{user \mapsto active\_roles(user) \cup roleset\}$
Conditions:
   $user \in USERS$
   $roleset \subseteq authorized\_roles(user)$
   $\forall r_1, r_2 \in roleset \cup active\_roles(user).(r_1, r_2) \notin dsd$

Hence in [GB98], the designer has to perform three steps: 1. define the consistency properties on the entire system, 2. derive from step 1 the conditions for each operation, and 3. prove that the execution of each operation, satisfying the condition in step 2, preserves the consistency properties defined in step 1. In contrast, in our approach the designer has to perform step 1 only, that is, the definition of the consistency properties of the system. The derivation in step 2 of the conditions for each operation from the consistency properties can be performed automatically following a theoretical construction proposed in [HW95]. The result of such an automatic construction is a set of graph rules which is *guaranteed* to satisfy the given consistency properties and therefore the complex proofs of step 3 are not needed anymore. Our approach also presents some advantages when the consistency properties must be modified in a system already specified. In such a case the designer can define a new consistency property and can use the automatic construction to change the existing rules for each operation to satisfy the new consistency properties. In [GB98], such an incremental modification requires a human intervention in all three steps described above.

In the following, we explain the automatic construction of the condition of an operation to guarantee the consistency properties, by discussing as an example the activate role operation. Consistency properties are specified by *graphical constraints*. A graphical constraint is a graph that depicts a forbidden or a required structure. A graph is *consistent* w.r.t. a graphical constraint that forbids (requires) a structure, if this structure does not occur (does occur) in the graph. The property (1) is specified by the graphical constraint in Fig. 5. The graphical constraint shows the structure that must not occur.

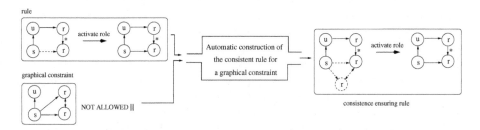

Fig. 5. *Automatic construction of a consistent rule from a graphical constraint.*

The double-headed edge between two roles specifies that the two roles are in the *dsd*-relation. On the left-hand side of the figure, rule *activate roles* from Fig. 4 is shown. This rule, if applied without modification, could produce an inconsistent state by creating an edge between a session node and a role which is in *dsd*-relation to another role of the session. Therefore, this rule has to be completed by adding a negative application condition which prevents the activation of incompatible roles. The negative application condition can be constructed automatically during the design phase. Figure 5 shows the overall scheme for this construction. We call the modified rule *consistent* w.r.t. the graphical constraint in the sense of the following theorem:

Theorem: Given a rule r, a graphical constraint gc, a graph G consistent w.r.t. gc, and the rule $r(gc)$ modified as above, the graph H resulting from an application of $r(gc)$ to G is consistent w.r.t. gc.

In the example in Fig. 5, the automatic construction adds a negative application condition to the rule. This condition forbids the rule application if an edge exists between the session node and an active role (modeled by the dashed role and the edge connected to the session node) in *dsd*-relation with the role that shall be activated. This rule can never create a state graph that violates the graphical constraint for the *dsd*-relation and therefore an "a posteriori check" is not needed. In a similar way, all the properties defined in [GB98] can be modeled by graphical constraints and for each of them a consistent rule can automatically be derived.

5   Decentralized Administration of Roles

There are some open problems in the decentralized administration of roles of the RBAC model stemming from the fact that the responsibility of a range of roles is not sufficient to guarantee the desired effect of an action performed inside the range by the administrative role for that range. To illustrate the problems, consider the concrete role hierarchy in Fig. 6 in the following discussion.

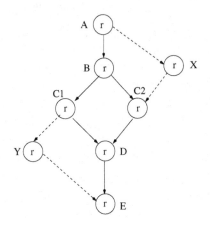

Fig. 6. *Problems of the RBAC model.*

Deletion of a user from a role: if a user is a member of roles $C1$ and B, by inheritance, the user is authorized for roles $B, C1, C2, D, Y$ and E. An administrative role ar with range $C1, D$ can remove the user from role $C1$. However, since the user is still a member of B, by inheritance he still has the permission of $C1$. Since the role B is not in the range of the administrator ar, he cannot remove the membership of the user from role B. The problem of this kind of user assignment revocation is called *weak revocation* [San98]. The case where the user must loose the authorization to the role if the assignment edge is deleted (*strong revocation*) may be more desirable but it requires a greater administrative effort.

Deletion of a permission from a role: This problem is dual to the previous one. A revocation of a permission from a senior role has no effect on the senior if a junior role still has this permission.

Deletion of roles: In the RBAC model, the range for an administrator is given by an interval over the partial order. Deleting the boundaries of the interval destroys the range definition, therefore only roles inside the interval can be deleted.

Special hierarchy graphs: If a special structure for the hierarchy graph for (administrative) roles is required, changes to the graph may destroy it. For example, if we require a partial order, an edge from E to A in Fig. 6 creates a cycle. Similarly if each range must have unique senior and junior roles (as in Fig. 6, B is the unique senior and D is the unique junior of the diamond range), the addition of the node X and an edge from X to $C2$ violates the constraint of the unique senior. The insertion of an edge (from $C2$ to $C1$) may also create a dependency between previously unrelated roles (X and Y), and therefore a local change by an administrator may have impact outside his/her range.

We propose now three models using graph transformation that tackle the first three problems. We introduce here only the rules for the user assignment; the rules for the assignment of permissions are similar. We will discuss in Sec. 6 how to deal with the last problem exploiting graph transformation concepts.

5.1 Static Single Assignment

The idea is to have at most one assignment per user, i.e. a user can be in at most one role. The assignment is static in the sense that it can only be changed by deleting it and inserting a new one. The deletion of the assignment implies the loss of the authorization for roles that was given by the assignment edge. The graph rules for the static single assignment are shown in Fig. 7. A user can be assigned to a role if he is not yet a member of a role. Membership is indicated by the color of the u node. A white u node indicates that the user is not yet in a role; a black one indicates that he is a member of a role. The rule **add to role** in Fig.7 changes the white user node to a black one when it sets the assignment. The removal of the assignment is simpler than in the model of Fig. 4, since the authorization of roles for this user is known, namely all roles reachable from the unique assignment edge. The rule **remove from role** removes the assignment edge and deactivates all sessions of the user. All sessions are deactivated since all activated roles for a session are authorized by the one assignment edge. There cannot be roles activated that are not authorized by this assignment. The user node is changed to white again. Moreover, the case where

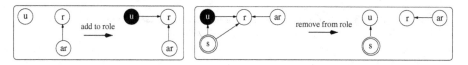

Fig. 7. *Graph rules for static single assignment.*

the removal of the assignment does not have an impact on the authorization is not possible in this model. Therefore, we need no rule corresponding to **remove from role without loss of authorization**. All other rules of the model in Fig. 4 remain unchanged.

This idea could be generalized to more than one "color". The model above uses one "color", namely black. The black color is valid for all roles in the hierarchy graph, i.e. one user can take the black "hat" to be assigned to an arbitrary role in the hierarchy graph. If there are several disjoint hierarchy graphs, each of them has a unique color and we could allow many assignments provided that there is only one assignment for each color. Problems occur in this model, if we want to connect two disjoint hierarchy graphs. Then, the two colors have to be "melt" into one color and assignments may have to be removed.

5.2   Dynamic Single Assignment

The approach of a dynamic single assignment follows the idea of one assignment per user. The rule `add to role` for adding a user to a role is equal to the corresponding rule in the static single assignment model. The difference of this model is that the assignment edge is not static anymore, but it can move through the role hierarchy graph. Only for the lowest role in the role hierarchy it is possible to delete the assignment, since the assignment cannot be moved down anymore. Whenever an administrator wants to assign the user to a role that is higher in the role hierarchy than the current assigned role, the assignment is simply moved up in the hierarchy. The authorization of roles for the user is only enhanced and no changes in the sessions are necessary as modeled by rule `move up`. When an administrator wants to remove a user from a role, the assignment is not deleted, but it is moved down in the role hierarchy with the rule `move down` and only this role has to be deactivated from all the sessions of the user. For the lower role it can again be decided whether the assignment remains or is moved down again. If a user was assigned to a role where there is no inheritance edge to another role, the assignment is deleted and the user is changed to a white node again. All sessions of the user can be deleted as well, since the user has no authorization for any role. This is done by rule `remove role`.

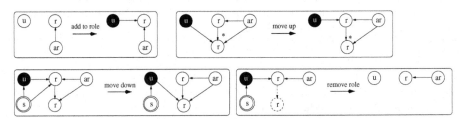

Fig. 8. *Graph rules for dynamic single assignment.*

5.3   (Strong) Multiple Assignment

The idea is to allow an arbitrary number of assignments and to defer the decision on the deletion of an assignment edge to a higher level in the role hierarchy. Any administrator can stop the propagation if she/he wants to keep the assignment and this decision is immediately propagated down. The actual deletion of the assignment can take place only at the top of the role hierarchy: since there is no higher role that may want to keep the assignment, the decision on the deletion can be made. Since we do not require any structure for the hierarchy graph of roles, there can be multiple branches. This means that one branch may decide to delete the role, while another one decides to keep the user in the role. In this case, the assignments of the branch which decided deletion are removed, since the user is not needed in this branch anymore, while at the intersection point the decision to keep the assignment is propagated down. The graph rules for this model are shown in Figure 9.

If an administrator wants to remove an assignment of a user to a role, she/he makes this visible to the administrators of higher roles by a special label. The graph rule `remove from role` inserts the label d on the edge for the assignment. This label can be seen from other administrators. By means of the rule `propagate up` the label d is moved up to the next higher role of which the user is a member. The rule ensures, by the negative application condition, that the label is propagated to the immediately higher role assigned to the user (no roles are skipped). This ensures that all memberships of the user in higher roles are checked. Whenever the label is set on the assignment edge between a user and a role, a responsible administrator can decide if the user shall be removed from the role or kept. The graph rule `veto no deletion` is applied, if the administrator wants to keep the assignment. The label is changed from d to $d-$ and the propagation of the label d to higher roles is stopped (rule `propagate up` is not applicable anymore). If the administrator wants to delete the assignment he propagates the label d by means of rule `propagate up` to a higher role. If the role is the highest role (w.r.t. a branch of the hierarchy) the up-propagation rule is not applicable anymore and the corresponding administrator can decide (beside no deletion, which is possible always) to delete the assignment. This is done by the graph rule `veto deletion` that changes the label d to $d+$. Its negative application condition ensures that the role is the highest role in the hierarchy w.r.t. one branch. After the decision, the label $d-$ or the label $d+$ is propagated down. The rule `propagate veto` $d-$ propagates the label $d-$ and the negative application conditions guarantees again that this propagation does not forget any assignment. The graph rule `propagate veto d+` is more complex, since the label $d+$ cannot be simply propagated down, because there may exist several branches and in some of them the label $d-$ is propagated down, in other ones the label $d+$ is. Since in this model keeping the assignment is stronger than removing the assignment, at an intersection point of two (or more) branches it must be decided which label is propagated further. Only if all the branches want to propagate the label $d+$, $d+$ is propagated further. If only one branch wants to propagate $d-$, $d-$ is propagated further. This condition is checked in the negative application condition of rule `propagate veto` $d+$. Only if there is no higher role with a $d-$ or a d label at an assignment, the $d+$ label is propagated by rule `propagate veto` $d+$. The step-wise propagation guarantees the second negative application condition. If the labels $d-$ and $d+$ are present, the graph rules `delete` and `no delete` can be applied. The rule `delete` is applicable if there is a label $d+$ and it removes the assignment edge, also deactivating the role from all the sessions of the user. This rule is also applied to branches of the hierarchy that have decided for deletion, even if the label $d+$ was not propagated completely down since other branches had decided to keep the assignment. When a label $d-$ is encountered, indicating that the assignment shall be kept, the label is simply deleted but the assignment remains.

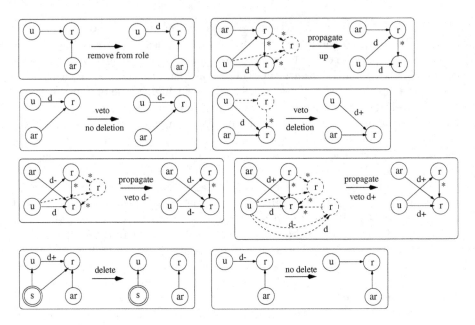

Fig. 9. *Graph rules for multiple assignment.*

6   Comparison of Proposals for Decentralized RBAC

The RBAC model has been described with the rules in Fig. 4 of Section 3 already in a setting that allows multiple administrators (explicit nodes of type ar). In the previous section, we have presented three graph specifications of the user-role assignment and deletion in the case of decentralized administration of roles. We discuss now how the four proposed specifications solve the issues of the RBAC model mentioned at the beginning of the previous section.

Deletion of a user from a role: The graph model in Fig. 4 can be seen as a *weak multiple assignment* model, because it models weak revocation and allows many assignments for a user. The three models proposed in Section 5 specify a strong revocation. Different assumptions are made to simplify the administrative effort. Adding an assignment is easy in all models. In the case of many assignments, no restrictions are needed for creation. In the case of a single assignment, creation is easy, since one has to check only, whether the user is already a member of a role or not. The main differences occur in the deletion of assignments. The single assignment models provide an easy deletion, since there is only one assignment and all authorization relations for the user are known. In the static case, the assignment is simply deleted. The many assignment models are more complex w.r.t. deletion of assignments, since the authorization relations for a user are not known. A more complex procedure is necessary to decide if the deletion of an assignment requires the deletion of other assignments or not. Altogether, the multiple assignment models are more flexible, but have a greater administrative effort. The following table summarizes the results.

policy	add assignment	remove assignment	comment
static single	easy	very easy	unflexible, restricted
dynamic single	easy	easy	more flexible
weak multiple	easy	not easy	more flexible but weak revocation
strong multiple	easy	complex	flexible and veto

Deletion of a permission from a role: This problem can be solved in a manner similar to the deletion of user from a role, by replacing user assignment with permission assignment.

Deletion of roles: This problem is solved by modeling the range of an administrator by a set of edges pointing to the roles the administrator is responsible for. By replacing the interval definition of a range in [SBM99] by a set definition, the deletion of a boundary role does not destroy the range of an administrator.

Comparing our model with [NO99], the algorithms presented there deal with the centralized administration of privileges (permissions) and roles. By explicitly introducing permission nodes, we could specify their model. For example, the deletion of a role while retaining its privileges could require the redirection of the edges to its permission nodes to other role nodes with a set of rules mimicking their algorithms.

Special hierarchy graphs: Our model does not require any structure for the hierarchy graph for (administrative) roles. Therefore, there are no special rules for maintaining a graph structure. If a special graph structure is required, the rules have to be constructed in such a way that they do not destroy the structure. Since these rules depend on the structure required, no general rules can be given. However, this problem could be solved by considering *graphical constraints* [HW95], which are a graphical means to express constraints like cardinality, mutual exclusion, prerequisite roles etc, and in particular, they can be used to define the desired structure of the hierarchy graphs. Constraints are also an important component of the RBAC model. Different constraints yield different access control models (see [San98,SBM99]). Graphical constraints can be automatically translated into negative application conditions for rules. The rules ensure the consistency w.r.t. the graphical constraint. That means for example, that the rules preserve the required graph structure.

7 Concluding Remarks

We propose a formalization of RBAC using graph transformations which is a graphical specification technique giving an intuitive visual description of the dynamic structures that occur in AC models. The use of graph structures allows a uniform treatment of user roles and administrative roles without the need for a meta-model to describe possible evolutions in the administrator structure. This formalization of the RBAC model can benefit from well-established results in graph transformations systems [Roz97]. Among them, the possibility of studying the sequential independence of rules (i.e. the final state is the same regardless of the order of application of two rules), the parallel application of rules (i.e.

the simultaneous application of two rules to produce an effect not attainable by their separate application), and in general the interference of rules.

Our approach is suitable for the specification and verification of the consistency requirement, as in [GB98], with the added feature of being able to systematically derive the new rules to reflect changes in the consistency conditions due to the evolution of an already designed system. Given a concrete specification (e.g., an assignment of names to roles and users) of a particular role-based system, properties can be verified using tools for graph transformations.

In [NO99], the authors present a specific way of implementing role-role relationships, representing as a graph the inclusion hierarchy generated by (part of) the powerset of the set of privileges. Here graph transformations are used as a general formalism to specify access control policies based on roles. No specific assumptions are made on the (arbitrary) structure of the role graph: if a particular structure is required, the graph rules can be adapted to satisfy the additional requirements. The algorithms there deal with the centralized administration of roles, while we focus on a decentralized administration of roles. By explicitly introducing permission nodes, we could specify their model. For example, the addition of a role node could require that it be explicitly connected to all the nodes representing its permissions (called effective privileges in [NO99]); the connection with other role nodes could be defined by a set of rules mimicking their algorithms, instead of being an arbitrary choice of the administrator as in **add connection** of Fig. 4

We also discuss and compare here several possible solutions to some of the issues left open in [San98]. In particular, we address the revocation cascade of users membership when administrative roles are decentralized, the out-of-range impact of local changes, and the removal of endpoint roles in an administrative range.

The proposed general framework is adequate for (but not restricted to) role-based access control policies. We are developing a methodology to compare different access control models within the graph grammar formalism and to analyse the effect of combining different access control policies [KMPP00]. A tool is under development to assist the systematic modification of rules in a system where the consistency condition may change.

Acknowledgement. Thanks to the anonymous reviewers for their pointed comments and usefull suggestions.

References

[EEKR99]   H. Ehrig, G. Engels, H.-J. Kreowski, and G. Rozenberg, editors. *Handbook of Graph Grammars and Computing by Graph Transformations. Vol. II: Applications, Languages, and Tools.* World Scientific, 1999.

[GB98]   Serban I. Gavrila and John F. Barkley. Formal Specification for Role Based Access Control User/Role and Role/Role Relationship Management. In *Proc. of 3rd ACM Workshop on Role-Based Access Control*, 1998.

[HW95]   Reiko Heckel and Annika Wagner. Ensuring consistency of conditional graph grammars - a constructive approach. In *Proc. of SEGRAGRA '95 Graph Rewriting and Computation*, number 2. Electronic Notes of TCS, 1995. http://www.elsevier.nl/locate/entcs/volume2.html.

[KMPP00] M. Koch, L. V. Mancini, and F. Parisi-Presicce. On the specification and evolution of access control policies. Technical Report SI-2000/05, Dip.Scienze dell'Informazione, Uni. Roma La Sapienza, May 2000.

[NO99]   M. Nyanchama and S.L. Osborne. The Role Graph Model and Conflict of Interest. *ACM Trans. of Info. and System Security*, 2(1):3–33, 1999.

[PEM87]   F. Parisi-Presicce H. Ehrig and U. Montanari. Graph Rewriting with Unification and Composition. In *Proc. 3rd Workshop on Graph Grammars. Lecture Notes in Computer Science 291*, Springer-Verlag, 1987, pp.496-514.

[Roz97]   Grzegorz Rozenberg, editor. *Handbook of Graph Grammars and Computing by Graph Transformations. Vol. I: Foundations*. World Scientific, 1997.

[San98]   Ravi S. Sandhu. Role-Based Access Control. In *Advances in Computers*, volume 46. Academic Press, 1998.

[SBM99]   Ravi Sandhu, Venkata Bhamidipati, and Qamar Munawer. The ARBAC97 model for role-based administration of roles. *ACM Transactions on Information and System Security*, 2(1):105–135, Feb. 1999.

A Formal Semantics for SPKI

Jon Howell[*] and David Kotz

Dartmouth College, Hanover NH 03755, USA
{jonh,dfk}@cs.dartmouth.edu
http://www.cs.dartmouth.edu/

Abstract. We extend the logic and semantics of authorization due to Abadi, Lampson, et al. to support restricted delegation. Our formal model provides a simple interpretation for the variety of constructs in the Simple Public Key Infrastructure (SPKI), and lends intuition about possible extensions. We discuss both extensions that our semantics supports and extensions that it cautions against.

1 Introduction

This paper provides a formal semantics for the Simple Public Key Infrastructure (SPKI), an Internet Experimental Protocol [1]. The current (2.0) version of SPKI is a merger of SPKI 1.0 and the Simple Distributed Security Infrastructure (SDSI) 1.0.

SPKI is an elegant practical system that addresses the problem of ensuring that a user is *authorized* to perform an action, not just the problem of identifying the user. This focus allows for much more flexible sharing of resources through delegation; in contrast, systems based on authentication with a conventional public-key infrastructure (PKI) plus authorization with conventional ACLs limit the available modes of resource sharing. SPKI does incorporate a notion of authentication as well: its linked local namespaces bind keys to names. This notion of authentication is more general than conventional hierarchical PKI naming, allowing it to escape the "trusted-root" problem.

Unfortunately, SPKI is not founded on a formal semantics that can provide intuition for what it does, what it promises, what it assumes, and how it may or may not be safely extended.

Abadi, Lampson, and others defined an authorization system called the Logic of Authentication [2,3]. This system provides delegation without restrictions. A user can encode restrictions by delegating control over "self as *role*" to another user, and adding the principal "self as role" to the ACL of the resource to be shared. The system is based on a formal semantics that explains how delegations interact with various combination operators for principals. Our formalism for SPKI is based on the semantics of the Logic of Authentication, extended to support restricted delegation and SPKI names.

Our formal treatment of SPKI is attractive for two reasons:

---

[*] Supported by the USENIX Association.

F. Cuppens et al. (Eds.): ESORICS 2000, LNCS 1895, pp. 140–158, 2000.
© Springer-Verlag Berlin Heidelberg 2000

First, it supplies intuition for what SPKI operations mean. The proliferation of concrete concepts in SPKI can be understood as applications of just three abstractions: *principal, statement,* and *name.*

Second, the formalism gives us guidance in extending SPKI. We give examples of dangerous extensions that the formalism advises against, and we give examples of extensions that the formalism supports and that we use in our concrete system implementation.

2   Related Work

Abadi provides a semantics for SPKI names [4], but its definition shares a flaw with that used for roles in the original logic [2]. We discuss Abadi's name semantics in Section 5.3.

Halpern and van der Meyden supply an alternate semantics for SPKI names [5], but it only encompasses the containment relation among names, and does not treat names as principals. As a result, it cannot relate names to compound principals nor relate names to other principals that are only connected by a restricted delegation.

Aura supplies a semantics for SPKI restricted delegation [6], but it is unsatisfying in that it essentially says what the reduction procedure says: a delegation is in place if there is a chain of delegation certificates and principals. It does not lend intuition about what the delegations mean. In contrast, our semantics connects restricted delegation to the logic of belief, a formal model that describes what a principal means when it delegates authority.

3   Background: The Original Logic of Authentication

For the reader unfamiliar with modal logic, we recommend the canoncial, concise introduction due to Hughes and Cresswell [7] or the gentler introduction of Fagin et al. [8]. The extended version of this paper [9] includes a brief introduction to each of the above topics, plus an overview of SPKI.

Abadi et al. apply modal logic to the access control problem by representing belief with the **says** operator. For example, if the proposition x means "it is good to read file X," then the statement A **says** x represents a principal A that wishes to read the file. The axiomatization of the Logic of Authentication begins with the standard axioms and rules of modal logic:[1]

> If σ is a tautology of propositional calculus,
>
> then $\vdash \sigma$ (Axiom S1)

---

[1] As is conventional in the modal logic community, the symbol $\supset$ is used for logical implication.

$$\frac{\vdash \sigma \quad \vdash \sigma \supset \tau}{\vdash \tau} \qquad \text{(Rule S2)}$$

$$\vdash A \,\textbf{says}\, (\sigma \supset \tau) \supset (A \,\textbf{says}\, \sigma \supset A \,\textbf{says}\, \tau) \qquad \text{(Axiom S3)}$$

$$\forall A, \; \frac{\vdash \sigma}{\vdash A \,\textbf{says}\, \sigma} \qquad \text{(Rule S4)}$$

Each entry in an object's access-control list (ACL) indicates that some principal establishes ground truth for the object. For example, if A *controls* x appears in the ACL for resource X, then when A **says** x, the server may conclude $\vdash x$: it is indeed good to read the file.

$$A \,controls\, \sigma \equiv ((A \,\textbf{says}\, \sigma) \supset \sigma) \qquad \text{(Definition A2)}$$

Much of the power of the Logic of Authentication derives from its calculus of principals. Two basic operators combine principals. The conjunction principal $A \wedge B$ believes only what *both* A and B believe. The quoting principal $B|A$ believes what B believes A believes. Access control decisions in the calculus focus on determining trust relationships among principals; these relationships are captured by the transitive *speaks-for* relation:

$$\vdash (B \Rightarrow A) \supset ((B \,\textbf{says}\, \sigma) \supset (A \,\textbf{says}\, \sigma)) \qquad \text{(Theorem P8)}$$
$$\vdash (B \Rightarrow A) \wedge (C \Rightarrow B) \supset C \Rightarrow A \qquad \text{(Theorem L1)}$$

The speaks-for operator itself serves to transmit authority. The quoting operator is how one principal asserts that it is working on behalf of another; if $B|A \Rightarrow A$ and A *controls* x, then principal B may access the resource by quoting A: if B **says** (A **says** x), then $B|A$ **says** x, so A **says** x, and we conclude $\vdash x$.

Imagine that someone other than A grants by an ACL that $B|A$ *controls* x. When $B|A$ accesses the resource, the system correctly concludes that the access is legitimate, but the result is misleading, since the decision is independent of any involvement by A. Abadi et al. capture delegation with a stronger concept, B **for** A:

$$(A \wedge (B|A)) \Rightarrow (B \,\textbf{for}\, A) \qquad \text{(Axiom D1)}$$

With the conjunction, when B **for** A appears in an ACL, we know that the mention of A implies A's involvement.

In this paper, we use the term *delegation* more generally than do Abadi et al.; we refer to any transfer of authority (such as establishing $B \Rightarrow A$) as a delegation, and we explore how we might make the language of delegation richer by adding the notion of restriction. We ignore the concept of **for** : where Abadi et al. use a **for** -delegation and an ACL entry, we use a restricted speaks-for delegation. Table 1 summarizes the notation we use for sets.

Table 1. The symbols used to represent sets in this article.

Set	Example members	Description
Σ	s, t, x	The set of primitive propositions. They represent resources.
Σ^*	σ, τ $s \wedge t$	The set of well-formed formulas (statements) constructed from Σ, $\wedge$, $\neg$, $\mathcal{A}$ **says**, and $\mathcal{B} \Rightarrow \mathcal{A}$
2^{Σ^*}	S, T, V	The set of sets of statements
P	A, B	The set of primitive principals. They represent agents, including people, machines, programs, and communications channels.
P^*	$\mathcal{A}, \mathcal{B}$ $A \wedge B$	The set of compound principals constructed from P, $\wedge$, $\mid$, and $\cdot N$
$\mathcal{N}$	N	The set of local names

4   The Logic and Semantics of Restricted Delegation

Lampson et al. mention in passing the idea of a restricted speaks-for operator [3, p. 272]. In this section, we introduce our *speaks-for-regarding* operator, which formalizes the notion of the restricted speaks-for operator. (The extended version of this paper proves the soundness of our axiomatization and the theorems mentioned here.) The new operator is written $B \overset{T}{\Rightarrow} A$, and read "$B$ speaks for A regarding the set of statements in T." T is any subset of Σ^*. The desired meaning is that when $\sigma \in T$,

$$B \overset{T}{\Rightarrow} A \supset ((B \,\text{\textbf{says}}\, \sigma) \supset (A \,\text{\textbf{says}}\, \sigma))$$

The power of the speaks-for-regarding operator $\overset{T}{\Rightarrow}$ is that A can delegate a subset of its authority *without modifying any ACLs*. Contrast the situation with the use of roles in the Logic of Authentication, where to delegate authority over a restricted subset of her resources, a user had to define a role and install that role in the ACLs of each resource to be shared.

Restricted speaks-for is transitive:

$$\vdash (\mathcal{C} \overset{T}{\Rightarrow} \mathcal{B}) \wedge (\mathcal{B} \overset{T}{\Rightarrow} \mathcal{A}) \supset (\mathcal{C} \overset{T}{\Rightarrow} \mathcal{A}) \qquad \text{(Axiom E1)}$$

We expect the $\wedge$ operation on principals to be monotonic over $\overset{T}{\Rightarrow}$:

$$\vdash (\mathcal{B} \overset{T}{\Rightarrow} \mathcal{A}) \supset (\mathcal{B} \wedge \mathcal{C}) \overset{T}{\Rightarrow} (\mathcal{A} \wedge \mathcal{C}) \qquad \text{(Axiom E2)}$$

Restricted control over two principals is the same as restricted control over their conjunct:

$$\vdash (\mathcal{C} \overset{T}{\Rightarrow} \mathcal{A}) \wedge (\mathcal{C} \overset{T}{\Rightarrow} \mathcal{B}) \equiv \mathcal{C} \overset{T}{\Rightarrow} (\mathcal{A} \wedge \mathcal{B}) \qquad \text{(Axiom E3)}$$

Let $\mathcal{U}$ be the universe of all well-formed formulas; that is, those formulas over which a model $\mathcal{M}$ defines $\mathcal{E}$.[2] Restricted speaks-for degenerates to the original speaks-for when the restriction set is the set of all statements:

$$\vdash (\mathcal{B} \overset{\mathcal{U}}{\Rightarrow} \mathcal{A}) \equiv (\mathcal{B} \Rightarrow \mathcal{A}) \qquad \text{(Axiom E4)}$$

If Bob speaks for Alice regarding a set of statements T, he surely speaks for her regarding a subset $T' \subseteq T$:

$$\vdash (\mathcal{B} \overset{T}{\Rightarrow} \mathcal{A}) \supset (\mathcal{B} \overset{T'}{\Rightarrow} \mathcal{A}) \qquad \text{(Axiom E5)}$$

Using Axiom E5, a chain of delegations can be collapsed to a single delegation, connecting the head principal in the chain to the tail, whose restriction set is the intersection of the restriction sets of each of the original delegations.

$$\vdash (\mathcal{C} \overset{S}{\Rightarrow} \mathcal{B}) \wedge (\mathcal{B} \overset{T}{\Rightarrow} \mathcal{A}) \supset (\mathcal{C} \overset{S \cap T}{\Rightarrow} \mathcal{A}) \qquad \text{(Theorem E6)}$$

This is not to say that $\mathcal{C}$ may not speak for $\mathcal{A}$ regarding more statements than those in the intersection; we address this topic further in Section 6.9.

If we have two restricted delegations from Alice to Bob, we might expect Alice to speak for Bob with respect to the union of the restriction sets. Because of the semantics we choose for $\overset{T}{\Rightarrow}$, however, this intuition does not hold.

$$(B \overset{S}{\Rightarrow} A) \wedge (B \overset{T}{\Rightarrow} A) \not\supset B \overset{S \cup T}{\Rightarrow} A \qquad \text{(Result E7)}$$

In the extended version of this paper, we describe a relation weaker than $\overset{T}{\Rightarrow}$ for which the intuitive statement holds.

The quoting operator ($|$) constructs compund principals such as $B|A$, read "B quoting A." When principal $B|A$ **says** σ, we conclude that B **says** $(A$ **says** $\sigma)$: B is asserting what he thinks A believes. The quoting operator is monotonic in both arguments over $\Rightarrow$. Quoting is still monotonic over $\overset{T}{\Rightarrow}$ in its left argument:

$$\vdash (\mathcal{B} \overset{T}{\Rightarrow} \mathcal{A}) \supset \mathcal{C}|\mathcal{B} \overset{T}{\Rightarrow} \mathcal{C}|\mathcal{A} \qquad \text{(Axiom E8)}$$

Our semantics does not justify monotonicity in the right argument, however:

$$(\mathcal{B} \overset{T}{\Rightarrow} \mathcal{A}) \not\supset \mathcal{B}|\mathcal{C} \overset{T}{\Rightarrow} \mathcal{A}|\mathcal{C} \qquad \text{(Result E9)}$$

Hence, when quoting others, principals cannot automatically invoke the same delegated authority they have when speaking directly. The same counterexample that shows Result E9 shows the same property for the weak speaks-for-regarding relation defined in the extended version of this paper, so it seems that the notion of quoting simply does not mix easily with restricted delegation. This result

---

[2] $\mathcal{E}$ is the extension function as in the formalism of Abadi et al. The function maps each logical formula to the set of worlds where the formula is true.

appears to limit the usefulness of quoting, because principals cannot employ quoting with the same ease as in the Logic of Authentication.

We can salvage some of the convenience of quoting, however, by propagating the quoted principal through the restriction set. Let T^* be the closure of T with respect to the propositional operators $\neg$ and $\wedge$: $T \subseteq T^*$, and if $\sigma, \tau \in T^*$, then $\neg\sigma \in T^*$ and $\sigma \wedge \tau \in T^*$. Furthermore let TC be the closure of T with respect to the modal operator C **says**: $T \subseteq TC$, and if $\sigma \in TC$, then $(C\,\textbf{says}\,\sigma) \in TC$. Now $(T^*)C$ is the modal closure applied to the propositional closure of some original set T. With these definitions, we can justify this axiom:

$$\vdash \left(B \overset{(T^*)C}{\Rightarrow} A \right) \supset \left(B|C \overset{T}{\Rightarrow} A|C \right) \qquad \text{(Axiom E10)}$$

When $T = \mathcal{U}$, this axiom reduces to showing right-monotonicity for the original speaks-for relation. This axiom means that A's restricted delegation to B must explicitly include any "quotes" of C about which it is willing to believe B. It seems awkward, but it is a useful result. Why? Because in any possible-worlds semantics wherein $(B \overset{T}{\Rightarrow} A) \supset (B|C \overset{T}{\Rightarrow} A|C)$ for *all* principals C, the relation representing A depends on every other principal relation. The introduction of malicious principals with cleverly-chosen relations into such a system can effectively expand T until $T = \mathcal{U}$.

4.1 Semantics of $\overset{T}{\Rightarrow}$

Like Abadi et al. [2], we use a semantics based on possible worlds, modeling a system with a *model* $\mathcal{M} = \langle W, w_0, I, J \rangle$. W is a set of possible worlds and $w_0 \in W$ the distinguished "real" world. The interpretation function I maps each primitive proposition to the worlds where it is true, and the interpretation function J maps each primitive principal to its possible-worlds visiblity relation.

The semantic definition of $\overset{T}{\Rightarrow}$ is based on the notion of *projecting* a model into a space where only the statements in set T are relevant. The idea behind this definition is that if one were to take the "quotient" of a model M with respect to the dual of T, the resulting model $\overline{M}$ would be concerned only with statements in T. $B \Rightarrow A$ in $\overline{M}$ should be equivalent to $B \overset{T}{\Rightarrow} A$ in the original model. The model $\overline{M}$ is a projection of M that only preserves information about statements in T.

We begin the construction by defining an equivalence relation $\cong_T : W \times W$ that relates two worlds whenever they agree on all statements in T:

$$w \cong_T w' \text{ iff } (\forall \sigma \in T, w \in \mathcal{E}(\sigma) \text{ iff } w' \in \mathcal{E}(\sigma)) \qquad \text{(Definition E11)}$$

Then we define the mapping $\phi_T : W \to \overline{W}$ that takes worlds from the original model to equivalence classes under $\cong_T$:

$$\phi_T(w) = \phi_T(w') \text{ iff } w \cong_T w' \qquad \text{(Definition E12)}$$

The equivalence classes belong to a set $\overline{W} = 2^T$; notice that worlds (equivalence class representatives) in $\overline{M}$ cannot be confused with those in M. The extended version of this paper gives a construction of $\phi_T(w)$.

Next we extend ϕ_T to the function $\phi_T^w : 2^W \to 2^{\overline{W}}$ that maps a set of worlds $S_w \subseteq W$ to a set of equivalence class representatives in the projected model:

$$\phi_T^w(S_w) = \{\overline{w} \mid \exists w \in S_w, \ \overline{w} = \phi_T(w)\} \qquad \text{(Definition E13)}$$

We use bar notation ($\overline{w}$) to indicate an equivalence class representative (member of a world of a projected model) as opposed to a member of W in the original model.

We can now give a semantic definition of restricted delegation:

$$\mathcal{E}(\mathcal{B} \overset{T}{\Rightarrow} \mathcal{A})$$
$$= \begin{cases} W \text{ if } \forall w_0 \left(\phi_T^w(\mathcal{R}(\mathcal{A})(w_0)) \subseteq \phi_T^w(\mathcal{R}(\mathcal{B})(w_0)) \right) \\ \varnothing \text{ otherwise} \end{cases} \qquad \text{(Definition E14)}$$

For the justifications of several of the axioms it is more convenient to shift the projection (ϕ) operation to one side of the subset relation. To do so, we define

$$\phi_T^+(R) = \{\langle w_0, w_1' \rangle \mid \exists w_1 \cong_T w_1', \ \langle w_0, w_1 \rangle \in R\} \qquad \text{(Definition E15)}$$

Think of ϕ_T^+ as a function that introduces as many edges as it can to a relation without disturbing its projection under T.

We can use ϕ_T^+ to give an equivalent definition of $\overset{T}{\Rightarrow}$:

$$\mathcal{E}(\mathcal{B} \overset{T}{\Rightarrow} \mathcal{A}) = \begin{cases} W \text{ if } \mathcal{R}(\mathcal{A}) \subseteq \phi_T^+(\mathcal{R}(\mathcal{B})) \\ \varnothing \text{ otherwise} \end{cases} \qquad \text{(Definition E16)}$$

The symbolic gymnastics of moving the projection to the right side of the $\subseteq$ relation is equivalent to the definition in terms of ϕ_T^w, but it makes some of the proofs more concise. The extended version of this paper shows the equivalence.

A casual intuition for this definition is that ϕ_T projects from the full model M down to a model in which worlds are only distinguished if they differ with regard to the truth of statements in T. If we collapse away the accessibility arrows that do not say anything about what is happening in T, and A's relation is a subset of B's relation in the projection, then A believes everything B believes about statements in T. This intuition is exactly what we want for restricted delegation.

What happens if we take an alternative semantic definition for restricted delegation? We explore one seemingly-natural but undesirable alternative and two other interesting alternatives in the extended version of this paper.

4.2 Additional Benefits of $\overset{T}{\Rightarrow}$

Introducing the $\overset{T}{\Rightarrow}$ operator to the logic not only provides the important feature of restricted delegation, but it simplifies the logic by replacing the *controls* operator, replacing roles, and providing a formal mechanism for the treatment of expiration times.

Supplanting *controls*. Now that we have the restricted speaks-for relation, we can dispense with the special *controls* operator for building ACLs.

Recall Abadi et al.'s special identity principal **1** [2, p. 718]. Because it believes only truth, $(\mathbf{1} \, \mathsf{says} \, s) \supset s$ for all statements s. That is, there is an implicit principal that controls all statements. We can replace every statement of the form $A \, controls \, s$ with an equivalent one: $A \overset{\{s\}}{\Rightarrow} \mathbf{1}$. This statement ensures that if $A \, \mathsf{says} \, s$, then $\mathbf{1} \, \mathsf{says} \, s$. Since the **1** relation only contains edges from a node to itself, a model can only satisfy this condition by selecting an actual world w_0 where s is true.

Supplanting Roles. Roles as originally defined are attractive, but they have the significant difficulty that introducing a new restricted role R_2 involves finding all of the objects that role should be allowed to touch, and adding $A \, \mathsf{as} \, R_2$ to each of those ACLs. When one of those objects does not allow ACL modifications by A, it is impossible for A to express the desired new role. The SPKI document gives a vivid example that shows how ACL management can become unwieldy [1, p. 17].

With the speaks-for-regarding relation, A can introduce a new role R_2 for itself by allowing $(A \, \mathsf{as} \, R_2) \overset{T_2}{\Rightarrow} A$. In fact, roles are no longer necessary at all, but the **as** and **for** operators, or operators like them, may still be useful for building tractable implementations.

Roles, as semantically defined by Abadi et al., can also have surprising consequences because they belong to a global "namespace." Imagine that both Alice and Bob use the role R_{user} in their ACLs. That means that the same relation $\mathcal{R}(R_{\mathrm{user}})$ encodes both the way that $A \, \mathsf{as} \, R_{\mathrm{user}}$ is weaker than A, and the way that $B \, \mathsf{as} \, R_{\mathrm{user}}$ is weaker than B. In the extended version of this paper, we give a detailed example model that demonstrates this problem.

Formalizing Statement Expiration. Lampson et al. treat expiration times casually: "Each premise has a *lifetime*, and the lifetime of the conclusion, and therefore of the credentials, is the lifetime of the shortest-lived premise" [3, p. 270]. It is likely that a formal treatment of lifetimes would be time-consuming and unsurprising, but the lifetimes are an unsightly element glued onto an otherwise elegant logical framework. Fortunately, the $\overset{T}{\Rightarrow}$ relation allows us to dispense with lifetimes.

Recall from [3, p. 271, note 4] that primitive statements such as s are meant to encode some operation in a real system. Assume that each s describes not only an operation, but the effective time the operation is to take place.[3] Further, assume a restriction set T in a delegation $B \overset{T}{\Rightarrow} A$ includes restrictions on the times of the operations under consideration. After the last time allowed by the set, the delegation remains logically valid, but becomes useless in practice. Furthermore,

---

[3] Like Lampson et al., we ignore the issue of securely providing loosely synchronized clocks.

restrictions on T can be more than expiration times; one can encode arbitrary temporal restrictions, such as only allowing a delegation to be valid on Friday afternoons.

5   The Semantics of SPKI Names

Recall from Section 4.2 how roles share a global "namespace," and the danger of crosstalk between applications of the same role. SPKI names have the same dangerous property: identical names have different meaning depending on the "scope" in which they appear. Hence treating names as roles will not do; we must extend the logic and semantics to model names.

We introduce to the logic a new set of primitive *names*, $\mathcal{N}$. We also extend principal expressions to include those of the form $\mathcal{A} \cdot N$, where $\mathcal{A}$ is an arbitrary principal expression and $N \in \mathcal{N}$. $\mathcal{A} \cdot N$ is read "$\mathcal{A}$'s N." For example, if Alice is represented by the logical principal A, and N_{barber} is the symbolic name "barber," then $A \cdot N_{\text{barber}}$ is a principal that represents "Alice's barber." That is, $A \cdot N_{\text{barber}}$ represents whoever it is that *Alice* defines as her barber. Should Bob delegate authority to the principal $A \cdot N_{\text{barber}}$, he is relying on a level of symbolic indirection defined by Alice. Should Alice change who has authority over $A \cdot N_{\text{barber}}$, she has redefined the subject of Bob's delegation.

Because $\cdot$ only accepts a principal as its left argument, there is no ambiguity in the order of operations; $\mathcal{A} \cdot N_1 \cdot N_2$ can only be parenthesized $(\mathcal{A} \cdot N_1) \cdot N_2$. For example, "Alice's barber's butcher" is "(Alice's barber)'s butcher." Parenthesizing the expression the other way, as "Alice's (barber's butcher)," is unnatural because it requires the ungrounded subexpression "(barber's butcher)."

5.1   The Logic of Names

What properties do we want names to have?

Local Namespaces. First, a principal should control the meaning of any names defined relative to itself:

$$\forall \text{ principals } \mathcal{A}, \text{ names } N :$$

$$(\mathcal{A} \text{ says } (\mathcal{B} \overset{T}{\Rightarrow} \mathcal{A} \cdot N)) \supset (\mathcal{B} \overset{T}{\Rightarrow} \mathcal{A} \cdot N)$$

We do not take this statement as an axiom for the same reason that Abadi, Lampson et al. do not accept the handoff axiom [2, p. 715], [3, p. 273]: our semantics does not support it in general. Instead, as with the handoff axiom, we allow the implementation to assume appropriate instances of it.

Left-Monotonicity. Name application should be monotonic over speaks-for. If Alice binds her name "barber" to Bob, and Bob binds his name "butcher" to Charlie, then we want "Alice's barber's butcher" to be bound to Charlie.

$$\vdash (\mathcal{B} \Rightarrow \mathcal{A}) \supset (\mathcal{B} \cdot N \Rightarrow \mathcal{A} \cdot N) \qquad \text{(Axiom E17)}$$

Using this rule, we can write the following to capture the desired intuition:

$$(\mathcal{B} \Rightarrow \mathcal{A} \cdot N_{\text{barber}}) \supset$$
$$\mathcal{B} \cdot N_{\text{butcher}} \Rightarrow \mathcal{A} \cdot N_{\text{barber}} \cdot N_{\text{butcher}}$$

Distributivity. We combine the following pair of results

$$\vdash (\mathcal{A} \wedge \mathcal{B}) \cdot N \Rightarrow (\mathcal{A} \cdot N) \wedge (\mathcal{B} \cdot N) \qquad \text{(Theorem E18)}$$
$$\vdash (\mathcal{A} \cdot N) \wedge (\mathcal{B} \cdot N) \Rightarrow (\mathcal{A} \wedge \mathcal{B}) \cdot N \qquad \text{(Axiom E19)}$$

to show that names distribute over principal conjunction:

$$\vdash (\mathcal{A} \wedge \mathcal{B}) \cdot N = (\mathcal{A} \cdot N) \wedge (\mathcal{B} \cdot N) \qquad \text{(Theorem E20)}$$

Here is a motivating example: If Alice has two doctors Emily and Fred, and Bob visits doctors Fred and George, then who is "(Alice and Bob)'s doctor?"

$$E \Rightarrow A \cdot N_{\text{doctor}}$$
$$F \Rightarrow A \cdot N_{\text{doctor}}$$
$$F \Rightarrow B \cdot N_{\text{doctor}}$$
$$G \Rightarrow B \cdot N_{\text{doctor}}$$

Applying Theorem E20, we conclude:

$$F \Rightarrow (A \wedge B) \cdot N_{\text{doctor}}$$

That is, Fred is the only person who serves as both people's doctor.

No Quoting Axiom. The principal $(\mathcal{A}|\mathcal{B}) \cdot N$ can be written, but we have yet to find a meaningful intuitive interpretation for it. $(\mathcal{A}|\mathcal{B}) \cdot N$ bears no obvious relation to $(\mathcal{A} \cdot N)|(\mathcal{B} \cdot N)$, for example. We allow the principal in the logic, but we offer no axioms for extracting quoting from inside a name application.

Nonidempotence. Finally, application of names should not be always idempotent. Unless some other speaks-for statement causes it, there is no reason that "Bob's barber's barber" should speak for "Bob's barber." We were initially tempted to model name application ($\cdot$) with role application, because roles satisfy Axiom E17; however, roles are idempotent. It may be the case that the application of a name can become idempotent; the extended version of this paper gives an example.

5.2   The Semantics of Names

Names and name application cannot be modeled with the roles and the quoting operator, because quoting a role is always idempotent. Furthermore, using the same role for multiple uses of the same name by different principals introduces crosstalk as described in Section 4.2.

Instead, we model names as follows. First, add a new element K to the tuple that defines a model. A model with naming consists of:

$$\mathcal{M} = \langle W, w_0, I, J, K \rangle$$

The new interpretation function $K : P \times \mathcal{N} \to 2^{W \times W}$ maps a primitive principal A and a name N to a relation. The idea is that principals only define the first level of names in their namespaces; all other names are consequences of chained first-level name definitions.

Next extend $\mathcal{R}$ to define the relations for principals formed through name application. We want to define $\mathcal{R}(A \cdot N)$ as the intersection of several other sets, each requirement ensuring a desired property. The definition, however, would end up circular (at requirement (I), with equal principals) if it were expressed in terms of set intersection. Instead, we define $\mathcal{R}(A \cdot N)$ as the largest relation (subset of $2^{W \times W}$) satisfying all of the following requirements:

$$\mathcal{R}(A \cdot N) \subseteq \mathcal{R}(B \cdot N) \tag{I}$$
$$(\forall B : \mathcal{R}(A) \subseteq \mathcal{R}(B))$$

$$\mathcal{R}(A \cdot N) \subseteq K(A, N) \tag{II}$$
$$(\text{when } A \in P)$$

$$\mathcal{R}(A \cdot N) \subseteq \mathcal{R}(B \cdot N) \cup \mathcal{R}(C \cdot N) \tag{III}$$
$$(\text{when } A = B \wedge C)$$

$$(\text{Definition E21})$$

Requirement (I) supports Axiom E17. Requirement (II) applies only to primitive principals, and allows each primitive principal to introduce definitions for first-level names in that principal's namespace. A system implementing instances of the handoff rule does so conceptually by modifying $K(A, N)$. Requirement (III) only applies to principal expressions that are conjunctions, and justifies Theorem E20.

There is no question some such largest relation exists. Since each requirement is a subset relation, at least the empty set satisfies all three. There is an upper bound, since every relation is a subset of the finite set $W \times W$. Finally, the largest relation must be unique. If there were two such relations, then any element in one must belong to the other, since it belongs to every set on the right-hand side of a subset relation in the requirements, and we arrive at a contradiction.

In our semantics, as in Abadi's, left-monotonicity (Axiom E17) turns out to be surprisingly powerful. In the extended version of this paper, we consider how to temper it. Note also that Axiom E17 applies only to unrestricted delegation ($\Rightarrow$). In the extended paper we consider a stronger version of left-monotonicity, generalized to the restricted-speaks-for relation ($\overset{T}{\Rightarrow}$), and discuss why it is difficult to support semantically. Because Theorem E20 derives from Axiom E17, it is similarly limited to the unrestricted case.

Table 2. A guide to translating between Abadi's notation and ours

Abadi's notation	Our notation
S	Σ
$\mu : S \times \mathcal{W} \to \{true, false\}$	$I : \Sigma \to 2^W$
$\rho : N \times \mathcal{W} \to 2^{\mathcal{W}}$	$K : P \times \mathcal{N} \to 2^{W \times W}$
$a \in \mathcal{W}$	$w \in W$
principals p, q	$\mathcal{A}, \mathcal{B} \in P^*$
$n \in N$	$N \in \mathcal{N}$
$[\![n]\!]_a = \rho(n, a)$	$\mathcal{R}(\mathcal{A} \cdot N)(w) = K(\mathcal{A}, N)(w)$
$[\![p\text{'s } n]\!]_a$	$\mathcal{R}(\mathcal{A} \cdot N)(w)$

5.3 Abadi's Semantics for Linked Local Namespaces

Abadi gives an alternate logic and semantics for SPKI-style linked local namespaces [4]. (He refers to SDSI, from which SPKI 2.0 derives.) Abadi's notation diverges from that used in the Logic of Authentication [2], but the semantics are the same. Table 2 helps translate the notation. Our semantics differs in three interesting ways.

First, SPKI has special global names, so that if N_G is a global name, $\mathcal{A} \cdot N_G = N_G$. The result is that the same syntactic construct can be used to bind a local name to another local name or to a globally-specified name. All names in linking statements are implicitly prefixed by the name of the speaking principal; but if the explicitly mentioned name is global, the prefix has no consequence. We consider this syntactic sugar, and leave it to an implementation to determine from explicit cues (such as a key specification or a SDSI global name with the special !! suffix) whether a mentioned principal should be interpreted as local to the speaker.

Second, Abadi's logic adopts the handoff rule for names, which he calls the "Linking" axiom. Here it is, translated to our terminology:

$$\mathcal{A} \text{ says } (\mathcal{B} \Rightarrow (\mathcal{A} \cdot N)) \supset (\mathcal{B} \Rightarrow (\mathcal{A} \cdot N))$$

He validates the axiom by the use of composition to model name application, with which we disagree.

Indeed, the third and most important way our semantics differs from Abadi's explains just why we disagree. Abadi's semantics models name application as quoting (composition). Each unqualified (local) name is mapped to a single relation. This property can introduce crosstalk between otherwise unconnected principals; recall the example from Section 4.2. Even when a name relation is not constrained to be a role, the same problem arises. For example, let N represent the name "doctor." Imagine that Bob assigns Charlie to be his doctor: $C \Rightarrow B|N$. This is fine; Charlie should be able to do some things on Bob's behalf, but not everything: If $B|N \overset{T}{\Rightarrow} B$, then Charlie can do the things in T.

Enter Alice, who is not only omniscient ($A = 1$), but serves as her own doctor ($A \Rightarrow A|N$). Abadi's semantics requires that $\mathcal{R}(1) \circ \mathcal{R}(N) \subseteq \mathcal{R}(1)$. At worst,

$\mathcal{R}(N) = \mathcal{R}(\mathbf{1})$, causing $B|N = B$, enabling Charlie's doctor to make investment decisions on Charlie's behalf. At best, $\mathcal{R}(N) \subset \mathcal{R}(\mathbf{1})$, and $B|N$ begins spouting off random statements, some of which may be in T, making Bob believe random statements. Our semantics escapes this fate by assigning to each use of a name its own relation, then ensuring the correct subset relationships remain among those relations.

In summary, defining a meaningful semantics to local applications of names from the same global namespace is nontrivial. Our semantics depends on an existential definition involving the "largest set satisfying the requirements," and is therefore more opaque than illuminating. Despite its limitations, we feel that it is better than an alternative that implies undesirable consequences.

6   Modeling SPKI

The original Logic of Authentication is useful because its principals are general enough to model several parts of a computing system, from users to trusted servers to communications channels. To formally model SPKI with our extended calculus, we first give a construction that models the delegation-control bit.

6.1   Delegation Control

The SPKI document gives the motivation for including a delegation-control bit in SPKI certificates. We disagree with the argument and fall in favor of no delegation control, and for the same reasons as described in the document: delegation control is futile, and its use tempts users to divulge their keys or install signing oracles to subvert the restriction. Such subversion not only nullifies delegation control, but forfeits the benefits of auditability provided by requiring proofs of authorization. Despite our opinion, we present a construction that models delegation control.

To model the delegation-control feature we wish to split the **says** modality into two separate modalities: "utterance," which represents a principal actually making a statement, and is never automatically inherited by other principals, and "belief," which is inherited transitively just as **says** is. Not only is introducing a new logical modality clumsy, but it would require us to support a dubious axiom, undermining the simplicity of the semantics.

Instead, we resort to an equivalent construct: we split each "real" principal $\mathcal{A}$ we wish to model into subprincipals $\mathcal{A}_u$ and $\mathcal{A}_b$. $\mathcal{A}_u$ shall say only the things that $\mathcal{A}$ utters (statements that are actually signed by $\mathcal{A}$'s key; recall that all certificate-issuing principals in SPKI are keys), and $\mathcal{A}_b$ shall say all of the things that $\mathcal{A}$ believes. $\mathcal{A}$ may inherit her beliefs from other principals (because she has delegated to other subjects the authority to speak on her behalf), and furthermore $\mathcal{A}$ should believe anything she utters. This last condition replaces the clumsy axiom we wished to avoid; instead we enforce it by explicitly assuming the following statement for all principals $\mathcal{A}$ and statements s:

$$\vdash \mathcal{A}_u \textbf{ says } s \supset \mathcal{A}_b \textbf{ says } s \qquad \text{(Assumption E22)}$$

Certificates issued by a concrete principal A are statements uttered by A asserting things that A believes, so we model them as statements about A_b said by A_u. The desirable outcome is that no principal can delegate authority to make herself utter something (make A_u say something); she may only utter the statement directly (by signing it with her key).

6.2 Restriction

Recall that a SPKI 5-tuple includes five fields: issuer, subject, delegation-control bit, authorization, and validity dates. Let I and S represent the issuer and subject principals. Let T_A represent the set of primitive permissions represented by the authorization S-expression, and T_V the set of primitive permissions limited by the validity dates (assuming the effective-time encoding of Section 4.2). The 5-tuple can be represented this way if its delegation-control bit is set:

$$I_u \text{ says } S_b \overset{T_A \cap T_V}{\Rightarrow} I_b$$

or this way if not:

$$I_u \text{ says } S_u \overset{T_A \cap T_V}{\Rightarrow} I_b$$

A 4-tuple has a name field (N) and no authorization field or delegation-control bit. It would be encoded:

$$I_u \text{ says } S_b \overset{T_V}{\Rightarrow} I_b \cdot N$$

It seems natural that a delegation bit is meaningless for a name binding, for in SPKI, a name principal can never utter a statement directly, only a key principal can. It is surprising, however, that SPKI name-binding certificates omit the authorization field. Why not allow a principal to say the following?

$$I_u \text{ says } (S_b \overset{\{shampoo\}}{\Rightarrow} I_b \cdot N_{\text{barber}})$$

As it turns out, our semantics does not support such restricted name bindings (see Section 5.2).

6.3 Linked Local Namespaces

The subject principals in the keys above may be either keys (each directly represented by a primitive principal) or a string of names grounded in a key. Hence namespaces are "local" in that names are meaningless except relative to a globally unambiguous key; namespaces are "linked" in that the naming operation may be repeated: If $K_1 \cdot N_1$ resolves to K_2, then $K_1 \cdot N_1 \cdot N_2$ is the same as $K_2 \cdot N_2$, perhaps defined as some K_3.

We give a logic and semantics for linked local namespaces in Section 5. We model the SPKI name subject "george: (name fred sam)" with the principal expression $K_{\text{george}} \cdot N_{\text{``fred''}} \cdot N_{\text{``sam''}}$. Substituting the principal expression for S_b, a 4-tuple takes on the general appearance:

$$I_u \text{ says } ((K_S \cdot N_1 \cdots N_k) \overset{T_V}{\Rightarrow} I_b \cdot N_0)$$

6.4   Threshold Subjects

A threshold subject is a group of n principals who are authorized by a certificate only when k of the principals agree to the requested action. Such certificates are really just an abbreviation for a combinatorially-long $\binom{n}{k}$ list of conjunction statements. For example, a certificate with a 2-of-3 threshold subject naming principals P_1, P_2, and P_3 and an issuer A can be represented as:

$$P_1 \wedge P_2 \Rightarrow A$$
$$P_1 \wedge P_3 \Rightarrow A$$
$$P_2 \wedge P_3 \Rightarrow A$$

Hence the logic easily captures threshold subjects, although any tractable implementation would obviously want to work with them in their unexpanded form.

6.5   Auth Tags

The "auth tags" used in authorization fields in SPKI represent sets of primitive statements. Therefore, we simply model them using mathematical sets.

6.6   Tuple Reduction

The SPKI access-control decision procedure is called "tuple reduction." A request is granted if it can be shown that a collection of certificates reduce to authorize the request. The reduced tuple's subject must be the key that signed the request; the tuple's issuer must represent the server providing the requested service; and the specific request must belong to the authorization tag of the reduced tuple.

It is clear that tuple reduction is sound with respect to the extended logic. When 5- and 4-tuples are encoded in the logic as shown in Section 5 and Section 6.2, tuple-reduction simply constructs a proof from several applications of Theorem E6 and Axiom E17.

6.7   Validity Conditions

An optional validity condition, such as a certificate revocation list, a timed revalidation list, or a one-time revalidation, can be encoded in the logic using a conjunction. For example, a certificate requiring a timed revalidation would be interpreted

$$A \textbf{ says } (B \wedge (R|H_1)) \Rightarrow A$$

to mean that the revalidation principal R must verify that this certificate (with hash H_1) is valid. Principal R signs a revalidation instrument I with a short validity interval T_V

$$R \textbf{ says } I \overset{T_V}{\Rightarrow} R$$

and a given revalidation instrument would agree with all valid outstanding certificates:

$$I \text{ says } \mathbf{0} \Rightarrow I | H_1$$
$$I \text{ says } \mathbf{0} \Rightarrow I | H_2$$

$$\vdots$$

The principal $\mathbf{0}$ has relation $\mathcal{R}(\mathbf{0}) = \varnothing$, so that every principal speaks for $\mathbf{0}$. Using the logic, we can reason that

$$\mathbf{0} \Rightarrow I | H_1 \stackrel{T_V}{\Rightarrow} R | H_1$$

and since $B = B \wedge \mathbf{0}$, $B \stackrel{T_V}{\Rightarrow} A$. Notice the treatment of a certificate's hash as a principal. In the logic, principals are general entities and can be used to represent many objects and actors.

Negative certificate revocation lists can be handled similarly; an implementation examining a revocation list would conclude $I \text{ says } \mathbf{0} \Rightarrow I | H_1$ for any H_1 *not* present in the list.

One-time revalidations are meant to be interpreted as having a zero validity interval. A system verifying a request s creates a nonce E, understanding $E \text{ says } s$, and sends it to the revalidator R. R replies with a statement meant to be interpreted

$$R \text{ says } E \stackrel{\{s\}}{\Rightarrow} R | H_1$$

Now both B and $E \stackrel{\{s\}}{\Rightarrow} R | H_1$ say s, so $A \text{ says } s$. Any future request of the same sort will require another revalidation, for its s will have a different effective time.

6.8   Safe Extensions

Our semantics suggests that SPKI may be safely extended to support a variety of principals other than public keys. Channels protected by secret keys or a trusted computing base, for example, are easily modeled as principals in the logic. In the examples in this article, we represent principals with symbolic names. Real principals, however, are represented by some mechanism that can verify that a given request comes from a particular principal. Examples of mechanisms for authenticating users include the UID mechanism in Unix, the Kerberos authentication server, and public key cryptography. Lampson et al. show that many common system components can be modeled as principals [3].

Compound principals let us represent useful trust relationships other than delegation. A conjunct principal $(A \wedge B)$, for example, represents a principal that only believes σ when both A and B believe σ. Hence a delegation to a conjunct principal is analogous to a check that requires two signatures to cash. Conjunct principals are not first-class entities in SPKI, although they can appear as threshold subjects; an extended SPKI might exploit Theorem E20. Quoting principals are also missing from SPKI; Lampson et al. give nice examples showing how quoting can help a multiplexed server or communications channel differentiate when it is working on behalf of one client versus another [3, Sections 4.3, 6.1, 6.2, and 7.1]. Without quoting, such a server has permission to make statements for either client, so it must perform an access-control check in advance of relaying a client's statement. Quoting lets the multiplexed server defer the complete access-control decision to the final resource server that verifies the proof. The result is improved auditability, since the gateway's role in the transaction is recorded at the server, and a smaller trusted computing base, since only a tiny part of the gateway code must be correct to pass on the authorization decision to the server.

6.9   Dangerous Extensions

In this section, we argue that SPKI auth tags should not be extended to represent logical negations. If $\mathcal{B}$ speaks for $\mathcal{A}$ regarding multiple restriction sets, the semantics suggest that $\mathcal{B}$ actually has some authority not explicitly mentioned in either set. For example,

$$(\mathcal{B} \overset{\{\sigma, \tau\}}{\Rightarrow} \mathcal{A}) \supset (\mathcal{B} \overset{\{\sigma \wedge \tau\}}{\Rightarrow} \mathcal{A}) \qquad \text{(Axiom E23)}$$

means that a principal believed on a set of statements is also believed on their conjuncts. This conclusion seems fairly natural, but it is interesting to note that a restriction set actually permits more statements than it represents explicitly.

With the semantics for restricted delegation we define in Section 4, not only does

$$(\mathcal{B} \overset{\{\sigma, \tau\}}{\Rightarrow} \mathcal{A}) \supset (\mathcal{B} \overset{\{\sigma \wedge \tau\}}{\Rightarrow} \mathcal{A}) \qquad \text{(Axiom E24)}$$

hold, but also:

$$(\mathcal{B} \overset{\{\sigma\}}{\Rightarrow} \mathcal{A}) \supset (\mathcal{B} \overset{\{\neg\sigma\}}{\Rightarrow} \mathcal{A}) \qquad \text{(Axiom E25)}$$

This result implies that given authority on a set of primitive statements, a principal also has authority on any propositional formula constructed from those statements. It is surprising, for even if only $\mathcal{B} \overset{\{s\}}{\Rightarrow} \mathcal{A}$ is explicitly granted, $\mathcal{B}$ can also cause $\mathcal{A}$ to say the negation of s.

Perhaps scarier still is that

$$\mathcal{B} \overset{\{\sigma\}}{\Rightarrow} \mathcal{A} \supset \mathcal{B} \overset{\{\sigma, \neg\sigma\}}{\Rightarrow} \mathcal{A}$$
$$\supset (\mathcal{B} \textbf{ says } \text{false}) \supset (\mathcal{A} \textbf{ says } \text{false})$$

The conclusion is the definition of Abadi's $\mapsto$ relation:

"Intuitively, $\mathcal{A} \mapsto \mathcal{B}$ means that there is something that $\mathcal{A}$ can do (say *false*) that yields an arbitrarily strong statement by $\mathcal{B}$ (in fact, *false*). Thus, $\mathcal{A} \mapsto \mathcal{B}$ means that $\mathcal{A}$ is at least as powerful as $\mathcal{B}$ in practice." [2, p. 713]

With these semantics, one might fear that no restriction is actually meaningful. How might we escape it? We might abandon the **K** axiom ($\mathcal{A}$ **believes** s $\wedge$ $\mathcal{A}$ **believes** $(s \supset t)$ $\supset$ $\mathcal{A}$ **believes** t), so that principals no longer believe every consequence of their beliefs. This option is undesirable because it cripples the logic to only operate outside the scope of belief operators.

A second option is to both disallow negative statements in restriction sets and to use the weaker $\mathcal{B} \overset{T}{\to} \mathcal{A}$ relation (described in the extended paper) instead of $\mathcal{B} \overset{T}{\Rightarrow} \mathcal{A}$ to model delegation.

A third option is to prevent principals from making contradictory statements. This is difficult in general in a distributed system. One approach is to prevent principals from making negative statements at all. SPKI takes this approach. Its tags, which represent both restriction sets and individual statements, cannot represent both a statement and its logical negation. We provide a formal treatment of tags in the extended version of this paper.

Another extension might be to allow SPKI name bindings (4-tuples) to include authorization restrictions. As mentioned in Section 5.2, our semantics suggests that this seemingly-natural extension has undesirable consequences.

We conclude that in certain dimensions, SPKI is as strong as it can be. Changing SPKI by allowing principals to make negative statements or by allowing negative statements in restriction sets would push SPKI "over the edge," making its restrictions meaningless. Those proposing to augment SPKI, or other systems based on a logic of restricted delegation such as that of Section 4, must be wary of this hazard.

7   Summary

We extend the Logic of Authentication and its underlying possible-worlds semantics to support restricted delegation, delegation control, and local namespaces. To define the semantics of restricted delegation, we project a model to a set of worlds distinguished only by statements in the restriction set. The resulting system provides intuition and a formal framework in which we reason about the current SPKI system and possible extensions to SPKI.

One of the advantages our formal framework is that it represents the many complicated features of SPKI with three simple concepts: *principal*, *statement*, and *name*. Features such as threshold subjects and on-line validations can be modeled with compound principals and idiomatic statements. The simplicity also suggests that SPKI may be safely integrated with systems with notions of "principal" other than SPKI's public keys; such principals are desirable because they can exploit fast local or secret-key-protected channels. The results are applied in just this way in a prototype system implementation [10].

Our formalism also warns of the danger of apparently-harmless extensions. In our semantics, allowing a principal to utter both a statement and its negation or allowing restricted delegation to a name binding would reduce restricted delegation to meaninglessness. It would be imprudent to so extend SPKI without developing an alternate semantics that gives the extension meaning. One might also assume that delegation over two sets of permissions should combine to represent a delegation over the union of the permissions, but Result E7 suggests that this is not the case.

Acknowledgements. Thanks to John Lamping, who patiently helped Jon understand logical proof systems and semantic models. Thanks also Jon Bredin, Valeria de Paiva, Mark Montague and Larry Gariepy for their discussions, which helped refine the idea. Thanks to the USENIX organization for funding our research on this topic.

References

1. Carl M. Ellison, Bill Frantz, Butler Lampson, Ron Rivest, Brian M. Thomas, and Tatu Ylonen. SPKI certificate theory, October 1999. Internet RFC 2693.
2. Martín Abadi, Michael Burrows, Butler Lampson, and Gordon Plotkin. A calculus for access control in distributed systems. *ACM Transactions on Programming Languages and Systems*, 15(4):706–734, September 1993.
3. Butler Lampson, Martín Abadi, Michael Burrows, and Edward Wobber. Authentication in distributed systems: theory and practice. *ACM Transactions on Computer Systems*, 10(4):265–310, November 1992.
4. Martín Abadi. On SDSI's linked local name spaces. *Journal of Computer Security*, 6(1-2):3–21, 1998.
5. Joseph Y. Halpern and Ronald van der Meyden. A logic for SDSI's linked local name spaces. In *Proceedings of the 12th IEEE Computer Security Foundations Workshop*, pages 111–122, 1999.
6. Tuomas Aura. On the structure of delegation networks. In *Proceedings of the Eleventh IEEE Computer Security Foundations Workshop*, pages 14–26, 1998.
7. G. E. Hughes and M. J. Cresswell. *A New Introduction to Modal Logic*. Routledge, 1996.
8. Ronald Fagin, Joseph Y. Halpern, Yoram Moses, and Moshe Y. Vardi. *Reasoning about Knowledge*. MIT Press, 1995.
9. Jon Howell and David Kotz. A Formal Semantics for SPKI. Technical Report TR2000-363, Dartmouth College, Computer Science, Hanover, NH, March 2000. Available at: http://www.cs.dartmouth.edu/reports/abstracts/TR2000-363/.
10. Jonathan R. Howell. *Naming and sharing resources across administrative boundaries*. PhD thesis, Department of Computer Science, Dartmouth College, 2000.

Formal Verification of
Cardholder Registration in SET

Giampaolo Bella[1], Fabio Massacci[2,3], Lawrence C. Paulson[1], and
Piero Tramontano[3]

[1] Computer Laboratory, Univ. of Cambridge — Pembroke Street, Cambridge
CB2 3QG, England
{gb221,lcp}@cl.cam.ac.uk
[2] Dip. di Ing. dell'Informazione, Univ. di Siena — via Roma 56, 53100 Siena, Italy
massacci@dii.unisi.it
[3] Dip. di Inform. e Sist., Univ. di Roma "La Sapienza" — via Salaria 113, 00198
Roma, Italy
{massacci,tramonta}@dis.uniroma1.it

Abstract. The first phase of the SET protocol, namely Cardholder Registration, has been modelled inductively. This phase is presented in outline and its formal model is described. A number of basic lemmas have been proved about the protocol using Isabelle/HOL, along with a theorem stating that a certification authority will certify a given key at most once. Many ambiguities, contradictions and omissions were noted while formalizing the protocol.

1   Introduction

The last ten years have seen the rapid development of formal methods for analyzing security protocols. At the same time, protocols have become much more complex. Early security protocols typically involved two or three agents and established a shared secret. Six pages were enough to describe the Needham-Schroeder protocol in 1978 [16]. But six hundred pages are not enough to describe the SET protocol [11,12,13]. Such a complex protocol is likely to contain errors, but verifying it formally is a huge challenge.

Meadows [14] notes a further problem: electronic commerce protocols are *systems* of protocols and their goals are difficult to express in terms of traditional protocol concepts such as authentication and secrecy. The SET protocol is split in many phases each of which can be seen as a protocol on its own and has quite different high-level goals.

Therefore, it is no surprise that we do not find many published works on its verification. After Kailar's [7] analysis of simple electronic commerce protocols, there have been attempts to model more realistic protocols such as Kerberos [3], TLS/SSL [19] and Cybercash coin-exchange [4,5]. However, to the best of our knowledge, the SET protocol has still been out of reach. Meadows and Syverson [15] have designed a language for describing SET specifications but have left the

F. Cuppens et al. (Eds.): ESORICS 2000, LNCS 1895, pp. 159–174, 2000.

actual analysis to future work. Kessler and Neumann [8] have designed a belief logic to analyse a single message of the payment phase of SET.

The present paper describes our work in the analysis of a complete phase of SET: Cardholder Registration.

2 The SET Protocol

The SET protocol [9,11,12,13] has been proposed and standardized by a consortium of credit card companies (VISA, Mastercard, American Express) and software corporations (Microsoft, Netscape, etc.). SET aims to protect sensitive cardholder information, to ensure payment integrity and to authenticate merchants and cardholders. It does not support non-repudiation.

The overall architecture of SET is based on a rooted hierarchy of *Certification Authorities* (CAs). The top level is a trusted *Root Certification Authority*, below which we find centralized CAs corresponding to credit card brands. One level down, there are geo-political subsidiaries and finally, two levels down, there are CAs (corresponding to banks) that actually interact with customers. The task of these CAs is to provide customers with digital certificates for signature and encryption. Customers must generate and safeguard their private keys.

Participants of the payment system are *Cardholders* (C) and *Merchants* (M). Their financial institutions are called *Issuers* and *Acquirers*, respectively; they act largely outside the protocol. *Payment Gateways* (PG) play the traditional role of clearing-houses: their task is to settle the payment requests made by merchants and cardholders when buying goods.

2.1 Overview of SET

The SET protocol consists of five phases. The first two phases are used by the agents participating in the protocol to register their keys and get the appropriate certificates. The remaining phases constitute the electronic transaction itself.

Cardholder Registration. This is the initial step for cardholders. The agent C sends to a certification authority CA the information on the credit card he wants to use. The CA replies with a registration form, which C completes and returns, together with the signing key that C wants to register. Then, CA checks that the credit card is valid (this step is outside the protocol) and releases the signature certificate for C who stores it for future use. All this information (such as credit card details) must be protected and this makes the protocol steps complicated. A couple of points are worth noting:

- C may register as many public keys as he wants to.
- C's identity is not stored in the certificate. It only contains the hash of the *primary account number* (PAN), loosely speaking the credit card number, and of a secret nonce (PANSecret). A merchant should not be able to verify a cardholder's identity from his certificate [11, pp. 7, 12 and 25].

- The certificates must assure the merchant (without his having to see the PAN) that there is a link between a cardholder, a card and a PAN that has been validated by the card issuer [11, pp. 8 and 25].

Merchant Registration. This phase performs the analogous function for merchants. In contrast with Cardholder Registration, the merchant M can not only register a public key for signature but also a public key for encryption. The process is shorter because there is no confidential information to be protected.

Purchase Request. We reach this phase if C has decided to buy something. C sends to M the order information and the payment instructions. M processes the order and starts the *Payment Authorization* phase by forwarding the payment instructions to the PG. This last step is needed because SET aims to keep the cardholder's PAN confidential; M cannot simply take this number, as done in telephone credit card transactions [17], and settle directly with the Issuer.

Payment Authorization. After receiving the payment instructions from the Merchant, the PG, in cooperation with Issuers and banks, checks that everything is fine. If so, it sends the payment authorization to M, who sends to C the confirmation and possibly the purchased goods. C acknowledges the result and M passes to the next stage.

Payment Capture. In this last phase, M sends to PG one or more payment requests and the corresponding capture tokens obtained during the previous steps. PG checks that everything is satisfactory and replies to M. The actual funds transfer from C to M is done outside the protocol.

To accomplish these tasks, SET uses numerous combinations of cryptographic functions. Even for the handling of certificates, SET makes many extensions to the PKCS standards by RSA-Security [20,21].

2.2   Cardholder Registration: A Closer Look

Our analysis concerns the Cardholder Registration phase of the protocol. Figure 1 [11, p. 36] provides a high-level view of this phase. We can distinguish three message pairs. The first pair starts the registration process; the second gives the cardholder an appropriate registration form; the last exchanges the completed registration form for the requested certificate. Let us describe them in a bit more detail.

Initiate Request. The cardholder C starts the protocol.

Initiate Response. When the CA receives the request, it transmits a signed answer and its certificates to the cardholder. The signature certificate is used to verify the signature affixed to the response. The encryption certificate provides the cardholder with the key necessary to protect the payment card account number (PAN) in the registration form request. The CA will identify the issuer of the card using the first six to eleven digits of the account number to select the appropriate registration form.

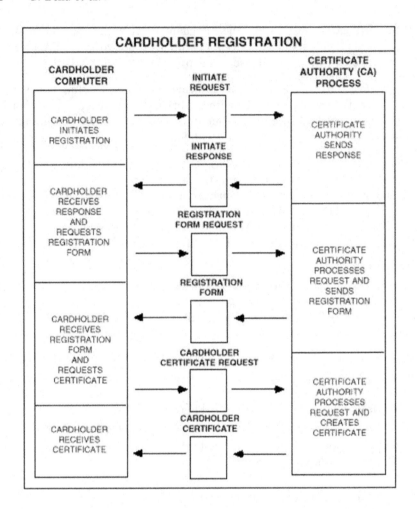

Fig. 1. Cardholder Registration in SET

$$1 . C \longrightarrow CA : C, N_{C_1}$$
$$2 . CA \longrightarrow C \quad : \text{Sign}_{CA}\{C, N_{C_1}\}, \text{CertE}_{RCA}\{CA\}, \text{CertS}_{RCA}\{CA\}$$
$$3 . C \longrightarrow CA : \{C, N_{C_2}, H(PAN)\}_{K_{C_1}}, \text{Encr}_{CA}\{K_{C_1}, PAN, H(C, N_{C_2})\}$$
$$4 . CA \longrightarrow C \quad : \text{Sign}_{CA}\{C, N_{C_2}, N_{CA}\}, \text{CertE}_{RCA}\{CA\}, \text{CertS}_{RCA}\{CA\}$$
$$5 . C \longrightarrow CA : \left\{m, \{H(m, PAN, N_{SecC})\}_{privSK_C}\right\}_{K_{C_3}},$$
$$\text{Encr}_{CA}\{K_{C_3}, PAN, N_{SecC}\}$$
$$\text{where } m = C, N_{C_3}, K_{C_2}, pubSK_C$$
$$6 . CA \longrightarrow C \quad : \{\text{Sign}_{CA}\{C, N_{C_3}, CA, N_{SecCA}\}, \text{CertS}_{CA}\{C\},$$
$$\text{CertS}_{RCA}\{CA\}\}_{K_{C_2}}$$

Fig. 2. High-level View of Cardholder Registration

Registration Form Request. C verifies the certificates of CA and the signature in the response. Then he sends a registration form request with his PAN. The request is encrypted with a random symmetric key that is encrypted along with the PAN in a digital envelope, sealed using the CA's public encryption key.

Registration Form. The CA unpacks the digital envelope, signs the appropriate registration form and returns it to C.

Cardholder Certificate Request. C verifies the certificate of CA and the signature on the received message. Now C fills in the registration form with the information the issuing bank deems necessary to identify him as a valid cardholder. C generates a signature key pair and a random number which will be used by CA to generate the certificate. Then, C creates a certificate request containing the registration form, the proposed public key and a random symmetric key used by CA to encrypt the response. This message is signed with C's private key. This signature yields no authentication—the corresponding public key is not yet certified—but it proves to CA that the requester knows the private key. The signed message is then encrypted with another fresh symmetric key; this key is encrypted along with the PAN and the random number, and the resulting message is sent to CA.

Cardholder Certificate. CA decrypts the request, checks C's signature and verifies the information on the registration form. In addition, CA should check that the key has not been registered by another cardholder; this obvious check is not mentioned in the specifications. Next, CA generates a random number and combines it with the one created by C to generate a secret value. Then CA generates the cardholder certificate by signing a message containing the public key and a hash of PAN and secret value. The certificate and a response message (with the CA half of the secret value) are encrypted with the symmetric key from the previous message and sent to C, together with CA's certificates.

Finally, before storing the certificate, C verifies it by comparing the hash contained in it with the correct value he can generate.

3   Making Sense of the Documents

The starting point of a formal analysis is defining an abstract model of the protocol. We eliminate technology dependent features and other inessential details. This must be done with care: keeping too many details results in an unmanageable model, while neglecting essential details allows unrealistic properties to be proved.

Usually, we can abstract away from particular cryptographic algorithms. The difference between SHA-1 and MD5 is inessential, since we merely expect hashing to be collision-free and non-invertible. We typically assume perfect encryption; in consequence, we can eliminate message components that are introduced only to circumvent the limitations of real-world cryptosystems.

The next obvious step is the elimination of all optional parts. But with SET, we found that this cannot be so easily done, as some options are not options at all. This is one of the major problems of the current SET specifications.

Here is an example. The task of the registration phases is to distribute certificates, which contain either encryption or signature keys. Both components are declared optional in the formal specification [12, p. 171], but omitting both 'options' would make the protocol vacuous. Only the informal text outside the definition [12, p. 170] says that at least one of them must be present.

Another example concerns symmetric keys. The specification of Cardholder Registration says that, at a certain stage, the cardholder C should send a symmetric key in order to get from the CA a message encrypted with that key. The field where the key is stored is tagged as optional [12, p. 171]. But the Programmer's Guide [13, p. 177] states that if the key field is missing then CA replies with an error message.

The SET designers do acknowledge this problem. The API reference guide to the SET reference implementation version 1.0 by Visa and MasterCard (available in the CD-ROM packaged with Loeb [9]) mentions this problem in the NOTES section at the end of the manual pages of the code:

> There is a difference between non-required and optional. Non-required fields may be omitted according to the SET protocol. Optional fields may be omitted according to ASN.1 encoding rules. In some messages, a field may be optional according to ASN.1, but still required by the SET protocol. In these cases, it is incumbent on the application to fill in these fields.

It is hard to believe that such a statement could be part of the specification of a security protocol. The manual pages do not distinguish the non-required and optional parts.

Another example is the use of certificates. According to the Business Description, CA always sends the certificates (or thumb-prints) for the signing keys. The reason, we think, is that Cardholder Registration is designed so that it can be interrupted and resumed later (we do not know whether this is intended) and that CA may want to offer C the possibility of always getting the most recent key. However, certificates for the encryption keys are sometimes missing, and this difference in managing the two different kinds of certificates is not explained. The handling of certificates can only be understood by making reference to the PKCS standards. So, to decide which message component is required for our analysis, we need a case-by-case analysis, which can only be done with a full comprehension of the protocol goals and structure.

Such problems of formalization are sadly typical of commercial protocols. Once a protocol reaches the stage of an RFC (Request for Comments), it is often specified in an elaborate but unsatisfactory manner. The meanings of the fields of a message are only given informally. Often it is hard to know precisely what the recipient of a message will do with it or when a particular message will be sent. It is often unclear what counts as a successful outcome. When it comes to syntax, we have the opposite problem: too much detail. The fields of each message are specified down to the last bit. Current verification technology cannot cope with detailed descriptions.

The SET protocol documentation suffers from the same problem. SET-Book 3 [12] provides a Formal Protocol Definition in ASN.1. It specifies each message field and yet it is not sufficient, as we have already noted. To resolve issues one must look elsewhere, such as in the Programmer's Guide [13] or in the Business Description [11], but sometimes they contradict each other. The SET designers state, 'In the event of discrepancy between this and any other description of the protocol, the ASN.1 in Part II takes precedence' [12, p. 1] but (as we have seen) this is sometimes impossible.

The Business Description [11] is most misleading — its figures especially. For instance, the description of the Payment Authorization phase suggests that each merchant will receive from the payment gateway a digital envelope containing in clear the primary account number of the customer [11, p. 66]. This contradicts the text which forbids such eventuality [11, p. 12]: 'SET ensures that in the cardholder's interactions with the merchant, the payment card account information remains confidential.' To complicate matters, in the fine print of the formal definition, a field in the certificate gives some merchants the privilege of receiving the cardholder account information in clear. The explicit requirement of confidentiality specified by the SET designers can then be overruled by an implementation which adheres to the specifications. The effect of this trap-door on the formal analysis of the payment phase remains to be seen.

We used the Programmer's Guide [13] as the ultimate reference. Other readers of the specification may resolve its ambiguities in other ways.

4   Cryptographic Functions for Cardholder Registration

This section presents the Cardholder Registration phase in a format similar to those used in security protocol papers. It also shows the relationship between the SET documentation and its Isabelle formalization. We introduce some notation and explain how we encode the complex combinations of hashing, strong and weak encryption that are used in SET and in the PKCS#7 standard.

Below, M and m denote messages, s denotes a sender, r denotes a receiver (s and r are SET entities). Here are the building blocks of our construction:

C, CA, RCA: entities involved in the CR-phase, respectively Cardholder, Certification Authority and Root Certification Authority
N_X, K_X: nonce N and symmetric key K generated by an agent X
$pubEK_X$, $privEK_X$: public and private encryption keys held by agent X
$pubSK_X$, $privSK_X$: public and private signature keys held by agent X
PAN_X: Primary Account Number of agent X
$\{X, Y, Z, \dots\}$: a sequence (tuple) of zero or more data elements
$H(X)$: hash of tuple X
$\{X\}_K$: encryption of X with key K

The *DigestedData* $DD(M)$ is a simple construction. It is defined as the concatenation of a message and its digest, but in this case the plain message is absent; so we have only $H(M)$ for a message M. The *Linkage L(M,m)* is a shorthand for $\{M, DD(m)\}$. It links m to M as only someone possessing m or a trusted hash of m can verify the linkage. The intuition is that m contains some pieces of M. We express it as $\{M, H(m)\}$.

The *Signature only* $SO(s, M)$ is the signature of entity s on message M, omitting the plaintext of M, and corresponds to a PKCS#7 *SignedData* with the 'Content' field set to 'absent.' In our notation it is $\{H(M)\}_{privSK_s}$. The *Signed message S(s,M)* is a shorthand for $\{M, SO(s, M)\}$. It represents a full signature, the concatenation of a message M and its signed digest, and corresponds to a PKCS#7 *SignedData*. In our model it is expressed as $\{M, \{H(M)\}_{privSK_s}\}$ and is abbreviated as $\mathtt{Sign}_s\{M\}$.

The *Asymmetric encryption* $E(r, M)$ uses a mixture of symmetric and asymmetric encryption. Given a message M, this is encrypted with a fresh symmetric key K and K itself is encrypted with the receiver r's public encryption key. It corresponds to the PKCS#7 *EnvelopedData* combining RSA encryption and Bellare-Rogaway Optimal Asymmetric Encryption Padding (OAEP). Since OAEP just aims at strengthening the cryptographic algorithms, we simply code this primitive as the pair $\{\{M\}_K, \{K\}_{pubEK_r}\}$ and abbreviates it as $\mathtt{Encr}_r\{M\}$.

The *Extra encryption with integrity* $EXH(r, M, m)$ is a more complex form of digital envelope. Here m is a message usually containing payment card information and a nonce useful to foil dictionary attacks. Extra encryption with integrity is implemented in accordance with the following procedure:

- The hash of m is concatenated to M (as in a linkage);
- this is encrypted with a fresh symmetric key K obtaining a message m';
- a digital envelope containing K, m, and the hash of M is encrypted with the receiver r's public key;
- m' and the envelope are concatenated.

After being expanded and simplified, $EXH(r, M, m)$ can be expressed as

$$\{\{M, H(m)\}_K, \{K, m, H(M)\}_{pubEK_r}\}.$$

Hashing is used to verify integrity, but this primitive uses no signature and cannot authenticate the sender.

Simple Encapsulation with signature $Enc(s, r, M)$ models both digital signature and digital envelope and is an instance of PKCS#7 *SignedData* encapsulated in *EnvelopedData*. The message M is first signed with the private key of s and then encrypted with a fresh symmetric key K sent to r in a digital envelope. Thus *Enc(s,r,M)* is equivalent to $E(r, S(s, M))$ and is expanded as $\{\{M, \{H(M)\}_{privSK_s}\}_K, \{K\}_{pubEK_r}\}$. This primitive authenticates the sender and provides confidentiality.

Simple Encapsulation with signature and provided key data $EncK(kd, s, M)$ is an instance of PKCS#7 *SignedData* encapsulated in *EncryptedData*. It models a message M first signed with the sender's private key and then encrypted with a symmetric key K. (The word 'provided' means that the key data must have been provided in advance by some other message of the protocol.) It is typically used if K is a symmetric key which has been previously sent by r. With this latter hypothesis, it guarantees both data confidentiality and sender's authentication. It boils down to $\{M, \{H(M)\}_{privSK_s}\}_K$.

The *Extra encapsulation with signature EncX(s,r,M,m)* is also a signed and sealed message, but it requires a more complex procedure:

- The DER[1] encoding of m is concatenated to M;
- the sender s signs a digest of the resulting message, yielding m';
- message m' is concatenated to M;
- the message resulting from the previous step is encrypted with a fresh symmetric key K, yielding a message m'';
- K and m are sealed using the public encryption key of r;
- finally m'' and this envelope are concatenated.

Since DER encoding is injective, we can replace $DER(m)$ with m. Expanding the primitive results in $\{\{M, \{H(M, m)\}_{privSK_s}\}_K, \{K, m\}_{pubEK_r}\}$.

SET certificates make reference to X.509 Version 3 certificates [6], but includes the use of X.509 extensions (as defined in PKCS#6 [20]) and further SET-specific extensions. The point of including a set of attributes is to extend the certification process to other information about an entity, not just its public key. For instance, such information includes whether a merchant is allowed to get hold of his customer's PAN.

For simplicity, our certificate has only the attributes relevant to the formal analysis. The obvious attributes to take into consideration include the *Subject* (the certificate owner's identity) and the *SubjectPublicKeyInfo* (the certified public key). The issuing certificate authority is identified by the key signing the certificate. Unusually, the CA signs the entire plaintext (not just an hash of it). So, a certificate containing information I is implemented as $\{I, \{I\}_{privSK_{CA}}\}$. Since an hash is much smaller than the actual message, by signing the whole message the CA might have a better defence against brute force cryptanalysis.

Several attributes specify which entity is the certificate owner, the intended use of the certified key and whether this key may be used to issue other certificates (the default answer is no). There is also a flag F to distinguish between signature and encryption certificates. We omit certificate thumbprints, validity periods and revocation lists. Finally we obtain the following encoding of the certificates for cardholders and certification authorities:

$$certC = \{\{H(PAN, PANSecret), pubSK_C, F\},$$
$$\{H(PAN, PANSecret), pubSK_C, F\}_{priSK_{CA}}\}$$
$$certCA = \{CA, pubK_{CA}, F\}, \{CA, pubK_{CA}, F\}_{priSK_{RCA}}\}$$

---

[1] DER (Distinguished Encoding Rules) is a set of rules for representing OSI's (Open Systems Interconnection) abstract objects as strings of ones and zeros.

Note that *PANSecret* is obtained as the exclusive 'or' of two nonces N_{SecC}, provided by the Cardholder C, and N_{SecCA}, provided by the Certification Authority CA.

We need a few more abbreviations. By $\mathtt{CertE}_{CA}\{X\}$ we denote the certificate of the public encryption key of X by the certification authority CA (the flag F is set to 0) and by $\mathtt{CertS}_{CA}\{X\}$ we denote the certificate of the public signing key of X by the certification authority CA (the flag F is set to 1).

Finally, we can compose all above constructs, fill the gaps in the specifications that we have mentioned in Sect. 3. We obtain the high-level model of SET Cardholder Registration (Fig. 2 above).

5   Modelling Cardholder Registration in Isabelle

Modelling SET-CR requires new techniques. The generation of a pair of asymmetric keys (step 5) and the verification preceding the issue of certificates (step 6) have never been formalised before. To deal with the incompleteness of the official SET specifications, we decided to adopt the following policy: *the model should allow everything that the official specifications do not forbid.*

Isabelle includes generic theories for analysing security protocols. In order to handle SET, we had to modify and extend them, especially the model of key management. In this section we assume familiarity with the *inductive approach* to verifying protocols [18].

5.1   Agents

First of all, we need to model the SET certification chain. The model reduces the four levels of the actual hierarchy of trust to two, bypassing brand CAs and geo-political CAs: we denote by RCA the root certification authority, and introduce an unbounded number of first-level certification authorities CA's.

```
datatype agent = RCA | CA nat | Friend nat | Spy
```

5.2   Messages

The Primary Account Number (PAN) of the payment card is exchanged during SET sessions. We do not model a PAN as a nonce because it has a long lifetime, while fresh nonces are chosen for each run. We extend the Isabelle datatype for messages with a constructor Pan to allow PANs as message components.

```
datatype msg = Agent agent | Nonce nat | Number nat | Key key |
               Pan nat | Hash msg | MPair msg msg | Crypt key msg
```

A datatype definition introduces injective type constructors with disjoint ranges. Here this asserts that PANs cannot be confused with other numbers. Injectivity also implies that hashing is collision free and that an encrypted message corresponds to exactly one plaintext.

The model presupposes that PANs cannot be guessed. Therefore, the spy can synthesize them from a set H of message components, only if they are already available in the set, as stated by the theorem

$$\mathsf{Pan}\, P \in \mathsf{synth}\, H \implies \mathsf{Pan}\, P \in H.$$

The function pan maps agents into naturals so that $\mathsf{Pan}\,(\mathsf{pan}\,A)$ formalises the message containing agent A's PAN.

5.3   Cryptographic Keys

Classical authentication protocols presuppose that each agent owns certain long-term keys and possibly acquires session keys. In contrast, certification protocols distribute long-term keys. We need to formalize this scenario and to understand new kinds of risks. In addition to distributing pairs of asymmetric long-term keys, SET-CR allows each agent to own several pairs, with the possibility of collision. The protocol uses different keys for different purposes: some for encryption, some for message signature, others for certificate signature. For simplicity, we identify the two kinds of signing keys. Thus, keys are associated to agents as follows.

- The root certification authority has a single pair of signature keys.
- A certification authority has a pair of encryption keys and a pair of signature keys. The SET specifications do not clearly state whether a CA may have more than one pair of each kind.
- A cardholder has no keys at the beginning but obtains them during a run. We assume that he can obtain more than one pair of keys regardless of which authority certifies them, as the SET specifications do not forbid this.
- The spy can obtain keys by running the protocol and also knows the keys of an unspecified set of certification authorities (see Sect. 5.4).

Note that the standard mapping of agents into keys by a single function is not acceptable: some keys that do not exist in reality would be associated to the cardholders. Hence, a bit more work is necessary for the Isabelle formalization.

Suitable rules state that all the keys existing before any protocol run are distinct. We call them *crucial* and put them in the set CrucialK.

5.4   Agents' Knowledge

Our model allows some certification authorities to collude with the spy in three different ways. An unspecified set badS of authorities has revealed their signature keys to the spy. Another set badE has revealed their encryption keys. A third set badN of authorities let the spy read any private notes, possibly containing crucial information, taken during the protocol sessions. The sets are unrelated and model many different scenarios. The Root CA is never compromised.

The existing formalisation of agents' knowledge [1,2] allows each agent to know the messages he alone sends or receives, while the spy knows all messages anybody sends or receives. This definition can easily be updated to capture the requirements stated above.

5.5 The Protocol Model

The signature of a message or of a certificate are two slightly different operations. Signing a message X by a key K returns the concatenation of X with the encryption by K of the hash of X. Signing a certificate X by a key K differs from the preceding operation by omitting the hashing. We model them as follows:

```
sign K X == {|X, Crypt K (Hash X)|}
signCert K X == {|X, Crypt K X|}
```

The protocol uses two different kinds of certificates: one issued by the cardholder, the other by the certification authorities. The cardholder issues a certificate by signing a message that contains his PAN and a nonce previously generated. The certification authorities issue certificates that bind an agent to a key. An extra parameter F distinguishes the encryption certificates ($F = 0$) from the signature certificates ($F = 1$).

```
certC PAN KA PS F SignK ==
    signCert SignK {|Hash{|Account PAN, Nonce PS|}, Key KA, Number F|}
certCA A KA F SignK == signCert SignK {|Agent A, Key KA, Number F|}
```

The formal protocol model is declared as a set of traces. A trace is a list of the events occurred during a particular history of the network.

```
consts set_cr :: event list set
```

The basic rules for defining set_cr provide the base of the induction, allow reception of the messages that have been sent and model the spy's illegal operations. They are omitted here, for they are common to all protocol models. The remaining rules formalise the protocol steps. Because of space limitations, we only quote the rules formalising the last two steps.

Rule SET_CR5. Two fresh nonces are needed: N_{C_3} establishes the freshness of the subsequent message, while N_{SecC} is used by the CA. The nonce N_{CA}, sent by the certification authority to verify the freshness of the subsequent message, is not sent back by the cardholder (it is optional in the formal definition), so its utility looks questionable. Two fresh symmetric keys are needed: K_{C_3} is used to create a digital envelope, K_{C_2} to encrypt the reply.

The cardholder generates a key *cardSK* that he wants certified as a public signature key. The only condition imposed on *cardSK* is that it should differ from the crucial keys. The model allows the cardholder to propose keys that have already been certified, possibly for a different cardholder or by a different authority.

```
[| evs5 ∈ set_cr; C ≠ (CA i);
    Nonce NC3 ∉ used evs5; Nonce NSecC ∉ used evs5; NC3≠NSecC;
    Key KC2 ∉ used evs5; isSymKey(KC2);
    Key KC3 ∉ used evs5; isSymKey(KC3); KC2≠KC3;
    ~isSymKey(cardSK); cardSK ∉ crucialK; invKey cardSK ∉ crucialK;
```

```
      Gets C {|sign (invKey SK) {|Agent C, Nonce NC2, Nonce NCA|},
               certCA (CA i) EK 0 priSK_RCA,
               certCA (CA i) SK 1 priSK_RCA |}  ∈ set evs5;
      Says C (CA i) {|Crypt KC1 {|Agent C, Nonce NC2,
                                  Hash (Account (pan C)) |},
                      Crypt EK {|Key KC1, Account (pan C),
                                  Hash {|Agent C, Nonce NC2|} |} |}
         ∈ set evs5 |]
  ==> Says C (CA i)
            {|Crypt KC3
                 {|Agent C, Nonce NC3, Key KC2, Key cardSK,
                   Crypt (invKey cardSK)
                     (Hash {|Agent C, Nonce NC3, Key KC2, Key cardSK,
                             Account (pan C), Nonce NSecC|} ) |},
                 Crypt EK {|Key KC3, Account (pan C), Nonce NSecC|} |}
            # evs5 ∈ set_cr
```

Rule SET_CR6. When the certification authority receives a certificate request, he checks that the proposed public key has been used to sign the hash. Then he generates a certificate, which includes the fresh nonce N_{SecCA}. The condition

$$\forall \text{ C'}. \text{ Key cardSK} \in \text{parts\{Y\}} \rightarrow \text{Says (CA i) C' Y} \notin \text{set evs6}$$

requires that the proposed key *cardSK* has never appeared in a message sent by the certification authority. So the cardholder can be assured that the same key has not been certified to some other agent. This condition is not explicitly required by the SET specifications, but the *Programmer's Guide* [13, p. 33] states the general principle that a certificate should 'bind a public key to a uniquely identified entity.' Our model does allow a private key of one agent to be certified as a public key of another one.

```
  [| evs6 ∈ set_cr;   (CA i) ≠ C;
     Nonce NSecCA ∉ used evs6;
     ∀ C'. Key cardSK ∈ parts{Y} → Says (CA i) C' Y ∉ set evs6;
     Gets (CA i)
           {|Crypt KC3
                {|Agent C, Nonce NC3, Key KC2, Key cardSK,
                  Crypt (invKey cardSK)
                    (Hash {|Agent C, Nonce NC3, Key KC2, Key cardSK,
                            Account (pan C), Nonce NSecC|} ) |},
                Crypt (pubEK i) {|Key KC3, Account(pan C), Nonce NSecC|}|}
           ∈ set evs6 |]
  ==> Says (CA i) C
          (Crypt KC2
             {|sign (priSK i)
                     {|Agent C, Nonce NC3, Agent (CA i), Nonce NSecCA|},
               certC (pan C) cardSK (XOR(NSecC,NSecCA)) 1 (priSK i),
               certCA (CA i) (pubSK i) 1 priSK_RCA|})
```

6   Mechanically Proved Properties

At the start, we had to prove all over again the properties of the modified theory of messages, which form the basis of Paulson's inductive method. This totals around 200 theorems. Isabelle's automation made this task easy, allowing us to concentrate on the novel aspects of the theories under study.

Security properties from the protocol verification literature [10,18,22], such as authentication and agreement, are often impossible to prove for the whole protocol run. A cause is the optional use of nonces, which are sent but need not be returned. So, it impossible to establish linkages of messages throughout the protocol.

For the analysis of Cardholder Registration, we have proved around 30 technical lemmas focussed towards the proofs of two major properties: a key is only certified as belonging to one agent (at least by the same CA), and the PAN remains confidential.

For the first property, we have been successful. Formally, if each authority should certify a given key only once, this means that if there exist two messages from a CA that certify the same key, then those messages are identical. This is stated by the following theorem.

Theorem 1.
```
[| evs ∈ set_cr
   Says (CA i) C
        (Crypt KC2
           {|sign (priSK i) {|Agent C, Nonce NC3, Agent(CA i), Nonce Y|},
             certC (pan C) cardSK X 1 (priSK i),
             certCA (CA i) (pubSK i) 1 priSK_RCA|}) ∈ set evs;
   Says (CA i) C'
        (Crypt KC2'
           {|sign (priSK i) {|Agent C, Nonce NC3', Agent(CA i), Nonce Y'|},
             certC (pan C) cardSK X' 1 (priSK i),
             certCA (CA i) (pubSK i) 1 priSK_RCA|}) ∈ set evs
|] ⟹ C=C' & KC2=KC2' & NC3=NC3' & X=X' & Y=Y'
```

In the proof, after induction and simplification, the subgoal arising from the modelling of the last step of the protocol requires further consideration. In this step, an authority CA i' certifies a key $cardSK'$. If either $i \neq i'$ or $cardSK' \neq cardSK$, then the inductive formula concludes the proof. Otherwise, the authority CA i has certified $cardSK$ twice, which our model forbids: contradiction.

While stressing that each authority certifies a specific key for a single cardholder, the theorem does not prevent different authorities to certify the same key for the same cardholder. Such a scenario is a subject for future analysis.

We have not managed to prove confidentiality of the PAN. In particular, we have not been able to eliminate a subgoal stating that no collection of keys can help the spy in getting the CAs' private keys. Again, the difference with other protocols is that here asymmetric key pairs are generated on the fly. The novelty of the problem seems to require novel proof techniques.

7   Conclusions

The introduction described other work concerning the SET protocol. But no previous work completely formalizes a phase of this protocol. One reason may be that the official specifications of SET [11,12,13] describe the composition of messages in minute detail, while failing to give them a satisfactory semantics.

Our inductive specification provides an operational semantics for the Cardholder Registration phase. We have unveiled some potentially dangerous omissions. We have proved that if a trusted CA keeps track of the registered keys, the protocol is robust enough to guarantee that two different agents will never get the same key certified by the same certification authority. However, different agents may collude and register the same key with different CAs. We have not investigated the consequences of this scenario, which might limit the accountability of the payment phase.

Our future work will cover the remaining phases of the protocol. Having digested the specifications, the greatest task is behind us. We expect to be able to derive further properties of SET with an acceptable amount of effort.

Acknowledgements. F. Massacci acknowledges the support of CNR and MURST grants. Part of this work has been done while P. Tramontano was visiting the Computer Laboratory in Cambridge under a visiting scholarship for master students by the University of Roma I "La Sapienza". L. Paulson was funded by the EPSRC grant GR/K57381 *Mechanizing Temporal Reasoning*.

References

1. G. Bella. Message reception in the inductive approach. Research Report 460, University of Cambridge — Computer Laboratory, 1999.
2. G. Bella. Modelling agents' knowledge inductively. In *Proceedings of the 7th International Workshop on Security Protocols*, volume 1796 of *Lecture Notes in Comp. Sci.* Springer-Verlag, 1999.
3. G. Bella and L. C. Paulson. Kerberos version IV: Inductive analysis of the secrecy goals. In *Proc. of the 5th Eur. Sym. on Res. in Comp. Sec.*, volume 1485 of *Lecture Notes in Comp. Sci.*, pages 361–375. Springer-Verlag, 1998.
4. S. Brackin. Automatic formal analyses of two large commercial protocols. In *Proceedings of the DIMACS Workshop on Design and Formal Verification of Security Protocols*, September 1997. Available on the web at http://www.arca.com/proj_papers/brackin/dimacs.pdf.
5. S. Brackin. Automatically detecting authentication limitations in commercial security protocols. In *Proceedings of the 22nd National Conference on Information Systems Security*, October 1999. Available on the web at http://www.arca.com/proj_papers/brackin/Nissc99.pdf.
6. CCITT. *Recommendation X.509: The Directory - Authentication Framework*, 1988. Available electronically at http://www.itu.int/itudoc/itu-t/rec/x/x500up/x509.html.
7. R. Kailar. Reasoning about accountability in protocols for electronic commerce. In *Proc. of the 14th IEEE Sym. on Sec. and Privacy*, pages 236–250. IEEE Comp. Society Press, 1995.

8. V. Kessler and H. Neumann. A sound logic for analysing electronic commerce protocols. In J. Quisquater, Y. Deswarte, C. Meadows, and D. Gollmann, editors, *Proc. of the 5th Eur. Sym. on Res. in Comp. Sec.*, volume 1485 of *Lecture Notes in Comp. Sci.* Springer-Verlag, 1998.

9. L. Loeb. *Secure Electronic Transactions: Introduction and Technical Reference.* Computer Science. Artech House, 1998. Enclosed a CD-ROM with SET Reference Implementation Version 1.0.

10. G. Lowe. A hierarchy of authentication specifications. In *Proc. of the 10th IEEE Comp. Sec. Found. Workshop*, pages 31–43. IEEE Comp. Society Press, 1997.

11. Mastercard & VISA. *SET Secure Electronic Transaction Specification: Business Description*, May 1997. Available electronically at `http://www.setco.org/set_specifications.html`.

12. Mastercard & VISA. *SET Secure Electronic Transaction Specification: Formal Protocol Definition*, May 1997. Available electronically at `http://www.setco.org/set_specifications.html`.

13. Mastercard & VISA. *SET Secure Electronic Transaction Specification: Programmer's Guide*, May 1997. Available electronically at `http://www.setco.org/set_specifications.html`.

14. C. Meadows. Open issues in formal methods for cryptographic protocol analysis. In *Proceedings of DISCEX 2000*, pages 237–250. IEEE Comp. Society Press, 2000.

15. C. Meadows and P. Syverson. A formal specification of requirements for payment transactions in the SET protocol. In R. Hirschfeld, editor, *Proceedings of Financial Cryptography 98*, volume 1465 of *Lecture Notes in Comp. Sci.* Springer-Verlag, 1998.

16. R. M. Needham and M. Schroeder. Using encryption for authentication in large networks of computers. *Comm. of the ACM*, 21(12):993–999, 1978.

17. D. O'Mahony, M. Peirce, and H. Tewari. *Electronic payment systems.* The Artech House computer science library. Artech House, 1997.

18. L. C. Paulson. The inductive approach to verifying cryptographic protocols. *J. of Comp. Sec.*, 6:85–128, 1998.

19. L. C. Paulson. Inductive analysis of the internet protocol TLS. *ACM Trans. on Inform. and Sys. Sec.*, 2(3):332–351, 1999.

20. RSA Laboratories. *PKCS-6: Extended-Certificate Syntax Standard*, 1993. Available electronically at `http://www.rsasecurity.com/rsalabs/pkcs`.

21. RSA Laboratories. *PKCS-7: Cryptographic Message Syntax Standard*, 1993. Available electronically at `http://www.rsasecurity.com/rsalabs/pkcs`.

22. S. Schneider. Verifying authentication protocols in CSP. *IEEE Trans. on Software Engineering*, 24(9):741–758, 1998.

Automating Data Independence

P. J. Broadfoot[1], G. Lowe[2], and A. W. Roscoe[1*]

[1] Oxford University Computing Laboratory, Wolfson Building, Parks Road, Oxford, OX1 3QD, UK, {Philippa.Broadfoot, Bill.Roscoe}@comlab.ox.ac.uk.
[2] Department of Mathematics and Computer Science, University of Leicester, University Road, Leicester, LE1 7RH, UK, gavin.lowe@mcs.le.ac.uk.

Abstract. In this paper, we generalise and fully automate the use of data independence techniques in the analysis of security protocols, developed in [16,17]. In [17], we successfully applied these techniques to a series of case studies; however, our scripts were carefully crafted by hand to suit each case study, a rather time-consuming and error-prone task. We have fully automated the data independence techniques by incorporating them into Casper, thus abstracting away from the user the complexity of the techniques, making them much more accessible.

Keywords: security protocols; data independence; automatic verification; model checking; Casper; CSP; FDR.

1 Introduction

Model checkers have been extremely effective in finding attacks on security protocols: see, for example, [9,12,13,14]. However, until a few years ago, their use in *proving* protocols had generally been limited to showing that a given small instance, usually restricted by the finiteness of some set of resources such as keys and nonces, is free of attacks.

In [16], Roscoe developed techniques borrowed from data independence and related fields to simulate, using the process algebra CSP [15], a system where agents can call upon an infinite supply of different nonces, keys, etc., even though the actual types remain finite. It was thus possible to create models of protocols in which agents could perform an unbounded number of sequential runs—although with a fixed, finite number of *concurrent* runs—and therefore claim that a finite-state check on a model checker, such as FDR [2], proved that a given protocol was free from attacks—subject to the same limit on the number of concurrent runs. These methods made it possible to prove far more complete results on model checkers than hitherto.

Our data independence techniques were further developed and successfully applied to a series of case studies in [17]; however, our scripts were carefully crafted by hand to suit each case study. This process proved to be time-consuming, error-prone and required a substantial knowledge of the CSP language and a good understanding of the theory underlying the data independence techniques.

---

* The authors received support from DERA Malvern and the US Office of Naval Research for the work reported in this paper.

F. Cuppens et al. (Eds.): ESORICS 2000, LNCS 1895, pp. 175–190, 2000.

In this paper we present the automation of our data independence techniques, by integrating them into Casper. Casper [10] is a compiler which takes a more abstract description of a security protocol (similar to that in the literature) and a specification of the properties to be verified; it automatically generates the CSP description, which can then be loaded directly into FDR.

Further, we present some generalisations of our methods, which allow a broader class of protocols to be modelled.

This work has already proved to be very useful for generating our CSP protocol models, since it only takes Casper a couple of seconds to perform the task, which in the past took us several weeks per protocol model.

2 Background

2.1 Modelling Security Protocols Using CSP and FDR

Security protocols are traditionally described in the literature as a series of messages between the various legitimate participants. The main example we will be using throughout this paper is a version of the Yahalom protocol closely based on the one suggested in [1]. Its five messages are:

$$
\begin{aligned}
\text{Message 1.} \quad & A \to B \;:\; N_a \\
\text{Message 2.} \quad & B \to S \;:\; N_b, \{A, N_a\}_{SKey(B)} \\
\text{Message 3.} \quad & S \to A \;:\; N_b, \{B, K_{ab}, N_a\}_{SKey(A)} \\
\text{Message 4.} \quad & S \to B \;:\; N_b, \{A, K_{ab}, N_b\}_{SKey(B)} \\
\text{Message 5.} \quad & A \to B \;:\; \{N_b\}_{K_{ab}}
\end{aligned}
$$

The only difference from the version in [1] is the way in which the server communicates message 4 directly to B rather than using A as a messenger. This type of re-direction has been shown in [3] to have no effect on security.

Such a description implicitly describes the role of each participant in the protocol and carries the implication that whenever an agent has, *from its point of view*, executed all the communications implied by the protocol, then it can take whatever action is enabled by the protocol. The above protocol is intended to *authenticate* A and B to each other. This particular version has a well known attack found by Syverson [19]. However, we will use it as our example throughout the paper to illustrate and clarify the techniques introduced.

We analyse security protocols using the process algebra CSP [15] and its model checker FDR [2]. We outline the traditional approach—without the application of data independence techniques—below. Further details can be found in [9,12].

Each honest participant of the protocol is modelled as a CSP process. These processes are relatively straightforward to derive from standard description of protocols presented in the literature.

The intruder is also modelled as a CSP process. This intruder can: overhear all messages that pass between the honest agents; prevent a message sent by one agent from reaching the intended recipient; generate new messages from those messages held initially or subsequently overheard, subject only to derivation rules that reflect the properties of the crypto-system in use; and send such messages to any agent, purporting to be from any other. We only allow the intruder to generate messages of size bounded by the message structure of the protocol, so we do not consider messages that do not correspond to part of a genuine protocol message. This is a standard assumption and one which can be justified in many cases, but it should be borne in mind that as with various points of our modelling, all our results are relative to it.

A system is created from a parallel combination of honest agents, together with an intruder. The system normally—but not necessarily—contains as many agents as are necessary for a complete run of the protocol (in the case of our example above, this would be two agents and one server).

One then seeks to show that any session that may occur between the honest nodes is secure, no matter what the actions of the intruder from the range above. This includes showing that if either of the nodes *thinks* it has completed a run of the protocol with the other, then it really has (see [11] for further details concerning specifications).

2.2   Casper

Model checkers (in our case, FDR) have proved to be extremely effective in checking for, and finding, attacks on security protocols. However, the process of creating the CSP protocol models is time-consuming, error-prone and requires a substantial knowledge of the CSP language. Casper [10] is a program which takes a more abstract description of a protocol and generates the corresponding CSP description. The CSP output file is such that it can be loaded directly into FDR, and the requested checks upon the protocol automatically tested. The style of the protocol descriptions in a Casper input file is based on that in the literature and is therefore familiar to users who are interested in modelling them. Casper has proved to be an extremely useful tool for generating these scripts and is accessible to a wide audience of users.

Figure 1 presents an example of a simple Casper script, namely the Yahalom protocol example we are using throughout this paper. There are two main parts to a Casper input script: a definition of the way in which the protocol operates (the first four sections); and a definition of the actual system to be verified (the last four sections).

2.3   Data Independence Techniques

A program P is said to be *data independent* in the type T if it places no constraints on what T is: the latter can be regarded as a *parameter* of P. Broadly speaking, P can input and output members of T, hold them as parameters, compare them for equality, and apply *polymorphic* operations to them such as tupling and list forming. It may not apply other operations such as functions

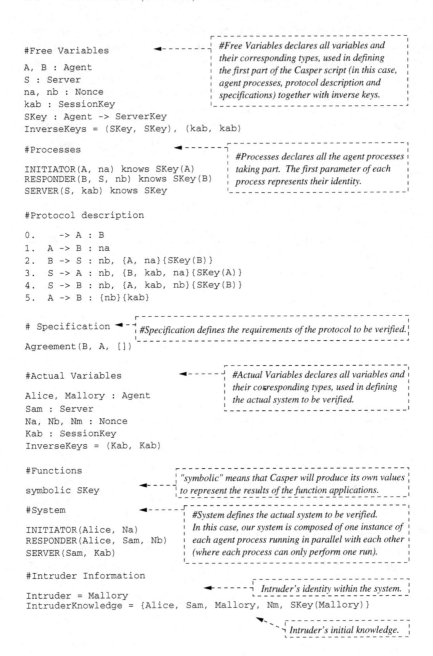

```
#Free Variables          ◄-------    #Free Variables declares all variables and
                                      their corresponding types, used in defining
A, B : Agent                          the first part of the Casper script (in this case,
S : Server                            agent processes, protocol description and
na, nb : Nonce                        specifications) together with inverse keys.
kab : SessionKey
SKey : Agent -> ServerKey
InverseKeys = (SKey, SKey), (kab, kab)

#Processes               ◄------
                                      #Processes declares all the agent processes
INITIATOR(A, na) knows SKey(A)        taking part. The first parameter of each
RESPONDER(B, S, nb) knows SKey(B)     process represents their identity.
SERVER(S, kab) knows SKey

#Protocol description

0.    -> A : B
1.  A -> B : na
2.  B -> S : nb, {A, na}{SKey(B)}
3.  S -> A : nb, {B, kab, na}{SKey(A)}
4.  S -> B : nb, {A, kab, nb}{SKey(B)}
5.  A -> B : {nb}{kab}

# Specification  ◄--    #Specification defines the requirements of the protocol to be verified.

Agreement(B, A, [])

#Actual Variables        ◄------      #Actual Variables declares all variables and
                                      their corresponding types, used in defining
Alice, Mallory : Agent                the actual system to be verified.
Sam : Server
Na, Nb, Nm : Nonce
Kab : SessionKey
InverseKeys = (Kab, Kab)

#Functions                       "symbolic" means that Casper will produce its own values
                          ◄----   to represent the results of the function applications.
symbolic SKey

#System                  ◄----
                                      #System defines the actual system to be verified.
INITIATOR(Alice, Na)                  In this case, our system is composed of one instance of
RESPONDER(Alice, Sam, Nb)             each agent process running in parallel with each other
SERVER(Sam, Kab)                      (where each process can only perform one run).

#Intruder Information

Intruder = Mallory       ◄------      Intruder's identity within the system.
IntruderKnowledge = {Alice, Sam, Mallory, Nm, SKey(Mallory)}

                                      Intruder's initial knowledge.
```

Fig. 1. Example of a Casper script for the Yahalom Protocol

that return members of T, or comparison operators such as $<$, or do things like compute the size of T. For further details and precise definitions, see [4,5,15].

The main objective of data independence analysis is usually to discover a finite *threshold* for a verification problem parameterised by the type T: a size of T beyond which the answer (positive or negative) to the problem will not vary. If we can verify a system for the threshold size of T, then we will have verified it for all larger values of T. This can be done successfully for a wide range of problems, as is shown, for example, in [15,6].

Several of the types used by crypto-protocol models have many of the characteristics of data independence. This is typically true of the type of nonces, types of keys that are not bound to a specific user, and may also be true of the type of agent identities. The main reason for this is that the abstract data type constructions used in the programs are polymorphic: there is no real difference between building a construction such as

```
Sq.<Nb, Encrypt.(SKey(A), <B, Kab, Na>)>
```

(the representation in our data type of a typical message 3) and building a list or tuple over the objects Nb, A, B, Kab and Na.

There are, however, several features of the protocol descriptions that mean the general purpose results for computing thresholds do not give useful results. Firstly, the assumption that each nonce or key generated is distinct means that there can be no hope of finite thresholds from standard results, because our program must at least implicitly carry an unbounded number of values in its state so it knows what to avoid next. The starting point for threshold calculations, in the context of equality tests, is the maximum number of values a process ever has to remember; so such calculations would give an infinite threshold in this case. Secondly, the nature of the intruder process causes difficulties because it also clearly has the ability to remember an unbounded number of values if they are available.

Since the general-purpose data independence results of the earlier papers had proved to be inapplicable, our approach (presented in [16,17]) was to apply some of the methods underlying the proofs of these results directly to the sort of CSP model that a protocol analysis generates. The aim was to take a "full-sized" model of a protocol (one with an unbounded number of other agents, and infinite sets of nonces, etc.) and to use these methods to reduce the problem of proving the correctness of a corresponding system for all parameter values to a finite check.

In [16], Roscoe showed how techniques borrowed from data independence and related fields can be used to achieve the illusion that nodes can call upon an infinite supply of different nonces, keys, etc., even though the actual types used for these things remain finite. It is thus possible to create models of protocols in which nodes do not have to stop after a small number of sequential runs, and to claim that a finite-state run on a model checker has proved that a given protocol is free from attacks that could be constructed in the model used. One proviso is that these techniques will only detect attacks that can be formed from the given degree of parallelism, and there remains the possibility that attacks could exist with a higher degree of parallelism. These methods were developed further and successfully applied to a number of case studies in [17].

These techniques were based around *manager processes*. In brief, for each data independent type T (for example, nonces or keys), we create a manager process MAN_T that gives the illusion of generating an infinite supply of fresh values, known as *foreground* values, when requested by participants. The manager process monitors the network so that, at all times, it knows which fresh values are stored by which participants. When such a value is no longer stored by any honest participant—when each honest agent that knew the value has terminated or withdrawn from the protocol run—the value can be *recycled*. The manager process is responsible for triggering the recycling mechanism, whereby forgotten foreground values get replaced by *background* values within the intruder's memory; the mapped values can then be reused. It is usually sufficient to include two background values of each type in the system: one that the intruder knows, and one that he doesn't. Roscoe showed in [16] that this recycling mechanism does not lose any attacks.

Our results rely on the fact that the intruder cannot perform any deductions based on the inequality of two objects with the same structures. Therefore, they only apply to intruders over a theory satisfying the *Positive Deductions* condition. What this essentially requires is that the generation of the deductions is symmetric in each data independent type T (i.e., treats all members of T equivalently) and never has an inequality requirement over members of T that appear on the left-hand side of a deduction (see [16] for further details).

3   Generalising Data Independence Techniques

In [17], these techniques were successfully applied to a number of case studies, the implementation being carefully crafted by hand to suit the protocol being modelled, in each case. All the case studies were for protocols obeying the following simple property:

> Each message M in the protocol introduces *at most* one variable V that is of a data independent type, and that is either *freshly* introduced by the sender or *newly acquired* by the receiver of M.

Message M might contain other variables $X_1, \ldots, X_n$ of data independent types in addition to V, as long as $X_1, \ldots, X_n$ are already known to the sender and receiver of M. This property simplifies the modelling strategy, but limits the class of protocols that can be modelled, because many protocols have multiple fresh variables introduced in one message, either of the same or different data independent types.

In this section, we present an overview of our new methodology for the application of these techniques. This makes them applicable to a broader spectrum of protocols, in particular, dropping the assumption above. It is also the key to how we fully automated their application within Casper (presented in Section 5).

3.1   Generalising Manager Processes

Previously, in [17], our manager processes were constructed with the assumption that the protocol models conformed to the property presented above; we refer to such managers as *one-dimensional*. This assumption makes the synchronisations between managers and monitored processes more straightforward, because a manager process does not have to handle multiple values in one synchronisation, and the managers collectively do not have to synchronise with each other.

We generalise the implementation of our techniques and abolish this limiting property above, by introducing *multi-dimensional* managers, as illustrated in the following example.

Example 1. Suppose the agent *Alice* is running some protocol and receives a message M in which she newly acquires two nonces and one key, where nonces and keys are data independent types:

$$... \rightarrow Alice : \{N_1, N_2, K_1\}_{K_2},$$

where key K_2 is assumed to be known to Alice already. Our *one-dimensional* managers could not handle this case. We require *multi-dimensional* managers where each manager process deals with *tuples* of values rather than a *single* value.

In this example, we would have two manager processes, MAN_N for nonces, and MAN_K for keys. MAN_N would have an event $told_N.X$ for every pair X of nonces. This message is subsequently renamed, so as to synchronise with the corresponding network message M, thereby allowing the manager to monitor multiple foreground values in a single synchronisation. Further, the key manager MAN_K will have its own event $told_K.Y$ for each 1-tuple Y of keys. The key manager must synchronise on the network message M, and hence will also synchronise with the nonce manager.

3.2   Stale Knowledge Generation

When applying these techniques, one runs into problems with the size of the state space of the protocol model. One reason for this is the gradual build up within the intruder of knowledge gathered from past protocol runs. All these messages have only background values in the places occupied by the data independent types, because all foreground values have been mapped to background values by the recycling mechanism.

If there are N such *stale* messages that the intruder might gain, then the effect is to multiply the total state space by as much as 2^N. To eliminate this problem, we observe that eventually the intruder can be expected to gain a complete set of this *stale knowledge* (with all values of data independent types mapped to background values), and can therefore exploit any such stale knowledge when attempting to perform attacks upon the protocol. So we simply calculate, at the start of a run, what the eventual set of stale knowledge ought to be and give this to the intruder as part of his initial knowledge. If done properly, this completely eliminates the state space explosion problem presented above.

In the case studies presented in [17], these sets of stale knowledge were calculated by hand. However, this proved to be error prone.

We have, therefore, automated the calculation of the stale knowledge by performing a series of *pre-run simulations* between combinations of agents, including cases where the intruder took some of the roles, taking care to distinguish those cases where the intruder does or does not know the values of data independent types included within the messages. These simulations do not affect the state space, since we do not perform any actual runs of the protocol. Instead, we make use of the existing computational methods that are used to calculate the intruder's initial knowledge from initially known values specified by the user, closed under the deduction rules. The simulations are performed by taking the set of messages that the intruder would see by observing a typical run, using the mechanism outlined above to calculate the closure under the deduction rules, and then mapping fresh values of data independent types to appropriate background values. Calculating these sets based on the model of the intruder allows us to automatically capture any subtleties within the intruder's specified behaviour.

4   Incorporating Honest Agents within the Intruder

Together with stale knowledge, a second strategy for reducing the state space of data independent protocol checks was introduced in [17]. This was to incorporate the functionality of some participant of the protocol into the intruder, thereby removing the need for an additional process in the system. An agent modelled this way is referred to as an *internal agent.*

It is only possible to do this easily for processes whose messages (or state of mind measured in some other way) are not directly examined by the specification we are using. Since such specifications tend to concentrate on the honest agents we have, to date, only incorporated server processes into the intruder. Henceforth, we will assume that it is a server that is being treated as internal.

In brief, the functionality of a server is captured within the intruder by means of an additional set of deductions and generations that the intruder can perform. As presented in more detail in [17], we classify internal agents into two categories. The first contains those that do not introduce any fresh variables of a data independent type at any point during the protocol. Internal agents in this first category are straightforward to incorporate into the intruder process and are captured with appropriate deductions (as demonstrated in the case studies presented in [17]). The second category are those internal agents that introduce fresh variables of data independent types at some stage in the protocol runs. Obvious examples of these are servers introducing fresh session keys like the one in the Yahalom example.

Deductions performed by the intruder are usually modelled by pairs of the form (X, f), where X is a finite set of facts and f is a fact that it can construct if it knows the whole of X, for example $(\{\{M\}_K, K\}, M)$. The functionality of the first sort of internal agent can be captured with this type of deduction within the intruder: we get a deduction (X, f) if, after the agent is told the messages in X, it can be expected to emit f (where f will be functionally dependent on X). The example given in [17] was the server in the TMN protocol ([12]) whose function was to receive two messages $M1$ and $M3$ and construct a corresponding third message $M4$, where $M4$ only contains variables in $M1$ and $M3$ (thereby not introducing any fresh variables into the system). The relevant deductions were therefore all valid instantiations of $(\{M1, M3\}, M4)$.

A special sort of "deduction" is required to model situations like that in our example protocol where an internalised server creates fresh values and may then put such values into several related packets (in our example, the second parts of messages 3 and 4). These *generations* have the form (t, X, Y), where t is a non-empty sequence of the fresh objects being created, X is the set of inputs the agent we are modelling requires to trigger it to produce the fresh values, and Y is the set of facts generated, which contain the fresh values that are produced. In our example, X would consist of a message 2, t would be a single fresh key, and Y would contain the second parts of messages 3 and 4:

$$t = \langle K_{ab} \rangle,$$
$$X = \{N_b, \{A, N_a\}_{SKey(B)}\},$$
$$Y = \{\{B, K_{ab}, N_a\}_{SKey(A)}, \{A, K_{ab}, N_b\}_{SKey(B)}\},$$

where K_{ab} is a fresh foreground value. (The first parts of messages 3 and 4 are not linked to the fresh value, and would be the subject of ordinary deductions.)

The sequence t (though it is rare for it to be more than length 1) synchronises with the appropriate manager(s), and the set Y is functionally dependent on X and t (i.e., if we know what messages went into our server, and what fresh values it generated in response, then we know what messages it will output).

Servers that generate fresh values create the most significant theoretical problem in our work. Namely, how can we reasonably limit the intruder's appetite for fresh values obtained from the server (whether internal or external) since it has the capability of requesting any number it wishes? The intruder can do this, for example, by using the same set X of inputs to the server to generate many different Y's, each characterised by a different key. Furthermore, it can often build up a store of these values and later use them one at a time with the honest agents. For essentially this reason, the recycling mechanism used elsewhere cannot be applied to these multiple Y's held within the intruder.

The only way to keep the number of fresh values manageable (or even finite) is to prevent the intruder storing many fresh values for later use. In automatically generated CSP scripts we are severe on the intruder: we stop it acquiring a new set of fresh values until one of the honest agents is ready to receive such a value "from the server". This bounds the state space satisfactorily, but how do we know we have not thrown away some attacks?

We are not aware of any real protocol where this simple approach does lose an attack, but that is not good enough since our objective is to provide a proof. On the assumption that the set Y that comes back from the server does indeed depend only on X and t, it is clearly true that any Y that the intruder could have acquired early for much later use could also be acquired just in time. Therefore, if the only thing the intruder does with the members of Y is to hand them on to honest agents, it is of no advantage to him to possess them early. The complications arise because the intruder might be in a position to make deductions from having many server-generated messages that affect his ability to produce other messages in advance of telling an honest agent about the fresh values.

We sketch below a solution which is guaranteed not to lose any attacks under the following additional assumptions:

- the server creates only one value of one type (so the t of each generation is a sequence of length 1);
- no agent learns any more than one value of this type at a time.

To simplify the presentation, we assume also that there is only one type being generated by the server (for example, there are not some generations of keys and some of nonces).

The solution to this is not unlike the background values used to enable the recycling of foreground values. We add extra, dummy values into the type being generated. These have the special characteristic that they are not accepted as genuine by any honest process (so the latter will never accept any message involving one). The intruder can use these values itself like any others, in particular doing deductions involving them. The trick is that we allow the intruder to perform, at any time, a "generation" based on a valid input set X, but unless there is a space in a honest agent for a value of the given type, the result will always be based on a dummy value. If there is a space, the result may be either a real or dummy value.

We can then argue that any trace of communications that take place between the intruder and agents in a model where there is an unbounded supply of values of the given type (and there is no restriction on how many times generations can occur) can be reproduced (with appropriate recycling mappings that occur in our existing model) in this intruder. For any message M that the intruder can generate when there is an unbounded supply of our type, it is possible to arrange that all the messages from the server that he uses to produce M are obtained after the last protocol message before M ("just in time"). This behaviour can be mapped onto a behaviour of the reduced system by mapping to dummy values all the values generated in these deductions other than the one value v freshly told to a trustworthy agent (if there is one), and making v the fresh value that the manager is still allowed to deliver to the intruder.

This use of dummy values therefore loses no attacks. However, there is the possibility that this technique introduces false attacks. An example would be where the value being introduced is a key K, and one of the messages contains something encrypted under K that the intruder would not otherwise learn; representing K by the dummy value, which the intruder could learn from elsewhere, would allow the intruder to deduce the contents of the message, as a false attack. The solution is to use two dummy values: one that is created in circumstances where we would expect the intruder to learn it legitimately, and one that is created in other cases. However, a single value appears to suffice more frequently than in the analogous case of background values.

There is no need to manage these dummy values via the manager process. Their "generation" can, in fact, be performed using ordinary deductions.

5 Full Automation of Data Independence Techniques

In this section, we begin by presenting an improvement to the CSP protocol models generated by Casper, which reduce the size of the state space; using data independence techniques increases the size of the state space, so these techniques would prove impractical without this balancing reduction. We then discuss the full integration of the data independence techniques within Casper.

5.1 Optimisation of Casper-Generated Scripts

The CSP protocol models generated by Casper make use of *signal events* that reflect the states of mind and beliefs of the honest processes running the protocol; these signal events are then used to specify security properties.

For example, suppose we want to test whether a protocol authenticates an agent Alice to another agent Bob, and whether they agree upon the value of some key k; we do this by testing whether if Bob thinks that he has completed a protocol run with Alice using a particular key k, represented by a signal event `signal.Commit.Bob.Alice.k`, then Alice thinks she was running the protocol with Bob using the same key, represented by an event `signal.Running.Alice.Bob.k`[1]. See [11] for fuller details, for example concerning details of the specifications and the placement of signals.

Previously, the definitions of the honest agents generated by Casper would interleave these signal events with the events representing the messages of the protocol. Unfortunately, these additional signal events greatly increases the number of traces of each process, and so greatly increases the state space. To overcome this problem, we redesigned our models so that instead of interleaving the signals with message events, the signals were introduced at the top most level, via an appropriate renaming of message events of the overall system process.

A problem arises, however, if the message event does not contain all the information needed to construct the corresponding signal event. To overcome this problem, we extended the CSP data structure representing the protocol messages by adding an additional field containing all the information required. (This field has *no* influence on the flow of messages in the protocol runs.) So, in our previous example, the message 5 corresponding to the desired signal event becomes `(Msg5, Encrypt.(kab, <nb>), <na>)`, where the extra field `<na>` completes the set of required variables for our signal event.

This optimisation on Casper has led to a dramatic reduction in the state space sizes of the protocols we model and check using FDR. For example, the

---

[1] We are simplifying the structure of the signal events slightly for ease of presentation.

number of states explored for the adapted Needham Schroeder Public Key Protocol [9] model (with two instances of the initiator and two of the responder agents running in parallel) using the new version of Casper is 15,050 states as opposed to the old version requiring 425,734 states; the value for the new version incorporates an optimisation inspired by and similar to one of those described in [18], namely that the intruder never acts when a trustworthy can output.

5.2   Incorporating Data Independence Techniques into Casper

Figure 2 presents an example of a Casper script modelling the same Yahalom protocol used in Figure 1, but this time incorporating our data independence techniques. The differences are minimal: we have abstracted away the design and complexity of our data independence techniques from the users of Casper, making our techniques much more accessible.

In brief, the main extensions to our Casper script are as follows. Firstly, the user must indicate which data types are to be treated as data independent. Within the #Processes section, variables of such types are indicated using the generates keyword: values for such variables will be freshly supplied by the corresponding manager processes. For example, in Figure 2 nonces and session keys are regarded as data independent, so the corresponding variables na, nb and kab are indicated as being generated in this way; by contrast, in Figure 1 these variables were introduced as parameters of the processes, with the parameters being instantiated in the #System section.

In the #Actual Variables section we declare the actual variables which will be used in our actual system; further, we now need to classify all variables of data independent types as either Foreground, KnownBackground or UnknownBackground values.

In the case of the foreground values, the user needs to estimate how many values the manager will need; if too few values are given, FDR will give a trace error, indicating that the manager process ran out of fresh values, and so was unable to allocate another value; in this case, the user can simply edit the Casper script to include an extra value. It is advisable to declare the minimum necessary number of foreground values for each type, since increasing this number will cause the state space of the system to grow dramatically. Finding methods for calculating the number needed is the subject of current work.

For each data independent type, the user must declare exactly one value as a KnownBackground value, and one as a UnknownBackground value.

The user can specify which roles should be modelled internally to the intruder process, using a line such as IntruderProcesses = SERVER, within the #Intruder Information section.

A further extension concerns the ability for the agent processes to withdraw *during* a session or not, captured by WithdrawOption = True / False. For full generality, one should allow agents to withdraw, but this increase the state space, so we make it an option.

```
#Free Variables

A, B : Agent
S : Server
na, nb : Nonce
kab : SessionKey
SKey : Agent -> ServerKey
InverseKeys = (SKey, SKey), (kab, kab)

#Processes

INITIATOR(A) knows SKey(A) generates na
RESPONDER(B, S) knows SKey(B) generates nb
SERVER(S) knows SKey generates kab
```

Values for na, nb, kab will be freshly supplied by the manager processes.

```
#Protocol description

0.    -> A : B
1. A -> B : na
2. B -> S : nb, {A, na}{SKey(B)}
3. S -> A : nb, {B, kab, na}{SKey(A)}
4. S -> B : nb, {A, kab, nb}{SKey(B)}
5. A -> B : {nb}{kab}


# Specification

Agreement(B, A, [])


#Actual Variables

Alice, Mallory : Agent
Sam : Server
N1, N2, N3 : Nonce (Foreground)
NBp : Nonce   (KnownBackground)
NBs : Nonce   (UnknownBackground)
K1, K2, K3 : SessionKey (Foreground)
KBp : SessionKey   (KnownBackground)
KBs : SessionKey   (UnknownBackground)
InverseKeys = (K1, K1), (K2, K2), (K3, K3), (KBp, KBp), (KBs, KBs)
```

Background values used for the recycling mechanism.

Declared foreground values used by the corresponding manager processes to generate the continous source of fresh values.

```
#Functions

symbolic SKey

#System

INITIATOR(Alice)
RESPONDER(Alice, Sam)
```
WithdrawOption = True / False

Optional: User can choose whether agents can withdraw at any point during a run or not.

```
#Intruder Information

Intruder = Mallory
IntruderKnowledge = {Alice, Sam, Mallory, NBp, KBp, SKey(Mallory)}
IntruderProcesses = SERVER
```

Functionality of SERVER process is to be captured within the intruder process.

Fig. 2. Casper script for the Yahalom protocol, using data independence techniques

5.3   Example

We now illustrate some of the advantages of our techniques by considering the results obtained when they are applied to the running example. The script in Figure 2 treats nonces and session keys as data independent. The script defines a system where a particular agent Alice can act both as initiator and responder, and can perform an unbounded number of sequential runs. The server is defined to be internal within the intruder process. The property we are interested in verifying is represented by the authentication specification Agreement(B, A, []) which, in brief, means that if A thinks she has successfully completed a run of the protocol with B, then B has previously been running the protocol, apparently with A, and furthermore, there is a one-to-one relationship between the runs of A and the runs of B. In our example, we test this authentication property between Alice (as responder) and herself (as initiator).

It is well known that this particular version of the Yahalom protocol is flawed. The attack we use for the purpose of illustrating our techniques is essentially the same as the well-known attack by Syverson (in [19]), except it is a self-authentication attack, between Alice and herself. We write $Alice_I$ and $Alice_R$ to differentiate Alice in her roles as initiator and responder, respectively.

- Message 1. $Alice_I \rightarrow Intruder_{Alice_R} : N_1$.
- The intruder performs the functionality of the server using message 1 from the current run, and an old message 2, namely $\{Alice, NBp\}_{SKey(Alice)}$, where NBp is the unknown background nonce, representing some old nonce used in a previous run. This allows the intruder to generate the two corresponding messages $\{Alice, K_1, N_1\}_{SKey(Alice)}$ and $\{Alice, K_1, NBp\}_{SKey(Alice)}$. If the server were implemented as a separate process, then this would be reflected in the following sequence of steps:

  Message 2. $Intruder_{Alice_R} \rightarrow Sam$: $N_1, \{Alice, NBp\}_{SKey(Alice)}$

  Message 3. $Sam \rightarrow Intruder_{Alice_I}$: $N_1, \{Alice, K_1, NBp\}_{SKey(Alice)}$

  Message 4. $Sam \rightarrow Intruder_{Alice_R}$: $N_1, \{Alice, K_1, N_1\}_{SKey(Alice)}$.

- Message 3. $Intruder_{Sam} \rightarrow Alice_I : \{Alice, K_1, N_1\}_{SKey(Alice)}$.
- Message 5. $Alice_I \rightarrow Intruder_{Alice_R} : \{N_1\}_{K_1}$.

Alice, as initiator, believes she has completed a run of the protocol with herself, as responder, when in actual fact, Alice did not participate in this latest run as responder.

This attack requires Alice to have run a session with herself previously, so in our previous models, without data independence techniques, we would not have caught this particular attack if we had defined a system where each agent could only perform one run each. When using data independent techniques, we do not need to worry about how many runs each agent has to perform in order to be sure we have captured potential attacks, since our techniques are such that the number of runs each instance can perform is unbounded.

Furthermore, this example nicely illustrates how effective the use of stale knowledge is in terms of state space. In the attack above, where we provided the intruder with stale knowledge, the attack was found in 223 states. However, if we remove the stale knowledge from the intruder's initial knowledge and perform the same check again, then we get the equivalent attack, but FDR now requires 258,967 states to find it. In systems where no attack is found, the difference becomes even larger.

6   Conclusion

In this paper, we presented some generalisations and the full automation of the data independence techniques developed in [17]. The first main generalisation involved dropping the assumption presented in Section 3.1, thereby making our techniques applicable to a broader spectrum of protocols. The second concerned the method used for calculating the stale knowledge sets: to ensure that the maximum set is correctly generated taking all sorts of subtleties within the model (for example, algebraic equivalences) into account, we based our new method of calculating them upon the existing computational methods that are used to calculate the intruder's initial knowledge.

The work on the application of data independence techniques presented thus far has successfully drawn us much closer towards complete correctness proofs automatically generated by Casper and FDR. We are now interested in expanding this work to be able to construct proofs for an arbitrary number of agents running the protocol in parallel with each other. We believe that our methods of incorporating honest agents into the intruder will prove useful for this.

Further planned extensions include the automation of the calculation of the number of foreground values required for each data independent type (as described in Section 5.2), a generalisation of the argument in Section 4 so as to do away with the additional assumptions, the incorporation of time stamps into our techniques, and the continued development of optimisation strategies within our models to reduce the state space size.

Data independence applies to a wide range of notations other than CSP, and we imagine that the same sort of ideas discussed here could profitably be used in other protocol model checkers. However, details will inevitably vary from notation to notation and require care. An encouraging development here is the work of Lazić and Nowak ([7]) which shows how Lazić's CSP data independence results can be transferred to a general setting.

References

1. Burrows, M., Abadi, M., Needham, R.: A Logic of Authentication. Proceedings of the Royal Society of London A, Vol. 426 (1989) 233-271
2. Formal Systems (Europe) Ltd: Failures-Divergences Refinement: FDR2 Manual (1997)

3. Hui, M., Lowe, G.: Fault-Preserving Simplifying Transformations for Security Protocols. Submitted for publication (2000)
4. Lazić, R.S.: A semantic study of data-independence with applications to the mechanical verification of concurrent systems. Oxford University D.Phil thesis (1998)
5. Lazić, R.S., Roscoe, A.W.: Using logical relations for automated verification of data-independent CSP. Proceedings of the Workshop on Automated Formal Methods (Oxford, U.K.). Electronic Notes in Theoretical Computer Science 5 (1997)
6. Lazić, R.S., Roscoe, A.W.: Verifying determinism of data-independent systems with labellings, arrays and constants. Proceedings of INFINITY (1998)
7. Lazić, R.S., Nowak, D.: A Unifying Approach to Data-independence. Proceedings of the 11th International Conference on Concurrency Theory (2000)
8. Lowe, G.: An Attack on the Needham-Schroeder Public-Key Authentication Protocol. Information Processing Letters, Vol. 56 (1995) 131-133
9. Lowe, G.: Breaking and fixing the Needham-Schroeder public-key protocol using FDR. Proceedings of TACAS '97. Springer LNCS 1055 (1996)
10. Lowe, G.: Casper: a compiler for the analysis of security protocols. Proceedings of 1997 IEEE Computer Security Foundations Workshop. IEEE Computer Society Press (1997)
11. Lowe, G.: A hierarchy of authentication specifications. Proceedings of 1997 IEEE Computer Security Foundations Workshop. IEEE Computer Society Press (1997)
12. Lowe, G., Roscoe, A.W.: Using CSP to detect errors in the TMN protocol. IEEE transactions on Software Engineering 23, 10 (1997) 659-669
13. Marrero, W., Clarke, E., Jha, S.: A Model Checker for Authentication Protocols. Proceedings of the DIMACS Workshop on Design and Formal Verification of Security Protocols (1997)
14. Mitchell, J.C., Mitchell, M., Stern, U.: Automated Analysis of Cryptographic Protocols Using Murϕ. IEEE Symposium on Security and Privacy (1997) 141-151
15. Roscoe, A.W.: The theory and practice of concurrency. Prentice Hall (1998)
16. Roscoe, A.W.: Proving security protocols with model checkers by data independence techniques. Proceedings of the 11th IEEE Computer Security Foundations Workshop (1998)
17. Roscoe, A.W., Broadfoot, P.J.: Proving security protocols with model checkers by data independence techniques. Journal of Computer Security. Special Issue CSFW11 (1999) 147-190
18. Shmatikov, V., Stern, U.: Efficient Finite-State Analysis for Large Security Protocols. Proceedings of the 11th IEEE Computer Security Foundations Workshop (1998)
19. Syverson, P.: A Taxonomy of Replay Attacks. Proceedings of the 7th IEEE Computer Security Foundations Workshop (1994) 131-136

Finding a Connection Chain for Tracing Intruders

Kunikazu Yoda and Hiroaki Etoh

IBM Tokyo Research Laboratory,
1623-14 Shimotsuruma, Yamato, Kanagawa 242-8502, Japan
{yoda,etoh}@jp.ibm.com

Abstract. Intruders usually log in through a chain of multiple computer systems to hide their origins before breaking into their targets, which makes tracing difficult. In this paper we present a method to find the connection chain of an intruder for tracing back to the origin. We focus on telnet and rlogin as interactive applications intruders use to log in through hosts.

The method involves setting up packet monitors at as many traffic points as possible on the Internet to record the activities of intruders at the packet level. When a host is compromised and used as a step-through host to access another host, we compare the packet logs of the intruder at that host to logs we have recorded all over the Internet to find the closest match. We define the 'deviation' for one packet stream on a connection from another, and implement a system to compute deviations. If a deviation is small, the two connections must be in the same connection chain. We present some experimental results showing that the deviation for two unrelated packet streams is large enough to be distinguished from the deviation for packet streams on connections in the same chain.

1 Introduction

In recent years, unauthorized accesses to computer systems are increasing as more and more commercial activities and services take place on the Internet. One characteristic of network break-ins is that it is very hard to trace the source of an intruder back to the origin after the incident has occurred. In order to hide their identities, intruders usually keep several computers under their control, called step-through hosts, from which they access another computer. Since there are many vulnerable hosts on the Internet and scanning tools are widely available and easy to use to locate these hosts, they are constantly gathering a collection of computers to be used as step-through hosts. Intruders don't log in directly to their targets from their own computers, but rather they first log into a step-through host and then another, and continue this step several times making a chain of hosts, before breaking into their targets. They usually erase logs on these step-through hosts. Even if logs remain on a particular host, we can only use it to trace back one link in the chain. Thus, we have to examine each host at a time to follow each of their predecessors in the chain in order to get to the

F. Cuppens et al. (Eds.): ESORICS 2000, LNCS 1895, pp. 191–205, 2000.

origin. Because the step-through hosts may be in different countries operated by administrators not paying much attention to their systems, it takes a lot of time and effort to get in touch with these administrators to investigate the chain of hosts step by step. Often we would end up at a host where no logs remained to continue the investigation [8]. Intruders know this and take advantage of the features of the Internet to preserve their anonymity.

When a user logs into a computer via a network, from there logs into another computer, and then another and so on, TCP connections are established between each pair of computers. We want to find this kind of 'connection chain'. (We will give the formal definition of the connection chain in Sect. 3.) Our approach to tracing considers the following problem: Given a stream of packets on a connection C^I an intruder used at some step-through host and a very large number of connections $C = \{C_1, C_2, \dots\}$ at various traffic points on the Internet, find $C' \subset C$ such that C^I and $\forall X \in C'$ are in the same connection chain. We are particularly interested in the case where $\forall X \in C'$ are connections closer to the origin than C^I. Although we don't have to trace the links in the chain one by one in our approach, the connection chain found will probably be partial. However, it may contain a host that is or is closer to the origin.

In this paper we provide a method to find a connection similar to a given one from very large traffic data. To cope with real-life traffic data, errors and variations of packet data at different connections on the same chain should be taken into consideration. Those problems include propagation delays through the chain, packetization variations because of TCP flow control, clock synchronization errors on time stamps, and others. We focus on telnet [4] and rlogin [2] as the interactive applications whose packets are transmitted through the connection chain. We define the 'deviation' for one stream of packets on a connection from another. It is the difference between the average propagation delay and the minimum propagation delay between the two connections. Experiments show that the deviation for streams of packets on the same chain is much smaller than that for a pair of unrelated streams.

The rest of the paper is organized as follows. Section 2 provides a survey of related work. We present our definition of deviation and describe our method in Sect. 3. We show some experimental results in Sect. 4. Finally, Sect. 5 concludes the paper and discusses future work.

2   Related Work

We briefly review several systems that have been proposed for tracing intruders in this section. DIDS (Distributed Intrusion Detection System) [5] is a system where all TCP connections and logins within the supervised network are monitored and the system keeps track of all the movement and the current states of users. A host monitor resides on each host in the network, gathering audit information about the host, which is transmitted to the central DIDS director, where the network behavior is accounted for.

CIS (Caller Identification System) [1] is a system to authenticate the origin of a user when the user attempts to log into a host at the end of a connection chain. When a user tries to log into the nth host, the nth host queries the $n-1$th host for a list of its predecessor hosts: $n-2, n-3, \ldots, 1$. The nth host then queries each of the predecessor host a list of their predecessor hosts. The nth host accepts the user's login only if those lists of predecessor hosts are consistent.

Caller ID [10] is a technique the United States Air Force employed to trace intruders. It breaks into the hosts of the chain in the same way as the intruder did to reach the target, going backwards up the chain towards the intruder. It does this while the intruder is active, using the same knowledge and methods as the intruder. However, it is often difficult or impossible to break into a host if the intruder closed the security hole after compromising the host. It is also still illegal to break into someone else's computer, even in response to the intruder's illegal act.

Generally, tracing methods can be categorized into two types: 'host-based' and 'network-based'. While host-based methods set up the components for tracing at each host, network-based methods set up components in the network infrastructure. Examples of host-based systems are [1,5,9]. The major drawback of these host-based systems is that if the tracing system is not used on a particular host or is modified by an intruder, the whole system can not function reliably once the intruder goes through that host. In the Internet environment, it is difficult to require that all administrative domains employ a particular tracing system on all hosts: every one of which must be kept secured from an intruder's attacks. Therefore, we believe that a host-based system is not feasible on the Internet.

Thumbprinting [6] is a network-based method which is based on the fact that the content of the data in a connection is invariant at all points on a connection chain, after taking into account the details of the protocols. A 'thumbprint', is a small signature which effectively summarizes a certain section of a connection and uniquely distinguishes a given connection from all other unrelated connections but has a similar value for any two connections in the same connection chain. These thumbprints can be routinely stored at many points in the network. When an intrusion is detected at some host, the thumbprint of that connection during the intrusion can be later compared to various thumbprints all over the network during the same period to find the other connections in the chain.

The advantage of a network-based approach is that it is useful even if part of the Internet employs it. That is, all the links of a connection chain will not be found sequentially, but parts of the links will be found separately at network locations covered by the system. Although there is still a chance that a tracing system in the network will be compromised by an intruder, it requires fewer components than we need in a host-based system, and these components can be special boxes which are only passively monitoring the traffic and have no other functions. We believe these 'traffic log boxes' can be made very secure.

The advantage of thumbprinting is that it requires a very small disk space to store thumbprints. But the special software needs to be installed on all hosts at traffic points for computing thumbprints and the saved thumbprints cannot be used for other purposes such as traffic analysis or intrusion detection. A thumbprint is a summary of contents of a connection for a certain fixed range of time. Because of clock synchronization errors or propagation delays, if a connection continues within one range of time, but another connection in the same chain crosses a boundary of the range, the three thumbprints might be quite different. While our method requires a relatively large disk space to store packet header data, they can be collected by packet capture software already installed on many hosts. The saved data can be used for other purposes and timing errors do not affect the result of our method.

3   Finding Connections in the Chain

We will describe the details of our method for tracing connections in this section. First, we formally define some terms.

Definition 1 (Connection Chain). *When a user on a computer H_0 logs into another computer H_1 via a network, a TCP connection C_1 is established between them. When the user logs from H_1 into another computer H_2, and then $H_3, \ldots, H_n$ successively in the same way, TCP connections $C_2, C_3, \ldots, C_n$ are established respectively on each link between the computers. We call this sequence of connections $C = \langle C_1, C_2, \ldots, C_n \rangle$ a connection chain.*

See Fig. 1 for an illustration of the above definition. H_0 is the source of an intruder and H_n is the target. $H_1, H_2, \ldots,$ and H_{n-1} are step-through hosts the intruder logs in through sequentially. C_i is a TCP connection established between H_{i-1} and H_i.

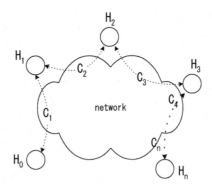

Fig. 1. Connection chain

Definition 2 (Upstream and Downstream Connection). *We say that C_i is an upstream connection of C_j, and C_j is a downstream connection of C_i when C_i and C_j are in the same connection chain $C = \langle \ldots, C_i, \ldots, C_j, \ldots \rangle$ and $i < j$.*

At any particular point of time, a TCP connection is uniquely determined by a 4-tuple: source IP address, destination IP address, source port number, and destination port number, thus we can tell which connection a given packet belongs to by looking at the IP and TCP header of the packet. An individual packet will either travel upstream or downstream. If we denote a connection as a 4-tuple (I_1, p_1, I_2, p_2), one direction is expressed as $(I_1 : p_1) \rightarrow (I_2 : p_2)$ and the other is expressed as $(I_1 : p_1) \leftarrow (I_2 : p_2)$.

Definition 3 (Packet Stream). *A packet stream on a connection is a series of packets on that connection moving in the same direction and listed in chronological order.*

There are two packet streams in one connection for each of the directions, but we currently treat each of them independently. Directions are defined with regards to an intruder's actual origin, so we say the direction of a packet stream is upstream if the packets are moving toward the intruder, and downstream if the packets are moving toward the target host.

3.1 Data Collection

In this section we describe how to record packet data at traffic points in networks.

Packets can be collected at various traffic points in the Internet backbone networks, which usually use optical fiber cables for their links. Optical splitters or some other device that replicates one input signal into multiple output signals can be placed at these links to retrieve a copy of data flowing through the backbone network without much effect on the existing network performance. With one side of the splitter connected to a network card of a computer, the time stamp, IP address, and TCP header of each packet passing through the line can be written to the hard drives of the computer by using packet capture software.

3.2 Problem Statement

Based on the definitions Def. 1, Def. 2, and Def. 3, the problem we address is stated as follows.

Problem 1 (Discovery of Connection Chain). Given a packet stream on a connection C_k in an unknown connection chain $C = \langle C_1, C_2, \ldots, C_n \rangle$, find packet streams on upstream connections C_is of C_k in the same connection chain from a large number of packet streams of connections.

To give a solution to this general problem, we need to be more specific about the conditions of the problem.

3.3 Conditions

In order to make the technology applicable to encrypted communications in the future and because of concerns regarding privacy issues, we do not use the message content of the TCP packets, but we principally use the time stamps of the packets and the sizes of the TCP packets. At this point we must explain more about the sequence numbers of the packets at different connections in the same chain.

The cumulative TCP data bytes transmitted since the start of a connection is measured by the sequence numbers in the TCP headers [3,7]. The sequence numbers are 32-bit integers assigned to the data bytes in the packets belonging to a particular connection. The initial sequence number for a connection is randomly determined at the establishment of the connection, and the number gets increased as data is transmitted using the connection. The sequence number field in the TCP header of a packet is the sequence number of the first data byte in the packet. Since an upstream connection generally starts earlier and stops later than a downstream connection on the same chain, we can filter out connections which transfer fewer data bytes than a given connection does to help identify possible upstream connections of the given one.

3.4   Basic Idea

Figure 2 (left) is a graph of a packet stream on a connection plotted with sequence numbers of the packets on the Y-axis and time stamps when the packets were captured on the X-axis. The data point should move down and to the right when a retransmission occurs, but because we take the upper bound of sequence numbers for each of the time stamps, the graph is monotonically increasing. We don't assume that an intruder runs a script on a host so that commands are automatically executed within a short time, but assume that an intruder manually inputs commands by hands and operates a host interactively for a longer time, so that graphs of the packet streams of those connections must show characteristic patterns for each intrusion. Therefore, it can be expected that graphs of packet streams of different connections will be similar if the proper parts of the graphs from the same chain are compared to each other. Therefore, we will introduce the 'deviation' for a packet stream from another packet stream as a metric of this similarity. If the value is small, one stream is likely to be in the same chain with the other. Otherwise they are probably unrelated.

Next we discuss what features remain unchanged and what features get changed between graphs of packet streams on different connections in the same connection chain. First we notice that while we are using telnet or rlogin in a normal way, the same TCP data bytes flow at any connections in the same chain when taking into account flow control and retransmissions of packets. Therefore, the height of the part of a graph which shows the increase in sequence numbers (which is the number of data byte transmitted) should be equal to others in the same connection chain. But since we cannot determine exactly what part of a graph corresponds to the other because of timing errors, we have to try every starting position of the graph to compare to the other.

We use the upper bound of the sequence numbers, and when a packet is lost and a retransmission occurs the data bytes following the lost data is not forwarded to the next connection in the chain until the lost data bytes are

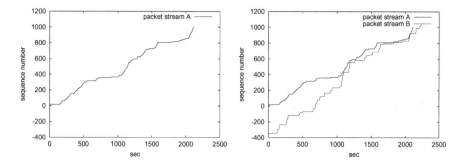

Fig. 2. Sample graph of a packet stream A (left) and the position of a graph of a packet stream B (right) where the average gap from A on the X-axis is the smallest.

retransmitted and acknowledged. Therefore, the propagation delay includes the retransmission time. Hence, if the clocks used by the packet capture software are accurate, a data byte at a downstream connection compared with the same data byte at an upstream connection is observed earlier if the direction of the packet is upstream and later if the direction is downstream, as is expected. However, the propagation delays may have large variances. If a graph is repositioned along the Y-axis so as to match the proper part of the other graph, that part of the graph may be distorted by being extended along the X-axis. Because we assume that an intruder is manipulating a host interactively, we also assume that the average propagation delay a packet travels between the first upstream connection and the last downstream connection is usually several hundred milliseconds and at most a few seconds. It would be too inefficient for an intruder to manipulate a host in a connection chain of a few seconds of delay each way.

3.5   Deviation for Packet Streams

We define the deviation for packet streams in this section. Suppose we have a graph of a packet stream A and a graph of another packet stream B. If we move graph B horizontally as well as vertically on the X-Y plane without crossing A so that B is as close as possible to A, the average gap on the X-axis between B and A will be small if the two are in the same connection chain and large if the two are unrelated. Intuitively, we define this average gap as the *deviation* for B from A. See Fig. 2 (right) for an example. In this figure, the position of the line showing the data for B is where the average gap between the two lines for B and A is the smallest. The formal definition of the deviation is as follows:

Definition 4 (Deviation for Packet Streams). *Given a packet stream A of n packets, the sequence number of the last data byte in the ith packet of which is a_i; the data size of the ith packet is $a_i - a_{i-1}$ bytes, and let $t(s)$ ($a_0 < s \leq a_n$) be the time at which the packet that contains the data byte associated with a sequence number s is observed, where a_0 is the initial sequence number of A. Similarly, let B be a packet stream of m packets, the sequence number of the last* *data byte in the ith packet of which is b_i, and let $u(r)$ $(b_0 < r \leq b_m)$ be the time at which the packet that contains the data byte associated with a sequence number r is observed, where b_0 is the initial sequence number of B. The deviation for B from A is defined as*

$$\frac{1}{d} \min_{0 \leq k \leq m'} \left\{ \left| \sum_{h=1}^{d} \left(T(h,k) - \min_{1 \leq h \leq d} \{T(h,k)\} \right) \right|, \left| \sum_{h=1}^{d} \left(T(h,k) - \max_{1 \leq h \leq d} \{T(h,k)\} \right) \right| \right\}$$

(1)

where $T(h,k) = u(b_k+h) - t(a_0+h)$, $d = a_n - a_0$ and $m' = \max\{i \mid b_i + d \leq b_m\}$.

Note that the sequence numbers associated with the data bytes in the ith packet of A are $a_{i-1} + 1, a_{i-1} + 2, \ldots, a_i$ and these are within a single packet so that $t(a_{i-1}+1) = t(a_{i-1}+2) = \cdots = t(a_i)$. The same is true for the sequence numbers and time stamps of B. The deviation for B from A is defined only if the total data size of B is larger than that of A, so we can assume that $b_m - b_0 \geq a_n - a_0$.

A deviation is a measurement of how far the graph of a packet stream B differs from the graph of a given packet stream A. It is basically the average horizontal distance between the two graphs computed along the vertical range of graph A. But we have to consider the position of graph B against A so that the average distance between the two is the minimum when computing the deviation.

Since we do not know in advance in what range of B be best matched to A, we have to try every range of B. This means we move B vertically to find out the vertical position where the average distance between the two graph is the minimum. The $\min_{0 \leq k \leq m'}$ of (1) treats this minimization.

We also have to consider the horizontal position. Because if the shapes of the two graphs are almost identical but the horizontal distance between the two graphs is large (due to for example long propagation delays), the deviation would be large, which is obviously not desired. So we move B horizontally as well as vertically to find out the position where the average distance between the two is the minimum. There are two directions for moving B horizontally since B cannot cross A. One is to move from left to right and the other is from right to left. The $\min_{1 \leq h \leq d}$ of (1) treats the minimization of the horizontal position moving from right to left and the $\max_{1 \leq h \leq d}$ of (1) treats the minimization of the horizontal position moving from left to right.

3.6   Analysis of Deviations

We analyze what a deviation, defined by Def. 4 means in this section. The following lemma gives an upper bound on the deviation.

Lemma 1. *Let A and B be packet streams on connections. If the connection of B is in the same connection chain with that of A and the directions of both streams are the same, the deviation for B from A is less than the average propagation delay minus the minimum propagation delay between connections of A and B.*

Proof. Let α and β be the differences between an accurate clock and the clocks of A and B respectively, and denote $\tilde{t}(s) = t(s) + \alpha$ and $\tilde{u}(r) = u(r) + \beta$. Since the connections of A and B are in the same connection chain and the packets of both are moving in the same direction, there exists k such that each data byte associated with a sequence number $b_k + h$ ($h = 1, 2, \ldots, d = a_n - a_0$) in B is equal to the data byte associated with a sequence number $a_0 + h$ in A. We denote $\tilde{T}(h, k) = \tilde{u}(b_k + h) - \tilde{t}(a_0 + h)$, and without loss of generality, will focus the proof on the case where $\tilde{T}(h, k) \geq 0$. This is the case covered by the first equation inside the braces of min in (1):

$$\frac{1}{d} \sum_{h=1}^{d} \left(T(h, k) - \min_{1 \leq h \leq d} \{T(h, k)\} \right) = \frac{1}{d} \sum_{h=1}^{d} \left(\tilde{T}(h, k) - \min_{1 \leq h \leq d} \{\tilde{T}(h, k)\} \right) \quad (2)$$

$$= E(\tilde{T}(h, k)) - \min_{1 \leq h \leq d} \{\tilde{T}(h, k)\} \quad (3)$$

where $E(\tilde{T}(h, k)) = \frac{1}{d} \sum_{h=1}^{d} \tilde{T}(h, k)$ is the average of $\tilde{T}(h, k)$. Note that $\tilde{T}(h, k)$ is the propagation time for the data byte associated with a sequence number $a_0 + h$ to travel from the network location at A to the network location at B as measured by accurate clocks. Therefore, the deviation calculated by (1) is less than the value of (3), which is the average propagation delay minus the minimum propagation delay between the connections of A and B.   □

Assuming that the average propagation delay a packet travels from the beginning of a connection chain to the end of the connection chain is at most a few seconds, the deviations for packet streams on those connections are also at most a few seconds.

3.7   Implementation

In this section, we show how to compute deviations, defined by Def. 4 in an efficient manner.

Suppose we have a given packet stream A as an array of n elements in main memory.

$$A : \quad \langle\, (t(a_1), a_1),\ (t(a_2), a_2),\, \ldots,\, (t(a_n), a_n)\, \rangle$$

Also suppose that we have traffic data S, packets in which are stored in chronological order as they were captured in a storage disk, which is a source of packet streams for comparing with A to compute deviations. It is essential that S should be scanned once sequentially for efficient implementation.

The entire structure of the implementation is described in the following steps.

1. Until we reach the end of S repeat the following.
   a) Take the next packet p to the previous one taken from S.
   b) Retrieve the entry of the packet stream to which p belongs from a hash, or create a new entry in the hash when there is no packet stream to which p belongs or p is the first packet of a connection.

c) Do some computation on the entry of the packet stream in the hash to update the values relating to the deviation for that packet stream.

2. Traverse the hash to iterate all the entries of the packet streams to get the deviations for them.

The key to the hash is the 4-tuple TCP connection parameters together with the direction of packet p. We will describe the details of the step (1c) in the next section. We denote that the entry of the packet stream B is retrieved at step (1b) and that the packet taken at step (1a) is the kth packet of B.

$$B: \quad \langle \; (u(b_1), b_1), \; (u(b_2), b_2) \;, \ldots, (u(b_k), b_k), \ldots \; \rangle$$

We also denote that $v(r, s) = u(r) - t(s)$.

Step (1c): Procedure when the kth packet b_k of B is taken from S.
For each $j = j_k, j_k + 1, \ldots, k$ $(j_1 = 1)$ do the following computations.

1. Compute $f(k, j)$
   When we move graph A and B along the Y-axis so that a_0 and b_{j-1} are at the same level 0 on the Y-axis, the two graphs (named as A' and $B(j)$) are repositioned as follows:

   $A': \quad \langle \; (t(a_1), a_1 - a_0), (t(a_2), a_2 - a_0), \ldots, (t(a_n), a_n - a_0) \; \rangle$
   $B(j): \quad \langle \; (u(b_1), b_1 - b_{j-1}), \ldots, (u(b_{j-1}), 0), \ldots, (u(b_k), b_k - b_{j-1}), \ldots \; \rangle$.

   $f(k, j)$ is the index of A' at which $a_{f(k,j)} - a_0$ is the lowest position above $b_k - b_{j-1}$, and is computed using $f(k - 1, j)$ as the starting position by the following equation.

   $$f(k, j) = \begin{cases} \min\{i \mid a_i - a_0 > b_k - b_{j-1}\} \\ \quad (= \min\{i \mid i \geq f(k - 1, j), \; a_i - a_0 > b_k - b_{j-1}\}) \\ n + 1 \quad \text{if } a_n - a_0 \leq b_k - b_{j-1} \end{cases} \qquad (4)$$

   $f(k, j) = n + 1$ is a special case indicating that the height of graph $B(j)$ above 0 exceeds that of A' so that no more packet b_i $(i > k)$ of B is needed for computing $M(i, j)$ for j.

2. Compute $g(k, j), l(k, j)$, and $M(k, j)$
   We then compute $M(k, j)$, the area surrounded by graph A' and $B(j)$ in the range $[0, b_k - b_{j-1}]$ on the Y-axis. $g(k, j)$ is the maximum difference and $l(k, j)$ is the minimum difference on the X-axis between A' and $B(j)$ in the range $[0, b_k - b_{j-1}]$ on the Y-axis. These values are computed using the values at $k - 1$ by the following equations.

$$M(k,j) = M(k-1,j)$$

$$+ \begin{cases} L(k,j) & \text{if } f(k-1,j) < f(k) \\ v(b_k, a_{f(k,j)}) \times (b_k - b_{k-1}) & \text{if } f(k-1,j) = f(k,j) \leq n \\ 0 & \text{if } f(k-1,j) = f(k,j) = n+1 \end{cases}$$

(5)

$$L(k,j) = v(b_k, a_{f(k-1,j)}) \times \big((a_{f(k-1,j)} - a_0) - (b_{k-1} - b_{j-1})\big)$$

$$+ \sum_{i=f(k-1,j)+1}^{f(k,j)-1} v(b_k, a_i) \times (a_i - a_{i-1})$$

(6)

$$+ v(b_k, a_{f(k,j)}) \times \big((b_k - b_{j-1}) - (a_{f(k,j)-1} - a_0)\big)$$

$$g(k,j) = \max\{g(k-1,j), \max\{v(b_k, a_i) \mid f(k-1,j) \leq i \leq f(k,j)\}\}$$
$$l(k,j) = \min\{l(k-1,j), \min\{v(b_k, a_i) \mid f(k-1,j) \leq i \leq f(k,j)\}\}$$

(7)

If $f(k,j) = n+1$, the last term of (6) is not added, and $v(b_k, a_{n+1})$ is not counted in (7) either.

3. Compute $\hat{M}(k,j)$

If $f(k,j) = n+1$, the range on the Y-axis of $B(j)$ covers the range on the Y-axis of A' ($[0,d] \subset [b_0 - b_{j-1}, b_k - b_{j-1}]$). Then $M'(k,j)$, the area surrounded by two graphs when we move $B(j)$ as close as possible to A' along the X-axis, can be computed by the following equation.

$$M'(k,j) = \min\{|M(k,j) - g(k,j) \times d|, |M(k,j) - l(k,j) \times d|\}$$

We can compute $\hat{M}(k,j) = \min\{M'(k,i) \mid i \leq j\}$ by the following equation if either $\hat{M}(k,j-1)$ or $M'(k,j)$ is defined.

$$\hat{M}(k,j) = \min\{\hat{M}(k,j-1), M'(k,j)\}$$

(8)

After all the computations for $j = 1, 2, \ldots, k$ are done, $M(k) = \hat{M}(k,k)$ is the area surrounded by graph A and $B(k)$ in the vertical range of A when $B(k)$ moves horizontally and vertically without crossing A so that $B(k)$ is as close as possible to A, where $B(k)$ is a sub array of B:

$$B(k): \quad \langle (u(b_1), b_1), \ldots, (u(b_k), b_k) \rangle$$

If $M(k)$ is not defined, the deviation for $B(k)$ from A cannot be defined. We can delete objects (such as b_j) associated with $j = j_k - 1, j_k + 1, \ldots, j_{k+1} - 2$ allocated in memory except for the ones at the minimum. (j_k is defined by $j_{k+1} = \max\{j \mid j \geq j_k, f(k,j) = n+1\}$ or $j_{k+1} = 1$ if $f(k,1) \leq n$.)

When we have finished processing all the packets in B and suppose the number of packets in B is m, the deviation for B from A is obtained by $M(m)/d$.

Computation Time. For each b_j (the last sequence number of data byte in the jth packet of B), the number of iterations in (4), (6), and (7) is $f(k,j) - f(k-1,j) + 1$ every time the kth packet of B is processed. So the total number of iterations for each b_j when all the packets in B are processed is at most $\sum_{k=1}^{m} (f(k,j) - f(k-1,j) + 1) = n + m$, where m is the number of packets in a packet stream B. This holds for any packet in S.

Suppose $O(m) = O(n)$, which is true for larger n in most cases. The computation time in computing deviations for every packet stream in S from A is $O(nN)$, where n is the number of packets in A and N is the number of packets in S.

3.8   A Solution to the Problem

Based on the definition Def. 4, a solution to the Problem 1 is briefly described in the following.

Solution 1.   1. Take any packet stream A on a connection which an intruder used to access through hosts.
  2. Compute deviations for every packet stream available on the Internet around some time period including the time period of A.
  3. Find small deviations and examine the connections they involve.
  4. Some of those connections could be found to be in the same connection chain if we examine the packets of those connections in detail.

4   Experiments

4.1   Distribution of Deviations

Since it might be possible that a small deviation could be computed from a packet stream unrelated to a given one, we examine experimentally with real-life data a distribution of deviations in this section.

We have implemented software which computes deviations for packet streams as defined by Def. 4. The program is written in C and runs under Linux (Red Hat 6.1) using libpcap[1] to read packet data recorded by tcpdump[1].

The first dataset we used is traffic data recorded at some Internet backbone network locations for an hour by tcpdump. The dataset contains about 2.4 million TCP packets, 5.6 % of which are packets of telnet or rlogin. We took only packets of telnet or rlogin connections which continue for at least one minute and where the size of the total data is at least 60 bytes. We computed deviations from each of the packet stream against all other packet streams (18733 deviations in total). Figure 3 is the distribution of deviations computed on this dataset.

We can see from Fig. 3 (right) that a deviation of less than three seconds is extremely rare. This indicates that if the deviation of a packet stream is in this

---
[1] available at `ftp://ftp.ee.lbl.gov/`

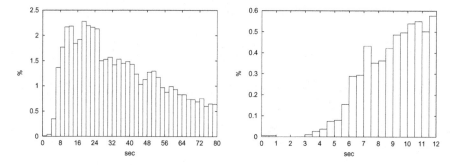

Fig. 3. Distribution of deviations computed on a dataset in the range [0,80) with a grid width of two seconds (left) and a closer look over the range [0,12) with a finer grid width of 0.5 seconds (right)

range, it is highly likely that the packet stream is in the same connection chain with the given one. We also notice that there are a few, actually two, deviations below one second. Examining the headers of the packets used to derive the deviation, we found that these are really packet streams of adjacent connections in a connection chain; the two deviations are for each direction of packets in the connection. Therefore, we can find a packet stream on a connection in the same connection chain with that of the given one by looking for connections whose average propagation delay minus minimum propagation delay is at most three seconds between the beginning and the end of the chain in this dataset. Generally, this upper bound of the average propagation delay minus the minimum propagation delay of a connection chain gets larger as the time period of a given connection is longer and more data bytes are available.

Next we used the data set of NLANR network traffic traces[2]. We chose traffic data whose file names begin with AIX, ANL, APN, MRT, NCA, NCL, ODU, OSU, SDC, TAU, or TXS under directory 20000115/, and performed the same analysis as we did for the first dataset. The number of deviations computed is in total 40,433. Figure 4 is the result.

We can see from Fig. 4 (right) that the frequency gradually decreases to zero as the deviation moves down to around three seconds just like we saw in Fig. 3 (right) for the first dataset, except in the range [1.0, 3.5). Almost all of the deviations in this range involve the same packet stream of a particular connection, so it is considered an error or an exception.

4.2   Performance in Computing Deviations

To measure the performance in computing deviations, we carried out an experiment to run our program for various data sizes. The program was run on a PC

---

[2] The dataset is provided by the National Science Foundation NLANR/MOAT Cooperative Agreement (No. ANI-9807479), and the National Laboratory for Applied Network Research, and is available from http://moat.nlanr.net.

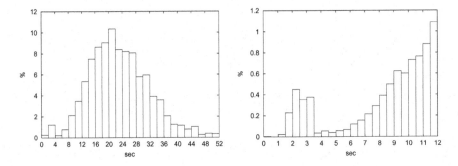

Fig. 4. Distribution of deviations computed on a data set of NLANR network traffic traces in the range [0,52) with a grid width of two seconds (left) and the closer look over the range [0,12) with a finer grid width of 0.5 seconds (right)

which has a 600 MHz Pentium III processor and 192 MB of main memory with an Ultra2 Wide SCSI hard disk attached to it.

Table 1 shows the execution time in seconds to compute all the deviations for packet streams in traffic data of N packets from a packet stream of n packets for varying n and N. In the top row of the table, the letter 'K' means thousand or 10^3, and the letter 'M' means million or 10^6. The result confirms that the computation time is $O(nN)$.

Table 1. Execution time (in seconds) to compute deviations

$n\backslash N$	1K	5K	10K	50K	100K	500K	1M
100	0.03	0.16	0.35	1.69	3.48	17.98	36.52
200	0.06	0.27	0.59	2.84	5.88	30.35	61.96
400	0.10	0.51	1.05	5.13	10.62	54.95	112.07
700	0.16	0.83	1.73	8.38	17.31	89.66	182.57

5   Conclusions

In this paper, we have presented a network-based tracing method which requires IP and TCP headers of packets and time stamps to be recorded at many places on the Internet. If a packet stream is given in which an intruder accessed a host in a connection chain with telnet or rlogin interactively for a long time, the system we developed computes a deviation for each of the packet streams at various Internet sites from the given stream, and the result would be small only if a packet stream is in the same connection chain as the given one, otherwise it will be large. Our method relies on the fact that the increase in sequence numbers is invariant at all points on a connection chain if the proper sections of packet streams that are in the same chain are compared. We use only time stamps and headers of the packets, not the contents of packets, so that the method would be applicable to encrypted connections such as those used in SSH or SSL telnet in the future. But the fact we mentioned above does not hold when some part of a connection in a chain is encrypted, so our method cannot apply directly in that case. Things get more complicated when compression is used as well as encryption in a connection, where the size of the data after compression and encryption also depends on the contents of the original data. As encrypted communications are becoming more widely used today, a future research question would be regarding a tracing method that is effective even if some of the connections are encrypted and compressed.

References

1. H. T. Jung et al. Caller Identification System in the Internet Environment. In *Proceedings of the 4th Usenix Security Symposium*, 1993.
2. B. Kantor. BSD Rlogin. *Request For Comments RFC 1282*, 1991.
3. J. Postel. Transmission Control Protocol. *Internet Standards STD 7*, 1981.
4. J. Postel and J. Reynolds. Telnet Protocol. *Internet Standards STD 8*, 1983.
5. S. Snapp et al. DIDS (Distributed Intrusion Detection System) - Motivation, Architecture, and An Early Prototype. In *Proceedings of the 14th National Computer Security Conference*, 1991.
6. S. Staniford-Chen and L. T. Heberlein. Holding Intruders Accountable on the Internet. In *Proceedings of the 1995 IEEE Symposium on Security and Privacy*, 1995.
7. W. R. Stevens. *TCP/IP Illustrated, Volume 1*. Addison Wesley, 1994.
8. C. Stoll. *The Cukoo's Egg*. Doubleday, 1987.
9. H. Tsutsui. Distributed Computer Networks for Tracking The Access Path of A User. *United States Patent 5220655*, Date of Patent Jun. 15, 1993.
10. S. Wadell. Private Communications. 1994.

A Full Bandwidth ATM Firewall

Olivier Paul*, Maryline Laurent, and Sylvain Gombault

ENST de Bretagne, 2 rue de la chataigneraie, 35510 Cesson-Sévigné, France.
{paul|mlaurent|sylvain}@rennes.enst-bretagne.fr

Abstract. In this paper we describe an architecture providing an high speed access control service for ATM networks. This architecture is based on two main components. The first one is a signalling analyser which takes the signalling information as an input and produces dynamically the configuration for our second module. This second module called IFT (Internet Fast Translator) is used to analyse the information located in the ATM cells and currently operates at 622 Mb/s. The complete architecture provides the access control at the ATM, IP and transport levels without packet reassembling.

1 Introduction

In the recent past, much attention has been paid developing security services for ATM networks. This resulted in the creation of many working groups within (and outside) the standardisation bodies. One of them is the ATM Forum security Working Group created in 1995, which released its version 1.0 specifications in February 1999. Confidentiality, authentication, integrity and some kind of access control have been considered. Access control as defined by the ISO in [1] is a security service used to protect resources against unauthorised use. The ATM technology has been specified to transport various kinds of flows and allows users to specify the QoS (Quality of Service) applying to these flows. Communications are connection oriented and a signalling protocol is used to set up, control and release connections. In this article we show that the classical approach supplying the access control service (commonly called firewall) is unable to preserve the QoS. We then describe a new access control architecture for ATM and IP-over-ATM networks. This architecture called CARAT does not alter the negotiated QoS. The next section analyses current solutions providing the access control service in the ATM and IP over ATM networks. Section 3 describes the CARAT architecture. This one is based on two main components. The first one is a signalling analyser which takes the signalling information as an input and produce dynamically the configuration of our second module. This second module called IFT (Internet Fast Translator) is used to analyse the information located in the ATM cells at 622 Mb/s. As a conclusion we perform a comparison between our solution and other proposed approaches and we show that CARAT is a good alternative to current solutions.

---

* This work is funded by DRET and done in collaboration France Telecom - RD

F. Cuppens et al. (Eds.): ESORICS 2000, LNCS 1895, pp. 206–221, 2000.

2   Related Work

Several solutions have been proposed in order to provide some kind of access-control in ATM and IP over ATM networks. This section is divided into four parts. In the first part we consider the adaptation of the Internet "classical" firewall architecture to ATM networks. In the second part we describe the solution proposed by the ATM Forum. In the third part we describe various solutions proposed to improve the "classical" firewall solution. Finally, part four compares existing solutions and highlights the main problems.

2.1   Classical Solution

The first solution [9] is to use a classical firewall located between the internal and public networks in order to provide access-control at the packet, circuit and application levels. As such the ATM network is considered as a level 2 layer offering point to point connections. As a result access-control at the ATM level is not possible and end to end QoS is no longer guaranteed. At the IP and circuit levels, IP packets are reassembled from the ATM cells. Access-control is supplied using the information embedded in the TCP, UDP and IP headers. Packets are filtered by comparing the fields in the headers such as the source and destination addresses, the source and destination ports, the direction and the TCP flags with a pattern of prohibited and allowed packets. Prohibited packets are destroyed whereas allowed packets are forwarded from one interface to the other. When the same QoS is negotiated on both sides of the firewall, the end to end QoS may be modified in the following ways:

- Reassembly, routing, filtering and deassembly operations increase the Cell Transit Delay.
- Internal operations done over IP packets may increase the Cell Loss Ratio.
- The time spent to reassemble and disassemble the packets is proportional to the packet sizes, which are variable. As a result, the Cell Transit Delay Variation may be different from the CDVT value negotiated on each side of the firewall.
- Routing and filtering actions operate at the software level. Thus the load of the system may cause variations in the Sustainable and Minimum Cell Rate.

Application procedures are then filtered at the application level by proxy applications in accordance with the security policy. Like with the IP or circuit level filters, the QoS is affected, but much more strongly, since the traffic has to reach the application level. Moreover since the filtering operations are provided in a multitasking environment, desynchronisation between the flows can occur. This kind of solution is reported to have performance problems in a high speed network environment [3, 5]. The latest tests [6] show that this access control solution is unsuccessful at the OC-3 (155 Mb/s) speed. Finally, [17] has shown that load balancing techniques between several firewalls could partially solve this performance problem but at a very high cost since the speedup/cost ratio generated by this technique is far from being linear.

2.2   The Access Control Service as Considered by the ATM Forum

The access-control service as defined in the ATM Forum security specifications [10] is based on the access- control service provided in the A and B orange book classified systems. In this approach one sensitivity level per object and one authorisation level per subject are defined. These levels include a hierarchical level (e.g. public, secret, top secret, etc.) and a set of domains modelling the domains associated with the information (e.g. management, research, education, etc.). A subject may access an object if the level of the subject is greater than the level of the object and one of the domains associated with the subject includes one of the domains associated with the object. In the ATM Forum specifications, the sensitivity and authorisation levels are coded according to the NIST [4] specification as a label, which is associated with the data being transmitted. This label may be sent embedded into the signalling, or as user data prior to any user data exchanges. The access-control is operated by the network equipment which verifies that the sensitivity level of the data complies with the authorisation level assigned to the links and interfaces over which the data are transmitted. The main advantage of this solution is its scalability since the access control decision is made at the connection set-up and does not interfere with the user data. However it suffers from the following drawbacks:

- The network equipment is assumed to manage sensitivity and authorisation levels. This is not provided in current network equipment.
- A connection should be set up for each sensitivity level.
- The access-control service as considered in traditional firewalls (i.e. access-control to hosts, services) is voluntarily left outside the scope of the specification.

2.3   Specific Solutions

The above limitations have been identified and many proposals have been made in order to supply the "traditional" access-control service in ATM networks. These solutions may be classified into two classes: industrial and academic solutions.

Industrial Solutions

The first industrial solution (Cisco [14], Celotek, GTE) uses a classical ATM switch that is modified to filter ATM connection set up requests based on the source and destination addresses. The problem with this approach is that the access- control is not powerful since the parameters are very limited. The second one (Storagetek [13]) is also based on an ATM switch. However this switch has been modified to supply access-control at the IP level. Instead of reassembling cells for packet headers examination like in traditional firewalls, this approach is expected to find IP and TCP/UDP information directly in the first ATM cell being transmitted over the connection. This approach prevents delays being introduced during cell switching. Storagetek also uses a specific memory called CAM (Content Addressable Memory) designed to speed up the research in the access-control policy. This approach is the first one taking into account the limitations introduced by the classical firewall approach. However some problems have not yet been solved:

- Access-control is limited to the network and transport levels. ATM and application levels are not considered.
- IP packets including options are not filtered since options may shift the UDP/TCP information in the second cell. This causes a serious security flaw.
- The device is not easy to manage especially when dynamic connections are required, since connection filters have to be configured manually.
- Performances of the device are not very scalable. An OC-12 (622 Mb/s) version of this product was announced in 1996 but has not been yet exhibited.

Academic Solutions

Both academic solutions being proposed are based on the above Storagetek architecture, but they introduce some improvements to cope with Storagetek problems.

The first approach [2] uses an FPGA specialised circuit associated with a modified switch architecture. At the ATM level, the access control at connection establishment time is improved by providing filtering capabilities based on the source and destination addresses. This approach also allows ATM level PNNI (Private Network to Network Interface) routing information to be filtered. At the IP and circuit levels the access-control service is similar to the one provided by the Storagetek product. This solution is interesting since it is the most complete solution being currently implemented. However it suffers from many limitations:

- Special IP packets (e.g. packets with optional fields in the header) are not processed.
- Only a small part of the information supplied by the signalling (i.e. source and destination addresses) is used.
- Access-control at the application level is not considered.
- Only a small part of the proposal has been implemented.

The second approach [11] is the most complete architecture being currently proposed. This solution provides many improvements in comparison with the Storagetek architecture. The most interesting idea is the classification of the traffic. The traffic is classified into four classes depending on the ATM connection QoS descriptors and on the processing allowed to be done over it. Class A provides a basic ATM access-control. ATM connections are filtered according to the information provided by the signalling (i.e. source and destination addresses). Class B provides traffic monitoring. The analysis of the traffic is made on a copy of the flow. When a packet is prohibited, the reply to this packet is blocked. Class C is associated with packet filtering. IP and transport packet headers are reassembled from the ATM cells and analysed. During this analysis the last cell belonging to the packet called LCH (Last Cell Hostage) is kept in memory by the switch. The analysis should be at least faster than the time spent by the whole packet crossing the switch. When the packet is allowed, the LCH is released, but when the packet is prohibited the LCH is modified so that a CRC error occurs and the packet is rejected. For class D, the access control processing is similar to that of the firewall proxy.

Table 1. Access Control Classes

Level/Application	With QoS Requirements	Without QoS Requirements
ATM	Class A	Class A
TCP/IP	Class B	Class C
Application	No Access Control	Class D

This classification expects the switch to separate traffic with QoS requirements from traffic without QoS requirements. As such the traffic with QoS requirements is allowed to cross the switch without being delayed. Table 1 gives the filtering operations depending on the level implementing the access control and the traffic QoS requirements.

This approach is very interesting since it introduces many improvements (traffic classification, LCH) over all the other proposals. However some problems remain:

- Few parameters are used to supply the access control service at the ATM level.
- Access control is not provided at the application level for applications requiring QoS.
- Traffic monitoring only applies to connection oriented communications, and UDP packets cannot be filtered using this technique.
- The LCH technique is useless against information leakage since an internal user can decide to bypass the integrity checks on two end systems on both sides of the firewall.
- This architecture is complex. No implementation has been exhibited.

2.4   Conclusion

As a conclusion, table 2 compares all the competing approaches designed to provide access control on both ATM and IP over ATM networks. The ATM forum proposal has not been included in this comparison since this solution requires deep changes in the existing equipment.

A comparison between the remaining proposals shows that several problems remain unsolved. For example, existing solutions only allow the security officer

Table 2. Comparison of different approaches

Property/Approach	Classical Firewall [9]	Filtering Switch [14]	ATM Firewall [13]	McHenry & al. [2]	Xu & al. [11]	CARAT
ATM level A.C.	No	Poor	No	Poor	Poor	Good
TCP/IP A.C.	Good	No	Average	Average	Average	Average
Application A.C.	Good	No	No	No	Good	No
Impact on the QoS	Large	Low	Low	Low	Low	Low
Manageability	Good	Good	Poor	Poor	Good	Good
Implementation	Yes	Yes	Yes	Partly	No	Yes
Bandwidth (Mb/s)	150	622	155	155	/	622

to filter ATM connections on addresses. One of the goals of CARAT is solve this problem by using an improved signalling analyser which allows the security officer to control almost all the parameters that can be used to describe an ATM connection.

Another point is the balance between performance, impact on the QoS and quality of the access control. Most of the current solutions either provide a good security level while offering poor performance and large QoS modifications or provide a lower security level while offering good performance and small impact on the QoS. The goal of CARAT in this field is to reach a security level similar to the one provided by a traditional stateless packet filter while offering better performance than the existing cell based proposals. Similarly to [11], CARAT can be easily extended to provide application level access control for applications without QoS requirements. As a consequence the security level provided by CARAT is at least as good as the Xu and al. proposal which has not been implemented.

The last point is that current cell based proposals rely on the caching of access control decisions in order to speed-up the cell classification process. This cache is filled through a slow cell classification process that analyses cells that can not be classified through the information located in the cache. However, as demonstrated in [18], these kind of architecture is subject to denial of service attacks because hackers can produce a traffic that will always generate cache misses thus forcing the cell classification process to work at the speed of the slow software classification scheme. These attacks can reduce dramatically the performance of cache based proposals. On the other hand, CARAT succeeds to store the complete access control policy [15] by using a policy compression technique and a patented storage method. Consequently CARAT is not subject to similar DoS attacks.

3   Proposed Solution

As depicted in figure 1, CARAT is based on two main parts. The first part is dedicated to the ATM signalling analysis. The result of this analysis is then used to build a dynamic configuration which is used by our second part to control

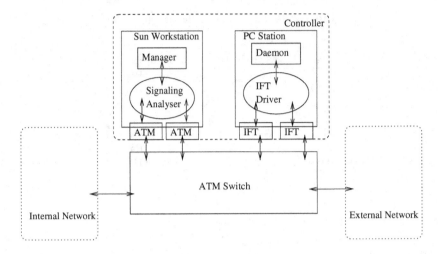

Fig. 1. Controller prototype architecture

the ATM cells. This second part is able to retrieve the ATM, IP and transport level information in order to decide whether a communication has to be allowed or denied. The configuration of the whole controller is made through a single language.

3.1   An Access Control Policy Definition Language

In order to express the access control policy we define an Access Control Policy Description Language (ACPDL). This language is based on draft proposal for a policy description language [7] which had been defined in 1998 by the policy working group at the IETF. In this language an access control policy is described by a set of rules. Each rule consists of a set of conditions and one action which has to be executed when the conditions are met. The following BNF (Backus-Naur Formalism) expression describes the rule syntax. Rule ::= IF <Conditions> THEN <Action>. All the conditions have the same generic structure (BNF notation):

```
Condition ::= <ACCESS CONTROL PARAMETER> <RELATIONAL OPERATOR>
<VALUE>
```

Depending on the level in the protocol stack, various access control parameters may be used:

- At the ATM level useful access control parameters have been described in [8], which include the traffic type, connection identifiers, addressing information, QoS descriptors and service identifiers.
- At the transport level most of the included parameters are commonly used to provide access control in firewalls (e.g. addressing information, ports, TCP flags, ICMP codes, etc.).

Actions also have a generic structure (BNF notation).

```
Action ::= <ACTION> <ACTION LEVEL>
```

The action can be to permit or to deny the communication. The level describes the layer (i.e. ATM, Transport) where the action has to be executed.

```
IF ( SRC ADDRESS = 47.007300000000000000002402.08002074E457.00 ) AND
( DST ADDRESS = 47.007300000000000000002404.0800200D6AD3.00 ) AND
(BHLI TYPE = 04 ) AND ( BHLI ID = 00A03E00000002 ) THEN DENY.
```

Fig. 2. Access Control Rule Example

Figure 2 provides an example of how a rule prohibiting connections between two ATM devices for the Video On Demand service can be expressed using the ACPDL. In this example both devices are identified by their ATM addresses and the video service is identified by the Broadband Higher Layer Identifier (BHLI).

3.2 The Manager

The policy defined by the security officer using this language is used to configure the two parts of our access controller. However the policy cannot be used directly by our access control tools. As a result the manager has to translate the access control policy in relevant access control configurations for both our components. The whole translation process is described in figure 3.

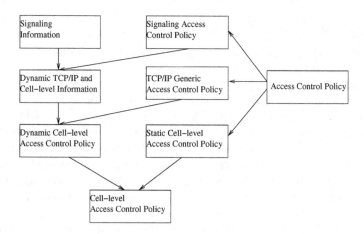

Fig. 3. Access Control Policy Generation Process

This translation process can be divided into two main parts. The first one translates the policy into three static sets of configuration data.

– At the ATM signalling level, this configuration includes a description of the communications that have to be controlled. Each communication is described by a set of Information Elements (IEs) and an action (DENY or ALLOW). This configuration is sent to the signalling analyser.
– At the TCP/IP level, the configuration includes a description of packets that have to be controlled. This part of the policy is generic which means that this configuration is not dedicated to a specific ATM connection.
– At the cell level, the configuration includes a description of the cells that have to be controlled. These cells are divided into a set of fields. The set of values that each field can take is described through a tree. This configuration is directly sent to the IFT modules.

The second part of the configuration process occurs when a connection request is received by the signalling analyser. Once the access control process has been completed, the signalling analyser sends to the manager the pieces of information needed to complete the dynamic configuration of the IFTs. This dynamic configuration process is important since it allows the size of the configuration stored in the IFTs to be reduced in comparison to a static configuration. The size of the configuration is an important issue because the delay introduced by the IFT during the access control process depends on it. The information provided by the signalling analyser includes:

– The Vci and Vpi connection identifiers.
– The source and destination ATM addresses.
– The service descriptor (Classical IP over ATM (CLIP), Native ATM Application). When an additional layer is used above the ATM model, the signalling analyser also provides the encapsulation (with or without SNAP/LLC headers).
– The direction of the communication.

In a CLIP environment, the manager uses the ATM source and destination addresses to find the corresponding IP addresses. This translation is done directly by using a local file describing the matching between ATM and IP addresses. However this process could be improved by taking advantage from an ATM Address Resolution Protocol Servers. The manager then uses the TCP/IP generic access control policy to find a match between the IP addresses and the TCP/IP level access control rules. The subset of matching rules is used along with the other pieces of information (addresses, encapsulation, connection identifiers, direction) to complete the configuration of the IFT cards. They are kept during the connection life. At the connection release, the manager receives a message from the signalling analyser to reconfigure IFTs cards and clean their configuration. The manager then destroys the information associated to the connection.

3.3   The Signalling Analyser

The signalling analyser process relies on two capabilities. The first one is to redirect all the signalling messages coming from our external and internal networks to a message filter located on a SUN workstation. The second one is the ability to decompose these messages according to the UNI 3.1 specification [12] and to forward or drop them according to the access control policy description provided by the manager.

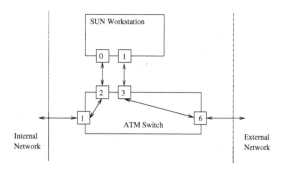

Fig. 4. ATM Switch Configuration

In order to redirect the signalling, the ATM switch has to be reconfigured to redirect signalling messages to the SUN workstation as described in figure 4. This configuration can be achieved by disabling the signalling protocol on interfaces 1, 2, 3 and 6. A Virtual Path has then to be defined between each pair of interfaces for each possible signalling virtual channel. These virtual channels are identified by the vci connection identifier 5.

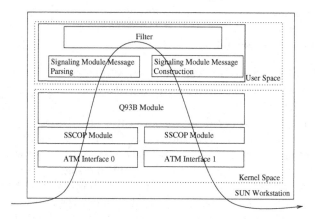

Fig. 5. Signalling Filtering Process

With the previous configuration, signalling messages coming from the external network reach the ATM interface 1 on the SUN workstation, whereas messages coming from the internal network reach the ATM interface 0. As described by figure 5, all signalling messages are usually multiplexed by the Q93B module whose goal is to establish, manage and release ATM connections. In order to prevent signalling messages from being rejected by the Q93B module, this module has to be modified to forward all the signalling messages to the filter application located in the user space without further analysis. In order to differentiate the filtering process for incoming and outgoing messages, signalling messages are associated with the originating ATM interface. This information is provided to the signalling filter by the Q93B module.

When signalling messages are received by the signalling analyser, these messages are parsed by the message parsing module into Information Elements (IEs) according to the UNI 3.1 specification. IEs are then parsed into basic connection descriptors such as addresses, connection identifiers, call reference, QoS descriptors and service identifiers. The analyser then checks whether the message can be associated with an existing connection through the type of the message and the call reference information. If the connection is new, a connection description structure is constructed. When the connection already exists, the structure is updated according to the new connection description parameters. The resulting set of parameters is associated with the connection state, the originating interface and identified by a connection identifier. The whole structure is then sent to the filter for analysis.

When the filter receives a new connection descriptor, it compares the connection parameters with the set of communications described by the access control policy. If a match is found, the filter applies the action described by the access control policy. When the action is to deny the communication, the filter destroys the corresponding connection description structure. Otherwise the connection identifier is sent to the message construction module. For CONNECT signalling messages, a subset of the connection parameters is sent to the manager as described in the previous section so that the dynamic part of the cell-level access control policy can be generated:

- Vci and Vpi are retrieved from the Connection Identifier IE.
- Source and destination addresses are retrieved from the Called and Calling Party Identifier IEs.
- The service descriptors can be retrieved from the Broadband Higher Layer Identifier (BHLI) and Broadband Lower Layer Identifier (BLLI) IEs.
- The direction is provided by the interface name associated with the connection identifier. For RELEASE COMPLETE messages, the connection identifier is sent to the manager. The communications between the filter and the manager are realised by using a shared memory segment which allows the manager to send the access control policy to the signalling analyser and the filter to send the results from the filtering process to the manager.

When the message construction module receives a connection identifiers from the filter, a new signalling message is constructed according to the information included in the connection description structure. The message is then associated with the outgoing interface and sent to the Q93B module. When the connection state associated to the connection identifier indicates that a RELEASE COMPLETE message has been sent to release the connection, the construction module frees the resources associated with the corresponding connection.

Another functionality provided by the message composition module is the ability to modify the ATM source address when the communication comes from the internal network to hide the structure of the network. This functionality is provided by changing the source address into the ATM address of the workstation external ATM interface.

The delay introduced by the whole signalling analysis process has few impact on the communication since the standardised signalling timeout values have been greatly oversized (for example a 14 seconds delay is allowed between SETUP and CONNECT messages).

3.4   IFT Cards

The Internet Fast Translator (IFT) card [15, 16] is a product designed and manufactured by the research branch of our industrial partner. These card have been originally designed to implement an high speed IP packet routing engine. However this card integrates several interesting features that can be used by our ATM firewall:

- It allows the first cell of the AAL5 frame to be analysed and the connection identifiers to be modified according to the analysis.
- The current prototype works at 622Mb/s thanks to a patented cell analysis scheme.
- The delay introduced by the cell analysis process can be bounded and depends on the cell analysis configuration.
- It can be configured dynamically during the cell analysis without interrupting ongoing operations.
- It can be integrated into an off the shelf personal computer using the Solaris x86 operating system.

Table 3 describes the information available for analysis in the first ATM cell with the CLIP and CLIP (without LLC-SNAP encapsulation) protocols. The UD and TD fields indicate the beginning of UDP and TCP data segments. However optional fields such as IP options have not been indicated and may shift TCP or UDP related information in a second ATM cell. Our policy for these kind of cells is currently to drop all the packets including IP options. One may consider this policy to be a severe limitation, however similar access control policies are usually implemented on traditional firewalls since these options are used most of the time by hackers to generate DoS attacks or bypass existing routing mechanisms.

The first part of the cell-level access control process is to direct all the traffic coming from the external and internal networks to the IFT cards. However the configuration of the switch needs to preserve the configuration used by the

Table 3. First ATM Cell Analysis

Byte	1	2	3	4	5	6	7	8	9	10	11	12
CLIP1	ATM Header					AA	AA	03	00	00	00	08
CLIP2	ATM Header					45		Length				
Byte	13	14	15	16	17	18	19	20	21	22	23	24
CLIP1	XX	45	Length								P	
CLIP2			P			Src IP Addr					Dst IP	
Byte	25	26	27	28	29	30	31	32	33	34	35	36
CLIP1		Src IP Addr				Dst IP Addr				Src Port		Dst
CLIP2	Addr	Src Port			Dst Port					UD		
Byte	37	38	39	40	41	42	43	44	45	46	47	48
CLIP1	Port					UD					D	
CLIP2			D							TD		
Byte	49	50	51	52	53							
CLIP1												
CLIP2												

signalling analysis process. As a result the switch has to be configured to create a virtual channel for each value of vci different from 5 and 31 between each pair of interfaces (1,4 and 5,6). Virtual channels identified by a 31 vci value and later called trash VCs are voluntarily left unconfigured to allow the switch to drop cells belonging to a communication that has to be denied.

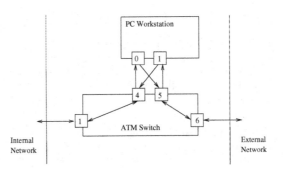

Fig. 6. ATM Switch Configuration

IFT cards allow only unidirectional flows to be controlled. This means that incoming and outgoing flows have to be separated. This operation is particularly simple when dealing with a Mono Mode Fibber physical support since emission and reception fibbers are physically separated. Figure 6 shows how emission and reception fibbers have to be connected between IFTs and switch ports on both sides of the switch.

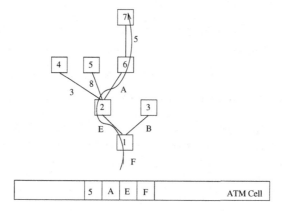

Fig. 7. Analysis Example

The second part is the configuration of the IFTs to provide the access control service. This configuration is done by the manager. IFTs have been originally designed to be managed remotely by concurrent managers. As a result an RPC daemon has been developed to serialise configuration requests to the IFT driver. On the manager side, a library gives access to configuration functions. This library translates the local calls to remote calls on the Solaris PC. The communication between the workstation and the PC are done through a dedicated external Ethernet network.

The IFT analysis process is based on the trie memory [19]. Trie memory is especially interesting in order to take advantage of the redundancy that can be found in access control policies. The configuration of this process relies on a description of the communications as a set of trees. Each branch within a tree describes a 4 bit value that can be matched during the analysis process. The root of each tree describes a gate by which to begin the tree analysis. An example of analysis is provided in figure 7. Additional information can be provided in a node to allow the analysis to jump from one tree to another or to terminate the analysis and return the connection identifiers values that have to be modified. Configuration functions allow the manager to build, update and remove this set of trees and entries within a given tree while the IFTs are operating. The translation between the information provided by the dynamic cell-level policy generation process and trees can be done as follows:

- Each possible field is coded into a tree. The values described by the security policy are then sliced in 4 bit words and attributed to the nodes of the tree. Range described by multiple conditions on the same field can be described by generating the nodes for each possible word inside the range.
- An AND operation between two conditions on two different fields is coded as a jump from one tree to another.
- The action (DENY or ALLOW) is coded through a special node ending the analysis process and returning the connection identifier that will be attri-

buted to the cells belonging to the corresponding AAL5 frame. A DENY action is coded by directing the frame to a trash virtual channel on the switch. An ALLOW action is coded by leaving the connection identifiers fields unmodified.

Preliminary experimental results [15] show that the use of trie memory makes it possible to store the complete TCP/IP level access control policy from a well know French ISP in 2.8M 4 bits words. This is far behind the capacity of the current IFT prototype which is 4M 4 bits words. Additional results [16] show that the worst case delay introduced by the access control process during the test was around 1.7ms.

4   Conclusion

In this article, we describe in detail how an ATM firewall can be constructed by using existing components. This ATM firewall has the ability to provide the access control service at the ATM, IP and transport levels at 622Mb/s while maintaining the QoS that has been negotiated. As we can see, our approach has the following advantages:

- Good access control at the ATM level.
- Small impact on the QoS thanks to a bounded delay cell level access control process.
- Improved access control speed at the cell level.
- Is not subject to performance DoS attacks like existing cache based architectures.
- Can easily be adapted to provide the access control service for other kinds of ATM usage (LANE, MPOA, MPLS) with reduced software developments.

Our proposal could be improved in the following directions:

- Application level access control could be easily provided for applications with no quality of service requirements by using the IFTs to direct the flows generated by these applications to a classical firewall where these flows could be analysed in depth. The filter would have to be modified to send a QoS flag to the manager along with the set of parameters currently used to describe the connection. This solution would also provide an answer to the IP options problem.
- The manager and the message filter could be modified to provide filtering capabilities for other kinds of ATM usage such as LAN Emulation, MPOA or MPLS.
- The access control speed could be improved. Our industrial partner is currently working on a new version of the IFT that would be able to handle a several gigabits bandwidth.

Acknowledgements. The authors would like to thank all the people that are involved in the CARAT project, namely Yves le Pape Anthony Lucas, Benoit Martin and Jean-Jacques Maret at DGA, Pierre Rolin, Christian Duret, Joel Lattmann and Jean-Louis Simon at CNET for their support and useful comments.

References

1. ISO, ISO 7498-2:1989, Information processing systems – Open Systems Interconnection – Basic Reference Model – Part 2: Security Architecture, 1989.
2. J. McHenry, P. Dowd, F. Pellegrino, T. Carrozzi, W. Cocks, An FPGA-Based Coprocessor for ATM Firewalls, in proceedings of IEEE FCCM'97, April 1997.
3. D. Newman, H. Holzbaur, and K. Bishop, Firewalls: Don't Get Burned, Data Communications, March 1997.
4. National Institute of Standards and Technology, Standard Security Label for Information Transfer, Federal Information Processing Standards Publication 188, September 1994.
5. J. Abusamra, ATM Net Management: Missing Pieces, Data Communications, May 1998.
6. Keylabs inc., Firewall Shootout Test Final Report, Networld+Interop'98, May 1998.
7. J. Strassner, S. Schleimer, Policy Framework Definition Language, draft-ietf-policy-framework-pfdl-00.txt, Internet Engineering Task Force, November 1998.
8. O. Paul, M. Laurent, S. Gombault, Manageable Parameters to improve Access Control in ATM Networks, in proc. of the 5th HPOVUA Workshop, April 1998.
9. M. Ranum, A network firewall, in proc. of the World Conference on System Administration and Security, 1992.
10. The ATM Forum Technical Committee, ATM Security Specification Version 1.0, February 1999.
11. J. Xu, M. Singhal, Design of a high-performance ATM Firewall, in proc. of the 5th ACM Conference on Computer & Communications Security, 1998.
12. The ATM Forum Technical Committee, ATM User-Network Interface Specification, Version 3.1 (UNI3.1), July 1994.
13. B. Kowalski, Atlas Policy Cache Architecture, White paper, Storagetek Corp., 1997.
14. Cisco Corp., LightStream 1010 Multiservice ATM Switch Overview, 1999.
15. M. Accarion, C. Boscher, C. Duret, J. Lattmann, Extensive packet header lookup at Gb/s speed for an application to IP/ATM multimedia switching router, in proc. of the WTC/ISS2000 Conference, May 2000.
16. Centre National d'Etude des Télécommunications - France Telecom, IP Fast Translator, FT.BD/CNET/DSE/SDL/226/CD, December 1999.
17. C. Benecke, A parallel Packet Screen for High Speed Networks, in proc. of the 15th Annual Computer Security Applications Conference, December 1999.
18. T.V. Laksham, D. Stiliadis, High-Speed Policy-based Packet Forwarding Using Efficient Multi-Dimensional Range Matching, in proc. of ACM SIGCOMM'98, September 1998.
19. E. Fredkin, Trie Memory, Communications of the ACM, Vol 3, September 1960, pp 490-499.

Analysing Time Dependent Security Properties in CSP Using PVS

Neil Evans and Steve Schneider

Department of Computer Science
Royal Holloway, University of London

Abstract. This paper details an approach to verifying time dependent authentication properties of security protocols. We discuss the introduction of time into the Communicating Sequential Processes (CSP) protocol verification framework of [11]. The embedding of CSP in the theorem prover PVS (Prototype Verification System) is extended to incorporate event-based time, retaining the use of the existing rank function approach to verify such properties. An example analysis is demonstrated using the Wide-Mouthed Frog protocol.
Keywords: Authentication Protocol Verification, Automated Theorem Proving, Timed Behaviour, CSP, PVS.

1 Introduction

There are many methods that model and analyse security policies of distributed systems. Typically, the policies concerning communication are achieved using security protocols in which the agents of a system are trusted to provide a degree of secure communication across the system's network.

The complexity of security protocols and the size of distributed systems have often been too great for analyses without a great deal of abstraction. This can lead to over-simplification and the possibility of missing some size-dependent flaws. This is prevented in analyses in which a (potentially infinite) number of agents can engage in arbitrarily many (possibly concurrent) runs of a security protocol.

Model checking, via highly automated tools, has proved to be an invaluable ally to those who wish to analyse protocols by searching for attacks. However, justifying the correctness of a protocol from a model checking analysis is more difficult because it is usually impossible the explore the entire state space. Indeed, to explore any reasonable amount of state space, one is often required to approximate the model by considering individual runs of the protocol with the minimal number of agents.

Theorem proving, on the other hand, does not suffer from the state space problem. It is easier to justify protocol correctness, via a successful proof, than it is to extract an attack from an unsuccessful proof. Assuming that the protocols of the future will not fail as readily as current protocols, these are obviously desirable qualities. The main disadvantage of theorem proving is the need for

F. Cuppens et al. (Eds.): ESORICS 2000, LNCS 1895, pp. 222–237, 2000.

intense user intervention. Current tool support technology for theorem proving provides relatively little automation, though the situation is improving. Two general purpose theorem provers that have been used in the context of security protocol analysis are Isabelle [10], and PVS [9]; in this paper we will use the latter.

In these analyses, time is often abstracted from the protocol descriptions and from the properties that are proven about them. However, there are situations in which sensitivity to time is required for an appropriate analysis, either because the protocol exhibits some time-dependent behaviour (for example comparing a received value of a timestamp with the current time, or using timeouts and delays in its flow of control) or because the required property is concerned with time (for example, that a ticket accepted by an authorising agent has not yet expired).

Introducing time into a protocol analysis framework brings complications. The use of explicit time increases the state space of the system by a significant factor, which means that for model-checking either even simpler versions of the protocol need to be analysed, or else more powerful computers or larger time-scales are required to perform an appropriate analysis. The introduction of explicit time in theorem-proving approaches generally introduces time as an additional data-type, but the special nature of time imposes restrictions on its use, and requires that care should be taken to ensure that it is modelled in sensible and realistic ways. This is feasible when it is used in simple ways (such as simply providing timestamps and checking if they are recent) but the more complex the time-dependent behaviour, the less confidence we can have in ad-hoc approaches to introducing time.

In this paper, we shall introduce event-based time into the process modelling language CSP, and we shall extend the corresponding embedding of CSP in the theorem prover PVS [5] to incorporate this approach to time. One benefit of the CSP approach is that the theory of *timewise refinement* [12] allows results to be translated between the untimed and timed models, enabling verifications to be carried out at their most appropriate level of abstraction and then combined if necessary from different models. The timed model will be illustrated by proving a time dependent property of the Wide-Mouthed Frog protocol [2].

The next section gives a review of the CSP embedding in PVS, a description of the general model of the network, and the message-oriented approach to authentication. We then extend the model by allowing *tock* events on which all agents (including the enemy) must synchronise. We then give an example analysis of a protocol that uses timestamps.

2   Review of Previous Work

2.1   Communicating Sequential Processes

CSP is a modelling language that allows the description of systems of interacting processes by means of a few language primitives. Processes execute and interact by means of performing *events* drawn from a universal set Σ. Some events are of the form $c.v$, where c represents a channel and v represents a value being passed along that channel. This allows messages to be communicated between processes.

The process *Stop* is a stopped process—it can perform no events. The process RUN_A is the process that will repeatedly be able to perform any event in the set of events A. The process $a \rightarrow P$ is initially willing to perform the event a, and then behave subsequently as P. The input process $c?x \rightarrow P(x)$ will accept a value x along channel P and then behave subsequently as $P(x)$; The output process $c!v \rightarrow P$ will output v along channel c and then behave as P. In general, communications and channels can have any number of message fields. For example, $rec.a.b.m$ can represent a channel $rec.a$ carrying a message $b.m$.

The choice $P \,\square\, Q$ offers the choice between processes P and Q. $P \,|[\,A\,]|\, Q$ executes P and Q in parallel, where they must synchronise on all events in the set A—this is how processes interact with each other. Processes may also be defined by means of recursive definitions.

Each CSP process description is identified with its set of traces: the sequences of events that it can perform. For example, the process $in?x \rightarrow out!x \rightarrow Stop$ has $\langle in.3, out.3 \rangle$ as a possible trace, but not $\langle in.3, out.5 \rangle$: it cannot output 5 after inputting 3.

A specification $S(tr)$ is a predicate on traces. A process P satisfies a specification, written P **sat** $S(tr)$, if all of its traces meet the predicate. Trace specifications are used to capture safety requirements on processes: they require that all executions should be of a particular form, and hence that no execution should violate the specification.

2.2   Embedding CSP into PVS

A PVS ascii syntax is provided for the required CSP operators. This is shown in Figure 1. Since we are interested in safety properties of security protocols, a CSP process is represented by its trace semantics in PVS. That is, given a fixed set, Σ, of all possible events, a process is represented by the set of traces of events from Σ that could be observed at the process interface. Recursive definitions are also possible by defining a monotonic functional, H, and then using the fixed point operator, mu, to generate its least fixed point, mu(H). A type-correctness condition (TCC) is generated by PVS requiring a proof of H's monotonicity. This is straightforward as all the CSP operators described above are monotonic with respect to their operand processes. (The ordering on processes is the subset ordering of their corresponding sets of traces.)

PVS support is provided in the form of theory files for general CSP trace semantics as follows:

- Traces
- Fixed point theory
- CSP operators
- specification and the **sat** relation

Operation	CSP	PVS
Stop	$Stop$	Stop
Prefix	$a \rightarrow P$	a $\gg$ P
Choice	$P \square Q$	P \/ Q
	$\square_{i \in I} P_i$	Choice! i: P(i)
Parallel Composition	$P \|[A]\| Q$	Par(A)(P, Q)
	$P \|\|\| Q$	P // Q
	$\|[A]\|_{i \in I} P_i$	Par(A)(lambda (i:I) : P(i))
	$\|\|\|_{i \in I} P_i$	Interleave! i: P(i)

Fig. 1. The PVS syntax for the CSP operators

2.3 Analysing Security Protocols

A protocol is described in CSP in terms of the activity required of the participating agents, which may include servers and trusted third parties as well as parties that want to communicate. They are described in terms of the messages they send along *trans* channels, and receive along *rec* channels, and the manipulations they carry out on those messages. For example, the protocol which has user A signing a nonce challenge with a signature key s_A would be described by

$$USER_A = rec.A?j?n \rightarrow trans.A!j!\{n\}_{s_A} \rightarrow Stop$$

In this description, $USER_A$ receives a nonce n, apparently from j, on its receive channel *rec.A*. It responds by transmitting $\{n\}_{s_A}$ back to j along its transmit channel *trans.A*, and finishes. We use $\{m\}_k$ to denote message m encrypted with key k.

To analyse the protocol in the context of a possibly hostile environment, we use the Dolev-Yao model of a network [4]. In this framework the set of agent processes communicate with each other only by passing messages on the *trans* and *rec* channels to an 'enemy' that is in full control of the communications medium. He has the potential to block, re-direct, duplicate or fake messages on the medium. When cooperating with a user, the enemy accepts messages on the agent's transmitting channel *trans* and passes the message to the appropriate agent's receiving channel *rec*. This architecture is depicted in Figure 2.

To capture the enemy's ability to produce new messages, a 'generates' relation, $\vdash$, is defined allowing a new message, m, to be generated from a set of messages, S, already known. This is written as $S \vdash m$. This model of communication is defined in CSP by allowing agents to communicate with the enemy using transmission and reception events only: *trans.i.j.m* is interpreted as agent i attempting to send message m to agent j, and *rec.i.j.m* means agent i receives

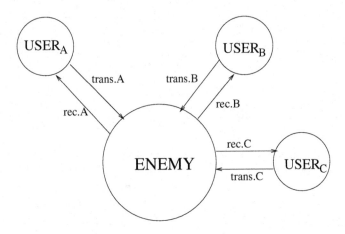

Fig. 2. Communication in a hostile environment—the Dolev-Yao model

message m apparently from agent j. The enemy is defined as a CSP process that is willing to synchronise with all agents on *trans* and *rec* events. Any message received by the enemy (a *trans* event) is added to his set of knowledge. Any message the enemy intends to send (a *rec* event) must have been generated from his set of knowledge using the relation ⊢. This is defined in the PVS embedding by the process **enemy**, defined recursively by the function F: enemy(S) = F(enemy)(S)

```
F(X)(S) : process =
        (Choice! i, j, m : trans(i, j, m) >> X(add(m, S)))
   \/ (Choice! i, j, (m | S |- m) : rec(i, j, m) >> X(S))
```

```
enemy : [set[message] -> process] = mu(F)
```

In [11], the network is defined as a CSP process, *NET* which is the parallel combination (synchronising on *trans* and *rec*) of the enemy together with all of the protocol agents and their possible communication partners. In PVS this is expressed as follows:

```
network : process =
        Par(trans? OR rec?)(enemy(INIT), Interleave(USER))
```

where `USER : [Identity -> process]` is the function defining the behaviour of all agents running the protocol, and `INIT` is the enemy's initial knowledge set.

Having defined the protocol in the worst possible environment, it is now possible to analyse the traces of this system and investigate whether certain properties relating to authentication hold.

2.4   Authentication Properties

We take an event-based approach to authentication in order to enable a formal analysis. We say that one set of events T authenticates another set of events

R if an occurrence of an event in T guarantees that some event in R occurred previously. This is easily expressed as a property on traces: if a trace contains an event in the set T, then it should also contain a previous event in the set R.

By choosing appropriate T and R, we can express properties on the entire system NET that give various flavours of authentication. For example, if $T = \{rec.B.A.m\}$ and $R = \{trans.A.B.m\}$, then for NET to meet this property it must be the case that whenever $USER_B$ receives message m apparently from A, then $USER_A$ did indeed earlier transmit this message to user B. Clearly this will not be true for arbitrary messages, since if the enemy can generate m then he can pass it to $USER_B$ as if it had come from user A. So an authentication protocol designed to provide this property will have to design the authenticating message m appropriately.

A significant body of theory [11] has been developed on top of CSP trace theory for verifying properties of this type. This is based around finding a *rank function*, which assigns an integer value to each possible message, in such a way that all messages that might ever appear in a protocol run have positive rank, and only messages that can never appear have non-positive rank. Thus the enemy can only ever generate positive rank messages if it only ever has positive rank messages; and protocol agents must be shown to preserve positive rank, never introducing non-positive rank messages if they are never provided with them. If all occurrences of R within the system are blocked, then we aim to find a rank function where all messages in T have rank 0, establishing that they cannot occur in the restricted system. Thus for any T to occur, R must occur previously.

This body of CSP theory has also been provided and verified within PVS [5], in the following PVS theories:

- authentication properties
- rank function properties
- enemy definition
- network definition and authentication theorem
- event datatypes
- rules for restricted parallel combinations (implemented from [11])
- rules for maintaining positive rank (implemented from [11])

The way PVS is used in practise is to find rank functions (where they exist) by carrying out a proof for the protocol in question providing only a 'blank' rank function, and then reducing all of the proof obligations on the correctness of the protocol to requirements on the rank function. These requirements often point the way to construction of a rank function, or alternatively they might be shown to be contradictory if the protocol is flawed, and might point the way to an attack.

The entire body of theory described thus far does not provide any general theoretical framework for handling time in the protocol descriptions or in the properties the system should meet. The contribution of this paper is the extension of the framework to include time.

3   Event-Based Time

Time can be introduced into CSP in a number of ways. The most natural way, from the theoretical point of view, would be to use the approach of Timed CSP [13], which is a mature modelling language in its own right. This approach integrates real-time in the form of the real numbers into the CSP language, and results in a sophisticated but complex semantic model which would require much of the PVS framework to be redeveloped.

The other main approach (which is preferred in model-checking approaches because of the discrete nature of time) is to introduce a new special event *tock* into the alphabet of all processes. The resulting language is called *tock*-CSP. The event *tock* is used to represent the passage of one unit of time, and must be synchronised on by all processes in the system to reflect the fact that time passes at the same rate in all processes. Delays are introduced by requiring a number of *tock*'s to occur, and other time-sensitive behaviour such as a timeout is also modelled easily in this framework. For example a fragment of a process which is repeatedly awaiting input but which will timeout and retransmit a value v if input is not received within one time unit might be described as

$$P(v) = in?x \rightarrow Q(x) \;\Box\; tock \rightarrow out!v \rightarrow P(v)$$

A detailed account of event-based time with illustrative examples can be found in [13].

By using an explicit event to mark the passage of time it is easier to integrate the handling of time into the existing PVS framework for CSP, which is based purely on events.

The modelling of time using this special event introduces some features that must be treated carefully. Care must be taken when defining processes in a timed environment. A process with no *tock* events does not mean that it is indifferent to the passage of time, but rather that it does not allow the passage of time. In our setting, all agents must synchronise on *tock* and none of them should have the power to impede time. Therefore, process definitions that prevent *tock* events suggest a flaw in the network model.

The *urgent* events of a process are events that occur before any *tock* event is possible. (They are urgent because they must be performed immediately). It is essential that urgent events are not blocked: an uncooperative environment that blocks an urgent event would prevent the occurrence of any *tock* events. When using CSP to describe a process, it is therefore essential to include sufficient *tock* events to ensure such blocking does not occur, and that only events which should be urgent are indeed modelled in this way.

For example, the one-pass copy process described in CSP as

$$OPC = in?x \rightarrow out!x \rightarrow Stop$$

does not allow any time to pass at all, since it has no *tock* events in its description. Since *in* should not be urgent, it should allow any number of *tock*'s to occur before *in*. If *out* is also not urgent, then the appropriate description in *tock*-CSP would be:

$$TOPC = in?x \rightarrow TOPC(x)$$
$$\square \ tock \rightarrow TOPC$$

$$TOPC(x) = out!x \rightarrow RUN_{tock}$$
$$\square \ tock \rightarrow TOPC(x)$$

Conversely, if the message should be passed on as soon as it is received (so *out* is urgent), then the description should be

$$TOPC' = in?x \rightarrow out!x \rightarrow RUN_{tock}$$
$$\square \ tock \rightarrow TOPC'$$

Once *in* occurs, then *out* must occur before any more time passes. It is essential that the rest of the system does not block *out*, or else the model will contain a timestop state.

The translation mechanism, Ψ, from [13] provides a systematic way of translating CSP processes P into *tock*-CSP processes $\Psi(P)$, so that all of the events are non-urgent. The resulting process can either perform one of the enabled events, or else it can perform a *tock* event and remain in the same state. For example, $\Psi(OPC) = TOPC$. This mechanism allows processes without time-critical behaviour to be described in CSP and then translated naturally into *tock*-CSP.

Adding event-based time to the PVS embedding of CSP causes no problems because all of the theories concerning this embedding are parameterised by the event type. Only two changes were made to the original set of theories defining the embedding. Firstly, a **tock** constructor was added to the abstract data-type defining the CSP events in PVS. Secondly, a PVS definition of the RUN process (as used in the translation mechanism above) was added allowing it to be viewed as a primitive process in a timed setting in the same way that *Stop* is viewed in an untimed setting.

3.1   The Timed Network Model

We retain the Dolev-Yao model of the network in which the enemy is in full control of the communications medium, and the agents continue to communicate with each other via the enemy. The revised enemy is simply the original enemy with time added by means of Ψ: the most general enemy has no time-critical behaviour.

However, protocol agents' behaviour can be sensitive to time for a number of reasons:

- The values they produce (e.g. timestamps) can depend on the current time, and so the agents will have to be described explicitly in *tock*-CSP rather than as untimed CSP descriptions translated through Ψ. In fact they will need to keep track of the current time, and increment it on every *tock*.
- The response to a particular message might depend on the relationship between the current time and a time value within the message (usually to check that it is recent enough).
- The implementation of the protocol might include time-dependent behaviour such as timeouts or explicit delays.

In such cases, the CSP description of the protocol cannot be given purely as an untimed process translated through Ψ. Instead the timed behaviour will have to be described explicitly as a *tock*-CSP process. Section 4 gives an example of how this is done.

Furthermore, time can be introduced into the authentication properties that need to be checked. It may be necessary to check that a message received was in fact sent relatively recently; or perhaps that an entire protocol run has taken no more than a certain amount of time. If timestamps appear in the messages then such properties can be expressed within the existing framework of using one set of events T to authenticate another set R. For example, if m is a message and l is a timestamp, then $\{rec.B.A.m.l\}$ might be used to authenticate $\{trans.A.B.m.l' \mid l - d \leqslant l' \leqslant l\}$: that the message was sent with a timestamp l' between $l - d$ and l.

Since the central rank function theorem remains true in the timed framework (as has been proved in PVS), this means that the existing rank function approach can be applied to verify that a time-sensitive protocol satisfies a timed authentication property expressed in this way.

4   An Example Analysis

The Wide-Mouthed Frog protocol is a simple protocol that uses timestamps. Its aim is to send a session key from one agent to another, via a server, using shared key cryptography. Timestamps indicate how recently a message was sent. The informal definition (taken from [2]) is stated as follows:

(1) $A \to S$: $A, \{B, Ta, Kab\}_{Kas}$
(2) $S \to B$: $\{A, Ts, Kab\}_{Kbs}$

where Ta and Ts are timestamps, Kas is the key that A shares with S, Kbs is B's shared key, and Kab is a new session key generated by A. Both the server, S, and the receiver of message 2, B in this case, check that the timestamps lie within a specified range. If either message is too old then the session key is ignored.

From this description we gather information about the types of messages involved, the capabilities of the enemy, and the definition of the agents.

4.1   The Agents

In general, an agent i can either initiate a protocol run with another agent (via the server), or he can respond to an agent who chooses to initiate a run of the protocol with i. In this case, the word 'respond' is somewhat misleading because the agent receiving the message in a protocol run does not give any response. However, we shall continue to use it to distinguish between the roles of the agents and to be consistent with the terminology of examples in the literature. The server does not behave like an initiator or a responder and, therefore, requires a separate process definition.

We allow an agent to initiate and respond to arbitrarily many runs of the protocol. $UINIT$ and $URESP$ describe an initiator and a responder run respectively. The numeric arguments of SERVER, UINIT, and URESP represent the current time - i.e. we can view the agents as having synchronised clocks. These values are incremented for each $tock$ event.

The definitions of UINIT and URESP are straightforward. Each deals with one non-urgent message, and so follows the style of the Ψ translation in ensuring that $tock$ is always possible. For example, $UINUT(i,j,k)(l)$ representing a user i at time l wishing to send key k to user j (via the server S) is defined in CSP as follows:

$$UINIT(i,j,k)(l) = trans.i!S!(i, \{j.l.k\}_{k_{is}}) \rightarrow RUN_{tock}$$
$$\Box\ tock \rightarrow UINIT(i,j,k)(l+1)$$

This is expressed in PVS explicitly as the fixed point of the function FUINIT. The responder is expressed in a similar style. We use E(k,m) to denote in ascii form the encrypted message $\{m\}_k$.

```
Y : VAR [nat -> process[event]]

FUINIT(i, j, k)(Y)(l) : process =
  (trans(i, s, conc(user(i),
   E(shared(i), conc3(user(j), time(l), session(k))))))
    >> RUN(tock))
 \/
  (tock >> Y(l + 1))

UINIT(i, j, k) : [nat -> process] = mu(FUINIT(i, j, k))

FURESP(i)(Y)(l) : process =
  (Choice! j, k, (l1 : nat | l >= l1 AND l1 >= l - d) :
   (rec(i, s, E(shared(i), conc3(user(j), time(l1), session(k)))))
    >> (RUN(tock))))
 \/
  (tock >> Y(l + 1))

URESP(i) : [nat -> process] = mu(FURESP(i))
```

Note that in FURESP we use PVS's dependent type capability to capture the notion a 'recent' message: the responding agent is willing to accept any message (apparently from the server s) whose timestamp value 11 lies between the current time 1 and the time 1 - d for a delay constant d.

The definition for SERVER requires the response to the receipt of a message to be urgent, and hence prevents a tock from occurring until the trans event has occurred. The server also performs the same check as the responder: that the timestamp 11 on the received message is no older than d units of time.

```
FSERVER(Y)(1) : process =
  (Choice! i, j, k, (11 : nat | 1 >= 11 AND 11 >= 1 - d):
   (rec(s, i, conc(user(i),
       E(shared(i), conc3(user(j), time(11), session(k)))))) >>
   (trans(s, j, E(shared(j), conc3(user(i), time(1), session(k))))
    >> (RUN(tock)))))
 \/
  (tock >> Y(1 + 1))

SERVER : [nat -> process] = mu(FSERVER)
```

It is appropriate to make the trans event urgent because the server has control over when the messages are sent. The enemy never blocks *trans* events, so no timestop will occur. On the other hand, rec events should not be urgent, since this would imply that the agent controls the time that messages must be received.

4.2   The Authentication Property

The property that we shall analyse is the following: if agent b 'responds' to a message containing timestamp value t then the protocol run was initiated at or after a time t - d, where d is the delay constant. Note that t would be the timestamp generated by the server. This is achieved by defining the sets T and R as:

```
T : set[mevent] =
    { e | e = rec(b, s, E(Kbs, conc3(A, time(t), Kab))) }

R : set[event] =
    { e | EXISTS (1 : nat | t >= 1 AND 1 >= t - d) :
        e = trans(a, s, conc(A, E(Kas, conc3(B, time(1), Kab)))) }
```

The theorem that we want to prove is:

```
authenticated : THEOREM network(enemy(INIT), USER) |> auth(T, R)
```

Now we have everything we need to perform the analysis except a definition for the rank function, rho, if one exists. In the usual way, we shall initially declare rho as an uninterpreted function, and then use the PVS theorem prover to extract the conditions that rho must satisfy. It is from these conditions that we can either build a rank function to complete the proof, or show, because of a contradiction in the conditions, that no rank function exists (indicating the possibility of an attack).

In fact, in attempting to construct a rank function, we find that the following derived condition is required:

authenticated.3.1.2.1.2.2.2.4 :

```
[-1]   t >= 11
[-2]   11 >= t - d
 |-------
[1]    11 = t
```

This is true only when d is 0. The problem is caused by the similarity in the messages that the server receives and the subsequent messages he transmits.

When $d > 0$ we can prove that the conditions required of the rank function are contradictory, and so we can conclude that no rank function can be constructed. From these derived conditions, it is possible to see the attack:

$$A \rightarrow S : A, \{B, Ta, Kab\}_{Kas}$$
$$S \rightarrow I(B) : \{A, Ta + d, Kab\}_{Kbs}$$
$$I(B) \rightarrow S : B, \{A, Ta + d, Kab\}_{Kbs}$$
$$S \rightarrow I(A) : \{B, Ta + 2d, Kab\}_{Kas}$$
$$I(A) \rightarrow S : A, \{B, Ta + 2d, Kab\}_{Kas}$$
$$S \rightarrow B : \{A, Ta + 3d, Kab\}_{Kbs}$$

In fact, this is an instance of an attack on the Wide-Mouthed Frog protocol given in [3]: the enemy can intercept a message sent by the server and, after prefixing the appropriate user identity to the message, send it back to the server as an initiator message. He can repeat this more than once providing that each interception occurs within the time delay, d. The effect of this is to keep the message's timestamp recent even though the age of the message could be more than the acceptable delay, d. This delaying tactic makes it possible for b to receive the message containing the key kab with timestamp Ta+3d (i.e. the event in T) even if the events in R (i.e. a transmitting with a timestamp between Ta+2d and Ta+3d) are blocked, since the original transmission with timestamp Ta is not blocked. If, as is implied by our problematic subgoals, d is set to zero then the problem does not arise because the enemy would have to act immediately and the message would not age. However, setting d to be zero would be an unrealistic assumption.

The alternative solution to this problem is to add an extra field to the encrypted part of the messages to distinguish between the initiator and responder messages. That is, the modified protocol becomes:

(1) $A \rightarrow S : A, \{B, Ta, Kab, initiate\}_{Kas}$
(2) $S \rightarrow B : \{A, Ts, Kab, respond\}_{Kbs}$

The corresponding modification to our PVS definition confirms this: re-running the proof easily yields a rank function which successfully verifies the amended protocol.

5   Discussion

Introducing Time

This report has documented the generalisation of the PVS embedding of CSP (presented in [5]) by implementing event-based time. This allows the analysis of protocols that use timestamps in order to fulfil one or more security properties. In our example, the intended property is the freshness of a session key. However, it is still possible to analyse security protocols that have no time critical features, and existing proofs of authentication properties for untimed protocols have been repeated in the timed setting without modification.

The strength of the framework is that it will also allow more complicated time-dependent behaviour of the protocol agents to be expressed naturally, and analysed. Protocols, when modelled for analysis, are generally (implicitly) considered to halt if they do not make progress. Yet their implementations may use a timeout mechanism which triggers retransmission of a message a number of times before eventually giving up on the protocol. Such mechanisms might have a bearing on protocol correctness, particularly where timestamps are involved, and a framework for describing and analysing them will be of benefit. Investigation of such examples is the subject of ongoing research.

Other theorem-proving and model-checking approaches such as those described in [6], [1], [14], [7] among others do not offer this benefit explicitly, though it should be possible to extend their work to a general framework for handling time-critical behaviour of protocols, for example by modelling timeouts by use of timeout events (which may or may not contain specific time values). However, the coding up required would make the complex behaviour difficult to understand, and it is preferable to use a language designed to express such real-time behaviour.

Lowe's Casper tool [6] allows timed authentication properties to be checked by including a separate clock process within the model and requiring that every event involving time should synchronise with the clock to ensure the correct value. Thus protocol agents are not themselves described as timed processes, but they treat time values as they do other data values and use the clock as the time server. Similarly, Paulson defines the timestamp provided on a message in terms of a function of the events that have already occurred, which is akin to Lowe's approach, in the sense that the time value is obtained from some source external to the protocol. Again, time values are considered as data values, and time-critical behaviour such as timeouts are not expressed within this framework. Strand spaces [14] can handle timestamps, but would need times associated with all messages (even those without timestamps) in order to handle time-critical agent behaviour. The NRL Protocol Analyser does not currently handle timestamps, though they can (and will) be introduced by means of coding up what is essentially a global clock [8].

PVS

The PVS type system is very expressive and makes theory definitions more succinct. We have used subtyping to generalise the set of events in our CSP embedding. Events are now either value passing (`trans` and `rec` are events that enable the exchange of messages) or pure synchronisations (such as `tock` events). Our example analysis has demonstrated the use of dependent types in process definitions. Recall that messages containing a timestamp were received only if their timestamp values were 'recent' according to a numeric argument representing the current time.

Altering the features of an existing PVS theory can be a nontrivial, time consuming exercise. Changes that are made to theories at the lower levels of a theory hierarchy can have a detrimental effect on the established proofs of theorems higher up the proof chain. The use of PVS's `status-proof` commands helps to indicate which proofs are affected. If, after the change, a lemma's status becomes `unfinished` then one can deduce that the change has had a direct effect on the lemma. Otherwise, if its status becomes `proved-incomplete` then there is an indirect effect on the lemma (the proof still works but refers to other `unfinished` lemmas). In our case, the addition of *tock* events has an (indirect) impact on the PVS implementation of the central authentication theorem. However, this work on the underlying theory needs to be done only once, and the payoff is a more general approach framework for analysing more classes of authentication protocol. In particular, a PVS proof shows that the central rank function theorem remains true in the more general semantic framework.

Figure 3 gives an approximation of the hierarchy of the theories that are influenced by the modification of the event data-type. This is just a small part of the total hierarchy because the theories that occur lower down (such as the definitions of the CSP trace semantics) are unaffected by changes to `event`. (In fact, they are polymorphic with respect to events.)

The PVS environment also provides some features that have assisted the development of this project. In particular, the proof status commands are a useful source of information.

The theorem prover is used in an analysis to derive the conditions that must be satisfied by a rank function prior to its construction. These conditions are the leaves of the open branches of the proof tree. Our analysis has shown that a set of conditions can be inconsistent, signifying that no such rank function can be constructed. We have also shown that once a rank function has been defined it can be used to close the branches of the proof tree. The PVS strategy `GRIND` can be used to close such branches. However, it is common for `GRIND` to generate multiple subgoals from one condition, and closing these branches can be very tedious.

Future Work

Investigation of this framework will benefit from a more significant example in which protocol agents exhibit time-critical behaviour. This does not require

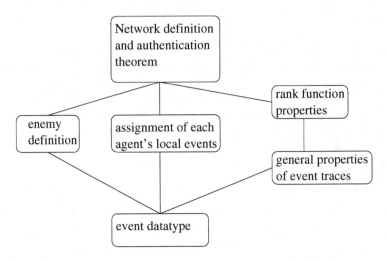

Fig. 3. The theory hierarchy

analysis of new protocols, but rather analysis of existing protocols in which the real-time behaviour of agents such as retransmission on timeout is modelled explicitly, rather than abstracted away. We need to understand the impact these implementation issues can have on protocol correctness, and may be able to obtain some general results about timing mechanisms.

As a tool for protocol analysis, this approach is not user friendly. The whole approach could benefit from a Casper-style interface [6] that allows a refined level of interaction. The construction of more specialised strategies that hide individual steps of a proof whilst allowing the user to intervene when some security or rank function expertise is needed. This automates the process and makes it more amenable to those with limited PVS knowledge by allowing communication at a level higher than primitive prover commands.

Acknowledgements. The authors would like to thank the anonymous referees for their comments, and are grateful to the UK EPSRC for funding under grant GR/M33402.

References

1. G. Bella and L.C. Paulson. Using Isabelle to prove properties of the kerberos authentication system. In *DIMACS Workshop on Design and Formal Verification of Security Protocols*, 1997.
2. M. Burrows, M. Abadi, and R. Needham. A logic of authentication. *ACM Transactions on Computer Systems*, 8, 1989.
3. John Clark and Jeremy Jacob. On the security of recent protocols. *Information Processing Letters*, 56(3):151–155, November 1995.

4. D. Dolev and A. C. Yao. On the security of public key protocols. In *IEEE Transactions on Information Theory*, volume 29(2), 1983.
5. B. Dutertre and S. Schneider. Embedding CSP in PVS. an application to authentication protocols. In Elsa Gunter and Amy Felty, editors, *Theorem Proving in Higher Order Logics: 10th International Conference, TPHOLs '97*, volume 1275 of *Lecture Notes in Computer Science*. Springer-Verlag, 1997.
6. G. Lowe. Casper: A compiler for the analysis of security protocols. In *Proceedings of the 10th IEEE Computer Security Foundations Workshop*, 1997.
7. C. Meadows. Language generation and verification in the NRL Protocol Analyzer. In *Proceedings of the 10th IEEE Computer Security Foundations Workshop*, 1996.
8. C. Meadows. personal communication, 2000.
9. S. Owre, J. M. Rushby, and N. Shankar. PVS: A prototype verification system. In Deepak Kapur, editor, *11th International Conference on Automated Deduction (CADE)*, volume 607 of *Lecture Notes in Artificial Intelligence*, pages 748–752, Saratoga, NY, June 1992. Springer-Verlag.
10. L. C. Paulson. *Isabelle: A Generic Theorem Prover.* Springer, 1994.
11. S. A. Schneider. Verifying authentication protocols in CSP. *IEEE Transactions on Software Engineering*, 1998.
12. S.A. Schneider. Timewise refinement for communicating processes. *Science of Computer Programming*, 28, 1997.
13. S.A. Schneider. *Concurrent and Real-time Systems.* Wiley, 1999.
14. J. Thayer, J. C. Herzog, and J. D. Guttman. Strand spaces: Proving security protocols correct. *Journal of Computer Security*, 1999.

Unwinding Possibilistic Security Properties

Heiko Mantel

German Research Center for Artificial Intelligence (DFKI)
Stuhlsatzenhausweg 3, 66123 Saarbrücken, Germany
mantel@dfki.de

Abstract. Unwinding conditions are helpful to prove that deterministic systems fulfill non-interference. In order to generalize non-interference to non-deterministic systems various possibilistic security properties have been proposed. In this paper, we present generic unwinding conditions which are applicable to a large class of such security properties. That these conditions are sufficient to ensure security is demonstrated by unwinding theorems. In certain cases they are also necessary. The practical usefulness of our results is illustrated by instantiating the generic unwinding conditions for well-known security properties. Furthermore, similarities of proving security with proving refinement are identified which results in proof techniques which are correct as well as complete.
Keywords: security models, information flow, unwinding, refinement

1 Introduction

Non-interference has been introduced by Goguen and Meseguer [GM82,GM84] as a concept to formalize restrictions on the information flow within a deterministic system. Although confidentiality as well as integrity requirements can be expressed using such restrictions, we focus on the former in this article and use the term security synonymously with confidentiality. Formally, non-interference is often defined in terms of execution sequences. Alternatively, it can be defined by *unwinding conditions* which demand properties of individual actions. While the first approach yields a more abstract definition of security, the second results in proof obligations which are easier to handle. The advantages of both approaches can be combined by an *unwinding theorem* which states that unwinding conditions imply an abstract definition of non-interference. Since the original work of Goguen and Meseguer, numerous articles have been published in which non-interference – among other improvements – has been extended to non-deterministic systems, e.g. [Sut86,Fol87,McC87,McL94,ZL97].

A possibilistic security property can be regarded as an extension of non-interference to non-deterministic systems. The underlying idea is that an observer cannot deduce confidential information if the set of possible behaviours which generate a given observation is large enough. However, the extension of non-interference to non-deterministic systems seems not to have one canonical solution. Different opinions on when the set of possible behaviours is large enough lead to different possibilistic security properties like non-inference [O'H90], generalized non-interference [McC87], restrictiveness [McC87], or the perfect security

F. Cuppens et al. (Eds.): ESORICS 2000, LNCS 1895, pp. 238–254, 2000.

property [ZL97]. In order to understand this variety, frameworks have been proposed in which possibilistic security properties can be represented in a uniform way and be compared to each other [McL94,ZL97,Man00].

Possibilistic security properties cannot be represented in the Alpern/Schneider framework [AS85] of safety and liveness properties [McL94]. As expected, this makes it difficult to prove that a system is secure for such a property. Thus, it is especially desirable to have unwinding conditions which simplify such proofs. Nevertheless, unwinding of possibilistic security has been mostly neglected (see [GCS91,Rya91,Mil94] for exceptions). This article seeks to fill the gap by deriving unwinding conditions for a large class of possibilistic security properties. All unwinding conditions presented are sufficient to guarantee security and some are also necessary. One novelty is that the unwinding conditions are based on orderings rather than on equivalences. This results in a correspondence between security and refinement which allows us to apply simulation techniques when proving security. In fact, our unwinding conditions turn out to correspond to forward simulation. Other simulation techniques can be transferred as well which results in proof techniques which are correct and also complete.

In Section 2, we recall how possibilistic security properties can be represented with event systems in our previously proposed framework [Man00]. We introduce state-event systems in Section 3. Unwinding conditions for a class of security properties are defined in Section 4 and shown to be sufficient as well as necessary. Unwinding conditions for a larger class of security properties are presented in Section 5. These unwinding conditions are sufficient to ensure security but they are not necessary. We clarify the relation to refinement in Section 6 and illustrate how simulation techniques can be applied. In Section 7 we outline how the results can be applied for various definitions of security. We discuss our achievements in Section 8 and compare them with related work. We conclude by summarizing our results and pointing out some areas for future work.

2   Possibilistic Security Properties

The confidentiality of classified information can only be ensured if direct as well as indirect flows of information are restricted. In order to prevent direct information flows certain aspects of the system behaviour must not be directly observable for observers who do not have the appropriate clearance. However, in general, an observer might still be able to deduce confidential information from other observations. In the worst case the observer has complete knowledge of the system, can construct all possible system behaviours which generate a given observation, and try to deduce confidential information from this set. The underlying idea of possibilistic security is to demand that this set is so large that the observer cannot deduce confidential information because he cannot be certain which behaviour has actually occurred. Thus, preventing indirect flows of information. The various possibilistic security properties differ in the set of behaviours which is required. Note that the possibilistic approach prevents certainty about deduced information and abstracts from probabilities.

The taxonomy in [Man00] distinguishes two dimensions of possibilistic security. In the first dimension, it is required that the occurrence of confidential events does not increase the "possible observations" at lower clearances. Otherwise, additional observations would be possible and one could deduce from such an observation that these confidential events have occurred. In the second dimension the occurrence of confidential events must not decrease the "possible observations". Otherwise, any of the observations which become impossible after these events, would lead to the conclusion that the confidential events have not occurred. How the term "possible observations" is formalized depends on the computational model under consideration. Common to many of these models is, that a prohibited increase of possible observations corresponds to *refinement*. The computational model we consider in this article is *trace semantics*. In trace semantics, two systems are *equivalent* if they have the same set of execution sequences, i.e. *traces*, and a system is *refined* by another systems if all traces of the latter are also traces of the former system. In the large body of work on non-interference in process algebras also other semantics like failure divergence in CSP [RWW94] or weak bisimulation in CCS [FG95] have been investigated. For a more general discussion of similarities between non-interference and process equivalence we refer to [RS99] and for an overview on other semantics to [vG90].

Event Systems. Following McCullough [McC87], we model systems by event systems. An *event* is an atomic action with no duration. We distinguish *input events* which cannot be enforced by the system from *internal* and *output events* which are controlled by the system. Input as well as output events can be observed from the outside while internal events cannot. The possible behaviours of a system are modeled as sequences of events. Note that we do not make the restricting assumption of input-totality, i.e. that input events are always enabled.

Definition 1. *An* event system *is a tuple* $ES = (E, I, O, Tr)$ *where E is a set of events, $I \subseteq E$, $O \subseteq E$ respectively are the input and output events, and $Tr \subseteq E^*$ is the set of traces. Each trace $t \in Tr$ is a finite sequence of events in E and Tr must be closed under prefixes, i.e. any prefix of a trace in Tr must also be in Tr.*

Given a set D of security domains, we associate a security domain $dom(e) \in D$ with each event $e \in E$. A security domain can be e.g. a group of users, a collection of files, or a memory section. A *security property* is composed of a *non-interference relation* $\not\leadsto \subseteq D \times D$ which formalizes a *security policy* by stating which domains may not interfere with others, together with a *definition of security*. As usual, we simplify and consider only two domains, a high H and a low level L, and the security policy which demands that H must not interfere with L, i.e. $H \not\leadsto L$. This simplification is possible because we investigate transitive security policies only, i.e. if domain D_1 interferes with D_2 ($D_1 \leadsto D_2$) and $D_2 \leadsto D_3$ then $D_1 \leadsto D_3$ where $\leadsto$ is the complement of $\not\leadsto$.

Notational Conventions. We denote the set of low- and high-level events, respectively, also by the names L and H of the security domains. The projection

$\alpha|_{E'}$ of a sequence $\alpha \in E^*$ to the events in $E' \subseteq E$ results from α by deleting all events *not* in E'. E.g. the projection $\alpha|_H$ of α to the high-level events results from α by deleting all low-level events. Hiding of E' in α is denoted by $\alpha\backslash_{E'}$ and results from α by deleting all events in E'. Thus, $\alpha\backslash_{E'} = \alpha|_{(E\backslash E')}$ holds. If τ is a trace of the event system $ES = (E, I, O, Tr)$ then $ES/_\tau$ denotes the event system (E, I, O, Tr') with $Tr' = \{\alpha \in E^* \mid \tau.\alpha \in Tr\}$ after the occurrence of τ.

Assembling Possibilistic Definitions of Security. Possibilistic definitions of security can be expressed in a modular way using the assembly kit from [Man00]. In that framework, each definition of security corresponds to a *security predicate* and is composed from *basic security predicates* (abbreviated by BSP in the sequel). This allows for a modular comparison of different security predicates. The framework seeks to combine the advantages of earlier frameworks [McL94,ZL97] while overcoming their limitations. Like in [ZL97], the perfect security property can be expressed within the framework which is not possible in [McL94], however, there is a correspondence between closure operations and security properties like in [McL94] which is not present in [ZL97].

As already pointed out in the beginning of this section, two dimensions of BSPs are distinguished in the framework. The first and second dimension, respectively, ensure that the occurrence of a confidential high-level event does not increase or decrease the "possible observations" at the low-level.

The observability of events is a subtle issue in the context of security. We assume that I and O specify the intended interface of a system when it is used properly. This interface should be used when properties apart from security are specified. However, an adversary may be able to observe also internal events (with some effort). Therefore, we specify a separate interface for security considerations. It may, but need not, coincide with the usual interface (I, O). Moreover, we relax the separation between H and L such that only events in $H_c \subseteq H$ must not be deducible. We distinguish two other sets of high-level events. $H_a \subseteq (H \setminus H_c)$ contains (adaptable) events which cannot be enforced, prevented, or observed by the low-level. However, we do not care if occurrences of these events are deducible. Events in $H_o = H \setminus (H_c \cup H_a)$ may even be directly observed on the low-level. Thus, $L \cup H_o$ is the interface which an adversary can access.

BSPs in the first dimension demand that the occurrence of a high-level event from H_c does *not add* possible low-level observations. Considering the system after a trace β has occurred, any observation $\overline{\alpha} \in (E \setminus (H_c \cup H_a))^*$ which is possible after $h_c \in H_c$ must also be possible if h_c has not occurred. If the observation results from $\alpha \in (E \setminus H_c)^*$, i.e. $\alpha|_{L \cup H_o} = \overline{\alpha}$, after h_c has occurred then some $\alpha' \in (E \backslash H_c)^*$ must be possible after h_c has not occurred where α' may differ from α only in events from H_a. Formally, we receive the schema BSD_{H_c,H_a} for BSPs which are based on the *backwards strict deletion of confidential events*.

$$BSD_{H_c,H_a}(Tr) \equiv \forall \alpha, \beta \in E^*. \forall h_c \in H_c.(\beta.h_c.\alpha \in Tr \wedge \alpha|_{H_c} = \langle \rangle)$$
$$\Rightarrow \exists \alpha' \in E^*. \alpha'|_{(E\backslash H_a)} = \alpha|_{(E\backslash H_a)} \wedge \beta.\alpha' \in Tr$$

BSPs in the second dimension demand that the occurrence of a high-level event from H_c does *not remove* possible low-level observations. The relation between

α and α' is like in the first dimension. The additional premise $\beta.h_c \in Tr$ ensures that the event h_c is admissible after β. Such a condition is necessary for non-critical dependencies of high-level on low-level events [ZL97,Man00]. We receive the schema $BSIA_{H_c,H_a}$ for BSPs which are based on the *backwards strict insertion of admissible confidential events*.

$$BSIA_{H_c,H_a}(Tr) \equiv \forall\alpha,\beta \in E^*.\forall h_c \in H_c.(\beta.\alpha \in Tr \wedge \alpha|_{H_c} = \langle\rangle \wedge \beta.h_c \in Tr)$$
$$\Rightarrow \exists\alpha' \in E^*.\alpha'|_{(E \setminus H_a)} = \alpha|_{(E \setminus H_a)} \wedge \beta.h_c.\alpha' \in Tr$$

In order to illustrate the relation to refinement let Tr_β and $Tr_{\beta.h_c}$ respectively be the set of traces of ES/β and $ES/\beta.h_c$. Then BSD_{H_c,H_a} demands that $(Tr_{\beta.h_c} \cap (H \setminus H_c)^*)\setminus_{H_a} \subseteq (Tr_\beta \cap (H \setminus H_c)^*)\setminus_{H_a}$ holds. This can be regarded as the requirement that $ES/\beta.h_c$ *refines* ES/β.[1] Similarly, $BSIA_{H_c,H_a}$ demands the inclusion/refinement in the other direction.

The parameterization of BSD and $BSIA$ by H_c and H_a is motivated by existing security properties. E.g. in generalized non-interference [McC87] only high-level inputs are considered as confidential, i.e. $H_c = H \cap I$. All other high-level events can be adapted in the construction of α' from α, i.e. $H_a = H \setminus I$. Since no such adaptation is allowed for β we refer to these BSPs as *backwards strict*. Considering all events in $L \cup H_o$ as observable on the low-level is a worst case assumption. Apparently, H_o and H_a allow for some information flow from the high- to the low-level. However, they cannot downgrade information about events in H_c and intransitive security policies are outside the scope of this article.

Inductive definitions of BSPs like the one for BSD and $BSIA$ above are encouraged by the framework in [Man00]. Unlike in the deterministic case, these inductive definitions are not already unwinding conditions (α is a sequence of events). However, they are helpful in the development of such conditions. The difference between H_o and H_a is important. Moving events from H_o to H_a results, on the one hand side, in a weaker security property. On the other hand, an adequate handling of events in H_a with unwinding is not easy. This will give rise to different unwinding conditions in Section 4 and 5.

Security predicates are constructed by conjoining BSPs. Often, one BSP from each dimension is taken. E.g. the *perfect security predicate PSP* from [ZL97] can be constructed as $BSD_{H,\emptyset} \wedge BSIA_{H,\emptyset}$. For a construction of other definitions of security in the framework we refer to Section 7 and to [Man00].

3   State-Event Systems

In order to express the pre- and post-condition of events, we enrich event systems by states. The pre-condition of an event e is the set of states in which e possibly can occur. The post-condition is a function from states to the set of states which may result after the event has occurred in the respective state. Each sequence of events leads to a state and, thus, states can be regarded as abstractions of the traces which lead to them. In our subsequent considerations the notion of state

---

[1] To be precise, events in H_a are hidden and events in H_c are disabled here.

will be transparent and the reader may assume his favored notion. One may take an intensional point of view by defining states as mappings from objects to values, an extensional point of view by identifying states with all sequences of events which are enabled, or alternatively, identify states with the history which led to them (if one really dislikes states). However, it is important to note that only events can be observed and that states are not directly observable.

Definition 2. *A state-event system is a tuple* (S, S_I, E, I, O, T) *where S is a set of states, $S_I \subseteq S$ are the initial states, E is a set of events, $I, O \subseteq E$ respectively are the input and output events, and $T \subseteq S \times E \times S$ is a transition relation.*

A *history* of a state-event system SES is a sequence of states and events. Starting and ending with a state, events and states alternate within a history. The set of histories $Hist(SES) \subseteq S \times (E \times S)^*$ for SES is defined inductively. If $s \in S_I$ then $s \in Hist(SES)$. If $\tau.s_1 \in Hist(SES)$ and $(s_1, e, s_2) \in T$ then $\tau.s_1.e.s_2 \in Hist(SES)$. Each state-event system $SES = (S, S_I, E, I, O, T)$ induces an event system $ES_{SES} = (E, I, O, Tr_{SES})$ where the set of traces $Tr_{SES} \subseteq E^*$ results from $Hist(SES)$ by deleting states from the histories.

Event systems and state-event systems are non-deterministic. While non-determinism in event-systems is caused only by the choice between different events, there are two potential sources for non-determinism in state-event systems. Non-determinism is caused by the choice of events as well as by the effect of events because two occurrences of an event in the same state might result in different successor states. In order to simplify our subsequent considerations we remove the second source of non-determinism in state-event systems and assume that the effect of events is deterministic. Moreover, we require that S_I is a singleton set. However, note that state-event systems are still non-deterministic because of the choice between different events and since internal events may have an effect. How to relax this assumption will be discussed in Section 6.

The *successor set* for $s_1 \in S$ and $e \in E$ is $succ(s_1, e) = \{s_2 \mid (s_1, e, s_2) \in T\}$ and the *predecessor set* is $pred(s_2, e) = \{s_1 \mid (s_1, e, s_2) \in T\}$. According to our simplification, $succ(s_1, e)$ has at most one element. We extend $succ$ and $pred$ to sets $S_1 \subseteq S$ of states and sequences $\alpha \in E^*$ of events.

$$succ(S_1, \alpha) \equiv if\ \alpha = \langle\rangle\ then\ S_1\ else\ let\ e.\alpha' = \alpha\ in\ succ(\textstyle\bigcup_{s \in S_1} succ(s, e), \alpha')$$
$$pred(S_1, \alpha) \equiv if\ \alpha = \langle\rangle\ then\ S_1\ else\ let\ \alpha'.e = \alpha\ in\ pred(\textstyle\bigcup_{s \in S_1} pred(s, e), \alpha')$$

The *pre-condition* of a sequence $\alpha \in E^*$ is the set of states defined by $pre(\alpha) \equiv pred(S, \alpha)$. The *enabledness* of a sequence of events α in a state s is defined by $enabled(\alpha, s) \equiv s \in pre(\alpha)$. A state s is *reachable*, i.e. *reachable*(s), if there is an initial state $s_I \in S_I$ and a sequence α of events such that $s \in succ(s_I, \alpha)$.

4   Unwinding Conditions for Possibilistic Security

Security properties like non-interference are usually defined in terms of execution sequences, like traces or histories. This implies that security often needs to be proved by tedious inductions. Unwinding conditions on the other hand are formulated in terms of single events and, thus, can be proved without induction. This makes the proof of security feasible. That a proof of the unwinding conditions indeed guarantees security needs to be ensured by an unwinding theorem. Unwinding conditions, can be regarded as schemas for proofs of security where the inductive part is justified once and for all. Unwinding conditions for possibilistic security properties are especially desirable. The reason is that a possibilistic security property, in general, corresponds to a *set of sets of traces* [McL94] and, thus, cannot be represented in the Alpern/Schneider framework [AS85] of safety and liveness properties in which properties correspond to sets of traces.

In this section we derive unwinding conditions for the case where the set H_a of adaptable events is empty and, thus, $H_o = H \setminus H_c$. We consider the families of basic security predicates $BSD_{H_c,\emptyset}$ and $BSIA_{H_c,\emptyset}$. The unwinding conditions are proved to be sufficient as well as necessary to guarantee security. Unwinding conditions for the case where H_a is not empty will be derived in Section 5.

Definition 3. *A low-level possibility (pre-)order is a reflexive and transitive relation* $\ltimes_L \subseteq S \times S$. *Let* $\bowtie_L$ *be defined by* $\bowtie_L = \ltimes_L \cap \ltimes_L$. $\ltimes_L$ *is antisymmetric if the equivalence relation* $\bowtie_L$ *is regarded as equality.*

The idea is to use $\ltimes_L$ as an ordering on states such that $s \ltimes_L s'$ holds if every observation which can be made starting in s is also possible in s'. To ensure this formally, we now present three unwinding conditions $osc_{H_c,\emptyset}$, lrf_{H_c}, and lrb_{H_c}. In Section 6 we will show that $\ltimes_L$ can be regarded as a refinement relation.

$osc_{H_c,\emptyset}$ ensures that SES is *output and step consistent* for $\ltimes_L$ if $H_a = \emptyset$. If $s_1 \ltimes_L s_1'$ and e is enabled in s_1 $((s_1, e, s_2) \in T)$ then e must also be enabled in s_1' $((s_1', e, s_2') \in T)$ and the resulting states must be related $(s_2 \ltimes_L s_2')$. Thus if $s_1 \ltimes_L s_1'$ then all one-step observations which are possible in s_1 are also possible in s_1'.

$$osc_{H_c,\emptyset} : \forall s_1, s_1' \in S.s_1 \ltimes_L s_1' \Rightarrow \forall e \in E \setminus H_c.\forall s_2 \in S.$$
$$[(s_1, e, s_2) \in T \Rightarrow \exists s_2' \in S.((s_1', e, s_2') \in T \wedge s_2 \ltimes_L s_2')]$$

lrf_{H_c} ensures that SES *locally respects* $\ltimes_L$ *forwards*. This demands that $\ltimes_L$ holds for the state after and the state before the occurrence of a confidential event, i.e. if s' results from the occurrence of h_c in s $((s, h_c, s') \in T)$ then $s' \ltimes_L s$.

$$lrf_{H_c} : \forall s, s' \in S.\forall h_c \in H_c.((reachable(s) \wedge (s, h_c, s') \in T) \Rightarrow s' \ltimes_L s)$$

lrb_{H_c} ensures that SES *locally respects* $\ltimes_L$ *backwards*. This demands that $\ltimes_L$ holds for the state before and the state after the occurrence of a confidential event. If s' results from the occurrence of h_c in s $((s, h_c, s') \in T)$ then $s \ltimes_L s'$. That h_c is enabled is ensured by the assumption $s \in pre(h_c)$.

$$lrb_{H_c} : \forall s \in S.\forall h_c \in H_c.((reachable(s) \wedge s \in pre(h_c)) \Rightarrow$$
$$\exists s' \in S.((s, h_c, s') \in T \wedge s \ltimes_L s'))$$

A similar style to present unwinding conditions has been used by Rushby [Rus92]. Note, however, that his work is limited to deterministic systems. Rushby formulates three conditions based on equivalence relations on states. His conditions *oc* and sc together correspond to our osc. Rushby has one condition lr for locally respects. Since we distinguish two dimensions and, thus, use orderings rather than equivalence relations, we receive two conditions lrf and lrb.

osc demands that $\ltimes_L$ is an ordering on one-step observations. The following lemma shows that osc implies that $\ltimes_L$ is an ordering on arbitrary observations.

Lemma 1. *If a state-event system SES fulfills $osc_{H_c,\emptyset}$ for $\ltimes_L$ then*
$$\forall s_1,s_1' \in S.s_1 \ltimes_L s_1' \Rightarrow \forall \alpha \in E^*.(\alpha|_{H_c} = \langle\rangle \Rightarrow (enabled(\alpha,s_1) \Rightarrow enabled(\alpha,s_1'))).$$

Proof. We prove the proposition by induction on the length of α. For $\alpha = \langle\rangle$, it holds trivially. In the step case, i.e. for $\alpha = e.\alpha_2$, assume that α is enabled in s_1. According to the definition of $enabled$, $s_2 \in succ(s_1,e)$ exists with $enabled(\alpha_2,s_2)$. Because of $e \in E \setminus H_c$ and $osc_{H_c,\emptyset}$ there is a $s_2' \in succ(s_1',e)$ such that $s_2 \ltimes_L s_2'$. The induction hypothesis yields $enabled(\alpha_2,s_2')$ and, thus, $enabled(\alpha,s_1')$. $\square$

The following unwinding theorem forms the theoretical basis for proving possibilistic security using our unwinding conditions.

Theorem 1 (Unwinding Theorem). *If SES fulfills $osc_{H_c,\emptyset}$ for some low-level possibility ordering $\ltimes_L$ then the following implications are valid:*

$$(1)\ lrf_{H_c} \Rightarrow BSD_{H_c,\emptyset}(Tr_{SES}) \qquad (2)\ lrb_{H_c} \Rightarrow BSIA_{H_c,\emptyset}(Tr_{SES})$$

Proof. 1. Let $\alpha,\beta \in E^*$ and $h_c \in H_c$ be arbitrary with $\beta.h_c.\alpha \in Tr_{SES}$ and $\alpha|_{H_c} = \langle\rangle$. S_I is a singleton set, i.e. $S_I = \{s_I\}$, and T is functional. Therefore, there are states s_1 and s_1' such that $\{s_1\} = succ(s_I,\beta)$ and $\{s_1'\} = succ(s_I,\beta.h_c)$. $(s_1,h_c,s_1') \in T$ and lrf_{H_c} imply $s_1' \ltimes_L s_1$. Because of $enabled(\alpha,s_1')$ and lemma 1, we infer $enabled(\alpha,s_1)$ and receive $\beta.\alpha \in Tr_{SES}$.

2. Let $\alpha,\beta \in E^*$ and $h_c \in H_c$ be arbitrary with $\beta.\alpha \in Tr_{SES}$, $\alpha|_{H_c} = \langle\rangle$, and $\beta.e \in Tr_{SES}$. We have $\{s_1\} = succ(s_I,\beta)$ and $\{s_1'\} = succ(s_I,\beta.h_c)$ for some $s_1,s_1' \in S$. $(s_1,h_c,s_1') \in T$ and lrb_{H_c} imply $s_1 \ltimes_L s_1'$. Because of $enabled(\alpha,s_1)$ and lemma 1, we infer $enabled(\alpha,s_1')$ and receive $\beta.h_c.\alpha \in Tr_{SES}$. $\square$

According lemma 1 $osc_{H_c,\emptyset}$ implies that $\ltimes_L$ is an ordering wrt. possible observations. The following lemma ensures that it is not too restrictive.

Lemma 2. *SES fulfills $osc_{H_c,\emptyset}$ for $\ltimes_L$ if $\ltimes_L$ is defined by*

$$s_1 \ltimes_L s_1' \equiv \forall \alpha \in E^*.(\alpha|_{H_c} = \langle\rangle \Rightarrow (enabled(\alpha,s_1) \Rightarrow enabled(\alpha,s_1'))) .$$

Proof. Assume $s_1 \ltimes_L s_1'$, $e \in E \setminus H_c$, and $(s_1,e,s_2) \in T$. Choose $\alpha \in (E \setminus H_c)^*$ with $s_2 \in pre(\alpha)$. $e.\alpha$ is enabled in s_1. Since $s_1 \ltimes_L s_1'$, $e.\alpha$ is also enabled in s_1'. Thus, s_2' exists with $(s_1',e,s_2') \in T$ and $s_2' \in pre(\alpha)$. Since α was arbitrary, S_I a singleton, and the effect of events is deterministic, we receive $s_2 \ltimes_L s_2'$ which implies $osc_{H_c,\emptyset}$. $\square$

The practical benefit of specifying $\ltimes_L$ by osc rather than defining it (as in lemma 2) is that smaller relations $\ltimes_L$ may be used in a proof of security. This results in more flexibility for proof construction.

The following theorem shows that our unwinding conditions are necessary to prove the basic security predicates $BSD_{H_c,\emptyset}$ and $BSIA_{H_c,\emptyset}$.

Theorem 2.

1. If $BSD_{H_c,\emptyset}(Tr_{SES})$ then SES fulfills $osc_{H_c,\emptyset}$ and lrf_{H_c} for some $\ltimes_L$.
2. If $BSIA_{H_c,\emptyset}(Tr_{SES})$ then SES fulfills $osc_{H_c,\emptyset}$ and lrb_{H_c} for some $\ltimes_L$.

Proof. In both cases we choose $\ltimes_L$ as in lemma 2 and, thus, $osc_{H_c,\emptyset}$ holds. It remains to be shown that SES locally respects $\ltimes_L$.

1. Assume $s_1, s_1' \in S$ and $h_c \in H_c$ with $reachable(s_1)$ and $(s_1, h_c, s_1') \in T$. If $\beta \in E^*$ reaches s_1 then $\beta.h_c$ reaches s_1'. $BSD_{H_c,\emptyset}(Tr_{SES})$ ensures for arbitrary $\alpha \in (L \cup H_o)^*$ with $\beta.e.\alpha \in Tr_{SES}$ that $\beta.\alpha \in Tr_{SES}$ holds. Thus, $s_1' \ltimes_L s_1$.

2. Assume $s_1, s_1' \in S$ and $h_c \in H_c$ with $reachable(s_1)$ and $(s_1, h_c, s_1') \in T$. If $\beta \in E^*$ reaches s_1 then $\beta.h_c$ reaches s_1'. $BSD_{H_c,\emptyset}(Tr_{SES})$ ensures for arbitrary $\alpha \in (L \cup H_o)^*$ with $\beta.\alpha \in Tr_{SES}$ that $\beta.e.\alpha \in Tr_{SES}$ holds. Thus, $s_1 \ltimes_L s_1'$.   □

In order to prove a given security predicate, all BSPs from which it is composed must be proved. The following example illustrates how our results can be applied.

Example 1. Assume we want to prove that a system which is specified by a state-event system SES is secure with respect to PSP [ZL97]. Recall that PSP is equivalent to $BSD_{H,\emptyset}(Tr_{SES}) \wedge BSIA_{H,\emptyset}(Tr_{SES})$. The BSPs can be verified separately. According to our unwinding conditions we have to construct orderings $\ltimes_L^1$ and $\ltimes_L^2$ such that SES fulfills $osc_{H,\emptyset}$ for $\ltimes_L^1$ and $\ltimes_L^2$. Furthermore, SES must fulfill lrf_H for $\ltimes_L^1$ and lrb_H for $\ltimes_L^2$. Theorem 1 ensures that this implies the validity of $BSD_{H,\emptyset}$ and $BSIA_{H,\emptyset}$. Note that different orderings may be used in the proofs of the BSPs. Although, theoretically, one can use the same ordering in both proofs without loosing completeness (because of the construction of $\ltimes_L$ in the proof of theorem 2), using different orderings offers more flexibility.

In this section, we have proposed new and simple unwinding conditions for a class of possibilistic security properties, the ones which can be assembled from $BSD_{H_c,\emptyset}$ and $BSIA_{H_c,\emptyset}$. As an example, we have derived the proof obligations for PSP. Deriving these unwinding conditions can be regarded as a two step process. In the first step we constructed inductive definitions of the BSPs and in the second step we decomposed the requirement on sequences of events (α in the inductive definitions) into unwinding conditions on the pre- and post-condition of single events. The unwinding theorem ensures that these conditions are sufficient to guarantee security. Theorem 2 shows that they are also necessary. In the following sections we generalize these results. In Section 5, we present unwinding conditions for a larger class of BSPs. In Section 7, we demonstrate how these can be applied to various security properties from the literature.

5   More Unwinding Conditions

We now consider the general case and allow a non-empty set H_a of adaptable events. This results in a larger class of security properties to which our results are applicable. We need to generalize osc_{H_c,H_a} for *step and output consistency*, but lrf_{H_c} and lrb_{H_c} are like in the previous section.

osc_{H_c,H_a} ensures that SES is *output and step consistent* for $\ltimes_L$. If $s_1 \ltimes_L s_1'$ and e is enabled in s_1 then some sequence $\gamma'.e.\delta'$ which yields the same observation as e must be enabled in s_1' and the resulting states must be related.

$$osc_{H_c,H_a}: \forall s_1, s_1' \in S.s_1 \ltimes_L s_1' \Rightarrow \forall e \in E \setminus H_c.\forall s_2 \in S.[(s_1, e, s_2) \in T \Rightarrow$$
$$\exists \gamma' \in (E \setminus H_c)^*.\exists s_2' \in S.(\gamma'|_{L \cup H_o} = e|_{L \cup H_o} \wedge s_2' \in succ(s_1', \gamma') \wedge s_2 \ltimes_L s_2')]$$

Lemma 3. *If a state-event system SES fulfills osc_{H_c,H_a} for $\ltimes_L$ then*
$$\forall s_1, s_1' \in S.s_1 \ltimes_L s_1' \Rightarrow \forall \alpha \in E^*.[(\alpha|_{H_c} = \langle \rangle \wedge enabled(\alpha, s_1))$$
$$\Rightarrow \exists \alpha' \in E^*.(\alpha'|_{E \setminus H_a} = \alpha|_{E \setminus H_a} \wedge enabled(\alpha', s_1'))] .$$

Theorem 3 (Unwinding Theorem). *If SES fulfills osc_{H_c,H_a} for some low-level possibility ordering $\ltimes_L$ then the following implications are valid:*

$$(1) \; lrf_{H_c} \Rightarrow BSD_{H_c,H_a}(Tr_{SES}) \qquad (2) \; lrb_{H_c} \Rightarrow BSIA_{H_c,H_a}(Tr_{SES})$$

The unwinding theorem is the justification for applying our unwinding conditions to a large class of possibilistic security properties which we illustrate in Section 7. In comparison to Section 4, the unwinding conditions are not necessary. In the subsequent section we discuss this issue and justify our results.

6 Similarities to Refinement and Simulation Proofs

Proofs by simulation are applied in the verification of non-deterministic systems. The goal of simulation is to verify that a system implements a specification. Such *refinements* are the basis for a stepwise development process. Unfortunately, the refinement of secure systems is difficult because the usual refinement relations do not preserve security. This is due to the well-known *refinement paradox* [Jac89].

In this section, we demonstrate that techniques from refinement nevertheless can be applied in the development of secure systems. However, the purpose is not to establish a refinement relation between specifications at different levels of abstraction, but rather to prove the security of some system or specification at a single level of abstraction. We illustrate the correspondence at the example of $BSIA_{H_c,H_a}$. The adjustment to BSD_{H_c,H_a} is a simple task.

We briefly recall basic concepts from refinement. For a more complete introduction we refer to [LV95]. A refinement relation $\leq_T$ holds for two state-event systems $SES^a = (S^a, S_I^a, E^a, I, O, T^a)$ and $SES^c = (S^c, S_I^c, E^c, I, O, T^c)$ (I and O must be identical), i.e. SES^c *refines* SES^a ($SES^c \leq_T SES^a$), if $OTr_{SES^c} \subseteq OTr_{SES^a}$. OTr_{SES} are the *observable traces* of a state-event system. They result from the histories by deleting all states and all internal events, i.e. for $SES = (S, S_I, E, I, O, T)$ we have $OTr = \{h|_{I \cup O} \mid h \in Hist(SES)\}$.

The requirements of $BSIA_{H_c,H_a}$ can now be reformulated. A state-event system $SES = (S, S_I, E, I, O, T)$ fulfills $BSIA_{H_c,H_a}$ if SES after any confidential event $h_c \in H_c$ has occurred refines the system in the state before the event has occurred. Formally, this requirement is fulfilled if

$$\forall \beta \in E^*.\forall h_c \in H_c.succ(S_I, \beta) \cap pre(h_c) \neq \emptyset \Rightarrow$$
$$(S, succ(S_I, \beta), E, \emptyset, L \cup H_o, T') \leq_T (S, succ(S_I, \beta.h_c), E, \emptyset, L \cup H_o, T')$$

holds for $T' = \{(s, e, s') \in T \mid e \notin H_c\}$. The classification of events is crucial. Events in H_a correspond to internal events, events in $L \cup H_o$ to external events[2], and events in H_c are disabled. For state-event systems, this formulation is equivalent to our original requirement. The benefit of the new formulation is that it allows us to use *simulation techniques* which have been developed for refinement proofs. Different kinds of simulation have been proposed. For a unified presentation and comparisons of various simulation techniques we refer to [LV95].

With the above correspondence to refinement the unwinding conditions *osc* and *lrb* are equivalent to *forward simulation* which is a popular simulation technique. To be precise, *lrb* establishes the simulation relation between initial states in $succ(S_I, \beta)$ and $succ(S_I, \beta.e)$ while *osc* establishes a stepwise simulation.

The correctness of forward simulation implies that lemma 3 and theorem 3 are valid. The correspondence gives us this result *for free*.

On Completeness. Forward simulation is only partially complete, therefore there cannot be a theorem for our unwinding conditions in Section 5 which corresponds to theorem 2. The reason is the non-empty set H_a which causes the similar problems in a proof security like hidden events in a simulation proof of a refinement. However, simulation techniques can be combined in order to achieve completeness. If a refinement relation holds between two systems SES_a and SES_c then a system SES_i can always be constructed such that SES_i is a forward simulation of SES_a and SES_c is a backward simulation of SES_i. The correctness of both simulation techniques yields that this is a proof technique which is both correct and complete. This and other results on correctness and completeness can be found in [LV95]. Since it is straightforward to reformulate these results in the context of security using our correspondence to refinement we refrain from doing this here.

The correspondence to refinement also suggests how our simplifying assumptions on state-event systems, that S_I is a singleton and that the effect of events is deterministic, can be relaxed because the results on simulation are applicable for the general case. Basically, the non-determinism which results from relaxing the assumptions is similar to the one which is caused by invisible events.

7   Proving Possibilistic Security Properties

In this section we demonstrate how the generic unwinding conditions can be used to prove the security of systems. We present a method for determining the appropriate unwinding conditions and apply it to several previously proposed

---

[2] Whether events in $L \cup H_o$ are viewed as inputs or outputs (as we do) is not important.

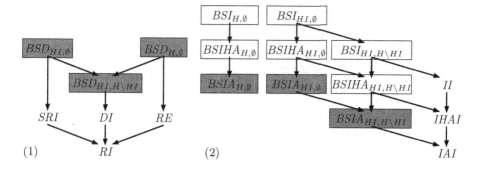

Fig. 1. Basic security predicates based on (1) deletion and (2) insertion of events

possibilistic security properties. This also shows that our results are applicable to a large class of such properties.

A collection of BSPs has been presented in our framework [Man00]. Their formal definition is not important for the purposes of this section. However, it is important that they can be ordered by implication as depicted in Figure 1. Each node in the diagrams corresponds to a BSP and the arrows indicate implications, e.g. the arrow from $BSD_{HI,\emptyset}$ to SRI indicates that $BSD_{HI,\emptyset} \Rightarrow SRI$ is valid ($HI = H \cap I$). For the BSPs which are surrounded by grey boxes we have presented unwinding conditions in Section 4 and 5. Unwinding conditions for the BSPs in white boxes are contained in the appendix. No unwinding conditions exist for the BSPs without boxes since they are not inductively defined or not backwards strict. However, only their position in the diagrams is of interest here.

Selecting appropriate unwinding conditions. How do we proceed if we want to prove that a system fulfills a given security property? First, the security property must be represented in our framework as a security predicate which is composed from one or more BSPs. Each BSP can be proved separately and if unwinding conditions exist for it, then they can be used in the proof. Otherwise, a stronger BSP must be retrieved (by traversing the arrows in Figure 1 in reversed direction) for which unwinding conditions exist. Of course, in general, there are cases where a system is secure for the given security property but does not fulfill the stronger BSPs. In these cases we cannot use our unwinding conditions and must prove the security property with other techniques.

Examples. *Non-inference NF* [O'H90] is a generalization of non-interference to non-deterministic systems. It can be represented in our framework by the single BSP RE. Since we have no unwinding conditions for RE (no box in the diagram), we use the ones for the stronger property $BSD_{H,\emptyset}$ instead, i.e. we have to construct a pre-order $\ltimes_L$ for which $osc_{H,\emptyset}$ and lrf_H hold. *Generalized non-inference GNF* [McL94] is a relaxation of *NF* which is more compatible with non-critical information flow from L to H. It corresponds to the BSP RI and, thus, the unwinding conditions for $BSD_{HI,H\setminus HI}$ are appropriate. *Generalized non-interference GNI* [McC87] is another generalization of non-interference for non-deterministic systems. It corresponds to $RI \wedge IHAI$. The two BSPs can be proved

Table 1. Proof obligations for well-known security properties

	$\ltimes_L^1$	$\ltimes_L^2$
NF	$osc_{H,\emptyset}, lrf_H$	
GNF	$osc_{HI,H\backslash HI}, lrf_{HI}$	
GNI	$osc_{HI,H\backslash HI}, lrf_{HI}$	$osc_{HI,H\backslash HI}, lrb_{HI}^{HAdm}$
SEP	$osc_{H,\emptyset}, lrf_H$	$osc_{H,\emptyset}, lrb_{HI}^{HAdm}$
PSP	$osc_{H,\emptyset}, lrf_H$	$osc_{H,\emptyset}, lrb_H$
$PGSP$	$osc_{HI,H\backslash HI}, lrf_{HI}$	$osc_{H,\emptyset}, lrb_H$

separately and the unwinding conditions for $BSD_{HI,H\backslash HI}$ and $BSIHA_{HI,H\backslash HI}$ can be used for this. *Separability SEP* [McL94] ($SEP \equiv (BSD_{H,\emptyset} \wedge BSIHA_{H,\emptyset})$) is a very restrictive security property which demands that high- and low-level are completely separated. The *perfect security property PSP* [ZL97] ($PSP \equiv (BSD_{H,\emptyset} \wedge BSIA_{H,\emptyset})$) is a relaxation of *SEP* which still prevents information flow from H to L completely. In fact, no weaker security property satisfies this. The *pretty good security predicate PGSP* [Man00] ($(RI \wedge BSIA_{H,\emptyset})$) is a relaxation of *PSP*. Consequently, it allows some information flow from H to L. However, it is less restrictive concerning information flow from L to H.

The proof obligations for these security properties are summarized in Table 1. For a proof of a security property by unwinding, $\ltimes_L^1$ and $\ltimes_L^2$ must be constructed such that the conditions in the table are fulfilled. For *NF* and *GNF* only $\ltimes_L^1$ needs to be constructed. The unwinding conditions imply the respective security property. For *PSP* they are also necessary as already discussed in example 1.

8 Discussion

We have presented unwinding conditions which are formulated in terms of pre- and post-conditions of events. Our investigations have been purely semantically and we have abstracted from syntactic formalisms in which such pre- and post-conditions are usually described. The intention was to avoid any bias to a particular syntactic formalism in order to receive results which can be applied in combination with a broad range of formalisms.

The unwinding conditions have been developed in a two-step process. In the first step, we constructed inductive definitions of the BSPs and, in the second step, derived unwinding conditions from them. Unlike in the deterministic case, inductive definitions are not already unwinding conditions because they involve sequences of events (α and β). It is surprising that our unwinding conditions involve only pre- and post-conditions of single events if one recalls that possibilistic security properties are outside the Alpern/Schneider framework of safety and liveness properties. A possibilistic security property corresponds to a set of sets of traces [McL94] which makes proofs of security more difficult. Nevertheless our unwinding conditions are similar to Rushbys conditions for the deterministic case. However, this does not imply that their proof will be always trivial.

Unwinding conditions for non-interference were first proposed in [GM84]. However, this original version of non-interference is limited to deterministic systems and based on a particular purge function. In [Jac90] the latter restriction was removed and unwinding conditions for a class of non-interference-like properties were derived using category theory. This class is parametric in the purge function. However, these results are not directly applicable to event systems because not every sequence of events is a valid trace but Jacobs work is based on monoids. In the presentation of our unwinding conditions we have used a similar style like Rushby [Rus92]. That work is also limited to deterministic systems and is based on equivalence relations rather than orderings. However, the results generalize to intransitive security policies.

Unwinding conditions for possibilistic security properties have been proposed before. In [GCS91] unwinding conditions were presented for a security property which is similar to *PSP*. These two unwinding conditions are similar to our output/step consistency and locally respects. A difference is that the equivalence relation is defined which is less flexible than specifying it, as in our approach (for the ordering). An unwinding theorem is provided but no completeness results. Ryan [Rya91] presented unwinding conditions which are also based on equivalence relations. He derived correctness as well as completeness results for a single possibilistic security property in the framework of CSP. Interestingly, these results were later re-proved in a slightly different setting by exploiting a correspondence between security and process equivalence [RS99]. The benefit was that the results could be achieved easily (like in our approach). Unwinding conditions for forward correctability, another possibilistic security property, were derived in [Mil94]. Again, the conditions are based on an equivalence relation. Although the unwinding conditions require the investigation of two-step transitions (caused by the peculiarities of forward correctability) they yield a substantial improvement compared to investigating complete traces.

The modular structure of the framework from [Man00] helped us to derive unwinding conditions for a whole *class* of possibilistic security properties. The use of BSPs as components of security predicates simplified the development of unwinding conditions while the ordering of BSPs provided useful guidance in determining appropriate (stronger) BSPs for which unwinding conditions exist. The use of pre-orders $\ltimes_L$ in the unwinding conditions has two advantages over using equivalence relations. First, it provides more flexibility when proving security because different orderings can (but need not) be used for each BSP. Second, more appropriate unwinding conditions can be used. E.g. for *NF* we can use $\ltimes_L$ with $osc_{H,\emptyset}$ and lrf_{HI}. To use an equivalence $\bowtie_L$ would require that $osc_{H,\emptyset}$, lrf_{HI}, and lrb_{HI} must hold for both directions. This means that we would have to prove *PSP*, a property which is much stronger than *NF*. A similar argument applies to *GNF* and *PGSP*. To use equivalence relations corresponds to using the same pre-order $\ltimes_L$ for all BSPs and additionally demanding that $\ltimes_L$ is symmetric. Thus, the use of pre-orders results in a major advantage of our approach.

9   Conclusion

We have presented unwinding conditions for a large class of possibilistic security properties. This class includes non-inference [O'H90], generalized non-inference [McL94], generalized non-interference [McC87], separability [McL94],

PSP [ZL97], and *PGSP* [Man00]. We are confident, that the unwinding conditions can be applied to many other security properties, once they have been represented as a security predicate in our previously proposed framework [Man00]. We have described how to select the appropriate unwinding conditions for a given security predicate. That these conditions are indeed sufficient to guarantee the respective security property has been ensured by unwinding theorems. For a sub-class of the security properties, the unwinding conditions are not only sufficient but also necessary. To our knowledge, all of these results are novel.

Moreover, we have discovered that a close correspondence between possibilistic security properties and refinement exists. This correspondence appeared because of our distinction between two dimensions of BSPs and allowed us to apply results on simulation techniques to prove the correctness of our unwinding conditions. Moreover, we clarified the correspondence such that well-developed simulation techniques can be used for proving security.

Plans for future work include the practical application of our framework in case studies as well as its extension to intransitive security policies.

Acknowledgments. The author would like to thank Serge Autexier and Alexandra Heidger for many valuable comments on the presentation.

References

[AS85]   Bowen Alpern and Fred B. Schneider. Defining Liveness. *Information Processing Letters*, 21:181–185, 1985. North-Holland.

[FG95]   Riccardo Focardi and Roberto Gorrieri. A Classification of Security Properties for Process Algebras. *Journal of Computer Security*, 3(1):5–33, 1995.

[Fol87]   Simon N. Foley. A Universal Theory of Information Flow. In *Proceedings of the IEEE Symposium on Security and Privacy*, pages 116–122, 1987.

[GCS91]   John Graham-Cumming and J.W. Sanders. On the Refinement of Noninterference. In *Proceedings of the IEEE Computer Security Foundations Workshop*, pages 35–42, 1991.

[GM82]   J.A. Goguen and J. Meseguer. Security Policies and Security Models. *Proceedings of the IEEE Symposium on Security and Privacy*, pages 11–20, 1982.

[GM84]   J.A. Goguen and J. Meseguer. Inference Control and Unwinding. In *Proceedings of the IEEE Symposium on Security and Privacy*, pages 75–86, 1984.

[Jac89]   Jeremy Jacob. On the Derivation of Secure Components. In *Proceedings of the IEEE Symposium on Security and Privacy*, pages 242–247, 1989.

[Jac90]   Jeremy Jacob. Categorising Non-interference. In *Proceedings of the Computer Security Workshop*, pages 44–50, 1990.

[LV95]   Nancy Lynch and Frits Vaandrager. Forward and Backward Simulations, Part I: Untimed Systems. *Information and Computation*, 121(2):214–233, September 1995.

[Man00]   Heiko Mantel. Possibilistic Definitions of Security –An Assembly Kit–. In *Proceedings of the IEEE Computer Security Foundations Workshop*, 2000.

[McC87]   Daryl McCullough. Specifications for Multi-Level Security and a Hook-Up Property. In *Proceedings of the IEEE Symposium on Security and Privacy*, pages 161–166, 1987.

[McL94]   John McLean. A General Theory of Composition for Trace Sets Closed
          under Selective Interleaving Functions. In *Proceedings of the IEEE Sym-
          posium on Research in Security and Privacy*, pages 79–93, 1994.
[Mil94]   Jonathan K. Millen. Unwinding Forward Correctability. In *Proceedings of
          the Computer Security Foundations Workshop*, pages 2–10, 1994.
[O'H90]   Colin O'Halloran. A Calculus of Information Flow. In *Proceedings of the
          European Symposium on Research in Computer Security, ESORICS 90*,
          1990.
[RS99]   P.Y.A. Ryan and S.A. Schneider. Process Algebra and Non-interference. In
          Proceedings of the 12th IEEE Computer Security Foundations Workshop,
          pages 214–227, 1999.
[Rus92]   John Rushby. Noninterference, Transitivity, and Channel-Control Security
          Policies. Technical Report CSL-92-02, SRI International, 1992.
[RWW94]   A.W. Roscoe, J.C.P. Woodcock, and L. Wulf. Non-interference through
          Determinism. In *Proceedings of the European Symposium on Research in
          Computer Security (ESORICS)*, LNCS 875, pages 33–53. Springer, 1994.
[Rya91]   P.Y.A. Ryan. A CSP Formulation of Non-Interference and Unwinding.
          Cipher, pages 19–30, Winter 1991.
[Sut86]   D. Sutherland. A Model of Information. In *Proceedings of 9th National
          Computer Security Conference*, 1986.
[vG90]   R.J. van Glabbeek. The Linear Time – Branching Time Spectrum. In *Pro-
          ceedings of CONCUR'90, Theories of Concurrency: Unification and Exten-
          sions*, LNCS 458, pages 278–297. Springer, 1990.
[ZL97]   A. Zakinthinos and E.S. Lee. A General Theory of Security Properties.
          Proceedings of the IEEE Symposium on Security and Privacy, pp. 94–102,
          1997.

Appendix

We provide formal definitions of the BSPs *BSI* and *BSIHA* and state corresponding unwinding conditions. *BSI* and *BSIHA* result from *BSIA* by modifying the
admissibility condition $\beta.h_c \in Tr$. *BSI* does not assume that h_c is enabled after
β. *BSIHA* assumes that it is enabled if one only looks at the confidential events
which is formally defined by $HAdm_{H_c}(Tr, \beta, e) \equiv \exists \gamma \in E^*.\gamma.e \in Tr \wedge \gamma|_{H_c} = \beta|_{H_c}$.

$$BSI_{H_c,H_a}(Tr) \quad \equiv \forall \alpha,\beta \in E^*.\forall h_c \in H_c(\beta\alpha \in Tr \wedge \alpha|_{H_c}=\langle\rangle)$$
$$\Rightarrow \exists\alpha' \in E^*.\alpha'|_{(E\backslash H_a)} = \alpha|_{(E\backslash H_a)} \wedge \beta.h_c.\alpha' \in Tr$$
$$BSIHA_{H_c,H_a}(Tr) \equiv \forall \alpha,\beta \in E^*.\forall h_c \in H_c(\beta\alpha \in Tr \wedge \alpha|_{H_c}=\langle\rangle \wedge HAdm_{H_c}(Tr,\beta,h_c))$$
$$\Rightarrow \exists\alpha' \in E^*.\alpha'|_{(E\backslash H_a)} = \alpha|_{(E\backslash H_a)} \wedge \beta.h_c.\alpha' \in Tr$$

The two modifications of the admissibility assumption results in new versions of
locally respects backwards. In comparison to lrb_{H_c}, the assumption $s \in pre(h_c)$
is omitted for *BSI* (in $lrb^*_{H_c}$) and, for *BSIHA*, replaced by HEn_{H_c} (in $lrb^{HAdm}_{H_c}$).

$$lrb^*_{H_c} : \quad \forall s \in S.\forall h_c \in H_c.(reachable(s) \Rightarrow \exists s' \in S.((s,h_c,s') \in T \wedge s \bowtie_L s'))$$
$$lrb^{HAdm}_{H_c} : \forall s \in S.\forall h_c \in H_c.((reachable(s) \wedge HEn_{H_c}(Tr_{SES},s,h_c)) \Rightarrow$$
$$\exists s' \in S.((s,h_c,s') \in T \wedge s \bowtie_L s'))$$

HEn_{H_c} results from $HAdm_{H_c}$ and is technically complicated. We expect that it is difficult to use as assumption in practice. However, this difficulty is caused by the use of high-level admissibility which has also other drawbacks as pointed out in [ZL97,Man00]. Formally it is defined as follows.

$$HEn_{H_c}(\mathit{Tr}_{SES}, s, h_c) \equiv \exists \beta, \beta' \in \mathit{Tr}_{SES}.\exists s^* \in succ(S_I, \beta).$$
$$(s \in succ(S_I, \beta') \land \beta|_{H_c} = \beta'|_{H_c} \land s' \in pre(h_c)))$$

Theorem 1, 2, and 3 are easily adapted to these BSPs and unwinding conditions.

Authentication and Confidentiality via IPsec*

Joshua D. Guttman, Amy L. Herzog, and F. Javier Thayer

The MITRE Corporation
{guttman, althomas, jt}@mitre.org

Abstract. The IP security protocols (IPSEC) may be used via security gateways that apply cryptographic operations to provide security services to datagrams, and this mode of use is supported by an increasing number of commercial products. In this paper, we formalize the types of authentication and confidentiality goal that IPSEC is capable of achieving, and we provide criteria that entail that a network with particular IPSEC processing achieves its security goals.

This requires us to formalize the structure of networks using IPSEC, and the state of packets relevant to IPSEC processing. We can then prove confidentiality goals as invariants of the formalized systems. Authentication goals are formalized in the manner of [9], and a simple proof method using "unwinding sets" is introduced. We end the paper by explaining the network threats that are prevented by correct IPSEC processing.

1 Introduction

The IP security protocols [7,5,6] (see also [8,4]), collectively termed IPSEC, are an important set of security protocols currently making their way into the commercial world. The IPSEC standards include protocols for ensuring confidentiality, integrity, and authentication of data communications in an IP network. The standards are very flexible, and this flexibility has led to great commercial interest; many IPSEC products are now available. The same flexibility also means that the protocol set is complex [2]. Hence, naïvely configured IPSEC products will often be set up wrong, making it hard to know what security goals have actually been achieved. Our rigorous treatment suggests an approach to constructing IPSEC configuration tools, and suggests specific checks by which a system administrator can ensure his goals are met, even without a tool.

IPSEC can be used in two different ways. It can be used end-to-end, in which case the source and destination hosts for a datagram are responsible for all cryptographic processing. It can also be used via gateways, in which case a system near the source host is responsible for applying cryptographic operations on behalf of the source, while a system near the destination is responsible for checking and decryption. A flow of packets in which at least one endpoint is an IPSEC gateway is called a *tunnel*.

---

* This work was supported by the National Security Agency through US Army CE-COM contract DAAB07-99-C-C201.

F. Cuppens et al. (Eds.): ESORICS 2000, LNCS 1895, pp. 255–272, 2000.

The IPSEC protocols work by prefixing special IP headers (or infixing special header fields). These headers contain an index (the Security Protection Index) by which the system applying the cryptographic operations specifies algorithms and keys to be used. The cryptographic operations are intended to provide authentication and integrity[1] for packets, or else confidentiality for packets. A single IPSEC header may provide both authentication and confidentiality, and indeed it is sound practice not to provide confidentiality without authentication [1]. Authentication is provided by means of keyed hashes, confidentiality by symmetric encryption. Hence, in both cases secrets must be shared between the systems applying and removing the cryptography. Manual key placement or cryptographic key exchange methods [4,8] may be used to create these shared secrets.

We will always regard the action of an IPSEC gateway as a matter of manipulating headers. To apply cryptography, a source host or a gateway wraps the datagram (including its non-IPSEC header information) in a new header. If this header offers authentication then it can be applied only by a system sharing the symmetric key. Moreover, the payload is protected from alteration in the sense that alteration can be detected, and will prevent delivery of the (damaged) payload. If the new header offers confidentiality, then it can be removed only by a system sharing the symmetric key. Headers are applied at one end of a tunnel and checked and removed at the other. We abstract from operations on the payload itself, namely encrypting it or calculating a hash over it, although of course these operations are necessary for IPSEC to be useful.

When IPSEC is used via gateways, the hosts (or the organizations operating them) delegate a degree of *trust* to certain gateways. The purpose of this paper is to study the logic of that trust. We will formalize exactly what assumptions are needed for the two types of goal, authentication and confidentiality, and explain how the trust assumptions depend on network topology. We regard this paper as an extension of a research program, begun in [3], which aims to analyze the local processing required to enforce network-wide security policies. In [3], we studied the local packet filtering behavior routers must be trusted to perform, in order to enforce network-wide firewall-like security goals.

In the next section, we formalize the security goals one can achieve via IPSEC, and introduce the notion of a *trust set*, which is central to our analysis. We then formalize the structure of networks using IPSEC (Section 3.1), the state of packets relevant to IPSEC processing (Section 3.2), and the properties of cryptographic operations (Section 3.3). We detail our behavior requirements, and prove that they are sufficient to ensure goal achievability (Section 4). We illustrate specific attacks that our approach prevents in Section 5. We end by summarizing, and discussing potential future work.

---

[1] For our purposes, integrity and authentication belong together. Jointly, they ensure that the packet has originated at a known system, and has remained unchanged since, except for such header manipulations required by IP routing and delivery mechanisms. We will speak henceforth only of authentication; it should be understood that integrity is also included.

2   Achievable Security Goals

We focus on authentication and confidentiality as security goals in our analysis. Concrete security goals select certain packets that should receive protection [7]; selection criteria may use source or destination addresses, protocol, and other header components such as the ports, in case the protocol is TCP or UDP.

2.1   Authentication Goals

The essence of authentication is that it allows the recipient to—so to speak—take a packet at face value. Thus, for a packet p selected for protection by a authentication goal,

> If A is the value in the source header field of p as received by B, then p actually originated at A in the past, and the payload has not been altered since.

We do not regard a packet as being (properly) received unless the cryptographic hash it contains matches the value computed from a shared secret and the packet contents. It will not be delivered up the stack otherwise, nor forwarded to another system after IPSEC processing.

2.2   Confidentiality Goals

We assume that confidentiality headers (as in the Encapsulating Security Payload (ESP) protocol [6]) provide authentication, and add encryption. We have two reasons for doing so. First, the IPSEC specification allows both authentication and confidentiality to be used with the ESP header; it is inadvisable to request only confidentiality when authentication can also be had at the same time, and at modest additional processing cost. Second, it seems hard to state precisely what data is kept confidential, if that data might change as the packet traverses the network. It is thus hard to say what protection has been achieved [1,2]. When using confidentiality headers, we are therefore attempting to achieve an authentication goal as well as a confidentiality goal.

A confidentiality goal for a packet with source field A, requiring protection from disclosure in some network location C, stipulates:

> If a packet originates at A, and later reaches the location C, then while it is at C it has a header providing confidentiality.

The cryptographic protection may refer to the ESP header more specifically, stipulating certain parameters (key length, algorithm, etc). The proviso that the packet was once at A is necessary, because in most cases we cannot prevent someone at C from creating a spoofed packet with given header fields. However, a spoofed packet cannot compromise the confidentiality of A's data if it has no causal connection to A.

2.3   Example Goals

Consider the network in Figure 1. Given this example network, a potential authentication goal could be that packets traveling from *EngineeringA* to *EngineeringB* should be authenticated, meaning that any packet with source field claiming to be from *EngineeringA* that reaches *EngineeringB* should in fact have originated in *EngineeringA*. An example confidentiality goal is that packets traveling from *FinanceA* to *FinanceB* should be encrypted whenever outside those areas. This means that if a packet has source field in *FinanceA*, and actually originated there, then if it reaches any other area *R*, it has an ESP header providing encryption while at *R*.

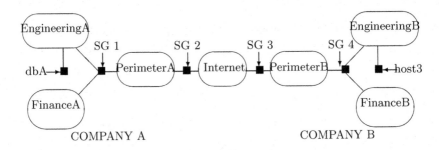

Fig. 1. Sample IPSEC Network Representation

One advantage to this form of expression is that it is semantically precise. Another is that policies expressed in this form appear to be intrinsically composable, in the sense that separate goals can always be satisfied together. Moreover, this form of expression often suggests placement of *trust sets*, in a sense we will now introduce.

2.4   Trust Sets

Once a packet enters an appropriate cryptographic tunnel, achieving a security goal does not depend on what happens until it exits. Thus, the set of locations in the network topology that are accessible to the packet from the source (before entering the tunnel) or accessible from the exit of the tunnel (before reaching the destination) are the only ones of real importance. We will call these locations a *trust set* for a particular security goal. A trust set is goal-specific; different goals may have different trust sets. For instance, an engineering group working on a sensitive project could easily have much more restrictive security goals than its parent corporation (in terms of trust).

Typically, a trust set is not a *connected* portion of the network. In many of the examples we will describe later, the trust set consists of two large connected portions, with a large public 'Internet' network between them. In some cases the trust set may consist of several islands, and the tunnels may not connect all of them directly. In this case, a packet may need to traverse several tunnels successively in order to get from one island of the trust set to a distant one.

The choice of trust set for a particular security goal is a matter of balance. Clearly, the source must belong to the same island of the trust set as the tunnel entrance, and the tunnel exit must belong to the same island as the destination (or the entrance to the next tunnel). This encourages creating trust sets as large as possible, since then a few tunnels may serve for many endpoints. However, the scope of a trust set must generally be limited to a set of networks on which it is possible to monitor traffic and check configurations. This encourages making the trust sets as small as possible. The art of using IPSEC effectively consists partly in balancing these two contrasting tendencies.

Boundaries. Of special importance are those systems inside a trust set with a direct connection to systems outside the trust set. We term these systems the *boundary* of the trust set. We assume that every device on the boundary of a trust set is capable of filtering packets. This may be a portion of its IPSEC functionality [7]. Alternatively, the device may not be IPSEC-enabled, but instead be a filtering router or packet-filtering firewall. We regard such devices as a degenerate case of an IPSEC-enabled device, one which happens never to be configured to apply any cryptographic operations.

3   Network Modeling

We begin talking about systems by viewing them as composed of networks and devices capable of IPSEC operations or packet filtering. A device has interfaces on one or more networks. Any machine (such as a switch or host) that performs no IPSEC operations or filtering we may simply ignore. We may also ignore a machine that can perform IPSEC operations, if it is not a member of the trust set for any security goal we would like to enforce. For instance, IPSEC-enabled machines elsewhere on the Internet can be ignored.

We regard a system as a graph with two kinds of nodes, representing the networks and the devices respectively. In the example shown in Figure 1, networks appear as ovals and devices appear as black squares. An edge represents the interfaces between a device and the network to which it is connected. We will never connect two networks directly via an edge; this would not give a security enforcement point to control the flow of packets between them. Instead, we will coagulate any two networks that are connected by a device that provides no security enforcement, representing them by the same oval. Figure 1 is a simple picture: for any two nodes, deletion of a single edge causes them to become disconnected. In other cases, there may be many disjoint paths between a pair of locations.

3.1   System Model

While the simple representation we have just described is useful for understanding one's network in terms of security policy, it is inconvenient for more rigorous examination. IPSEC processing depends heavily on which interface a packet is traversing, as well as the direction in which the packet is traversing that interface. Therefore it is convenient to have a system model in which there are two nodes corresponding to each interface. They represent the conceptual location of a packet when IPSEC processing is occurring, either as it traverses the interface inbound into the device or as it traverses the interface outbound from the device. We call these conceptual locations *directed interfaces*.

We introduce a model consisting of a directed graph containing three kinds of nodes. These represent networks, devices, and directed interfaces. To construct a model from a system representation in the style of Figure 1, for each edge between a device g and a network r we two directed interface nodes, which we will call $i_g[r]$ and $o_g[r]$. These represent inbound processing for a packet traveling from r to g and outbound processing for a packet traveling from g to r respectively. We add four directed arcs:

1. $r \to i_g[r]$ and $i_g[r] \to g$, the inbound arcs, and
2. $g \to o_g[r]$ and $o_g[r] \to r$, the outbound arcs.

For instance, the result of applying this process to the system representation shown in Figure 2 produces the enriched model shown in Figure 3.

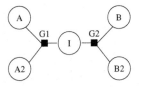

Fig. 2. Unenriched System Representation

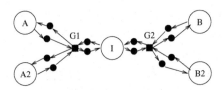

Fig. 3. Enriched System Representation

We will assume an enriched system representation $G = (V, E)$ throughout the remainder of this section. A location ℓ is a node, i.e. a member of V.

3.2   Packet States

Let P be a set of values we call protocol data. We may think of its values as the elements of IP headers other than source and destination. For instance, an IP header may specify that the protocol is TCP, and the embedded TCP header may specify a particular source port and destination port; this combination of protocol and port information may be taken as a typical member of P.

Let $A \subset P$ be a set we call authenticated protocol data; it represents those headers that provide IPSEC authentication services. Let $C \subset A$ be a set we call confidentiality protocol data; it represents those headers that provide IPSEC confidentiality services. The assumption $C \subset A$ codifies our decision not to consider ESP headers that provide only confidentiality (cf. Section 2.2).

A *header* is a member of the set $H = V \times V \times P$, consisting of a source location, a destination location, and a protocol data value. Packet states are members of H^*, that is, possibly empty sequences $\langle h_1, \ldots, h_n \rangle$. We use $\cdot$ as prefixing operator: $h \cdot \langle h_1, \ldots, h_n \rangle = \langle h, h_1, \ldots, h_n \rangle$.

Let K be a set of "processing states," with a distinguished element ready $\in K$. Intuitively, when an interface has taken all of the processing steps in the Security Association (SA, see [7]) for a packet p, then it enters the processing state ready, indicating that the packet is now ready to move across the arc from that interface. If this is an outbound interface, it means that the packet may now go out onto the attached network; if it is an inbound interface it means that the packet may now enter the device, typically to be routed to some outbound interface or for local delivery. Other members of K are used to keep track of complex IPSEC processing, when several header layers must be added or removed before processing is complete at a particular interface. These clusters of behavior represent IPSEC Security Association bundles.

We regard the travels of a packet through a system as the evolution of a state machine. The packet may not yet have started to travel; this is the start state. The packet may no longer be travelling; this is the finished state. Every other state is a triple of a node $\ell \in V$, indicating where the packet currently is situated; a processing state $\kappa \in K$, indicating whether the packet is ready to move, or how much additional processing remains; and a packet state $\theta \in H^*$, indicating the sequence of headers nested around the payload of the packet.

Definition 1. $\Omega(G, K, P, A, C)$ *is the set of network states over the graph* $G = (V, E)$, *the processing states* K, *and the protocol data* P *with* $C \subset A \subset P$. $\Omega(G, K, P, A, C)$ *is the disjoint union of*

1. start,
2. stop, *and*
3. *the triples* (ℓ, κ, θ), *for* $\ell \in V$, $\kappa \in K$, *and* $\theta \in H^*$.

The transition relation of a network state machine is a union of the following parameterized partial functions. We define what the resulting state is, assuming that the function is defined for the state given. We also constrain when some of these functions may be defined; different IPSEC security postures are determined by different choices of domain for each of these partial functions (subject to the constraints given).

Definition 2. *A network operation is any partial function of one of the following forms:*

1. *Packet creation operators* $\mathsf{create}_{\ell,h}(\mathsf{start}) = (\ell, \mathsf{ready}, \langle h \rangle)$, *when defined, for* $(\ell, h) \in V \times H$. $\mathsf{create}_{\ell,h}$ *is not defined unless its argument is the state* start.
2. *The packet discard operator* $\mathsf{discard}(\ell, \kappa, \theta) = \mathsf{stop}$, *when defined.* $\mathsf{discard}$ *is undefined for* start.
3. *Packet movement operators* $\mathsf{move}_{e,\kappa}(\ell, \mathsf{ready}, \theta) = (\ell', \kappa, \theta)$, *when* $e \in E$, $\ell \overset{e}{\to} \ell'$ *and* $\kappa \neq \mathsf{ready}$. $\mathsf{move}_{e,\kappa}$ *is undefined for all other network states.*
4. *Header prefixing operators* $\mathsf{prefix}_{h,\kappa}(\ell, \kappa', \theta) = (\ell, \kappa, h \cdot \theta)$ *when defined. The function* $\mathsf{prefix}_{h,\kappa}$ *is nowhere defined when* $h \notin A$.
5. *Header pop operators* $\mathsf{pop}_{\kappa}(\ell, \kappa', h \cdot \theta) = (\ell, \kappa, \theta)$ *when defined.*
6. *Null operators* $\mathsf{null}_{\kappa}(\ell, \kappa', \theta) = (\ell, \kappa, \theta)$ *when defined.*

A transition relation $\to \subset (\Omega(G, K, P, A, C) \times \Omega(G, K, P, A, C))$ *is a union of operators* create, $\mathsf{discard}$, move, prefix, pop, *and* null.

The assumption that $\mathsf{prefix}_{h,\kappa}$ is nowhere defined when $h \notin A$ means that the only nested headers we consider are IPSEC headers.

We call the assumption that $\mathsf{move}_{e,\kappa}(\ell, \kappa', \theta) = (\ell', \kappa, \theta)$ is not defined when $\kappa' \neq \mathsf{ready}$ the **motion restriction**. We call the assumption that it is not defined when $\kappa = \mathsf{ready}$ the **inbound motion restriction**. The motion restriction codifies the assumption that a device will not move a packet until it is ready. The inbound motion restriction codifies the assumption that there will always be a chance to process a packet when it arrives at a location, if needed, before it is declared ready to move to the next location.

Given a packet p, we call the address in the source header field of its topmost header $\mathsf{src}(p)$. We call the address in the destination header field of the topmost header $\mathsf{dst}(p)$. We also call a packet p an IPSEC packet if its outermost header is an AH or ESP header; an ESP packet if its outermost header is an ESP header; and an AH packet if its outermost header is an AH header.

Definition 3. *A trust set* S *for* $G = (V, E)$ *consists of a set* $R \subset V$ *of networks, together with all devices* g *adjacent to networks in* R *and all interfaces* $i_g[*]$ *and* $o_g[*]$.

The inbound boundary of S, *written* $\partial^{in} S$ *is the set of all interfaces* $i_g[r]$ *or* $i_g[g']$ *where* $g \in S$ *and* $r, g' \notin S$.

The outbound boundary of S, *written* $\partial^{out} S$ *is the set of all interfaces* $o_g[r]$ *or* $o_g[g']$ *where* $g \in S$ *and* $r, g' \notin S$.

In the remainder of this section, fix a trust set S and locations $a, b \in S$. We will use the following notation: Suppose $x = (\ell, \kappa, \theta)$ is a network state where $x \neq \mathsf{start}, \mathsf{stop}$.

- $\ell(x) = \ell$,
- $\kappa(x) = \kappa$,
- $\theta(x) = \theta$.

A transition $x \to y$ is *header non-augmenting* iff it is of the form $(\ell, \kappa, \theta^\frown \theta') \to (\ell, \kappa', \theta')$, where θ' is a final segment of the concatenation $\theta^\frown \theta'$.

3.3   Cryptographic Assumptions

We will make two assumptions about the IPSEC cryptographic headers. First, we assume that cryptographic headers cannot be spoofed; in other words, that if we receive a message with an authenticating header from a source "known to us,"[2] then the entity named in the source field of the header is the entity that applied the header, and the payload cannot have been changed without detection. Second, confidentiality headers have the property that packets protected with them can be decrypted only by the intended recipient, i.e. the device named in the ESP header destination field. More formally, using a dash for any field that may take any value, we stipulate that for any transition:

$$(\ell, \kappa, \langle [s', d', -], \ldots \rangle)$$
$$\downarrow$$
$$(\ell, \kappa', \langle [s, d, \alpha], [s', d', -], \ldots \rangle)$$

$\alpha \in A$ and $s \in S$ implies $\ell = s$. Moreover, for any transition:

$$(\ell, \kappa', \langle [s, d, \gamma], [s', d', -], \ldots \rangle)$$
$$\downarrow$$
$$(\ell, \kappa, \langle [s', d', -], \ldots \rangle)$$

$\gamma \in C$ and $s \in S$ implies $\ell = d$.

These properties axiomatize what is relevant to our analysis in the assumption that key material is secret. If keys are compromised then security goals dependent on them are unenforceable.

4   Security Goal Enforcement

Given an environment in which one can rigorously reason about packet states, and precise specifications of security goals, how does one ensure the goals are enforced? This section focuses on answering that question, by detailing formal behavior requirements for systems and then proving they guarantee enforceability.

In our reasoning, we will assume that security goals are stated in the form given in Section 2.3.

4.1   Authentication

Our authentication problem can be stated in the following way. Suppose a and b are network nodes. What processing conditions can we impose such that an authentication goal holds?

---

[2] Presumably as certified by some public key infrastructure, and certainly assumed to include those devices which are shown as nodes in the system model.

To make this precise, let us say an *authenticated state* is one having the form $(a, \kappa, \langle[a, -, -]\rangle)$ and an *acceptor state* is one of the form $(b, \mathsf{ready}, \langle[a, -, -]\rangle)$. The symbol authentic denotes the set of authenticated states, accept denotes the set of acceptor states. Our question can be stated thus: exhibit a set of processing restrictions which ensure the following:

> For any path $\mathsf{start} \longrightarrow^* \omega$ where $\omega \in \mathsf{accept}$ there is an intermediate state ω' so
> $$\mathsf{start} \longrightarrow^* \omega' \longrightarrow^* \omega$$
> where $\omega' \in \mathsf{authentic}$.

Thus, whenever an acceptor state is reached, an authenticated state must have occurred earlier in the state history. In this sense, the prior occurrence of an authenticated state is guaranteed when an acceptor state is observed. This use of "authenticated" for the states $\omega' \in \mathsf{authentic}$ follows Schneider [9].

Achieving authentication requires two types of behavior restrictions on trusted nodes, depending on whether the system in question is in the boundary or not. We list behavior restrictions for each.

First we list a constraint that is required for the proofs, but is vacuous in IPSEC [7], where inbound processing can only remove packet headers (but never add them).

Prefix Ready Rule.

$$(\ell, \kappa, \theta)$$
$$\downarrow$$
$$(\ell, \kappa', h \cdot \theta)$$

If $\ell \in \partial^{in} S$ then $\kappa = \mathsf{ready}$.

Authentication Tunnel Constraints. In order to achieve authentication, there are two rules that must be observed by every IPSEC-enabled device in the trust set. The first of these is that nodes in S must not spoof packets with sources in S.

Creation Rule. For any transition

$$\mathsf{start}$$
$$\downarrow$$
$$(\ell, \kappa, \langle[s, -, -]\rangle)$$

if $\ell \in S$ then $\ell = s$.

For the second rule, fix a trust set S. Whenever an IPSEC-enabled device in S processes an IPSEC packet p with $\mathsf{src}(p) \notin S$, and removing this header leads to a packet p' with $\mathsf{src}(p') \in S$, p' must be discarded. It codifies the idea that only nodes in S should be trusted to certify a packet as coming from S.

Pop Rule. For any transition

$$(\ell, \kappa, \langle [s, d, A], [a, -, -]\rangle)$$

$$\downarrow$$

$$(\ell, \kappa', \langle [a, -, -]\rangle)$$

If $\ell \in S$ then $s \in S$.

Authentication Boundary Constraints. Given the authentication goal above, boundary systems must only abide by one extra processing constraint: they must not pass an inbound packet that did not present any authentication headers.

Inbound Ready Rule.

$$(\ell, \kappa, \theta)$$

$$\downarrow$$

$$(\ell, \mathsf{ready}, \langle [a, -, -]\rangle)$$

If $\kappa \neq \mathsf{ready}$ and $\ell \in \partial^{in} S$, then $\theta = \langle [s, d, A], [a, -, -]\rangle$.

Unwinding. We prove that the processing restrictions formulated above are sufficient to ensure the authentication goal. To do so, we exhibit an *unwinding set G*.

Definition 4. *An* unwinding set G *is a set such that*

1. $\mathsf{start} \notin G$,
2. $\mathsf{accept} \subseteq G$,
3. $\mathsf{authentic} \subseteq G$,
4. *For any transition* $x \to y$ *with* $x \notin G$ *and* $y \in G$ *then* $y \in \mathsf{authentic}$.

Proposition 1 *A sufficient condition for the authentication condition to hold is the existence of an unwinding set.*

PROOF. Any path $\mathsf{start} \longrightarrow^* \omega$ with $\omega \in \mathsf{accept}$, must have the form

$$\mathsf{start} \longrightarrow^* x \to y \longrightarrow^* \omega$$

with $x \notin G, y \in G$. By the unwinding condition 4, $y \in \mathsf{authentic}$. ∎

We now exhibit an unwinding set G.

$$G = \mathsf{accept} \cup \mathsf{authentic} \cup \mathsf{continue}$$

where continue is defined:

Definition 5. (Continuing States) *A state is a continuing state if it belongs to one of the three disjoint classes below:*

C1 $(\ell, \mathsf{ready}, \langle [a, -, -] \rangle)$ *for* $\ell \in \partial^{in} S$;
C2 $(\ell, \kappa, \langle [a, -, -] \rangle)$ *for* $\ell \in S \setminus \partial^{in} S$,
    i.e. for locations in the portion of S *other than the inbound boundary;*
C3 $(\ell, \kappa, \langle \cdots [s, d, A], [a, -, -] \rangle)$ *for* $s \in S$ *and any* ℓ.

Proposition 2 *G is an unwinding set.*

PROOF. Suppose $x \to y$ with $x \notin G, y \in G$. The proof is a completely mechanical enumeration of cases. In each case, we show either that either it cannot really occur or that $y \in$ authentic.

Case I: $y \in$ accept. By definition of accept, y is of the form $(b, \mathsf{ready}, \langle [a, -, -] \rangle)$.

1. $b \in \partial^{in} S$.
    a) $x \to y$ is a motion. The **inbound motion restriction** excludes this case.
    b) $x \to y$ is non-augmenting. By the **inbound ready rule**, x is of the form
$$(b, \kappa, \langle \ldots, [s, d, A], [a, -, -] \rangle)$$
    with $s \in S$. This implies $x \in$ **C3** $\subseteq$ continue $\subseteq G$.
    c) $x =$ start. In this case, by the **creation rule** $b = a$. Thus $y \in$ authentic.
2. $b \in S \setminus \partial^{in} S$.
    a) If $x \to y$ is a motion, then x must be of the form $(\ell, \mathsf{ready}, \langle [a, -, -] \rangle)$ By definition of network boundary of S, $\ell \in S$. This implies $x \in$ **C1** $\cup$ **C2** $\subseteq G$. This case is thus excluded.
    b) Otherwise x must be of one the forms
        i. $(b, \kappa, \langle [s, d, A], [a, -, -] \rangle)$ with $s \in S$, so $x \in$ **C2** $\subseteq G$, which excludes this case also.
        ii. start. In this case, by the **creation rule** y is of the form $(b, \kappa, \langle [s, -, -] \rangle)$ with $b = s = a$. Thus $y \in$ authentic.

Case II: $y \in$ **C1**. Thus $y = (\ell, \mathsf{ready}, \langle [a, -, -] \rangle)$ for $\ell \in \partial^{in} S$.

1. $x = (\ell', \kappa, \theta)$. The **inbound motion rule** excludes this case.
2. $x = (\ell, \kappa, \theta)$. By the **inbound ready rule**, the transition $x \to y$ must be a pop. In this case, by the **pop rule** x must be of the form $(\ell, \kappa', \langle [s, d, A], [a, -, -] \rangle)$ for $s \in S$, so $x \in$ **C3** $\subseteq G$, which excludes this case also.
3. $x =$ start. In this case, the **creation rule** implies $\ell = a$, so $y \in$ authentic.

Case III: $y \in$ **C2**. In this case y is of the form $(\ell, \kappa, \langle [a, -, -] \rangle)$ for $\ell \in S \setminus \partial^{in} S$.

1. $x = (\ell', \kappa', \theta)$ with $\ell' \neq \ell$. In this case, the transition $x \to y$ must be a location change. By definition of border, $\ell' \in S$ and by the motion ready restriction, $\kappa' = \mathsf{ready}$. In this case $x \in$ **C1** or $x \in$ **C2** depending on wehether $\ell' \in \partial^{in} S$ or $\ell' \in S \setminus \partial^{in} S$. Thus this case is excluded.
2. $x = (\ell, \kappa', \theta)$. In this case, the transition $x \to y$ must be a pop. By the **pop rule** x must be of the form $(\ell, \kappa', \langle [s, d, A], [a, -, -] \rangle)$ for $s \in S$, so $x \in$ **C3** $\subseteq G$, which excludes this case also.
3. $x =$ start. In this case, the **creation rule** implies $\ell = a$, so $y \in$ authentic.

*Case IV: $y \in$ **C3**.* y is of the form $(\ell, \kappa, \langle \cdots [s, d, A], [a, -, -] \rangle)$ for $s \in S$.

1. If $x \to y$ is a motion, then $x \in$ **C3**
2. If $x \to y$ is a non-augmenting header transition, then x must also be of the form **C3**.
3. If $x \to y$ is a push, then either $x \in$ **C3** or x is of the form $(\ell, \kappa', \langle [a, -, -] \rangle)$. By cryptographic restriction, $\ell = s \in S$. In this case $x \in$ **C1** or $x \in$ **C2** depending on wehether $\ell \in \partial^{in} S$ or $\ell \in S \setminus \partial^{in} S$. Thus this case is excluded. ■

4.2   Confidentiality

We will consider the following confidentiality problem: Suppose a and b are network nodes. What conditions can we impose on the enclave nodes' processing to ensure that packets travelling from a to b are encrypted whenever they are not in the trust set S? More formally, given some set of processing restrictions,

> If we start with a packet of the form $(a, \mathsf{ready}, \langle [a, b, p] \rangle)$, where $a, b \in S$, then it will never be the case that $(\ell, \kappa, \langle [a, b, p] \rangle)$ if $\ell \notin S$.

Achieving confidentiality is even simpler than authentication. There are two simple constraints, one on all devices in the trust set, and an additional constraint for boundary members.

Confidentiality Tunnel Constraints. Fix a trust set S. The constraint on all trust set members requires them not to "tunnel" packets requiring protection out to a dangerous area. Our constraint will ensure that whenever a system inside S adds a confidentiality header to a packet which would require protection, the source and destination of the added header are also in S.

Destination Prefix Rule. For any transition

$$(\ell, \kappa, \langle [s_1, d_1, p_1] \cdots [a, b, p] \rangle)$$

$$\downarrow$$

$$(\ell, \kappa', \langle [s_2, d_2, p_2][s_1, d_1, p_1] \cdots [a, b, p] \rangle)$$

if $\ell \in S$, $s_1, d_1 \in S$, and $p_1 \notin C$, then $s_2, d_2 \in S$. We include the case where $\langle [s_1, d_1, p_1] \cdots [a, b, p] \rangle = \langle [a, b, p] \rangle$.

Confidentiality Boundary Constraints. As with authentication, we impose one constraint on boundary members. If a packet p is traversing an outbound interface on the boundary of S, and p could contain a packet $p_0 \in P$ with no confidentiality header, discard p.

One way to safely implement this is to pass a packet p only if its topmost layer is a confidentiality header, or else it has no IPSEC headers and $p \notin P$.

Outbound Ready Rule. For any transition

$$(\ell, \kappa, \theta)$$

$$\downarrow$$

$$(\ell, \mathsf{ready}, \theta')$$

if $\ell \in \partial^{out} S$, then either $\theta' = \langle [s, d, C], \ldots [a, b, p] \rangle$ for $s, d \in S$, or else $\theta' = \langle [s', d', -], \ldots \rangle$ where either s' or d' not in S.

Invariant. We will prove that the processing restrictions formulated above are sufficient to ensure the confidentiality goal using an invariant of our state machine. We will first show that the invariant holds, then prove that given the invariant, our confidentiality goal holds as well.

Proposition 3 *Suppose that Σ is a state machine satisfying the outbound ready rule and the destination prefix rule, and suppose that (ℓ, κ, θ) is the state resulting from a sequence of actions beginning with* $\mathsf{create}_{a,[a,b,p]}$*, where $a, b \in S$.*

1. *If $\ell \in S$, then either*
   a) *whenever $[s_1, d_1, p_1]$ is any layer of θ, then $s_1, d_1 \in S$ and $p_1 \notin C$, or*
   b) *there is a final segment of θ of the form $\langle [s_k, d_k, C] \cdots [s_i, d_i, p_i] \cdots \rangle$ where $s_k, d_k \in S$ and for each $i < k$, $s_i, d_i \in S$ and $p_i \notin C$.*
2. *If $\ell \notin S$, then there is a final segment of θ of the form $\langle [s_k, d_k, C] \cdots [s_i, d_i, p_i] \cdots \rangle$ where $s_k, d_k \in S$ and for each $i < k$, $s_i, d_i \in S$ and $p_i \notin C$.*

PROOF. We will examine each of the possible state transitions in turn, showing for each that they cannot violate the invariant.

Case 1: create and discard. In the case of the create operator, we know that the first transition in our state machine is the following (which does not violate the invariant):

$$\mathsf{start}$$

$$\downarrow$$

$$(a, \mathsf{ready}, \langle [a, b, p] \rangle)$$

The invariant imposes no constraints on the finish state, thus the discard transition is irrelevant.

Case 2: pop. Assume that we are at location ℓ. The state transition we are interested in is $\mathsf{pop}_\kappa(\ell, \kappa', h \cdot \theta) = (\ell, \kappa, \theta)$. Our cryptographic assumptions prevent any location from removing an encryption layer not destined for them. Thus, no location can remove the necessary confidentiality protection (provided it was applied), and the invariant is not violated.

Case 3: prefix. Assume once again we are at location ℓ. The transition is $\mathsf{prefix}_{h,\kappa}(\ell, \kappa', \theta) = (\ell, \kappa, h \cdot \theta)$. The only case which has bearing on the invariant is that where $\ell \in S$, and there is no encryption layer in θ. By the Destination Prefix rule, $src(h), dst(h) \in S$ as well. If h is a confidentiality header, the packet now satisfies the second invariant condition for locations in S. If h is not a confidentiality header, the packet satisfies the first invariant condition for locations in S.

Case 4: null. The invariant imposes no constraints on κ.

Case 5: move. Again, assume we are at location ℓ. The transition is

$$\mathsf{move}_{e,\kappa}(\ell, \mathsf{ready}, \theta) = (\ell', \kappa, \theta)$$

Since this involves no change of state, the only case which could violate the invariant is that where $\ell \in \partial^o S$ and $\ell' \notin S$. The Outbound Ready rule ensures that the top layer of θ is either $[s, d, C]$ with $s, d \in S$ or $[s', d', -]$ with $s', d' \notin S$. The Destination Prefix rule ensures that below the bottom-most confidentiality layer, all layers have source and destination in S. So, regardless of which portion of the Outbound Ready rule is appropriate, the invariant is not violated.

Thus, the given invariant holds for our state machine. We now must show it implies enforecement of the confidentiality goal.

The confidentiality goal is ensured if it is never the case that $(\ell, \kappa, \langle [a, b, p] \rangle)$ if $\ell \notin S$. Condition 2 of the invariant provides this: suppose that we're at $\ell \notin S$. Then there is at least one layer $[s, d, C]$ with $s, d \in S$, and no layers with external sources 'beneath' that layer.

5   What Can Go Wrong

We have seen that the restrictions of Sections 4.1 and 4.2 suffice to ensure that authentication and confidentiality goals are achieved. In this section, we argue less formally that they are necessary. We illustrate the problems that can otherwise arise, by presenting example attacks, focusing first on authentication. In all examples, we use the example network described in Figure 1.

5.1   Failures of Authentication

Corresponding to our three authentication constraints, there are three ways that IPSEC (incorrectly configured) may fail to achieve authentication goals.

Spoofing near source or destination. The first of these problems arise if locations within a trust set spoof packet addresses.

Consider the following security goal: packets traveling from *EngineeringA* to *EngineeringB* should be authenticated. If, in this case, one host in *EngineeringA* creates a packet claiming to come from another, the security gateway applying the cryptographic headers (either *SG1* or *SG2*, here) would be unable to determine that the packet was not legitimate. A similar situation could arise if a host in *EngineeringB* created packets with source header field of an *EngineeringA* system.

Tunneling packets to a point near source or destination. The second attack becomes possible if machines inside the source region do not ensure that removed layers correspond to an acceptable authentication tunnel.

Suppose again that the security goal is to authenticate packets traveling from *EngineeringA* to *EngineeringB*. Further suppose that the device which performs outbound cryptographic processing for Company A is *SG1*.

Consider, then, the following case: a machine in the region *Internet* creates a packet with an forged source of a host in *EngineeringA*, and a destination in *EngineeringB*, and then adds a tunnel mode authentication header destined for the host *dbA*, which performs IPSEC processing.

The packet goes via *SG2*, which routes it through *PerimeterA*, and past *SG1*. When it reaches the destination *dbA*, that host removes the tunnel-mode AH header and successfully checks the cryptographic checksum against the payload and tunneled header. The result of removing the tunnel-mode header is a non-IPSEC packet with source header field in *EngineeringA* and destination header field in *EngineeringB*. The normal routing mechanism causes it to pass back to *SG1*, which adds the "appropriate" authentication header. As a consequence it reaches Company B with a cryptographic header purporting to guarantee that it originated in *EngineeringA*.

The same effect is obtained if the machine in the region *Internet* creates the same packet initially, and then adds a tunnel mode authentication header destined for the host *host3*. Clearly, the IPSEC-enabled devices *dbA* and *host3* must be configured to compare the source address on the IPSEC header, namely the *Internet* machine, against the source address on the inner, non-IPSEC header (which claims to be in *EngineeringA*). The **Pop Rule** ensures that they will discard the forged packet when it emerges from the authentication tunnel with source outside the trust set *S*.

Entry of packets near source or destination. The third problem arises if systems on the *boundary* of the trust set *S* allow incoming packets to enter, even if the packets claim to have originated inside.

Again consider the security goal that all traffic between *EngineeringA* and *EngineeringB* must be authenticated. Suppose further that *SG1* and *SG4* are the endpoints of the authentication tunnel. Then, if *SG1* does not perform inbound filtering on packets arriving from *Perimeter A* to check that they do not have source header field from any system in *EngineeringA*, a machine in the region *Internet* could create a packet with source in *EngineeringA*, use source routing (or another routing attack) to send it into *EngineeringA*, where it would then be sent to *EngineeringB*.

5.2   Failures of Confidentiality

Again corresponding to our behavior constraints, there are two types of attacks that IPSEC, configured incorrectly, cannot protect against. Assume that the corporations Company A and B wish to protect the confidentiality of traffic flowing from *EngineeringA* to *EngineeringB*, by ensuring that it is always encrypted while in the public Internet.

Tunneling to a point distant from source and destination. The tunnel endpoints are *SG2* and *SG3* in this example. If *SG4* is misconfigured, it may insert the packets decrypted by *SG3* into another tunnel, intended for a different sort of traffic. The exit from that tunnel may be on the public Internet, say in Company C, with which Company B has some commercial relation, but which is a competitor of Company A. This would be a failure of confidentiality. Company C might even have been surprisingly helpful when the system administrators in Company B designed their IPSEC configuration.

Our *Destination Prefix Rule* (Section 4.2) prevents this sort of occurrence.

Escape to a point distant from source and destination. In this example, the tunnel endpoints are *SG1* and *SG4*. If *SG4* or *SG3* is not set up to prevent back-flow of packets with source header field in *EngineeringA* and destination header field in *EngineeringB*, then these packets could be re-routed out past *SG4* and *SG3* after having traversed *SG4*, the point at which the ESP header was removed. The risk that this may be a reasonable routing strategy (or a feasible attack on routing in *Engineering B*) increases if *Engineering B* consists of a large collection of networks, and if it is more richly connected to the outside world than in our sample diagram.

Hence, systems on the boundary of the trust set must inspect packets before passing them on; this sort of attack is not possible if the *Outbound Ready Rule* (Section 4.2) is in effect.

6   Conclusion

In this paper, we formalized the main security goals IPSEC is suited to achieve, and we formalized IPSEC-relevant aspects of networks. We then provided criteria entailing that a network with particular IPSEC processing achieves its security goals. Achieving these security goals requires identification of a *trust set* for each goal.

Our approach has several benefits.

- It is rigorous: provided the behavior restrictions are enforced, the security goals are formally guaranteed.
- It explains clearly exactly which systems must be trusted, and in exactly what ways.
- Its security management discipline can largely be enforced by software that checks the configurations of nodes within the trust set.

Future work will include the development of such a software tool. In addition, it seems likely that other related security protocol sets (for example, PPTP) could be analyzed in the same way; additional security goal types—such as traffic flow confidentiality or firewall-like restrictions on types of traffic, in the manner of [3]—could also be added.

References

1. Steven Bellovin.   Problem areas for the IP security protocols.   In *Proceedings of the Sixth USENIX UNIX Security Symposium*, July 1996.   Also at ftp://ftp.research.att.com/dist/smb/badesp.ps.
2. Niels Ferguson and Bruce Schneier. A cryptographic evaluation of ipsec. Counterpane Internet Security, Inc., available at http://www.counterpane.com/ipsec.html, 1999.
3. Joshua D. Guttman. Filtering postures: Local enforcement for global policies. In *Proceedings, 1997 IEEE Symposium on Security and Privacy*, pages 120–29. IEEE Computer Society Press, May 1997.
4. D. Harkins and D. Carrel. *The Internet Key Exchange (IKE)*. IETF Network Working Group RFC 2409, November 1998.
5. S. Kent and R. Atkinson. *IP Authentication Header*. IETF Network Working Group RFC 2402, November 1998.
6. S. Kent and R. Atkinson. *IP Encapsulating Security Payload*. IETF Network Working Group RFC 2406, November 1998.
7. S. Kent and R. Atkinson. *Security Architecture for the Internet Protocol*. IETF Network Working Group RFC 2401, November 1998.
8. D. Maughan, M. Schertler, M. Schneider, and J. Turner. *Internet Security Association and Key Management Protocol (ISAKMP)*. IETF Network Working Group RFC 2408, November 1998.
9. Steve Schneider. Security properties and CSP. In *Proceedings, 1996 IEEE Symposium on Security and Privacy*, pages 174–87. IEEE Computer Society Press, May 1996.

A Security Framework for a Mobile Agent System

Ciarán Bryce

Object Systems Group, University of Geneva, Switzerland
Ciaran.Bryce@cui.unige.ch

Abstract. This paper describes a distributed security infrastructure for mobile agents. The first property of the infrastructure is *believability*; this means that mechanisms are provided for authenticating information furnished by an agent. A second security property is *survivability*. This means that an agent computation can be programmed to survive attacks by malicious hosts on individual agents; this is achieved through encryption as well as agent replication and voting. The main feature of the infrastructure is that mobile agents are themselves used to enforce the security properties.

1 Introduction

Mobile agents offer a promising approach to Internet programming. An agent is a program that executes on a host, that can be stopped and then have its execution continued on another host [25]. The advantage of mobile agents is twofold. First, they enable computation to be moved closer to where the resources that they require reside on the network; studies confirm that this can save network bandwidth for applications [21]. Second, they enable application functionality to be dynamically deployed to hosts. With applications of the technology including active networking [24] and mobile computing, mobile agents could bring a new dimension to Internet programming, so their security is crucial.

Security remains a major problem for the agent paradigm. It is difficult to prevent a *malicious agent* from stealing or corrupting information on its host and in other agents on the host, or from launching denial of service attacks by over-consuming resources. Further, a *malicious host* can steal or corrupt agent information, or even kill the agent [26]. An agent infrastructure must work around these security problems and offer compensating security properties.

Most work on agent security has focussed on the malicious agent problem, and notably on techniques for *isolating* agents that execute on a host. However, security for agent-based applications requires more than isolation. Two further properties are *survivability* and *believability*. Survivability is about ensuring that an agent computation can survive attacks on individual agents by malicious hosts or agents. Believability is about ensuring that the information furnished by an agent visiting some host can be verified.

F. Cuppens et al. (Eds.): ESORICS 2000, LNCS 1895, pp. 273–290, 2000.

This paper presents a security framework for mobile agents. A key feature of the framework is that mobile agents themselves are used to implement believability and survivability. As an example, sensitive computations can be migrated to safe areas, or agents could move policy components to client sites so that the client can work off-line (that is, without having to use the network). We give several examples of these benefits throughout the text. With respect to survivability, agents help by having computation parts replicated and sent on different itineraries in an effort to tolerate single attacks [9]. With respect to believability, an agent carries signed credentials that verifies its bindings, e.g., public key to agent, agent to owner. A credential can be a disactivated agent, that when activated, executes a task that verifies the binding in question. Such a credential is known as an *active credential*. For instance, to verify that an agent is not a daemon, an active credential would verify that it has not been sent a `kill` signal by its owner. Using programs for credentials brings much flexibility to the security framework.

The plan of this paper is the following. Section 2 gives the background to the security framework, and explains why agents themselves are used to implement it. We motivate the survivability and believability security properties with the aid of two examples: an Internet auction room [20] and Internet newspaper service [18]. Section 3 presents the agent security framework, in the form of a small language, and Section 4 overviews its implementation in a Java-based mobile agent system [6]. Section 5 discusses related work and Section 6 concludes.

2   Background

This section outlines the main design choices for the security infrastructure. Section 2.1 gives an overview of the mobile agent paradigm. The two example applications are outlined in Section 2.2. We explain why these applications use mobile agents, and give their security requirements. Section 2.3 identifies the security properties of the agent infrastructure. Finally, Section 2.4 explains why agents themselves are used as a basic mechanism for security enforcement.

2.1   The Mobile Agent Paradigm

A mobile agent is a program or object that can be moved between network hosts during its execution [25]. The first benefit of agents is that computation can be moved closer to where the data it needs resides, and this can often save expensive network bandwidth [21]. A second benefit is that it enables application programs to be dynamically deployed to hosts on which one had not foreseen to run these programs. Mobility is already exploited by the active networking community [24], where programs are distributed in packets to routers; this allows application functionality to be taken away from centralized servers. Mobile computing is another avenue for mobile agents, as users may transfer programs between portable devices and their main stay-put sites.

Despite the attraction of mobile code and agent technology, security is still a major concern. One reason is the *malicious agent problem*, where an agent that executes on a host attacks other agents or local resources. The problem is that to support mobility over heterogeneous hardware platforms, agents usually execute on software or virtual machines. This means that software techniques are used to isolate agents from one another, and these are not always effective. Java-based agent systems for instance isolate agents by running each agent in a different type-space, e.g., [12]. This approach means that an attempt by an agent to reference an object in another agent provokes a type error. However, basic Java classes are shared by all agent type spaces and can be used to bypass the typing security [6]. Another kind of attack comes from agents over-consuming resources, with the intent of launching denial of service attacks.

A second security concern with the agent paradigm is the *malicious host problem* [26]. An agent is under complete control of its host, which may steal or modify agent information or even destroy the agent. No general solution exists for this problem, though *privacy homo-morphisms* (programs that are "encrypted" in such a way that they operate on encrypted data and produce the result in encrypted form) exist for a small class of problems [8,23]. This can prevent information from being disclosed to a host, though cannot prevent it from being destroyed.

Most of the research work into security is concentrating on the malicious agent issue, by advancing techniques that isolate the execution of agents from the rest of the system. However isolation on its own is only a first step for security. A security framework for an agent architecture must furnish further properties. For instance, an agent that visits a trustworthy host must be able to authenticate the information that it furnishes. Further, a host that sends an agent out onto the network on an errand must possess ways to increase its agent's survivability (a.k.a. chances of survival). An agent owner does this to cater for malicious hosts that the agent can meet on its itinerary.

2.2   Example Scenarios

This section outlines some properties for an agent security framework for the JavaSeal mobile agent system [6]. In particular, the framework is inspired by two agent applications that run over JavaSeal.

Example 1: HyperNews. HyperNews is a medium-sized electronic commerce system for the sale of newspaper articles [18]. The system was designed in cooperation with Hebdo - a Swiss journal - and aims to allow several newspaper *providers* to sell articles on the Internet. HyperNews is implemented using mobile agent technology. Once an article is published by a provider, it is encapsulated within, and carried around by, an agent. The reason for this choice is that an article must be self-contained. It must contain all of the procedures necessary for payment and reading. In addition, a client must be able to read an article without having to contact the provider server. The latter property is needed for off-line operation (allowing a client to read an article while disconnected), and in particular for *anonymity* (which means that a client can read an article without having his identity revealed to the provider).

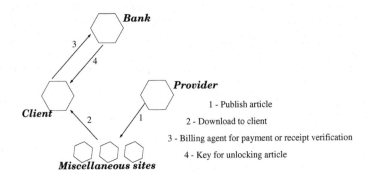

Fig. 1. The network interactions for article usage.

Apart from anonymity, the fundamental security requirement for HyperNews is that a client must pay a provider for each article of that provider that he reads.

The HyperNews schema is shown in Figure 1. The article contents are encrypted with a symmetric key k known only to the bank and provider. When the client reads the article for the first time, a *billing* agent is created and sent to the bank (communication 3 in Figure 1). The bank deducts the price of the article from the client's account, and then returns the key k to the client. The client environment decrypts the article, destroys the key and can read the contents in a tailored browser. The reply message from the bank also contains a receipt. When the client subsequently reads the article, the receipt must be validated. Steps 3 and 4 of Figure 1 are repeated except that the receipt is transferred in message 3 with k being returned. In the system, messages of steps 3 and 4 are encrypted with a symmetric session key established with the bank by each client[1].

Each provider has a proxy environment installed on the host of each client that reads one of its articles. This environment is represented by an agent termed a *news feed*. The news feed agents can enforce extra security checks before access to an article is granted, and they store receipts for articles of their provider. Billing agents transfer receipts between clients and the bank; key agents distribute the encryption keys (c.f., steps 3 and 4 of Figure 1).

One interesting feature of HyperNews is that security policy components (within news feeds) are agents. For instance, new access control policies for the news feeds can be distributed just as easily as news article agents. This is an example of the network savings feature of agents being exploited for security, as well as the dynamic distribution of programs.

---

[1] A recent implementation of HyperNews uses JavaCards for payment.

Example 2: Internet Auctions. This example is taken from a project currently in its design phase, whose aim is to build a reliable Internet auction room [20]. The architecture consists of a set of replicated auction servers distributed around the globe. The servers communicate using a specialized server to server protocol. This protocol includes a transaction phase for bid consistency when the auction participants are distributed. Clients access the auction through a standard web browser.

An important quality of service in this system is *off-line operation*. That is, a user should be able to deposit a bid for an item, log off and connect later to see if his bid has succeeded. Furthermore, the bid might be for an item not yet on sale, or for an item that might go on sale. In this case, the bid is activated when a corresponding item goes on sale. For these reasons, bids in the architecture are encapsulated within mobile agents. These agents contain the user's "instructions" for the bid process.

The main security requirement is that a bidder not be able to modify a competitor's bid. This means for instance, that the auction must be able to authenticate the information furnished by a bid, e.g., the owner identity, the value of the bid, etc. The eBay auction service was recently the subject of well-published bad practices where users posed fake bids for their item in the aim of pushing up the price. This example shows the importance of being able to validate all bid information. Another security requirement for the agent-based auction room is that an agent must be able to survive attacks on it on its way to, and at, the auction servers.

2.3 Mobile Agent Security Policies

The first issue raised when designing a security framework is the kind of security policies that agents and hosts must support.

One security requirement inherited from traditional distributed system security is **isolation** - that user programs and agents must be protected from each other, and the host must be protected from agents. This is a requirement on the underlying agent architecture, and is no different to the security requirement of any system.

In contrast to traditional programs, an agent is written to execute in different environments, and even to move during its execution. The owner of the agent can have different levels of trust in each host. An agent must therefore be **adaptable** to the environment in which it runs. This means that it must be programmed to respond to the differing trust levels of the hosts that it visits, and to adapt its defenses accordingly. For instance, a host may decide to encode a digital signature into its agent before sending it to another host, in order to authenticate that same agent when it returns. Similarly, an agent may decide to encrypt some of its data before moving to a less trustworthy host.

In our framework, two further properties are defined for agent applications. The first is **survivability**. In the auction application for instance, it is especially important that a bid survive attacks. This means being able to replicate an agent and send the replicas on different itineraries. Replica results can then be voted upon.

A further security property is **believability**. This means that there must be a way to verify the information furnished by an agent. A HyperNews agent for instance must prove that the contents it furnishes are the same as those published by the provider; a user must prove that the sum of money in his wallet is not forged. The auction example also shows a range of bindings that a bid agent has to prove to an auction server:

– Bid to user binding: in order to defeat masquerade attacks where an attacker forges a bid.
– Bid to quote binding: in order to detect attacks on the integrity of the bid's information by a competitor.
– Bid activeness: that a bid that presents itself is still valid, for instance that it has not received a `kill` signal from its owner.
– Bid to public key binding: that no revoke has been issued on the public key carried by an agent.

2.4 Mobile Agent Security Mechanisms

When designing mechanisms for the security framework's properties of adaptability, survivability and believability, one question considered was how mobile agents themselves could be used for security. After all, there are several existing examples of mobile code and agents aiding security.

E.g., Data Verification. One feature of the Semper electronic commerce framework is its conflict mediation functions that are used during transactions [2]. The role of these functions is to keep each party informed of his obligations at each stage of a transaction and to propose corrective actions in the event of a protocol going awry. The functions could run (as an agent) at the host of each transaction party instead of at a third party host. This approach has the advantage of allowing security checks to happen "off-line". Another verification approach for programs down-loaded to hosts is *proof carrying code* [19]. This is a proof of program correctness that is evaluated as the program executes. This is close to the agent model in that the security program is dynamically distributed to hosts. ◇

E.g., Login Applets. A simple login applet reads a name, password and perhaps other information and then brings this data back to the server. Such applets are quite common on the Internet. The reason for using an agent is that the server does not need to block threads for the client while he is typing the password. The server can process the request fully and completely when the applet returns. Also, the login procedure for the user need not be known to him in advance. ◇

E.g., Active Networking. Active networking, where programs can be distributed to network nodes to intelligently process application packets, is a natural target for security processing such as key management. The approach has already been used for mobile fire-walls and intrusion detection, e.g., [3]. ◇

There are two ways in which agents are being used in these examples. First, to move security processing nearer to the user or server; second, to dynamically distribute security programs. This can be further exploited for survivability and believability. For survivability, the platform can help increase the chances of an agent's survival by providing replication mechanisms so that a computation can be split and sent on different routes in order to tolerate attacks on individual agents from different hosts.

For believability, *active credentials* can be executed to verify properties of agents. Agents acting as credentials have the advantage that they add behavior and flexibility to the framework. The case of verifying that an agent has not received a `kill` signal for instance is more conveniently done using agents since the meaning of validity is application-specific, and so requires code specific to the application. Active credentials are thus similar in spirit to proof-carrying code.

Caveat. Our goal is not to argue that agents are a panacea for security, but that their use can sometimes make sense. In practice, security policy modeling in the Internet context must include risk analysis. For instance, the commonly cited airline reservation scenario where an agent visits the server of competing airlines to learn the cheapest fare [26] is becoming the reference example for the mobile host problem. The security risk is that a malicious server can alter the quote of a competing company. The scenario is too risky; A less risk prone use of agents in the airline example is for intelligent or batch bookings. For instance, an agent is sent to a server with a request "I want 2 seats on a flight to Paris with an overnight stopover in Bonn. If this costs me more than 100EUR, then reserve a direct flight". In this case, the request is being shipped to the server side for execution; the agent approach is useful because the client-server interaction is happening on the same machine, unaffected by slow network connections, and the user can be off-line. From the client's security viewpoint, the cost of an attack on his agent is the same as the cost of an attack on the messages that he would exchange with the airline server in the client-server approach.

Considering risk analysis in the HyperNews example, the key k used to decrypt the article on the client host is destroyed after the decryption to reduce the risk of the key being illegally copied. The browser used to view the articles is tailored, and does not possess printing or file saving capabilities. Of course, if the HyperNews platform has been tampered with, then the security is broken since access to the article key can be got and distributed, thus avoiding the need for payment. However, the security policy for HyperNews was designed as part of a *business plan* and contained an in-depth risk assessment. It was felt that the effort needed by an ordinary user to subvert his Java platform exceeds the gain - free access to a few articles which only cost a few centimes anyway.

3   The Security Framework

This section presents the security framework for mobile agents. Agents, naming, messaging and migration are described in 3.1. Agent security policies are described in 3.2, and the believability and survivability properties in 3.3. We close the section in 3.4 with some HyperNews agents written in the framework.

3.1   General

The network is composed of a set of inter-connected hosts or *places* where *agents* execute. Every component at a place is modeled as an agent, from mobile programs to immobile servers. An agent is an object that responds to a specific set of messages.

Naming. Agents' variables bind to other agents, places, and primitive data. The primitive data types are strings, encrypted values and agent name values or pointers (for treating agent names as first class values). Each agent has a *local name space* (LNS) for interpreting names. A place also has a name space.

Whereas an agent's name space resolves names for primitive types, it delegates resolution of agent names to its place's space. This is because name bindings change with agent migration. The name stdio held by an agent at a place might refer to the I/O component at that place. During migration, this binding is broken and a new binding for stdio to the I/O component at the destination place is formed.

There are two reserved names in the architecture. When evaluated in an agent, Env yields the agent's current place, and the name Self denotes the agent itself.

An agent name value or pointer is also a primitive type. Thus, while the binding $n \mapsto \sigma$ in a space means that the variable n in that space is bound to agent σ, an entry $n \mapsto m$ means that n is bound to the agent/place denoted by m in the space. The name value m can be a compound name, represented as a sequence, e.g., $\langle n_1, n_2, n_3 \rangle$ meaning that the name n is bound to the agent or place denoted by the name n_3 in the place named n_2 by the place named n_1 in the current local name space. A name value is got from an agent linked to variable v using the expression $n := \mathbf{ref}\ v$. The reverse transformation is done using the cast $v := (A)n$ where A is the class of the agent (see below).

Communication. The platform on which the framework runs assures isolation. This means that agents only communicate by exchanging messages. Communication is not restricted to agents of the same host. Messages are sent and received using the commands:

$$\textbf{Send } m \textbf{ to } a_1 \quad \text{and} \quad \textbf{Receive } m \textbf{ from } a_2$$

respectively. The send command names a recipient agent a_1. The receive command names a sending agent a_2, meaning that it will accept a message from a_2. The receiving agent may also use the expression "$\mathbf{any}(a_2)$" to name the sender. This means that it is willing to receive a message from any agent. After the message transfer occurs, the sending agent is bound to a_2.

A message m is a sequence composed of primitive types (strings, encrypted values or name values). The receiver may specify an agent, a primitive type or a free variable. In the former case, the value must match the sender's for the send and receive commands to match. If the latter case, the receive can match with any sender data, and the variable becomes bound to that data afterwards.

For instance, **Send** ("hello", n) **to** n_1 matches with **Receive** ("hello", n) **from any**(n_2), with **Receive** (**any**(s), **any**(n_3)) **from any**(n_2), though not with **Receive** ("goodbye", n) **from any**(n_2).

Mobility. Agents can be exchanged between places. An agent may move itself to a place named p using the command **MigrateTo** p. An agent may also be explicitly moved using a **SendAgent** command, for which there must be a corresponding **ReceiveAgent** command at the destination place:

$$\textbf{SendAgent } a_1 \textbf{ to } p_1 \quad \text{and} \quad \textbf{ReceiveAgent } a_2 \textbf{ from } p_2$$

As with the message exchange commands, the receiver may explicitly name the sending place and migrating agent, or use a free expression in which the variable is updated after the communication. After migration, an agent resumes its execution by having its **Restart** command executed. All local binding's in an agent's name space remain in tact during the migration; only agent bindings – those for which the environment is responsible – change.

Creating and Terminating Agents. An agent's *class* defines the variables and code of an agent. An agent is created with the command **New**, which specifies a class and a local variable to name the agent. The newly created agent executes its **Start** command at the same place as its creator. An agent is terminated with **Terminate** n.

Agent programming model. A "reaction style" of programming is chosen for agents. Whenever an agent is subject to an *event e*, it reacts by executing a list S of commands. An agent's class is a series of $e{\rightarrow}S$ event-reaction pairs. An event could be the **Start** signal from the environment on creation, or the **Restart** signal sent to the agent following its migration. Another event type is the message or agent **Receive** action. Agents can execute in parallel, though an event within an agent is not scheduled until a currently executing reaction list completes. This choice of programming model is based on experience gained in programming mobile agent systems (in Java) [6,18]. We have found that for communicating agents that move around the network, the real programming effort is spent in identifying all event scenarios that the agent can be subject to, and programming the agent to adapt to these [6,18].

Simplifications. The architecture has some simplifications. For instance, a host must control in practice the agents that can move and the termination of agents; this is the case in the JavaSeal platform [6] over which this security framework is implemented. However, the primitives suffice for the purposes of this discussion, since we only want to show how the security properties of adaptability, survivability and believability are programmed.

3.2   Security Policies

As mentioned, an important security notion in the framework is *adaptability*. This means that an agent's security policy is designed to adapt to its changing environment, by modifying the access rights for its environment and for other agents following events (e.g., message receipts, migrations).

An agent's security policy is self-contained. An agent defines a set of access *groups*, where a group represents a set of access rights. An agent a associates a group with its environment and each other agent that a knows is also given a group. If a associates a group g with some agent, then that agent possesses the rights implied by g for a. Reacting to events can involve changing the group that an agent associates with the environment or other agents, to model the change in trust that the event brought. An agent's decision to service a request from an agent A can depend on the group that the agent currently accords A.

The architecture contains a command that binds a group to a name in an agent's LNS, and a Boolean expression that queries the group of an agent:

$$a \text{ becomes G} \quad \text{and} \quad a \text{ has group G}$$

An example of an agent class (and security policy) is given in Section 3.4 for the HyperNews system. Here an article changes the group it associates with the environment each time it migrates. Only after an authentication phase involving a billing agent does the article agent change its group for the environment to CLIENT. An article only responds to read requests from users in CLIENT environments.

Simple Example. A mobile user wishes to compress a file of his that is stored on a file server. However, the user does not trust his current network and prefers to send the compression program in an agent to the file server to do the compression there. In this way, `file` is never exposed on the network. Of course, the compress program can be corrupted on the network but the user assumes that the server can verify sufficient integrity properties of the code down-loaded (e.g., via a MAC). The alternative to this is to encrypt the file contents while it is on the network, but why encrypt contents when one can transfer the compress program? The former solution requires two network transfers of a whole file instead of a single transfer of a program, as well as two encryptions and decryptions. Both `compress` and `file` are encapsulated as agents. The two places are `client` and `server`. The `file` agent class defines two groups: FOREIGN and FRIENDLY. The file policy is programmed to survey the environment in which it resides, to ensure that it remains FRIENDLY.

There are four event-reaction constructs in `file`'s class:

Restart at `client` $\rightarrow$ **Env becomes** FOREIGN

Receive ("password") **from `compress`   and (Env has group** FRIENDLY)
       $\rightarrow$ `compress` **becomes** FRIENDLY

Start $\rightarrow$ **Env becomes** FRIENDLY; **server** := ENV

Receive ("read") **from** compress   **and** (compress **has group** FRIENDLY)
    $\rightarrow$ **Send** Contents **to** compress

The first event-action pair states that when the enclosing agent moves to the client place, it assigns the group FOREIGN to the environment. This captures the fact that the file considers any environment other than the server place as unsafe. The second reaction governs the authentication of compress to file. The event is that of the compress agent sending the valid password, which in this case is the string "password". This action is only taken if the environment is trusted. The reaction states that the compress agent is assigned the group FRIENDLY. The third construct states that file trusts the environment that creates it. The fourth construct means that the agent only responds to read requests from authenticated compress agents (with the String contents of the file). On arrival at a host, a compress agent must authenticate itself to the file; this is modeled with the following construct which is part of compress's class.

Restart at Server $\rightarrow$ **Send** ("password") **to** file

3.3   Believability and Survivability

Encryption is needed to ensure the secrecy and integrity of messages and agents exchanged over the network. Keys are carried within a predefined class of agent. The key carried by a key agent k is denoted k.key. In HyperNews for instance, keys are always carried by agents; the advantage of this is that keys are distributed and protected in the same manner as articles. Once a key is created – whether it be symmetric or asymmetric – it is packaged inside of an agent before it leaves its creating environment. The choice of keys to distribute is application-specific; this depends on the properties that the application wishes to enforce.

A key can be used to encrypt a string or an agent, yielding an encrypted value. Encrypting an agent is equivalent to *serializing* its code and data (in Java parlance [1]) and then encrypting the serialized form with the key; this means transforming its state to a byte sequence format which is suitable for transfer to disk or over the network.

The architecture contains two commands for encrypting and decrypting:

$$\textbf{Encrypt}(n_1, n_2, n_3)   \text{ and }   \textbf{Decrypt}(n_1, n_2, n_3)$$

The first parameter in the encrypt command is the primitive value or agent to encrypt; the second parameter is the encryption key agent. The name n_1 is freed after the encryption. The encrypted value is bound to n_3 in the invoking agent's LNS. The decrypt reverses this procedure. Decrypting an encrypted agent instantiates that agent, which receives the **Restart** event.

Believability is concerned with the credibility of information. The traditional example of this is the use of certificates that validate a user's public key [11,7]. In this paper's framework, a credential can be a string message or, as we explained in Section 2, another agent. The latter is known as an *active credential*.

EncodeCredential(n_1, n_2, n_3)   and   **ExtractCredential**(n_1, n_2, n_3)

The encode command adds a credential to the string, agent or encrypted value named by n_1. The credential is the string (or serialized agent) named by n_3. The credential is encrypted using the key agent designated by n_2. The extract command binds the decrypted credential string or agent to n_3.

Another utility of credentials is to describe the behavior of agents. For instance, a provider may wish to bind to his articles the string "This agent is an article from the Times". Since serialized agents have credentials, this information can be encoded into the transfer format through the credentials. When a client receives a serialized agent, it can conduct an authentication phase without having to deserialize the agent, run it and await an authentication message. This is convenient in agent systems.

Survivability has as its goal that an agent computation be able to tolerate attacks on individual agents and places. This is an important issue, because the malicious host and malicious agent problems are still significant. Tolerating attacks requires encryption, being able to encode credentials into data and programs, as well as computation replication and voting [9] typically used in fault tolerant and intrusion tolerant systems. For this reason, the agent architecture supports the following two commands:

Replicate n **As** $\langle n_1, n_2, .., n_m \rangle$ and   **Receive** $\langle m_1, m_2, .., m_j \rangle$ from $\langle n_1, n_2, .., n_j \rangle$

The first command replicates an agent n as a sequence (n_1 to n_m) of agents. The second command is a multi-receive; the receiver blocks until it has received j messages from any number j of sources. The results can then be used in a vote.

3.4   Example

Figures 2 and 3 show the HyperNews article and billing agents written in the framework. There are some simplifications; for instance, the exchanges between hosts should be encrypted and the data structures in the real HyperNews system are richer. The example illustrates the use of the reactive security policy model for agents that allows them to *adapt* to their new environments, the use of agents for security components, and the use of active credentials. In particular, the billing agent is an *active credential* of the reader agent (whose code is not shown); when a request is made to read the article, this credential verifies that the reader has enough money to pay for it. Billing agents are replicated to increase tolerance of malicious hosts.

Class Article
       / Key words are in bold face */*
       String Contents, myCode; */* article text and credential tag */*
       EValue E-Contents; */* encrypted article contents */*
       Billing b1,b2; */* Billing agents*/*
       Key key, k;/* Keys to encode article text and Billing credential */
       User reader; */* browser agent */*
       Ref kn; */* reference to key agent */*
       Place site, creator, bank; */* places of interest: the current site, the publisher and the bank */*
       / Policy Groups */*
       Groups = {PREPAID, CLIENT, MYPROVIDER}

/ Start*/*
start → */* on provider site */*
       Env **becomes** MYPROVIDER; creator:=Env;

/ Initialisation of data structures */*
Receive (Contents,kn,bank) **from** Env **and** (Env **has group** MYPROVIDER) →
       key := (Key)kn;
       Encrypt(Contents,key,E-Contents); */* encrypt contents */*
       myCode := "This is my agent";

/ Download of document requests*/*
Receive ("download") **from any**(site) →
       MigrateTo site;

/ Event signalling migration of agent */*
Restart at site → */* security update */*
       if Env=creator **then** Env **becomes** MYPROVIDER **else** Env **becomes** PREPAID **fi**;

/ Reading the article - must initiate payment so send a credentially signed billing agent*/*
Receive ("open") **from any**(reader) **and** (Env **has group** PREPAID) →
       ExtractCredential(reader, k, b1); */* The billing agent is an active credential of the reader agent */*
       encodeCredential(b,k,myCode);
       Replicate b1 **as** b2; */* replicate agents for safety */*
       SendAgent b1 **to** bank; **SendAgent** b2 **to** bank;

/ Await return of one billing agent; verify credential on arrival */*
Receive ("Billing is back") **from any**(b) →
       extractCredential(b, k, myCode);
       if myCode <> "This is my agent" **then** */* fails authentication */*
         Terminate k; **Terminate** b; **fi**

Receive "receiptOK" **from** b ← */* payment made */*
       Env **becomes** CLIENT;

Receive ("open") **from any**(reader) **and** (Env **has group** CLIENT) →
       Decrypt(Contents,key,E-Contents);
       Send Contents **to** reader;
       Encrypt(Contents,key,E-Contents); */* encrypt contents again and throw away the key*/*
       Terminate key;

End Article.

Fig. 2. The Article Agent class.

Class Billing
         /* Local variable names */
         Place client; /* Where agent is sent from */
         Article a; /* The article that the billing agent is working for /
         Ref key; /* The key that the bank sends back to decrypt the article */
         String result; /* carried to client */
         /* Policy Groups */
         Groups = {DEFAULT}

/* Start*/
start →
         Env **becomes** DEFAULT;
         client := Env;

/* get the name of the key to ask for at the bank */
Receive any(key) **from** any(a) →
         skip;

/* Arrival at bank site*/
Restart at bank →
         Send (**ref** client) **to** Env;

/* get result of access decision from bank */
Receive any(result) **from** Env →
         SendAgent (Key)key **to** client;
         MigrateTo client;

/* return to client site and send hopefully "receiptOK" to article */
Restart at client →
         Send result **to** a;

End Billing.

Fig. 3. The Billing Agent class.

4   Implementation Notes

The security framework runs over a Java-based agent system called JavaSeal [6]. JavaSeal is an agent kernel that runs HyperNews. The implementation of the framework is not very specific to this platform, and can easily be adapted to other systems, e.g., D'Agents [13], Aglets [15] and Ajanta [16].

An agent is termed a *seal* in JavaSeal, and is an instance of a subclass of JavaSeal.seal. Agents are named using Name objects. JavaSeal was designed with agent isolation as a key goal. An agent's data is the set of all reachable user objects from the main seal object. To prevent direct sharing between agents, each agent possesses a distinct Java class loader. This means that an attempt by an object of one agent to reference an object of another space is treated as a type error [1]. This mechanism is used to ensure that agents do not communicate through hidden channels, but use the provided *channel* objects of the JavaSeal kernel. This is how JavaSeal achieves isolation for agents.

A credential in JavaSeal is assignable to each agent A. The credential is made from a credential *tag* which is string or (serialized) agent T, from an encryption key k, and bound into the agent A. The format of a credential is $\{A_I, T\}_k$, where X_K denotes the data X encrypted with key K. In the credential, I is an identity value associated with agent A. Each agent is given a relatively unique

512 byte array at creation; this partly consists of a hash on its code array and is partly randomly generated. When another agent is used as the tag, it is first transformed into its transfer format. When an agent is transformed to its transfer format (for the network), its data is serialized and the credentials are added to the serialized data. The I value is needed so that the kernel can correctly associate a credential with the agent that it was bound to.

```
package JavaSeal.security;

protected class Credential {
    protected Credential(String tag) {..}
    protected Credential(Name tag) {..}
}

public class AgentTransferUnit {
    public AgentTransferUnit() {..}
    public void activateUnderName(Name n) /* start agent with name n */
    public static void AgentTransferUnit disactivate(Name n)
    public void encodeCredential(Credential tag, Key k)
    public Credential extractCredential(Key k) /* returns null if no
    match */
    public void saveToDisk(String fileName)
    public void readFromDisk(String fileName)
}
```

An agent is exchanged in a *transfer format*. This has three components: a credential, a class archive and the serialized copy of the agent's data. The API of the credential and transfer formats are shown above.

The kernel provides communication channels that agents use to exchange messages. Over this, a library-level RMI mechanism is provided for each agent. There is an agent method for each event; the method's body contains the corresponding reaction. A *dispatch object* is instantiated on agent creation that contains a thread which listens for requests on communication channels, and which translates these requests to method calls within the agent. This dispatch mechanism contains the access control list mapping agent names to groups, and defining the operations that each group permits. The **become** command is implemented by the dispatch object to change this access control list.

5   Related Work

Much work has been done on agent security. Ajanta is one example of a running agent-based system that includes mechanisms for protecting agents and hosts [16]. Cryptographic based techniques implement read-only agent state, append-only agent state as well as secure host to host channels. The implementation of credentials in this paper resembles Ajanta's read-only state. However, Ajanta does not exploit mobility for application security.

PolicyMaker was one of the first security frameworks in which a certificate is more than a data structure that simply verifies the binding of a name to a public key [4]. A certificate in PolicyMaker actually validates the binding between a key and an access right. The motivation here is that the end-user's identity is often irrelevant; the important goal is to verify that a program that presents a right did not fabricate or steal that right. Credentials in this paper extend this notion of certificates. The SPKI-SDSI security architecture adopted the PolicyMaker approach for their attribute certificates [10,22]. These architectures do not have program mobility.

Existing examples of mobile code and agents in security architectures are intrusion agents and proof-carrying code [19]. Proof-carrying code is a form of executable certificate that is dynamically distributed, and that attests to a program's correctness. Mobile agents are used in intrusion detection systems to detect suspect behavior [3]. The goal in this case is to decentralize the intrusion detection mechanisms for scalability and efficiency reasons.

Other work worth mentioning include BirliX [14] and L3 [17] from the operating systems field. These systems encode security policies within programs. The advantage is that the policy that controls program interaction is more expressive than that expressible with mechanisms such as capabilities and ACLs.

The goal of the work presented in this paper differs from these related works in that it 1) seeks to exploit general mobility for security, and 2) outlines a security policy model for agents.

6   Conclusions

This paper introduced a security architecture for agents that uses agents. It is argued that using agents can bring security benefits, despite the malicious host and malicious agent problems. The ideas presented in this paper have been implemented in the JavaSeal mobile agent platform.

The syntax and semantics of the language presented are given in an extended version of this paper [5]. This is being used to continue the work in several directions. First, the semantics can be used for a proof system for properties of an agent such as, "the agent can never arrive in an environment that it does not trust", e.g., $\neg\Diamond$(**Env has group** UNFRIENDLY). Second, agent and host security policies can be extended to include notions of resource control and accounting, so that resource usage can be charged to some principal. A third extension to this work is to formally integrate risk analysis into the agent security policy modeling process so that the impact of agents on security can be more formally measured.

Program mobility is becoming an omnipresent feature of the Internet, through models such as active networking, network computing and mobile devices. Future security architectures should not ask with whether mobile agents are a component of the architecture, but rather what type of agents the architecture uses, e.g., police agents, traffic control agents, auditors, secret service agents, etc.

References

1. K. Arnold and J. Gosling. *The Java Programming Language*. The Java Series. Addison-Wesley, Reading, MA, second edition, 1998.
2. N. Asokan, E. V. Herreweghen, and M. Steiner. Towards a framework for handling disputes in payment systems. Research Report RZ 2996, IBM Research, Mar. 1998.
3. J. Balasubramamiyan, J. Fernandez, I. Isacoff, E. Spafford, and D. Zamboni. An architecture for intrusion detection using autonomous agents. In *Security Applications Conference*, Security Applications Conference, Oakland, CA, Dec. 1998. ACM, ACM.
4. M. Blaze, J. Feigenbaum, and J. Lacy. Decentralized trust management. In *SympSecPr*, Research in Security and Privacy, Oakland, CA, May 1996. IEEE Computer Society,Technical Committee on Security and Privacy, IEEECSP.
5. C. Bryce. A security framework for a mobile agent system. In *Technical Report, University of Geneva*, 2000.
6. C. Bryce and J. Vitek. The javaseal mobile agent kernel. In D. Milojevic, editor, *Proceedings of the 1st International Symposium on Agent Systems and Applications, Third International Symposium on Mobile Agents (ASAMA'99)*, pages 176–189, Palm Springs, May 9–13, 1999. ACM Press.
7. CCITT. X509, the directory - authentication framework, Nov. 1987.
8. R. A. DeMillo, D. P. Dobkin, A. Jones, and R. J. Lipton, editors. *Foundations of Secure Computation*. Academic Press, New York, 1978.
9. Y. Deswarte, L. Blain, and J.-C. Fabre. Intrusion tolerance in distributed computing systems. In *Proceedings of the 1991 IEEE Computer Society Symposium on Research in Security and Privacy (SSP '91)*, pages 110–121, Washington - Brussels - Tokyo, May 1991. IEEE.
10. C. M. Ellison, B. Frantz, B. Lampson, R. Rivest, B. M. Thomas, and T. Ylonen. SPKI certificate theory. Internet Draft, Mar. 1998. Expires: 16 September 1998.
11. S. Garfinkel. *PGP: Pretty Good Privacy*. O'Reilly & Associates, Inc., 103a Morris Street, Sebastopol, CA 95472, USA, Tel: +1 707 829 0515, and 90 Sherman Street, Cambridge, MA 02140, USA, Tel: +1 617 354 5800, 1995.
12. L. Gong. *Inside Java 2 platform security: architecture, API design, and implementation*. Addison-Wesley, Reading, MA, USA, 1999.
13. R. S. Gray, G. Cybenko, D. Kotz, and D. Rus. D'Agents: Security in a multiple-language, mobile-agent system. In G. Vigna, editor, *Mobile Agent Security*, Lecture Notes in Computer Science, pages 154–187. Springer-Verlag, 1998.
14. H. Härtig, O. Kowalski, and W. Kühnhauser. The BirliX security architecture. *Journal of Computer Security*, 2(1):5–21, 1993.
15. G. Karjoth, D. B. Lange, and M. Oshima. A security model for aglets. *Lecture Notes in Computer Science*, 1419:188–199, 1998.
16. N. Karnik and A. Tripathi. Security in the ajanta mobile agent system. Research Report RZ 2996, University of Minnesota, May 1999.
17. J. Liedtke. Improving IPC by kernel design. In B. Liskov, editor, *Proceedings of the 14th Symposium on Operating Systems Principles*, pages 175–188, New York, NY, USA, Dec. 1993. ACM Press.
18. J.-H. Morin and D. Konstantas. Commercialization of electronic information. *Journal of End User Computing*, 12(2):20–32, Apr.-June 2000.
19. G. C. Necula. Proof-carrying code. In *Proceedings of the 24th ACM Symposium on Principles of Programming Languages*, Paris, France, Jan. 1997.

20. F. Panzieri and S. Shrivastava. On the provision of replicated internet auction services. In *Proceedings of the Workshop on Electronic Commerce, Symposium on Reliable Distributed Systems (SRDS)*, Oct. Lausanne, 1999.

21. A. Puliafito, S. Riccobene, , and M. Scarpa. Which Protocol Should I Use? An Analytical Comparison of the Client-Server, Remote Evaluation and Mobile Agents Protocols. In *First International Symposium on Agent Systems and Applications (ASA'99)/Third International Symposium on Mobile Agents (MA'99)*, Palm Springs, CA, USA, Oct. 1999.

22. R. L. Rivest and B. Lampson. SDSI – A simple distributed security infrastructure. Presented at CRYPTO'96 Rumpsession, Apr. 1996. SDSI Version 1.0.

23. T. Sander and C. Tschudin. Towards mobile cryptography. In *SympSecPr*, Research in Security and Privacy, Oakland, CA, May 1998. IEEECSP.

24. D. L. Tennenhouse, J. M. Smith, W. D. Sincoskie, D. J. Wetherall, and G. J. Minden. A survey of active network research. *IEEE Communications Magazine*, 35(1):80–86, Jan. 1997.

25. J. Vitek and C. Tschudin. *Mobile Objects Systems*. Springer Verlag, Berlin, 1997.

26. B. S. Yee. A sanctuary for mobile agents. Technical Report CS97-537, UC San Diego, Department of Computer Science and Engineering, Apr. 1997.

A Distributed Access Control Model for Java

Refik Molva and Yves Roudier

Institut Eurécom, BP 193, 06904 Sophia-Antipolis - France
{molva,roudier}@eurecom.fr

Abstract. Despite its fully distributed and multi-party execution model, Java only supports centralized and single party access control. We suggest a new access control model for mobile code that copes with the shortcomings of the current access control model of Java. This new model is based on two key enhancements: the association of access control information with each mobile code segment in the form of attributes and the introduction of intermediate elements in the access control schema. The combination of the current ACL-based approach with the capability scheme achieved through mobile code attributes allows the new access control model to address dynamic multi-party scenarios while keeping the burden of security policy configuration at a minimum. We finally sketch the design of an access control system based on the proposed model using Simple Public Key Infrastructure (SPKI) certificates.

Keywords: Java, access control model, distribution, SPKI, capabilities

1 Introduction

The Java runtime environment (JRE) offers a rich set of security mechanisms for mobile code. The security features of the JRE evolved from the confinement-based sandbox approach of release 1.0 and 1.1 to a full-fledged access control model [GMPS97,Sun98,KG98] as implemented in release 1.2, also called Java 2. Java 2 offers fine-grained access control whereby the operations of mobile code segments on the local resources are controlled via access control lists (ACL) represented by a set of permissions. Each mobile code segment is granted a set of access rights defined as permissions. Access control is enforced during runtime by verifying the permissions of the mobile code for each operation attempting an access to a protected resource.

This access control solution suffers from a strong limitation: despite the truly distributed nature of its execution model, access control in Java 2 is based on a centralized security model. The JRE and the Java language offer a perfect environment for distributed computing in the sense that not only components from various sources can be dynamically integrated with an application at runtime, but also mobile programs can seamlessly run in remote environments like the Java virtual machine. The basic assumption underlying the execution model of Java is that each program may consist of various components and that each component can be generated by independent parties that can be geographically distributed. Such an execution model can be qualified as truly distributed, whereas the access control model of Java 2 seems to be based on a centralized

F. Cuppens et al. (Eds.): ESORICS 2000, LNCS 1895, pp. 291–308, 2000.

model. In the security model of Java 2, each distributed component needs to be designed in compliance with the security policy of the target environment and the security policy of the target environment needs to fulfill the requirements of each potential component that might be imported by the target environment. The only reasonable way to assure a meaningful collaboration between distributed components and a local environment governed by the security policy seems to place both the remote components and the local security policy under the jurisdiction of a single party. This is a serious limitation in the face of a fully distributed scenario taking advantage of the distributed nature of Java that affords a multi-party execution model including components from multiple sources and runtime environments with varying security policies.

In this paper, we suggest a new access control model for mobile code that copes with the shortcomings of the current access control model of Java. Section 3 describes the new model that is based on two key enhancements: the association of access control information with each mobile code segment in the form of attributes and the introduction of intermediate elements in the access control schema. The combination of the current ACL-based approach with the capability scheme achieved through mobile code attributes allows the new access control model to address dynamic multi-party scenarios while keeping the burden of security policy configuration at a minimum. Section 4 presents the design of an access control system based on the proposed model using SPKI certificates.

2   Access Control in Java 2

If we summarize the goal of access control as the enforcement of a model defining the authorized operations between active components called *subjects*, and resources called *objects*, in the JDK 1.2 access control model, subjects correspond to *protection domains*, and objects to local resources like files or system services. The protection domain of a class is identified by the CodeSource of that class and the CodeSource consists of the CodeBase or URL from which the class was loaded, and the signature of the CodeBase on the class file. In the recent JAAS extension to JDK, the protection domain concept also encompasses the identity of the user who runs the code within the JVM, thus allowing multi-user operations within a single JVM. Access rights are in turn represented by Java 2 constructs called *permissions* that include the details of an operation authorized on a protected resource. Access rights are granted to subjects by assigning permissions to protection domains in a policy file during configuration. The default implementation of the JVM supports two policy files defined respectively by the system administrator and the user.

The actual enforcement of access control at runtime is based on the reference monitor concept. The reference monitor can be implemented either by the *SecurityManager* class or the *AccessController* class. During its execution each object is labeled as belonging to a protection domain and will be granted an access based on this annotation.

Different permissions can be granted to a <protection domain, resource> tuple. The default policy is to deny all access to protected resources unless otherwise stated. The effective access permission as derived by the reference monitor corresponds to the intersection of all permissions of objects that are part of the execution thread, that is, the intersection of permissions from several protection domains. The only exception to this rule is the "privileged code" mark that enables a trusted code to keep its permissions from being shared by its callers.

3   Shortcomings

Unlike the Java execution model that is fully distributed, the access control mechanisms of Java 2 are based on a centralized security model. As depicted in the previous section, in the default implementation of JDK 1.2, the access rights of each mobile component are defined in a configuration file located in the runtime environment. This file includes the mapping between each mobile component and the permissions granted to the component during its execution on the local runtime environment. The reliance of access control decisions on the local configuration file results in two major limitations from the point of view of a distributed environment. First, each possible remote component or mobile code that can be authorized to access local resources must be identified beforehand and registered in the policy configuration of the runtime environment. Second, each component designer or mobile code programmer must take into account the access control restrictions of all potential target runtime environments at the design stage.

Apart from numerous practical difficulties in terms of programming, these limitations hinder the deployment of a dynamic distributed environment by requiring a static definition of all distributed components and their security attributes at once.

Further analysis points to the fact that these limitations are due to the centralized nature of the underlying access control model for Java 2. This model, which is based on the access control list (ACL) concept, requires that all the access control information be located near the resources that are subject to access control. Since the access control information includes both the identities and the attributes of all the potential subjects that might issue access requests, the resulting access control system necessarily needs to keep a centralized and static information base including all potential components and their attributes. Figure 1 depicts the centralized and single party access control model of Java 2.

Even though an ACL-based model can quite efficiently suit a centralized organization whereby a single party manages the security policy of all the components, it does not meet the requirements of dynamic multi-party scenarios akin to Internet applications. Multi-party environments require that the access control decisions be shared between the local party that manages the resources, or

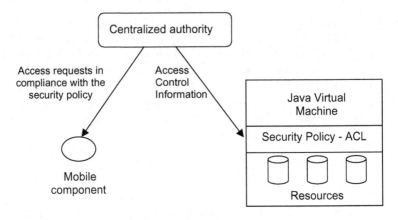

Fig. 1. Centralized and single party access model of Java 2.

objects in the access control terminology, and the remote parties that generate mobile code components, or *subjects*. Dynamic scenarios on the other hand call for a solution that suits dynamic populations both in the subject and object categories. A dynamic solution would then allow mobile code components to join and leave the set of potential subjects as well as a variable number of runtime environments to offer a variable set of resources for access by mobile components.

Another shortcoming of the single party model of Java 2 is that it does not properly exploit the public key infrastructure (PKI) on which it relies for authentication. Java 2 requires authentication of each mobile component based on digital signature verification using identity certificates defined as part of an X.509 PKI. The main objective of a PKI based on X.509 is to allow any two parties to be able to authenticate one another without any prior knowledge or without any bilateral trust relationship between those parties other than a trust chain that can be established through the global certification tree. Because of its centralized and single party access control model, Java 2 does not take advantage of the underlying PKI's global communication capabilities. Instead of a global PKI, a simple authentication model based on shared keys or a flat public key infrastructure using a single certification authority would as well be sufficient to meet the authentication requirements of Java 2.

As a result of the limitations in its access control model, Java 2 does not seem suitable for scenarios that are inherently multi-party or applications that involve dynamic populations of mobile code producers and consumers. For example, an extranet that consists of two or more interconnected corporate networks or intranets raises an access control problem that is inherently multi-party. Let's consider a mobile code access scenario whereby a mobile code component from intranet A attempts to access the resources of intranet B. The access control decision should take into account not only the security policy of intranet B with respect to its local resources but also the attributes of the mobile code component as defined by intranet A. Using Java 2's single party model in this scenario would require intranet B to incorporate into its access control information the attributes of authorized mobile code components from intranet A.

4 Towards a Distributed Access Control Model

In order to alleviate the limitations of Java's centralized and single party access control model, this paper suggests a new access control model that allows for distributed and multi-party operations.

This model enhances the existing access control model with two new concepts:

- access control attributes located with the mobile code segments, in addition to the access control information located within the runtime environment;
- intermediate access control elements that allow for the independent configuration of access control attributes accompanying the mobile programs and access control information located in the runtime environments.

4.1 Access Control Attributes

As depicted in section 2, a mobile code producer and its consumer are different parties: this requires both parties to cooperate in order to define a security policy that suits both parties. Each mobile code component has its own resource usage pattern that is a priori unknown by potential code consumers. In the current access control model of Java 2, the mobile code programs do not carry any access control information other than some identity certificate and a digital signature required for the purpose of authentication.

The first enhancement suggested in this paper consists in associating part of the access control information with the mobile code using a new type of component annotation called **attribute**. Attributes define a mobile code's authorizations in terms of access requirements, behavior, and software compatibility. Attributes are the basic means through which multi-party access control can be achieved, i.e. parties other than the runtime environment can participate in the access control process.

Similarly, the security requirements of dynamic distributed environments can be met thanks to the distributed definition of access control information using attributes. The other part of the access control information is not defined for specific components, but rather as general rules for generating a specific permission. A typical access control process using attributes should thus include an additional operation called attribute resolution. The main purpose of attribute resolution is to combine the information contained in the attribute with the access control rules stored in the local security policy in order to derive local access permissions and rules for the compatibility of the mobile component with the runtime environment or with other components. Once attribute resolution is complete, access enforcement during runtime is performed based on the existing Java 2 model.

4.2   Intermediate Elements

Even if each mobile code was tagged with attributes, the configuration of access control information in a dynamic environment might still be very complex. If access control information included in the attributes were defined in terms of (*subject, object, right*) tuples, each party defining an attribute for a mobile code would need to be aware of individual resources (*objects*) available at potential target runtime environments and, conversely, access control information included in each runtime environment would still have to enumerate all possible mobile code components (subjects). In this case, the advantage of introducing attributes over the existing Java 2 access control model would merely be limited to multi-party extension. Because of the inherent complexity, this solution would still not scale to large populations of code producers and consumers.

In order to cope with this complexity, we suggest a second enhancement that consists in factoring the access control information represented by the basic (subject, object, right) relation used in Java 2 into two simpler relations: (subject, *intermediate_element*) and (*intermediate_element*, object, right) (Figure 2). Parties involved in the access control process have to agree on **intermediate elements** that are abstractions of existing subjects and objects. Suitable instances for intermediate elements could be source authorizations (roles, groups) or predefined levels of execution contexts (library requirements, dynamic resource requirements, acceptable behavior, etc.).

The resulting access control information offers several advantages in terms of reduced complexity and independence of multi-party operations:

- an access control model for n subjects, m objects using p intermediate_elements can be described using $(n + m) \times p$ entries whereas the simple model would require $n \times m$ entries; there is a clear advantage when n and m are very large with respect to p;
- the two relations can be defined independently; in particular, subject and object populations can be managed in a totally independent manner;
- the first relation, (subject, *intermediate_element*), lends itself perfectly to the definition of attributes whereas the second one, (*intermediate_element*, object, right), is suitable for the description of access control rules stored with the runtime environment.

Another argument speaks for the use of intermediate elements. In the suggested distributed model, a mobile code is to carry its security attributes. If a simple model were used, these attributes would grow with the number of potential execution sites, since each would have different resources and different

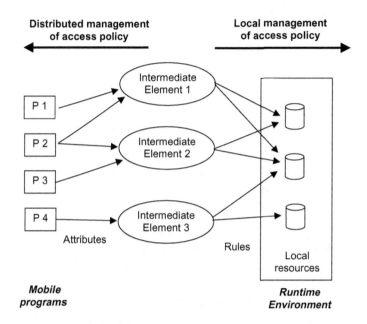

Fig. 2. Intermediate elements.

policies applied to them. With the use of intermediate elements, we can achieve to define the resources needed by a mobile code for several runtime environments simultaneously.

4.3   Advantages over the Centralized Model

The main improvement of the suggested model is the independence between code producers and code consumers with respect to the definition of access control policy. Unlike the current Java 2 model, the new model does not require the mobile code consumer to keep track of each mobile code component that can potentially be integrated or executed on the local runtime environment. Conversely, the code producer does not need to know any detail about the runtime environment at the time of code writing. Nonetheless, he can specify as part of the attributes the features relevant for the successful execution of his code. As a result of this independence, access control for mobile code can be achieved in very dynamic and complex environments with a large number of code producers and code consumers. In particular, the security policy of the runtime environments does not need to be updated when new parties produce mobile code components destined to these environments.

Thanks to the use of intermediate elements, access control does not rely on mobile components' identities. Like in *capability* schemes, the verification of attributes granted to a mobile code component does not require the knowledge of any identity. Consequently, this model can potentially achieve anonymity with mobile code components.

4.4   Deployment Cases

Possible deployment cases of the proposed model are depicted for some generic scenarios.

Single Party Case. This case is similar to the usual Java 2 scenario whereby a single party, the code consumer, defines all the access control information for the runtime environment. Even in this simple case, our model offers an advantage over the access control of Java 2 in that a dynamic mobile code population can be supported through the grouping of their common features with intermediate elements without increasing the complexity of the security policy configuration on the code consumer side.

Two-Party Case. The two-party case fully takes advantage of the new access control model.

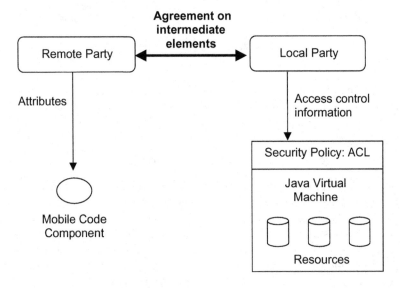

Fig. 3. Two-party case.

As depicted in Figure 3, access control is ruled by two different parties: the *local party* associated with the run-time environment sets the access control information concerning the resources located at the run-time environment whereas the *remote party* associated with the mobile code defines the attributes of the mobile code. The intermediate elements used in the definition of the access control information and the attributes can either be defined through a negotiation between the local party and the remote party or they can simply consist of pre-defined values. For instance, the local party might define two permission sets, one for games, and one for professional applications, each corresponding to several smaller-grained permissions about local resources. It might also define attributes to enable the mobile code to check if a given freeware library is installed or not before running, but forbid the same inquiry about a commercial library, and so on. If a number of such intermediate elements were established as a minimal standard, existing mobile code programs might be retrofitted with a flexible yet simple access control policy.

Three-Party Case. In the three-party case (Figure 4), the local party associated with the runtime environment sets the access control information governing the access to the resources managed by the runtime environment as in the two-party case.

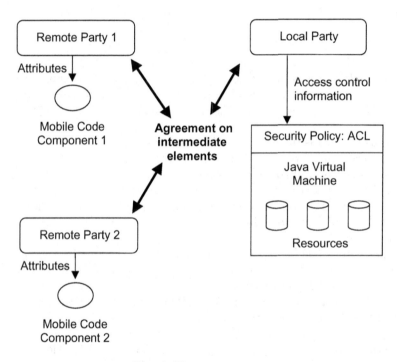

Fig. 4. Three-party case.

In this scenario a different remote party is associated with each of the two mobile code segments. Most interactions between the three parties occur in fact between one of the remote parties and the local party. These interactions thus resolve to two-party case interactions. However, some interactions involve the three parties at the same time. This occurs for instance in the following conditions: a component from remote party 1 that introduces new permissions is used in a program from remote party 2; remote party 2 ignores the identity of remote party 1, the access to component 1 being enforced by the local party. In that instance, the agreement on intermediate elements mentioned in the previous scenario involves the three parties. After an agreement has been reached on a given intermediate element determined either implicitly or explicitly, each remote party can annotate its mobile code components separately, in a distributed manner. Reaching an agreement might be as simple as defining a role for each participant.

5   Design of a Distributed Access Control System for Java

The previous section presents a distributed access control model as an alternative to the centralized Java 2 access control model. This section presents the design of a solution based on the new model using the Simple Public Key Infrastructure (SPKI) framework as a basis for implementing intermediate elements.

5.1   SPKI

The Simple Public Key Infrastructure (SPKI) [EFL+98a,EFL+98b,EFL+99] was started as an authorization-based infrastructure destined to answer access control problems in wide-scale networks. SPKI is now supported by IETF.

The focus of SPKI is the definition of authorization certificates. An SPKI authorization certificate is the encoding of an access control capability: it states that a given subject is granted a set of permissions by an authority, called the issuer, and under some conditions (for instance a given duration), called the validity. This statement is corroborated by the accompanying signature of the issuer and the certificate also includes the public key of the issuer.

As opposed to X.509 [IT88], SPKI does not require the identification of a party as a prerequisite to the access control decision concerning an operation requested by that party. SPKI allows instead to verify the rights of a party regardless of the party's identity. In addition, like X509, SPKI also allows for the representation of identities in public key certificates.

Furthermore, systems designed using SPKI often rely on delegation. Delegation means issuing an authorization certificate for a certain set of rights to another issuing authority. This authority can then itself issue certificates granting a subset of these rights, and so on. Delegation provides support for the distributed definition of authorizations. SPKI defines a precise semantics describing how to reduce a chain of delegated authorization certificates.

In addition to the basic authorization and identity certificates, SPKI has borrowed a mechanism for group certificates from the SDSI framework [RL96,Aba98]: an SDSI group certificate refers to a group of certificates. Group certificates allow treating a set of entities as a single entity. It is thus possible to grant or revoke rights to/from a set of users in a single authorization certificate. A key, that is, a subject, is considered to possess its own namespace corresponding to a group.

In summary, three types of certificates coexist in SPKI:

- public key certificates that can be modeled as $< K_{issuer}, name_{subject}, K_{subject}, validity >$ 4-tuples: the issuer states that subject $name_{subject}$ is identified by key $K_{subject}$
- group certificates, corresponding to $< K_{issuer}, name_{group}, name_1...name_n, validity >$ 4-tuples: the issuer says that the name chain "$name_1$ ... $name_n$" is identified by $name_{group}$ in his namespace; "$K_{issuer2} \, name_{group2}$" is an example of a name chain defining the name group2 in the certificate namespace of issuer2.
- authorization certificates, that is, $< K_{issuer}, name_{subject}, delegation, authorization, validity >$ 5-tuples: the issuer states that $name_{subject}$ has been granted some authorization; if $delegation$ is true, it states that the subject has also been granted the right to issue certificates stating the same privileges than those he was granted, or a subset of these privileges, to another subject.

An issuer can conclude the correctness of a set of certificates only when it can establish a chain of certificates starting from a self-signed certificate. The process through which a certificate chain is verified is named "reduction" in SPKI.

For many access control matters, SPKI now supersedes X.509. The delegation mechanism of SPKI is far superior to the simple cross-certification, and can implement it in a straightforward way. Moreover, with group certificates, SPKI can now specify role-based access control policies.

5.2   Components of the Design

Let's now focus on how SPKI certificates are used to support the annotation of mobile code attributes in our design. SPKI group certificates offer a perfect ground for the definition of intermediate elements, as depicted in Figure 5(a). Group certificates link the namespace of the local party with the namespaces of remote parties. Group certificates may also be used as a declaration of the intermediate element to the remote party. For instance, the certificate that we abbreviate as $< K_{LP}, group1, K_{RP1} \, group1 >$ means that the local party (identified by its key K_{LP}) will declare $group1$ to the remote party $RP1$ (identified by its key K_{RP1}). $Group \, 1$ will be referred under the same name in the namespaces of both parties and in subsequent certificates.

A mobile code component is identified by a public key certificate issued by its producer. It can also be identified by an SPKI group certificate issued by its producer and that can be ultimately identified by a public key certificate. Attributes will be written as SPKI group certificates attached to components. The latter group certificates will be issued by a remote party, but they must be chained with a certificate issued by the code consumer in order to be interpreted. An attribute reflects which intermediate element - be it a role, a user community, or an execution context - a mobile code is mapped to. A given mobile code can carry several such certificates. In Figure 5(b), remote party 2 issues the certificate $< K_{RP2},\ group3,\ K_{MC2} >$ associating mobile code $MC2$ with $group\ 3$.

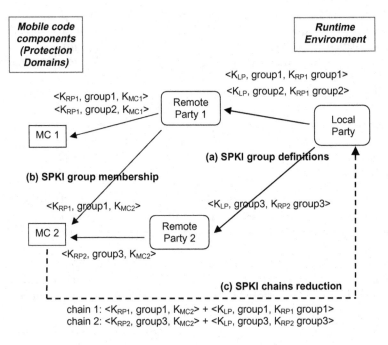

chain 1: $<K_{RP1}$, group1, $K_{MC2}> + <K_{LP}$, group1, K_{RP1} group1>
chain 2: $<K_{RP2}$, group3, $K_{MC2}> + <K_{LP}$, group3, K_{RP2} group3>

Fig. 5. Issuing and resolving access control attributes.

Attribute-policy resolution rules specify how intermediate elements should be translated into resource access rights, i.e. effective Java 2 permissions concerning the JVM local resources. These rules can be stored within SPKI authorization certificates. With intermediate elements interpreted as subjects, the rules provide a summary of the potential ACL entries for the runtime environment. The rules also seem to be a useful tool for making the inspection and revocation of access rights an easier task.

Let's now outline a typical attribute-policy resolution as depicted in Figure 5(c). Each certificate chain carried by the mobile code is reduced with the SPKI engine into a summary certificate that is issued by the local party. The summary certificate defines the mapping of the attribute to an intermediate element. Certificates issued locally may not be included with the mobile code in order to assure the compatibility of mobile components with a wide range of run-time platforms, and in particular to avoid the need for a specific version of components for each consumer. In that case, the certificate missing from an SPKI chain must be stored locally, possibly in an intranet server. This certificate can be retrieved at the time of reduction. The second part of resolution occurs when the mapping between the attribute and the intermediate element has been established. The local party has then to map the intermediate element obtained to an effective set of Java 2 permissions. This is achieved using the translation rules mentioned above. The resulting permissions are then included in the existing ACL definitions.

A problem might persist in this scenario due to the verification of validity conditions included in the certificates: checking the summary certificate only once at class loading is not sufficient to verify the validity of all the individual certificates referenced by the summary certificate. The validity of the summary certificate should be limited to the intersection of validity conditions of each individual certificate. Two alternative solutions can be envisioned to solve this problem:

- The validity of the summary certificate is re-evaluated at every access. In Java 2, a class is marked as pertaining to a protection domain, which means that the implementation associates a set of access control permissions to a protection domain. Based on this technique, the runtime environment could be extended so that it also stores and checks the validity conditions of the certificates along with the permissions of the protection domains.
- The policy configuration is refreshed periodically. This can be achieved by adding a background thread periodically calling the Policy.refresh() method. However, the refreshed policy may not change the policy set for classes already loaded, depending on the caching strategy of the class loader. Additional mechanisms might be required in existing Java 2 implementations.

The latter solution is preferable, because of its relatively minor impact on the performance of access control operations and the flexibility it offers with respect to the definition of the refreshment frequency.

5.3   Example

In this section we turn to an example where our design is used to implement a role-based access control system. Let's assume that a remote party, Bob, needs to define security restrictions on the applets he downloads from the Internet. Applets should be enabled to perform read operations on disk, but strictly forbidden write operations except for the gaming applets written by Alice or Brian. Bob might define two different applet roles, namely "browsing" and "gaming".

Suppose Alice and Brian have defined a role named "game" corresponding to gaming applets. Alice and Brian would then issue SPKI group certificates under this name and attach them to their various gaming applets. Bob will also issue an SPKI group certificate for each of the roles that he defined, as well as corresponding rights: the "browsing" certificate group will be used as the role attached by default to any applet entering Bob's intranet with read access. The "gaming" group certificate will be issued for Alice's and Brian's applets which share the same access needs. This certificate will link Bob's certificate namespace to Alice's (respectively Brian's) certificate namespace so that Alice's "game" might be seen as Bob's "gaming" role. Roles of authorized applets thus form a chain starting at Bob, who acts as his own authority. Based on the SPKI principles, Alice and Brian are only identified by their public keys, as stated in the group certificate issued by Bob.

As part of the local access control policy, Bob must have configured the rights associated with the "gaming" role. When an applet from Alice is loaded into a machine in Bob's intranet with Alice's "game" certificate, a chain starting from Bob using the "gaming" certificate stored in Bob's machine can be established and matching writing rights are associated with the applet. Alice's and Brian's applets share the same role: the same translation will therefore result in the same set of Java rights for Brian's applets.

Within the global definition of the "gaming" role, sub-roles can be defined by Alice and Brian who might decide to use routines from other parties and further grant them the same rights their applet was granted by Bob. SPKI thus allows Bob to delegate Alice or Brian the management of rights originally granted by Bob. This would be achieved for instance by Alice's issuing new certificates indicating that Mike's "high-score routine" is part of Alice's "game".

In this example, intermediate elements are just roles, but provide a simple common denominator: Alice's applets would run on Fred's browser as well, provided that he configured his runtime environment so that Alice's "game" is recognized as a role and is granted enough access rights. Other types of intermediate elements might be introduced, for instance, Alice might also state in a certificate that a particularly complex game needs a powerful CPU. Reducing such a certificate would mean that Bob has installed a plugin so that the SPKI engine performing the attribute-policy resolution can check the microprocessor of his machine.

5.4   Application: An Extranet Using Mobile Code

A federation of intranets or extranet offers another interesting example highlighting the suitability of our design for distributed and multi-party scenarios. An extranet access control system has to cope with an inherently multi-party scenario in that objects belong to several domains and each object can be accessed by several subjects from different domains. Suppose that applications programs in that extranet consist of Java mobile codes. In such an extranet, application deployment will require the granting of rights to mobile code components. These rights will concern the resources of the runtime environments where each mobile code can possibly be executed. The same mobile code must however be granted rights for local resources of all potential consumers, that is, all intranets that are part of the extranet. Enumerating all the combinations would be too complex and cumbersome. Even worse, adding a new intranet to the extranet would impact the attribute definitions in all the existing mobile codes segments.

Using the intermediate elements of our model, this deployment scenario becomes much simpler. For instance, instead of defining a hard disk or a printer as a resource, an intranet might advertise two sets of resources, one dedicated to a professional use, and another to a personal use; or define a set of resources available to all users of a given intranet. These sets will be declared as intermediate elements of access control.

In that particular application, each intranet advertises intermediate elements as SPKI group certificates to other intranets that are part of the extranet. These elements can then be viewed as standard service interfaces between the different intranets. As in X.509-based solutions, a cross-certification process is needed. It amounts to the exchange of the keys of certificate issuers. Our model otherwise directly supports the distributed nature of an extranet. Certificate reduction (the resolution of access control attributes into effective permissions) can be automated. Another major benefit of intermediate elements in this example is that new intranets can join the extranet without any impact on the access control definitions of existing components.

6   Related Work

A proposal by Nikander and Partanen [PN98,NP99] also addresses the issue of how to enhance access control in Java. In order to cope with the current Java's requirement on each end-user to individually set and update the security policy file on his machine, the authors suggest to store permissions in a distributed fashion together with applets. Their design is based on a modified version of SPKI whereby SPKI authorization certificates serve as a tool to store Java 2 permissions. This solution only applies to applets stored in an intranet or destined to an intranet, because permissions defined as part of that solution only refer to local resources and to a local access control policy. It cannot provide a solution for defining the access control in a distributed way, as in the examples provided in the previous section. It should be noted in particular, that the suggested model still relies upon Java's centralized and single party security model.

In comparison, our work focuses on the definition of a truly distributed and multi-party access control model. The definition and resolution of access control attributes attached to Java mobile code are completely independent from the definition of permissions associated with target resources. Like Nikander and Partanen, we also presented a possible implementation using SPKI. However, unlike their solution, our design is not based on authorization certificates of SPKI, but on the group mechanism of SPKI. In addition, in our design, SPKI certificates are used to store only attributes, not access control information, these attributes being only interpreted at attribute-policy resolution. Since the bulk of the access control information remains in the policy file as in Java 2, very few certificates need to be resolved when loading a mobile code component. This should be contrasted with the access control checking performed in Nikander and Partanen's work: it amounts to an SPKI chain reduction for every permission, performed each time the code requests access to a protected resource of the runtime environment.

[WBDF97] also proposed to integrate predefined sets of typical privileges to web browsers in order to help non-technical users. Our goal is similar, but we believe that even technical users, and especially network administrators, need new tools to cope with the wide-scale and pervasive deployment of mobile code. This is why our proposal puts the emphasis on the distributed and multi-party nature of the definition of the mobile code access control policy, which is a much broader concept than the grouping of access rights.

[AF99] argues that the information used for authentication might be specialized on demand for particular applications without the requirement for a special infrastructure for each new application. Based on this idea, specific intermediate elements might probably be encoded in a cleaner manner than with SPKI. However, the focus of our proposal is quite different from that of [AF99] since the latter does not address access control, but only how to introduce specialized attributes in authentication infrastructures.

Proof-Carrying Code (PCC) [Nec97,NL98] aims at verifying the safety of a mobile program with an original approach based on type checking. In this approach, the code consumer specifies a set of safety properties that should be met by the mobile code. The code producer demonstrates that its mobile code conforms to the properties explicitly indicated and bundles this proof together with the mobile program. When the runtime environment receives the mobile code and the proof, it decides whether the mobile program can be safely executed based on the verification of the proof. Checking that the proof is well formed gives the assurance that the program sent indeed corresponds to the program on which it has been proven.

Even though it relies on an approach fundamentally different from our solution, PCC shares some similarities with our proposal: safety properties are a kind of intermediate elements, on which an agreement must be reached between the code producer and the code consumer before establishing any proof. After verifying that the behavior is "safe", no safety checks are needed anymore. Although very promising, PCC has some drawbacks, the first being the basic difficulty of generating proofs. PCC also does not seem to address the distributed and multi-party access control issues discussed in this paper.

7   Conclusion

We proposed a new access control model for Java components addressing the problem of multi-party policy definition that has not been solved by the current model of Java. This new model is based on two key enhancements. Each mobile code component bears associated access control information or attributes. Intermediate elements are introduced in the access control schema to factorize access control policy definition. This model combines the current ACL-based approach with a capability scheme achieved through mobile code annotation with attributes to enable the description of dynamic multi-party systems while keeping the burden of security policy configuration at a minimum. We presented a possible design based on this model using SPKI certificates and the existing Java 2 run-time environment.

References

[Aba98]   Martin Abadi. On SDSI's Linked Local Name Spaces. *Journal of Computer Security*, 6:3–21, 1998.

[AF99]   Andrew Appel and Edward Felten. Proof-Carrying Authentication. In *Proceedings of the 6th ACM Conference on Computer and Communications Security, Singapore*, November 1999.

[EFL+98a]   Carl M. Ellison, Bill Frantz, Butler Lampson, Ron Rivest, Brian M. Thomas, and Tatu Ylonen. Simple Public Key Certificate, Internet Draft <draft-ietf-spki-cert-structure-05.txt>, March 1998.

[EFL+98b]   Carl M. Ellison, Bill Frantz, Butler Lampson, Ron Rivest, Brian M. Thomas, and Tatu Ylonen. SPKI Examples, Internet Draft <draft-ietf-spki-cert-examples-01.txt>, March 1998.

[EFL+99]   Carl M. Ellison, Bill Frantz, Butler Lampson, Ron Rivest, Brian M. Thomas, and Tatu Ylonen. SPKI Certificate Theory, RFC 2693, September 1999.

[GMPS97]   Li Gong, Marianne Mueller, Hemma Prafullchandra, and Roland Schemers. Going Beyond the Sandbox: An Overview of the New Security Architecture in the Java^{TM} Development Kit 1.2. In *Proceedings of the USENIX Symposium on Internet Technologies and Systems, Monterey, California*, December 1997.

[IT88]   ITU-T. Recommendation X.509: The Directory - Authentication Framework, 1988.

[KG98]   Lora Kassab and Steven Greenwald. Towards Formalizing the Java Security Architecture in JDK 1.2. In *Proceedings of the European Symposium on Research in Computer Security (ESORICS'98), Leuven-la-Neuve, Belgium*, LNCS. Springer, September 1998.

[Nec97]   George C. Necula. Proof-Carrying Code. In *Proceedings of the 24th ACM Symposium on Principles of Programming Languages, Paris, France*, January 1997.

[NL98]   George C. Necula and Peter Lee. Safe, Untrusted Agents using Proof-Carrying Code. Number 1419 in Lecture Notes in Computer Science. Springer-Verlag, 1998.

[NP99]   Pekka Nikander and Jonna Partanen. Distributed Policy Management for JDK 1.2. In *Proceedings of Network and Distributed System Security Symposium, San Diego, California*, February 1999.

[PN98]   Jonna Partanen and Pekka Nikander. Adding SPKI Certificates to JDK 1.2. In *Proceedings of the Nordsec'98, the Third Nordic Workshop on Secure IT Systems, Trondheim, Norway*, November 1998.

[RL96]   Ron Rivest and Butler Lampson. SDSI - A Simple Distributed Security Infrastructure. In *Proceedings of the 1996 Usenix Symposium*, 1996.

[Sun98]   Sun Microsystems Inc. Sun.   JDK 1.2 Security Documentation,
            http://java.sun.com/products/jdk/1.2/docs/guide/security/index.
            html, April 1998.
[WBDF97]   Dan Wallach, Dirk Balfanz, Drew Dean, and Edward Felten. Extensible
            Security Architectures for Java. In *Proceedings of the 16th Symposium on
            Operating Systems Principles, Saint-Malo, France*, October 1997.

Using Reflection as a Mechanism for Enforcing Security Policies in Mobile Code

Ian Welch and Robert J. Stroud

University of Newcastle-upon-Tyne, United Kingdom NE1 7RU
{I.S.Welch, R.J.Stroud}@ncl.ac.uk,
WWW home page:http://www.cs.ncl.ac.uk/people/
{I.S.Welch, R.J.Stroud}

Abstract. Several authors have proposed using code modification as a technique for enforcing security policies such as resource limits, access controls, and network information flows. However, these approaches are typically ad hoc and are implemented without a high level abstract framework for code modification. We propose using reflection as a mechanism for implementing code modifications within an abstract framework based on the semantics of the underlying programming language. We have developed a reflective version of Java called *Kava* that uses byte-code rewriting techniques to insert pre-defined hooks into Java class files at load time. This makes it possible to specify and implement security policies for mobile code in a more abstract and flexible way. Our mechanism could be used as a more principled way of enforcing some of the existing security policies described in the literature. The advantages of our approach over related work (*SASI, JRes*, etc.) are that we can guarantee that our security mechanisms cannot be bypassed, a property we call *strong non-bypassability*, and that our approach provides the high level abstractions needed to build useful security policies.

1 Introduction

We are interested in applying ideas of behavioural reflection [11] to enforcing security mechanisms with mobile code. Mobile code is compiled code retrieved from across a network and integrated into a running system. The code may not be trusted and therefore we to need ensure that it respects a range of security properties. The Java security model provides a good degree of transparent enforcement over access to system resources by mobile code but it does not provide the same degree of transparency for control over access to application level resources. A number of authors [4][5] have tackled this problem and made use of code modification in order to add more flexible enforcement mechanisms to mobile code. However, although they have provided higher level means of specifying the security policies they wish to enforce, they have used code modification techniques that have relied upon structural rather than behavioural changes. We argue that reflection can be used to provide a model for behavioural change that is implemented using code modification. This provides a greater degree of separation

F. Cuppens et al. (Eds.): ESORICS 2000, LNCS 1895, pp. 309–323, 2000.
© Springer-Verlag Berlin Heidelberg 2000

between policy and implementation than the current systems provide. It also addresses some of the drawbacks of existing schemes. In particular, it makes it possible to specify security policies at a more appropriate level of abstraction. Another advantage of our approach is that it provides a property we call *strong non-bypassability*. This guarantees the enforcement of security mechanisms by removing the opportunity to bypass them using the same mechanisms that were used to produce them. For example, approaches that use renaming are vulnerable to attacks that discover and exploit the real name of the underlying resource.

The paper is structured as follows. In section 2 we introduce the Java security model, describing its evolution and pointing out some of its drawbacks. In section 3 we describe our use of reflection to enforce security and introduce our reflective Java implementation *Kava*. In section 4 we provide two examples of how *Kava* can be used and show how it integrates with the existing Java security model. In section 5 we describe and evaluate some related work. Finally in section 6 we conclude with a discussion of the advantages and disadvantages of our approach.

2   Evolution of Java Security Model

Java [10] is a popular choice for researchers investigating mobile code technologies. Java has strong support for mobility of code and security. The Java class loader mechanism supports mobile code by allowing remote classes to be loaded over the network, and a security manager enforces checks on the use of local system resources by the mobile code. The ability to supply a user-defined class loader and security manager makes it possible to customise these mechanisms to a certain extent.

In the past few years the Java security model has undergone considerable evolution. In the JDK1.0 security model [9] any code run locally had full access to system resources while dynamically loaded code could only access system resources under the control of a security manager. System libraries have predefined hooks that cause `check access` methods provided by the security manager to be called before sensitive methods were executed. The default security manager sandbox provided minimal access and in order to support a different security model a new security manager would have to be implemented.

The concept of trusted dynamically loaded code was introduced in JDK1.1 [14]. Any dynamically loaded code that was digitally signed by a trusted code provider could execute with the same permissions as local code.

Recently JDK1.2/Java2 [15][16] (see figure 1) has introduced an extensible access control scheme that applies both to local code and dynamically loaded code. Fine-grained access to system resources by code can be specified in a policy file on the basis of the source of the code, the code provider (indicated by who cryptographically signed the code), and the user of the code. Unlike earlier versions of the JDK this policy file allows the security model to be adjusted without writing a new security manager. This is because the security manager has standard access control checkpoints embedded in its code whose behaviour is determined by the selection of permissions enabled in the policy file. The

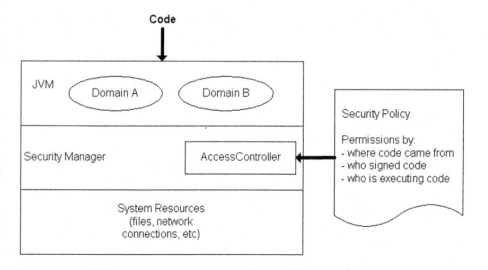

Fig. 1. Overview of Java2 Security Architecture

evaluation of the permissions is handled by an access controller that defines how different permissions are reconciled to give an overall access control decision. New permissions can be defined but explicit checks for the permissions must be added to the security manager or application code if the permissions apply to application resources rather than system resources.

2.1   Example: Extending the Java Security Model

To provide a flavour of the problems of the current Java security model we provide the following example of the definition of a customised security policy.

Imagine that an application developer has created a program for watching television broadcasts over the Internet called *WorldTV*. We may want to impose a security policy on the application to constrain which channels a user may watch. For example, if a machine is provided in a public place we might restrict the channels to a selection of local news channels.

The recommended steps for customising the Java security model in order to support such a policy [8] are:

- Define a permission class.
- Grant permissions.
- Modify resource management code.

A new permission class that represents the customized permission to *watch a channel* must be defined. It is realized by defining a class `com.WorldTV.Channel Permission` that subclasses the abstract class `java.Security.Permission`.

312   I. Welch and R.J. Stroud

Then the appropriate permission must be granted by adding entries into the security policy. In the example below we allow any application to watch channel 5.

```
grant
{
  permission com.WorldTV.ChannelPermission "5", "watch";
}
```

Finally, we must add an explicit check into the application's resource management code that calls `AccessController`'s `checkPermission` method using a `com.WorldTV.ChannelPermission` object as the parameter. If the application has not been granted the permission then an `AccessControlException` is raised. `AccessControlException` is a runtime exception so does not need to be declared in the class' interface.

```
public void watchChannel(String channel) {
  com.WorldTV.ChannelPermission tvperm = new
            com.WorldTV.ChannelPermission(channel, "watch");
  AccessController.checkPermission(tvperm);
  ...
}
```

2.2 Discussion

The ability to define application specific permissions makes the Java security model easily extensible. In previous versions of the Java security model the only way to implement application specific policy was to create a new `SecurityManager` class. For the example above a new method `checkChannel` would have had to been added to the `SecurityManager` class. By the time all possible checks had been added to `SecurityManager` the resulting interface would be too large and unwieldy for use and analysis. Through the use of typed access-control permissions and an automatic permission handling mechanism (implemented in the `AccessController` class) only a single method `checkPermission` is required. This represents an extensible and scalable architecture.

However, the application developer must still identify where the permission checks should be added into the application code and manually insert the checks. This means that security code is tangled with application code and this makes management and maintenance difficult. Whenever a new permission type is added then the application developer must access the source code of the application and modify then recompile. This raises the possibility of error as the modifications are made, and it is possible in the case of mobile code that the source code itself is not available.

A better approach would be to use something similar to the `SecurityManager` approach for system classes where hooks are added to the system classes that force the check methods of the `SecurityManager` to be invoked when certain critical methods are executed. Essentially it should be possible to take application code and automatically add hooks that invoke security mechanisms at appropriate places. For example, instead of manually modifying `watchChannel` the application developer should just be able to specify that the permission `ChannelPermission` is checked before this method can be invoked. This would result in a better separation of concerns between application code and security code.

3   A Reflective Approach Using *Kava*

Our approach is based on the use of metaobject protocols to provide flexible fine-grained control over the execution of components. The metaobject protocol implements the security mechanisms that enforce security policies upon application code. This effectively allows security checks to be inserted directly into compiled code, thus avoiding the need to recode applications in order to add application specific security checks. Figure 2 below presents the *Kava* reflective security architecture. We discuss each aspect of the architecture in the following sections.

3.1   Reflective Object Oriented Model of Computation

A reflective computational system [12] is a system that can reason about and make changes to its own behaviour. Such a system is composed of a base level and a meta level. The base level is the system being reasoned about, and the meta level has access to representations of the base level. Manipulations of the representations of the base level at the meta level result in changes to the behaviour of the base level system.

These notions of reflection have been extended to include the concept of the metaobject protocol [11] where the objects involved in the representation of the computational process and the protocols governing the execution of the program are exposed. A *metaobject* is bound to an object and controls the execution of the object. By changing the implementation of the metaobject the object's execution can be adjusted in a principled way.

In order to use reflection as a mechanism to enforce security properties we need to be able to control all interactions between the object and its environment. Therefore we need to be able to control all interactions with an object. This includes self-interactions. Thus, we need to control the following behaviours:

- Method invocation by an object.
- Method execution.
- Setting and getting of state.
- Object instantiation.
- Object construction.
- Exception raising.

The metaobject bound to the object defines the object's behaviour. Security enforcing mechanisms can be implemented by the metaobject in order to realise a security policy. In order to provide a guarantee that the security properties are honoured it must be impossible to bypass the metaobject. We call this property strong non-bypassability. We have implemented a reflective Java that implements this reflective model of object oriented computation and also has the property of strong non-bypassability.

In the next two sections we introduce the reflective version of Java we have developed and describe how it achieves this property we call strong non- bypassability.

3.2   Kava Metaobject Protocol

We have developed a reflective Java called *Kava* [19] that gives the control over the behaviour of objects that is required to add security enforcement at the meta layer. It uses byte code transformations to make principled changes to a class' binary structure in order to provide a metaobject protocol that brings object execution under the control of a meta level. These changes are applied at the time that classes are loaded into the runtime Java environment. The meta layer is written using standard Java classes and specifies adaptations to the behaviour of the components in a reusable way. Although neither bytecode transformation nor metaobject protocols are new ideas, our contribution has been to combine them. Byte code transformation is a very powerful tool but it is in general difficult to use, as it requires a deep knowledge of class file structure and byte code programming. What we do is use a load-time structural metaobject protocol (such as provided by Joie [1] or JavaClass [3]) in order to implement a runtime metaobject protocol. Working at the byte code level allows control over a wide range of behaviour. For example, the sending of invocations, initialisation, finalization, state update, object creation and exception raising are all under the control of *Kava*.

3.3   Meta Level Security Architecture

Security policy enforcement (see figure 2) is built on top of the runtime metaobject protocol provided by *Kava*. Metaobjects implement the security mechanisms that enforce the policy upon the application. Each object has a metaobject bound to it by *Kava*. In effect each metaobject acts a reference monitor for each application object. The binding is implemented by adding hooks directly into the binary code of the classes. As this binding exists within the component itself instead of in a separate wrapper class we argue that we are achieving a strong encapsulation of components. Outside parties cannot bypass the wrapping and therefore the security implemented in the metalevel by simply gaining an uncontrolled reference to the object because no such references exist. This type of binding we refer to as *strong non-bypassibility*. There are two common techiques for adding interceptions to Java classes : creation of a proxy class, or renaming methods in the class and replacing them with proxy methods. The proxies add

Fig. 2. Overview of *Kava* Security Architecture

the security enforcement. These approaches only support weak non-bypassability as there is the possibility that a reference to the real class might escape or the name of the real method might be discovered. This would make it possible to bypass the security enforcement.

The *Kava* system, binding specification and the metaobjects must form part of the trusted computing base. The *Kava* system and binding specification are installed locally and can be secured in the same way as the Java runtime system. However, the metaobjects may exist either locally or be retrieved across the network. This raises the possibility that the metaobjects themselves might be compromised. In order to counter this threat we use a specialised version of a classloader that verifies the identity and integrity of the metaobject classes using digital signing techniques. Each metaobject is digitally signed using a private key of the provider of the metaobject. The public key of the provider exists in the local public key registry on the host where the *Kava* system is installed. The digital signature of the downloaded metaobject is then verified using the local copy of the provider's public key. If there is discrepancy then a security exception is raised and the system halts. This prevents malicious combinations of application objects and metaobjects.

4   Example

In this section we provide two examples of how *Kava* can be used as the basis for implementing security enforcement mechanisms using metaobjects. The first example reworks the simple example from our discussion of the Java security model (an example of static permissions), and the second example is of a security policy that limits the total number of bytes that can written to the local file system by an application (an example of dynamic permissions).

4.1   Overview of Approach

Our approach leverages upon the existing Java security model. As pointed out earlier in section 2, the main problem with the Java security model is the lack of automatic addition of enforcement code to application code. *Kava* provides a principled way of doing this.

The enforcement *Kava* adds depends on the particular security policy being enforced, and the structure of the application. There are two particular phases in the *Kava* system. These are loadtime and runtime.

Loadtime. At loadtime *Kava* must determine what operations are trapped. These decisions are encapsulated by a `MetaConfiguration` class. There should be one for each security policy to be enforced. For example, there might be one configuration for a multilevel policy where all interactions between object must be trapped and another configuration for a simple access control policy where only method invocations are trapped. The `MetaConfiguration` class is responsible for parsing the *policy file* which provides additional information about the application that the security policy is being applied to and the particular policy settings for that application. For example, what metaobjects to bind to which classes, and what types of operation to trap. The *policy file* uses an extended form of the standard JDK1.2 syntax for security policies.

Runtime. At runtime the traps inserted under the control of the `MetaConfiguration` class switches execution for the base level (the application code) to the meta level (the metaobject associated with each object). The metaobject performs the permission checks necessary to implement the particular security policy. A specialised `Policy` object associates the permissions with the loaded classes. This is a specialisation of the default `Policy` class because it has to map additional permissions against classes in order to support the security policy.

4.2   Example: *WorldTV*

Using the *Kava* approach the developer carries out the first two steps of defining a permissions class and granting permissions as necessary. However, instead of taking the application code and editing it the application programmer defines a new `Metaobject` class and places the enforcement code here. For example,

```
import kava.*;
public class EnforcementMetaobject implements Metaobject
{
  public boolean beforeReceiveMethod(Reference source,
    Method myMethod, Value[] args)
  {
    com.WorldTV.ChannelPermission tvperm = new
            com.WorldTV.ChannelPermission(
```

```
        (String)args[0].getValue, "watch");
    AccessController.checkPermission(tvperm);
    return Constants.INVOKE_BASE;
  }
}
```

This redefines how a method invocation received by an object is handled. It enforces a check before the execution of the method invocation that the correct `ChannelPermission` is held by the thread executing the code.

The next step the application programmer must do is to specify which methods of which class are controlled by this enforcement metaobject. This is included in the expanded version of the standard Java policy file.

```
bind
{
    kava.EnforcementMetaobject *::watchChannel(String);
}
grant
{
    permission com.WorldTV.ChannelPermission "5", "watch";
}
```

The *bind* specification indicates to the `MetaConfiguation` class which methods of which class should be trapped. In this case any method named `watch` Channel with a single parameter of type `String` belonging to any class will be trapped and have security checks enforced upon it.

4.3   Example : LimitWrite

The previous example is a traditional fairly static access control security policy. *Kava* can also enforce dynamic security policies that depend upon changing state. The following example shows that *Kava* could be used to enforce a policy that places a million-byte limit on the amount of data that may be written to the file system.

The first task is to define a new permission type that has a dynamic behaviour. We define a permission class `FileWritePermission` that subclasses `java.security.Permission`. This new permission's constructor defines the maximum number of bytes that may be written to the file system. It also adds a new method `incrementResourceCounter(long n)` that increments the global count of the number of bytes written to the file system. Finally it defines the `implies` method so that when the `AccessController` calls the `implies` method to see if the permission being checked is held, the current number of bytes written is compared with the maximum to determine if this is true or not.

The second step is to specify the enforcement metaobject. It has a straightforward structure as the security policy decision is specified within the `Permission` class.

```
import kava.*;
public class FileEnforcementMetaobject
  implements Metaobject
{
  public boolean beforeSendMethod(Reference source,
  Method myMethod, Value[] args)
  {
  FileWritePermission perm = new
            FileWritePermission();
  perm.incrementResourceCounter(Integer.toLong(args[2].
  getValue());
  AccessController.checkPermission(perm);
  return Constants.INVOKE_BASE;
  }
}
```

Here the behaviour of an object sending an method invocation to another object is redefined. We do this because *Kava* cannot rewrite library classes unless the JVM is changed. A new FileWritePermission is constructed with a throwaway value. Then the context for the permission is updated by calling setPermissionContext using the number of bytes written to the file. Here we are exploiting the knowledge that the third argument always the number of bytes to be written to the file.

The third step is to specify the policy file :

```
bind
{
  kava.FileEnforcementMetaobject
      (* extends FileWriter).write(*, int, int);
}
grant {
  FileWritePermission "1000000";
}
```

The policy file determines which methods of which classes are brought under the control of the metaobject. It specifies that any invocation of write method of any subclass of FileWriter is to be trapped and handled by the metaobject FileEnforcementMetaobject. In this way we can ensure that no checks are accidentally omitted from the source code because of a software maintenance oversight.

Unlike the previous example we trap invocations made by an object rather than the execution of a particular method of an object. This is because *Kava* cannot rewrite system classes without the use of a custom JVM and so we trap calls made to the controlled object rather than modify the implementation of the object itself.

5   Related Work

The principle of separating security policy and dynamically enforcing security on applications is not new. In this section we discuss and evaluate four approaches to implementing this principle.

5.1   Applet Watch-Dog

Applet Watch-Dog [6] exploits the ability of the execution environment to control code execution. Here the threads spawned by applets are monitored and controlled in order to protect hosts from denial of service attacks. It is a portable approach that requires no changes to the Java platform in order to work. When applets are loaded in conjunction with the *Applet Watch-Dog* their use of memory, priority of threads, CPU usage and other resources is monitored and displayed in a window. The user can choose to stop or suspend threads as required. A security policy for resource usage can also be specified so that a thread is automatically stopped if it exceeds the prescribed maximum usage of a resource.

The *Applet Watch-Dog* approach can prevent a large class of denial-of-service attacks. However, it cannot prevent other attacks such as privacy attacks. The example given by the authors is that it cannot prevent an applet from forging mail as this would require monitoring port usage. The scope of policies enforceable by a Watch-Dog is obviously limited by the scope of control the execution environment has over code execution. For example, if the capability to monitor ports does not exist then attacks exploiting port access cannot be controlled. Another problem is that specifying a new type of security policy requires the rewriting of the *Applet Watch-Dog*.

5.2   Generic Wrappers

Generic wrappers use wrappers to bring components under the control of a security policy. The wrappers act as localised reference monitors for the wrapped components. A well developed example of this approach is found in [7]. Here the emphasis is on binary components and their interaction with an operating system via system calls. Wrappers are defined using a Wrapper Definition Language (WDL) and are instantiated as components are activated. The wrappers monitor and modify the interactions between the components and the operating system. Generic policies for access control, auditing, intrusion detection can be specified using the WDL.

The use of *generic wrappers* and a wrapper definition language is an attractive approach as it is flexible and is generalisable to many platforms. However, there are some drawbacks. Wrappers can only control flows across component interfaces and cannot control internal operations such as access to state or flows across outgoing interfaces. Also the wrappers are not at the right level of abstraction. The level of abstraction is at a lower level than the application level. This makes it difficult to specify security policies that control both access to system resources and application resources.

5.3   SASI - Security Automata SFI Implementation

SASI [4] uses a security automaton to specify security policies and enforces policies through software fault-isolation techniques. The security automaton acts as a reference monitor for code. A security automaton consists of a set of states, an input alphabet, and a transition relationship. In relation to a particular system the events that the reference monitor controls are represented by the alphabet, and the transition relationship encodes the security policy enforced by the reference monitor.

The security automaton is merged into application code by a *rewriter*. It adds code that implements the automaton directly before each instruction. The rewriter is language specific (the authors have produced one for x86 machine code, and one for Java bytecode). Partial evaluation techniques are used to remove unnecessary checks.

The current system does not have any means for maintaining security related state which makes some application level security policies difficult to express. The authors propose extending *SASI* to include the ability to maintain typed state.

One of the problems the authors found when applying *SASI* to x86 machine code was the lack of high level abstractions. For example, the lack of a concept of *function* or *function calls* meant that the *SASI* rewriter had to be extended to include an *event synthesizer*.

SASI is very powerful and can place controls on low level operation such as push and pop allowing rich security policies to be described. However, the security policy language is very low level with the events being used to construct the policies almost at the individual machine language instruction level. The Java implementation was at a slightly higher level, mainly because the Java machine code is a high level machine code for an object oriented machine, but still the policies were quite low level. The authors plan to investigate a Java implementation that exposes more high level abstractions and make use of high level security policies. We would argue that reflection provides an appropriate model for solving this problem.

5.4   Naccio - Flexible Policy-Directed Code Safety

Naccio [5] allows the expression of safety policies in a platform-independent way using a specialised language and applies these policies by transforming program code. A *policy generator* takes resource descriptions, safety policies, platform interface and the application to be transformed and generates a policy description file. This file is used by an *application transformer* to make the necessary changes to the application. The application transformer replaces system calls in the application to calls to a policy-enforcing library. *Naccio* has been implemented both for Win32 and Java.

Naccio relies on wrapping methods, the original method is renamed and a wrapper method with the same name added. The wrapper method delegates the actual work to the renamed method but can perform policy checking before and after the call to the renamed method.

Naccio provides a high level way of specifying application security that is platform-independent but it is limited in what can be controlled. For example, *Naccio* cannot specify a safety policy that prevents access to a particular field of an object by other objects. Also because *Naccio* relies on renaming of methods there is the possibility that the enforcement mechanisms could be bypassed.

5.5   Evaluation

The *Applet Watch-Dog* approach makes good use of existing capabilities in the execution environment to prevent denial-of-service attacks. However, it is limited in the scope of security policies it can support because it relies upon the capabilities already present in the execution environment. It also is difficult to specify new types of security policy as this requires the rewriting of the *Applet Watch-Dog*.

Generic wrappers, *SASI* and *Naccio* provide greater control over code execution and more flexible policy specification. *SASI* and *Naccio* extend earlier work that used code rewriting for security enforcement that was more ad hoc in nature and focused on specific classes of security policy. For example, Java bytecode rewriting has been used to implement fine grained access control [13], and resource monitoring and control policies [2].

However, there are problems with the level of abstraction and expressiveness of these approaches.

Generic wrappers work at a low level of abstraction, essentially the level of the operating system. This limits them to enforcing security policies that control access to system resources. Although it is possible that a number of application level security policies could be expressed, the lack of high level abstractions makes this task difficult.

SASI operates at the level of machine code which provides it with a lot of power. However, it has difficulties when dealing with application level abstractions where the operations that need to be intercepted are related to the object-oriented computational model. With the Java version there is the concept of higher level operations because the Java virtual machine bytecode explicitly uses object-oriented concepts. A higher level approach would be to base the security policy automata primitives on an abstract model of object oriented computation. This could be mapped to required behavioural changes which would then be realized in a platform dependent way.

To some extent *Naccio* supports application level abstractions. However, it lacks a rich model for expressing the program transformations. If it had a model based on behavioural change then it could specify richer policies but still in a platform independent way.

In our opinion the metaobject protocol [11] approach provides a good basis for the implementation of security policies. It provides both a high level, abstract model of the application but also a principled way to describe and implement changes to the behaviour of the application. The approaches discussed here implement the security policies at too low a level. Instead of implementing traps for individual machine code instructions or system calls the better approach is to work at the level of the object oriented computational model. For example, instead of trapping Java `invokevirtual` instructions and adding security enforcement mechanisms at this level, the metaobject approach would trap invocations sent from an object and specify before and after behaviour that invoked required security mechanisms. The actual mapping to code rewriting would be handled by the metaobject protocol allowing the security policy developer to work at a high level. This is the approach that we are taking with our system *Kava*.

6   Conclusions and Further Work

Using *Kava* to implement security mechanisms in Java allows security policy to be developed separately from application code and then be combined at loadtime. This makes it ideal for flexible security for securing mobile code where the policies that the code must obey are defined by the host and the code is delivered in a compiled form.

As we have shown *Kava* can be integrated with the current Java security model and uses high level abstractions in order to specify policy. The difference between using the standard Java security model and using *Kava* is that the permissions checking takes place in metaobjects that are separate from the application objects. The metaobjects are only bound at loadtime allowing security policy to be changed independently of the application code.

Due to the use of bytecode rewriting *Kava* achieves a strong degree of non-bypassability than other systems proposed. This is important for making the case that the metaobject can act as a non-bypassable reference monitor for the associated object.

The *Kava* metaobject protocol allows control over more aspects of the behaviour than a system such as *Naccio*, *generic wrappers*, or the *Applet Watch-Dog* and at the same time provides higher level abstractions than a system such as *SASI*.

A direction for future work is the development of general policy frameworks for use with *Kava*. Currently, as shown in the examples, the security policy is developed manually. This is a useful feature in some situations but ideally there should be policy frameworks available that free the developer from having to develop their own set of permissions and metaobjects . We have proposed elsewhere some frameworks for implementing the Clark-Wilson security model [17] and a Resource Management security model [18]. We are currently integrating this work with *Kava* to provide high level support for application security.

Acknowledgements. This work has been supported by the UK Defence Evaluation Research Agency, grant number CSM/547/UA and also the ESPIRIT LTR project MAFTIA.

References

[1] Cohen, G. A., and Chase, J. S. : Automatic Program Transformation with JOIE. Proceedings of USENIX Annual Technical Symposium 1998

[2] Czajkowsik, G., von Eicken, T., JRes: A Resource Accounting Interface for Java, ACM OOPSLA Conference, October 1998.

[3] Dahm, M. : Bytecode Engineering, Java Informations Tage 1999

[4] Erlingsson, U., Schneider, F. : SASI Enforcement of Security Policies: A Retrospective. Proceedings New Security Paradigms Workshop, 1999

[5] Evans, D., Twyman, A. : Flexible Policy-Directed Code Safety. IEEE Security and Privacy, Oakland, CA., May 9-12, 1999

[6] Florio, M.F., Gorrieri, R., Marchetti, G. : Coping with Denial of Service due to Malicious Java Applets. Computer Communications Journal, August 2000

[7] Fraser, T., Badger, L., Feldman, M. : Hardening COTS Software with Generic Software Wrappers. IEEE Security and Privacy, Oakland, CA., May 9-12, 1999

[8] Gong, L. : Inside Java(TM) 2 Platform Security. Addison-Wesley, 1999

[9] Gosling, J., Frank Yellin, and the Java Team, "Java API Documentation Version 1.0.2", Sun Microsystems, Inc., 1996

[10] Gosling, J., Joy, B., Steele, G. L. : The Java Language Specification, The Java Series, Addison-Wesley, 1996

[11] Kiczales G., des Rivieres J. : The Art of the Metaobject Protocol. MIT Press, 1991.

[12] Maes, P. : Concepts and experiments in computational reflection, OOPSLA, 1987

[13] Pandey, R., Hashii, B., Providing Fine-Grained Access Control for mobile programs through binary editing, Technical Report TR98-08, University of California, Davis, August 1998

[14] Java Team, JDK 1.1.8 Documentation", Sun Microsystems, Inc., 1996-1999

[15] Java Team, Java 2 SDK Documentation", Sun Microsystems, Inc., 1996-1999

[16] Java Security Team, "Java Authentication and Authorization Service", Sun Microsystems, Inc., http://java.sun.com/security/jaas/index.html, 1999

[17] Welch, I. : Reflective Enforcement of the Clark-Wilson Integrity Model, 2nd Workshop on Distributed Object Security, OOPSLA, 1999.

[18] Welch, I., Stroud, R. J. : Supporting Real World Security Models in Java. Proceedings of 7th IEEE International Workshop on Future Treads of Distributed Computing Systems, Cape Town, South Africa, December 20-22, 1999

[19] Welch, I., Stroud, R. J. : Kava : A Reflective Java based on Bytecode Rewriting. Springer-Verlag Lecture Notes in Computer Science LNCS 1826, 2000

Author Index

Lecture Notes in Computer Science

For information about Vols. 1–1825
please contact your bookseller or Springer-Verlag

Vol. 1865: K.R. Apt, A.C. Kakas, E. Monfroy, F. Rossi (Eds.). New Trends Constraints. Proceedings, 1999. X, 339 pages. 2000. (Subseries LNAI).

Vol. 1866: J. Cussens, A. Frisch (Eds.), Inductive Logic Programming. Proceedings, 2000. X, 265 pages. 2000. (Subseries LNAI).

Vol. 1867: B. Ganter, G.W. Mineau (Eds.), Conceptual Structures: Logical, Linguistic, and Computational Issues. Proceedings, 2000. XI, 569 pages. 2000. (Subseries LNAI).

Vol. 1868: P. Koopman, C. Clack (Eds.), Implementation of Functional Languages. Proceedings, 1999. IX, 199 pages. 2000.

Vol. 1869: M. Aagaard, J. Harrison (Eds.), Theorem Proving in Higher Order Logics. Proceedings, 2000. IX, 535 pages. 2000.

Vol. 1872: J. van Leeuwen, O. Watanabe, M. Hagiya, P.D. Mosses, T. Ito (Eds.), Theoretical Computer Science. Proceedings, 2000. XV, 630 pages. 2000.

Vol. 1873: M. Ibrahim, J. Küng, N. Revell (Eds.), Database and Expert Systems Applications. Proceedings, 2000. XIX, 1005 pages. 2000.

Vol. 1874: Y. Kambayashi, M. Mohania, A M. Tjoa (Eds.), Data Warehousing and Knowledge Discovery. Proceedings, 2000. XII, 438 pages. 2000.

Vol. 1875: K. Bauknecht, S.K. Madria, G. Pernul (Eds.), Electronic Commerce and Web Technologies. Proceedings, 2000. XII, 488 pages. 2000.

Vol. 1876: F. J. Ferri, J.M. Iñesta, A. Amin, P. Pudil (Eds.). Advances in Pattern Recognition. Proceedings, 2000. XVIII, 901 pages. 2000.

Vol. 1877: C. Palamidessi (Ed.), CONCUR 2000 – Concurrency Theory. Proceedings, 2000. XI, 612 pages. 2000.

Vol. 1878: J.P. Bowen, S. Dunne, A. Galloway, S. King (Eds.), ZB 2000: Formal Specification and Development in Z and B. Proceedings, 2000. XIV, 511 pages. 2000.

Vol. 1879: M. Paterson (Ed.), Algorithms – ESA 2000. Proceedings, 2000. IX, 450 pages. 2000.

Vol. 1880: M. Bellare (Ed.), Advances in Cryptology – CRYPTO 2000. Proceedings, 2000. XI, 545 pages. 2000.

Vol. 1881: C. Zhang, V.-W. Soo (Eds.), Design and Applications of Intelligent Agents. Proceedings, 2000. X, 183 pages. 2000. (Subseries LNAI).

Vol. 1882: D. Kotz, F. Mattern (Eds.), Agent Systems, Mobile Agents, and Applications. Proceedings, 2000. XII, 275 pages. 2000.

Vol. 1883: B. Triggs, A. Zisserman, R. Szeliski (Eds.), Vision Algorithms: Theory and Practice. Proceedings, 1999. X, 383 pages. 2000.

Vol. 1884: J. Štuller, J. Pokorný, B. Thalheim. Y. Masunaga (Eds.), Current Issues in Databases and Information Systems. Proceedings, 2000. XIII, 396 pages. 2000.

Vol. 1885: K. Havelund, J. Penix, W. Visser (Eds.), SPIN Model Checking and Software Verification. Proceedings, 2000. X, 343 pages. 2000.

Vol. 1886: R. Mizoguchi, J. Slaney /Eds.), PRICAI 2000: Topics in Artificial Intelligence. Proceedings, 2000. XX, 835 pages. 2000. (Subseries LNAI).

Vol. 1888: G. Sommer, Y.Y. Zeevi (Eds.), Algebraic Frames for the Perception-Action Cycle. Proceedings, 2000. X, 349 pages. 2000.

Vol. 1889: M. Anderson, P. Cheng, V. Haarslev (Eds.), Theory and Application of Diagrams. Proceedings, 2000. XII, 504 pages. 2000. (Subseries LNAI).

Vol. 1890: C Linnhoff-Popien, H.-G. Hegering (Eds.), Trends in Distributed Systems: Towards a Universal Service Market. Proceedings, 2000. XI, 341 pages. 2000.

Vol. 1891: A.L. Oliveira (Ed.), Grammatical Inference: Algorithms and Applications. Proceedings, 2000. VIII, 313 pages. 2000. (Subseries LNAI).

Vol. 1892: P. Brusilovsky, O. Stock, C. Strapparava (Eds.), Adaptive Hypermedia and Adaptive Web-Based Systems. Proceedings, 2000. XIII, 422 pages. 2000.

Vol. 1893: M. Nielsen, B. Rovan (Eds.), Mathematical Foundations of Computer Science 2000. Proceedings, 2000. XIII, 710 pages. 2000.

Vol. 1895: F. Cuppens, Y. Deswarte, D. Gollmann, M. Waidner (Eds.), Computer Security – ESORICS 2000. Proceedings, 2000. X, 325 pages. 2000.

Vol. 1896: R. W. Hartenstein, H. Grünbacher (Eds.), Field-Programmable Logic and Applications. Proceedings, 2000. XVII, 856 pages. 2000.

Vol. 1897: J. Gutknecht, W. Weck (Eds.), Modular Programming Languages. Proceedings, 2000. XII, 299 pages. 2000.

Vol. 1898: E. Blanzieri, L. Portinale (Eds.), Advances in Case-Based Reasoning. Proceedings, 2000. XII, 530 pages. 2000. (Subseries LNAI).

Vol. 1899: H.-H. Nagel, F.J. Perales López (Eds.). Articulated Motion and Deformable Objects. Proceedings, 2000. X, 183 pages. 2000.

Vol. 1900: A. Bode, T. Ludwig, W. Karl, R. Wismüller (Eds.), Euro-Par 2000 Parallel Processing. Proceedings, 2000. XXXV, 1368 pages. 2000.

Vol. 1901: O. Etzion, P. Scheuermann (Eds.), Cooperative Information Systems. Proceedings, 2000. XI, 336 pages. 2000.

Vol. 1902: P. Sojka, I. Kopeček, K. Pala (Eds.), Text, Speech and Dialogue. Proceedings, 2000. XIII, 463 pages. 2000. (Subseries LNAI).

Vol. 1906: A. Porto, G.-C. Roman (Eds.), Coordination Languages and Models. Proceedings, 2000. IX, 353 pages. 2000.

Vol. 1912: Y. Gurevich, P.W. Kutter. M. Odersky, L. Thiele (Eds.), Abstract State Machines. Proceedings, 2000. X, 381 pages. 2000.

Vol. 1913: K. Jansen, S. Khuller (Eds.), Approximation Algorithms for Combinatorial Optimization. Proceedings, 2000. IX, 275 pages. 2000.

Vol. 1923: J. Borbinha, T. Baker (Eds.), Research and Advanced Technology for Digital Libraries. Proceedings, 2000. XVII, 513 pages. 2000.

Vol. 1924: W. Taha (Ed.), Semantics, Applications, and Implementation of Program Generation. Proceedings, 2000. VIII, 231 pages. 2000.

Vol. 1926: M. Joseph (Ed.), Formal Techniques in Real-Time and Fault-Tolerant Systems. Proceedings, 2000. X, 305 pages. 2000.